Zero Cost Living

exploring extreme frugality

by James R. Delcamp

Verdant Publishing Company
2010

Published by Verdant Publishing Company
which may be contacted through e-mail at
jrdel@access4less.net

ISBN 1 – 4392 – 4621 - 1

first edition, revised

Printed in the United States

CONTENTS: Page:

ILLUSTRATIONS: Page:

TABLES: Page:

WHAT THIS BOOK IS ABOUT:

This book is a guide to living zero cost, thereby achieving economic security and financial freedom without having a fortune. Living zero cost is achieved by the practice of **extreme frugality** and the creation of your own **personal economy** wherein you build up an array of knowledge, skills, tools, materials, technology, etc. that efficiently produce most of the things required to meet all of your basic needs (food, shelter, clothing, transportation, recreation, etc.) so you need spend little or no money for these things.

By achieving zero cost living you can insulate yourself, your family, and your community from the ongoing storm of economic instability and insecurity inflicted upon too many folks by big business, corporations, governments, and the volatile global economy.

And, you can make time your own, instead of wasting your life on business, job, earning money, buying and spending, etcetera – thereby living a more full and free life unleashed from the chains of economic necessity.

WARNING

This book is a general guide to extreme frugality, revealing how living zero cost may be possible. In it, you will not find complete instructions on how to find wild food, operate a solar greenhouse, build your own house and car, etcetera. However, it will direct you to books, websites, magazine articles, etc. providing complete instructions. So don't complain to me, (your author) if you don't find in a book of only 400 pages as much detail as you would like on a topic. I doubt 4,000 pages would cover it all – 10 more books (an encyclopedia of thrift, maybe?). To find all of the details you need you may have to do more research. In the web site **http://0costliving.com** I intend to fill in more details and provide links to useful web sites.

"Money is not required to buy one necessary of the soul."
Henry David Thoreau

FOREWORD:

Is it possible to live in comfort without spending money, to live zero cost? And, if possible, how can zero cost living be achieved. In this book I answer these questions.

Here I will explore extreme frugality - going way beyond frugal, making mere frugality seem like extravagant luxury. I will not just squeeze a dollar, but squeeze the need for it out of existence. I will take things to the edges of legality and beyond in an unrelenting effort to achieve Zero Cost Living.

No other book or web site so relentlessly and thoroughly considers the problems and pursues the solutions to extremes; from wild plant substitutes for soap to cities designed so folks can live in comfort at minimal cost. Other books and web sites dabble in the problem; present collections of tips, suggestions, and little tricks. Here, I go further, much further.

"I have enough money for the rest of my life," said Jackie Mason; "as long as I don't buy anything." No doubt he got a laugh out of his remark. Seriously, is it possible to reach a point where you don't have to buy anything?

I'll examine the idea, and prove, I believe that Zero Cost Living is possible. Of course, anyone would agree it is possible to live zero cost in poverty and misery, but the goal here is Zero Cost Living in comfort and ease. By using money (gained by whatever means) wisely and doing the right things most, or all of your cost of living can be eliminated from your budget without sacrificing a pleasant life.

Why would you want to live zero cost?

You don't fit into clock ruled timetables, routines, schedules, and agendas. You can't stand to be directed, managed, supervised and administered by of layers of bosses above you. You haven't won the lottery or inherited a fortune. Your artwork is not selling; you can't find a publisher for your novel; your band can't get a gig. You can't get a paying acting job. Your singing didn't impress the judges of American Idol. You got voted off of Survivor. You didn't develop the personal computer in your garage. Your parents have disowned you.

Or maybe you are a victim of the volatile global economy. Technology has made your job skills obsolete. Your job has been downsized, outsourced, off-shored. Your business is bankrupt. The only job you can get is a dead end low wage service industry job.

You have no money, no prospects, no economic future, perhaps even no home. Your path in life is on the hard road of reality. You face the prospect of living in poverty, anonymity and freedom. (You may find very appealing, the freedom possible through a zero cost lifestyle). You are a candidate for Zero Cost Living.

And, Living Zero Cost may reduce, stop, even prevent your contribution to humanity's waste of natural resources, destruction of forests, extinction of species, and degradation of land, water and climate.

Some will read this book because they are slumming. Slumming – visiting the hovels of the down and out to feel better about your own life. And, rather than actually paying a visit, comfortable successful folk often revel in reading about the travails and ingenuities of desperate people. You know who you are and what you are doing. I know because I've done it - for example when I read ***The Road*** by Jack London.

My book is meant primarily for those who practice Zero Cost Living (ZCL) because they are not well off. They may be destitute, living on an insufficient income, or living with a moderate income by means of double jobs and endless toil. They certainly are not wealthy.

But, slummers, I invite you to read on. Put aside your secure moneyed life and step into the real world. And consider; circumstances can change. A bad investment, a job loss, a debilitating illness, and you may find yourself seriously considering living zero cost.

Live without spending money? Some expenses are irreducible - you may think. Or are they? Gasoline, property taxes, toilet paper, house insurance, electricity, medicine - we will explore ways to minimize or eliminate these expenses without giving up a comfortable, secure life. ZCL is like going on a diet, not just a food diet, but a diet encompassing all forms of consumption. Ordinary dieting is difficult. A ZCL consumption diet is much more difficult.

Costs that cannot be eliminated will have to be covered by savings interest, investments, or (God forbid) a job. Many jobs in the future unfortunately, are likely to pay far less (after adjusting for inflation) than they did in the past. But ZCL, practiced diligently, could eventually liberate you from the need to be a wage slave and set you free. You could achieve financial freedom, economic independence without a fortune.

Zero Cost Living will take you on a journey to the hard edge of real life. It will give a "reality" slap in the face to folks too long immersed in TV, web surfing, books, games, blogs, cell phones, esoteric intellectual pursuits, useless sports, impractical kinds of hobbies and the million trivial and meaningless distractions of modern life that threaten to make life itself meaningless.

ZCL in some ways is like a fascinating challenge, an intricate puzzle, or an enthralling game played in the real world - a 'Reality Game'. Unlike games, puzzles, or sports, at the end something real will have been accomplished.

Parts of the puzzle that is ZCL exists out there in books, magazines, and web sites. Here I put them all together, showing the whole picture. In this book I hope to achieve and believe I have achieved a rather comprehensive overview of the subject, more comprehensive than anywhere else. Nevertheless, this is an introductory guide for a subject worth many volumes.

I hope this book will help you quit and escape from stupid and meaningless jobs, get off public assistance, cope with loss of job and income, and live well in retirement without a fortune. I hope the book will help you make time your own and not use time, your most precious resource, to enrich businesses, corporations and governments that only undermine your independence, and reduce you to a meek, powerless, subservient consumer, welfare case, employee and taxpayer. Know this: you are surrounded by people and institutions that seek to reduce you to subservience, one way or another, even in supposedly free America. They have already done it to most people.

Living ZC you may dump the superfluous burdens of decadent civilization. No longer waste your time and money on nonsense, on fashion, on keeping up appearances, on mindless distractions and trivial pursuits, but live real, and basic and practical, in health and comfort.

"A penny saved is a penny earned," wrote Ben Franklin. And, "waste not want not". Bens' ***Poor Richard's Almanac*** expounded on frugality at the time of America's birth. Americans knew the value of frugality and it was the bedrock of their liberty. Liberty made the practice of frugality more possible, and frugality made liberty thrive – by freeing folks from economic burdens imposed upon them - whether by governments, aristocrats, landlords, bankers, financiers, cartels, companies, or corporations.

Today we have lost our skill at frugality and the economic burdens jettisoned by Americans at the time of the Revolution have come back to haunt us, overwhelm us, undermine our prosperity and our liberty.

Today, as we buy the products of low wage workers in the global economy middle class American incomes erode and jobs disappear as manufacturing jobs, and more recently many service and high tech jobs go overseas seeking the lowest wages. A flood of cheap imports undermines American companies who dare to hire Americans. At the same time, a flood of illegal immigrant labor undermines wages here. As our incomes erode, we may be faced with the prospect of living more like folks in the poorer parts of the world. Extensive, unprecedented debt: government, trade, and personal temporarily props us up, and only delay the inevitable reckoning.

Possibly, if we do the right things; even with income loss, we can live better than people do in the 'third world', and better than we do with high incomes.

Americans have forgotten how to save and how to live efficiently. Here I hope to reawaken the old frugality that they once excelled at. Learn and practice it now while you have the luxury to begin gently and deliberately, or be forced to do it in the future under the gun of necessity. In an era of unprecedented economic insecurity, and unexpected economic decline, no book is needed more. In a world full of people and institutions trying to take your money, here I'll show how to keep it.

ACKNOWLEDGEMENTS:

Many thanks to these folks:

My father for reviewing this book and giving me invaluable advice.

My family for their patience while I was writing and for enduring Zero Cost Living techniques I have practiced over the years.

Friends and relatives who offered invaluable advice useful for thrifty and frugal living.

The public Library of Brighton, Michigan, for getting me books from remote sources; books from libraries as far away as Spartanburg, South Carolina and Boise, Idaho - and for the use of their computers, up-to-date computer programs, fast internet access, and extensive expertise.

And thanks to innumerable web sites full of free information applicable to Zero Cost Living.

ABOUT THE AUTHOR:

Having experienced the vicissitudes of life, J. R. Delcamp - James Raymond Delcamp (your author) has become all too familiar with methods necessary to live with little or no money. Some of his experiences living zero cost have included: living homeless; living out of cars, tents, and trailers, building and living in shanties and sheds, and repairing damaged old houses to make them livable. And, he has built simple, practical houses, doing almost all of the work himself.

In the midst of these vicissitudes he was able to get a Masters degree in Urban Planning from the University of Michigan. He worked as a City Planner in Florida and Michigan. Later he worked for 12 years as vehicle designer under contract to General Motors.

He has made mistakes and taken side-tracks in his quest to achieve Zero Cost Living and he hopes that by reading this book you will be spared them.

He is currently writing more around the theme of Zero Cost Living - expanding the idea presented in this book in a new edition.

ABOUT THE BOOK:

The thing about an idea is, if it not written down, it is often forgotten. Hence, the need for writing. There are vast arrays of ideas and methods useful for living almost zero cost - making it impossible to keep them in mind so you can make use of them when the relevant situation comes up. Hence, the need for writings about living zero cost. And, there are masses of writings: websites, books, pamphlets, magazines relevant to zero cost living so it is impossible to keep all the information needed handy for reference. With so many books and web sites out there, the material needed may be difficult to find. Hence, the need for this book.

This book was initially just a mass of notes written by the author for his own use as a personal guide, so he could keep a concise record of these practices. These notes consisting of hundreds of pages were written (in true ZCL style) on scrap paper. Later the author realized these notes might be organized into a book and be made useful to others. The rough draft of this book, consisting of a chaotic mass of ideas and methods was, (again, consistent with ZCL) written on more scrap paper. Years were spent writing it. Decades of hard experience and extensive research are reflected in its pages. Here I introduce a philosophy and a way of life. I hope you find it useful.

The book introduces various methods, but does not try to explain every detail of a technique, such as the complete plans for an inexpensive house for example, but shows where to look to get complete details. The author has continued to discover more methods suitable for ZCL and expects to issue updates on his web site.

WEB SITE:

Visit the web site **http://0costliving.com** for updates, elaborations, personal experiences, more ideas, and more sources.

ABOUT SOURCES:

In this book are presented a collection of techniques and methods to live low cost and zero cost. Some methods are based on my own experience and knowledge, such as house building and foraging. But, I have had little or no personal experience with some ZCL methods, so my presentations on these are based the experiences of others as revealed in their books and websites. For example, because I have had only a little experience at it, I will refer to accounts of others in my discussion of seasteading; living on the water. I have no experience at hunting or keeping farm animals. Practiced with efficiency, I believe they could be viable method of augmenting a ZC lifestyle I do not discuss them in this book. Thousands of other books discuss these topics.

Most source references are written into the text. Therefore, in the source list at the end of the book (books and web sites) I include mostly sources not already referred to in the text. Also, my book references do not include complete publisher information. In the Internet age you can find these in an instant by simply typing the title or author in a search engine like ***google***.

ORGANIZATION OF THE BOOK:

The topics of this book sometimes do not lend themselves to a neat categorized organization. Foraging for stuff for example permeates the topic and will come up again and again.

General organization:

Chapter 1: 'Introduction' considers the meaning of the term Zero Cost Living, and motives, attitude and inspirations necessary to achieve it.

Chapter 2: 'Extreme Thrift ' explores frugal living as it applies to the varied economic circumstances described in chapters 3 through 6.

Chapters 3 through 6 take the reader on a journey from 'homeless destitution' to 'comfortable living' in a series of steps.

At the end of chapters 2, 4, 5 and 6 I will present a series of vignettes or short stories to make more real the circumstances, situations and practices of Zero Cost Living.

Chapter 7: 'Society Practicing ZCL' describes communities, societies and cultures as they might appear and evolve if Zero Cost Living was widely practiced.

Chapter 8: 'Society Verses ZCL' explores how society and civilization has affected folks living ZC in the past and may affect attempts to live ZC in the present and future.

Chapters 3 through 6 are organized to cover each of the basic elements you need to establish your own 'personal economy'. These elements include food, health care, shelter, utilities (such as electricity and heat), mobility (or transportation) miscellaneous (such as clothes and furniture) and recreation.

***

Chapter 1: INTRODUCTION to Zero Cost Living:

Contents: **Page:**

1.1 WHAT is Zero Cost Living?

Today: success equals money. Get lots of money. Be rich; obtain wealth and the toys to go with it. If you don't get it you're a failure. Our society incessantly and obsessively thrusts this message into your eye, ear and mind. Buy, buy, buy, more stuff equals more happiness.

Here, for once hear the opposite message. Here, one lone voice, I advise you to don't buy, to spend less, or even spend nothing.

Is it possible to live without spending any money? Yes, you may think, as a bum, a hobo, or a vagrant; in jail, entirely on charity, as a hermit in the wilderness, or perhaps as an ascetic Buddhist Monk. But I mean is it possible to live a comfortable life without spending any money? And the answer, well, you will discover the answer as you read this book.

DEFINITION: In this book 'Zero Cost Living' means living comfortably, not just surviving - with virtually no income except enough to pay certain irreducible costs such as property taxes - if you own land. Interest from savings or investments, or earnings from a job or business must cover irreducible expenses. I'll examine "irreducible" expenses too; to determine how they might be reduced.

In this book, as a convenience, I use the acronym ZCL for the term 'Zero Cost Living' or sometimes I use the acronym ZC for the term 'Zero Cost'. I capitalize to provide a little emphasis to these terms which (surprise) you will find much used in this book.

Note: All costs and prices in his book are in 2009 dollars. Adjust for the inevitable inflation as the years roll by. 3% per year is about average.

In this book I look at life from a unique perspective; the perspective of ZCL, a vantage point outside of the conventional lifestyle of the consumer. From the ZCL perspective, or point of view most activities and things that cost money can be done for free or almost free. And, they can be done legally, or mostly legally, and without harm to others or the environment. Indeed, you may find yourself able to help others, even able to help our much-abused environment. Living conventionally, you add more carbon dioxide and other greenhouse gases to the atmosphere, threatening us all with global warming and eventual catastrophe as explained by dozens of recent books. (A good one is ***Under a Green Sky*** by Peter D. Ward). Living ZC you may be able to pull more carbon dioxide out of the atmosphere than you spew into it - becoming part of the solution.

Are you looking for squalor, misery, and desperation in this book? You won't find it! Instead you will find ways out of these conditions. There is no reason living in relative poverty need not be comfortable if it's done right. For example, a solar greenhouse in your yard or attached to your house can provide hundreds or even thousands of dollars worth of produce per year to eat or sell. It lowers your cost for food. It eliminates packaging, trucking and distribution costs of food and the profits of wholesalers, middlemen, and retailers. It provides food out of season when prices are highest. Only a few minutes of pleasant work a day, providing healthy exercise, are required to operate it. A solar greenhouse could be built for a few hundred dollars. Using mostly recycled materials the cost could be well under a hundred dollars. And in true ZCL style a solar greenhouse could be built entirely of recycled and salvaged materials for nothing. Plans and methods of construction are detailed later in this book in chapter 5 on 'Homesteading'.

You must have money to live money free, not all that much money, certainly not millions. You can't live on nothing without having invested first in tools, structures, equipment and in learning skills that make it unnecessary to spend any money. For example: It is possible to design a house to have zero heating and zero electricity costs - sometimes called a zero energy house. But, you must build or buy such a house, or renovate an old house, so you must have the dollars and skills to do so.

"Oh great," you may say, "I have practically nothing and you tell me I must acquire a house". And I reply, "If you want to achieve a comfortable zero cost lifestyle as described in chapter 6 of this book you must have a house, a zero energy house. From the beginning, envision it, plan on it, and then get the money for it. By practicing ZCL you can save money that you can eventually apply to your own efficient house.

You may choose to avoid the land, and property taxes, and live on the water as described in chapter 4 but then you must get money for a used boat or at least money for the materials and tools for a boat you build yourself.

Instead of investing in the risky stock market or real estate, or a savings account that is eaten by inflation, invest in tools, methods, technologies, and in learning skills that lower your 'cost of living' (or 'COLA'). Government, business, and most people think your COLA is fixed. Your COLA is not fixed, but amenable to your way of life.

Practicing ZCL, you can keep the money you get - instead of letting it flow away from you in wasteful streams. Thus, you may achieve financial freedom without having a fortune.

It is possible to live at less than zero cost, that is, to live ZC, and build up a surplus of $ or assets. How? One example: photovoltaic panels - that produce electricity from sunlight - on your roof and/or in your yard feed excess electricity you don't need back into the power grid, and in a scheme called net energy metering make your electric meter run backwards. If you had enough solar panels, you might cover all of your living expenses and more. Currently solar panels for electricity are too expensive to make this a paying proposition, but in the future, they may be cheaper.

1.2 WHY practice Zero Cost Living?

ZCL can take the pressure of need away. No longer will you be compelled by economic necessity. It may be possible to cut your cost of living far beyond what you think is possible. You may be healthier and more comfortable than you'd be with more assets and expenditures.

You may attempt ZCL out of desire rather than need. It is a challenge, living almost money free. It is an interesting, even fascinating challenge requiring considerable physical and intellectual skills. As a challenge it might rank up there with climbing Mount Everest or perhaps even climbing K2 (far more dangerous than Everest); so few people have done it, or even attempted it. You will have to research methods, (everything isn't covered in this book) invent things, build things, and accomplish tasks ordinary folks rarely try.

Living ZC, you can be financially independent without having a fortune, not millions, not even a million (which barely qualifies you as wealthy anymore), but with a few tens to a few hundreds of thousands – within the range of most people.

ZCL may be more necessary than ever today given the decline of wages, income, and personal wealth in America and the ongoing destruction of the middle class thanks to outsourced jobs, cheap imports, illegal immigrant labor, corporate greed, increasing disparities of wealth, and the tsunami of economic instability provoked by the global economy.

Living ZC for the rest of your life may seem like a bleak future. You may have visions of endless misery, impoverishment, of barely getting by, eating badly, poor housing, etc. but by homesteading and building a place suitable for comfortable living as described in chapters 5 and 6 you can get beyond all of that.

1.3 WHO?

Who should attempt to live Zero Cost?

These situations may motivate you to attempt ZCL:

- Your income is low, but you don't want your income to limit your life to mere survival.
- You are retired and have only social security to live on.
- You are living off welfare, charity, or relatives but want to take care of yourself.
- You are physically or mentally challenged but still want to take care of yourself.
- You are young and new to the working world or old and near the end of your working life. You can only get low wage service industry jobs and want to escape them as soon as possible.
- Regardless of you age, you have been relegated to the undesirable, the miserable, the dead end jobs of society

• Your job is being outsourced; you face a coming layoff, or you are already laid off with no job opportunities in sight.
• You don't have a talent, or have one but can't make it pay (at least not now).
• You are an inventor, writer, artist, or entertainer. You want to pursue your ideas and dreams but you must have food, shelter, etc. so you must work many hours at tedious and low paying jobs that eat up your time and sap your energy and creativity. By practicing ZCL you may get out of that trap so more, even most of your time goes to what you really want to do.
• You want to escape the miserable world of business. It is a world of unbridled greed, cutthroat competition, and stepping on coworkers to get ahead, euphemistically called the 'rat race'. Maybe, you don't want to compete, you just want to live a pleasant, comfortable, agreeable life.
• Your job is stressful - physically or emotionally unhealthy. You need to escape the pressure of your job to reduce stress, relax and preserve/restore your health.

Better, maybe for folks who are not already rich, to learn and plan early to set up a ZC lifestyle. Sure everybody has big ideas and expects to get rich, but what if you don't? Shouldn't you have a backup plan? This book is one such plan. Most of us will not end up wealthy and should plan and act accordingly. And, the day must come when the world cannot afford the wasteful extravagances of the wealthy anymore, and then they will have to live like real people too. (When wealthy folks waste resources, such a driving gas wasting cars, they make the cost of gas go up for everybody, because they accelerate the depletion of the resource).

ZCL need not be practiced full time by more affluent folk. Possibly it may be tried as an interesting, challenging, fascinating hobby and/or recreation. Make ZCL your hobby and you will do things that are useful and practical, unlike most sports or hobbies that eat time and money. The Boy and Girl Scouts do this already - learn skills applicable to ZCL.

Folks living in poverty and/or on government assistance might attempt ZCL as a path up out of poverty, handouts, and dependence. It is my sincere hope that this book will serve as a guide for that purpose. Chapters 3 through 6 provide a step-by-step process by which destitute and homeless folks might eventually achieve a comfortable life.

I believe practicing extreme thrift as described in chapter two at each step in ZC Living will enable folks to save money and learn skills they can apply to achieving the next step towards ZCL.

Who should not attempt Zero Cost Living?

Maybe you're securely ensconced in a job you love. Maybe you inherited a fortune. If you are wealthy, and/or you have a good job, you are happy, you love your work, you are doing something interesting, valuable and satisfying you may not have any interest in ZCL. (So why are you reading this book?). Of course most people, the vast majority are not in these situations, and ZCL might have some, even a lot of appeal.

And even if you are well off and happy, things can change. Consider what happened when Hurricane Katrina struck. So prepare, build your fortress against adversity, against the wolf at your door now, while you can.

Ill health or an injury could make you unable to work. Medical bills could eat up your money. Better perhaps to "be prepared" (the Boy Scout motto), to have a plan or have everything in place to achieve ZCL should it become necessary. For example: design your expensive trophy house so it can be modified easily to be a zero energy house.

So, given these considerations, I believe that almost everybody should make an effort to study, learn, and live Zero Cost.

INSPIRING PEOPLE: Famous people who lived Zero Cost.

Buddha, Socrates, Diogenes, Jesus, Thoreau, Van Gogh, Gandhi, these folk had little or no money. Yet they did not live their lives in miserable squalor, but pursued great passions, dreams and purposes. They are among the few, the very few, who have lived beyond the bounds of ordinary economics. They were without wealth or power, yet they are studied, revered and followed as great teachers. What is the reason for our fascination with these folks?

One reason is that they lived free, pursing their dreams, almost without money. Why they did it and how they did it are intriguing questions. They didn't let lack of money get in their way. This is the essential idea of Zero Cost Living.

Buddha:

He chose to live with extreme frugality, believing right living, right thinking, and self-denial would enable the soul to reach a divine state of release from earthy and bodily pain, sorrow, and desire. His life is beautifully explained in the book ***Siddhartha*** by Hermann Hesse.

Socrates:

He lived for philosophy, to think and analyze the world, to critique society, to take or leave his civilization on his terms. He lived with frugality by choice so he could pursue his passion. "An unexamined life is not worth living," said Socrates.

He examined the assumptions of his society and found them to be faulty. As we examine modern society from a ZCL perspective perhaps some contemporary assumptions will be found at fault too.

Diogenes the Cynic:

He was a Greek philosopher who lived around 400 B.C, not long after Socrates. He is most famous for running through Athens in the night carrying a lamp and looking for an honest man. He was the first widely known person in European history who lived in poverty by conscious choice. He was a beggar who made his home in the streets of Athens. He made a virtue of extreme poverty. When he saw a peasant boy drinking water out of his hands he threw away his cup, one of his few possessions. He taught that wisdom and happiness belong to the man who is independent of society. He was contemptuous of dependency and of the master who could do nothing for himself. Alexander the Great, thrilled to visit him, asked if there was any favor he might do for him. Diogenes replied, "Stand out of my sunlight." Alexander said of him, "If I were not Alexander then I would wish to be Diogenes." Admired and emulated in the Ancient Greek world, I think a modern Diogenes might be considered a psychotic freak in the contemporary world.

Jesus:

Did Jesus live a ZC lifestyle? What did it cost for him to live? His cost of living was low by any standard, and his income negligible or nonexistent. He didn't own anything except the clothes on his back. He never hoarded any money or bought anything. Any money that came his way was given to the poor. He was homeless traveler, frequently sleeping out in the open. Sometimes he was invited to a "set down" supper (to use Jack London's hobo terminology). He had no house, no car, or beast of burden. He wore the simplest clothes, ate the simplest food. He was always among working folk; fishermen, farmers, shepherds. He helped fishermen catch more fish. He healed the sick (and raised Lazarus from the dead). It is impossible to apply the tired measurements of wealth used by conventional accounting to his life.

He taught simple rules for living. “Do unto others as you would have them do unto you.” “Love your neighbor as yourself.” Following these rules could make ZCL much easier. His simple rules make social co-operation practical. And if folks can co-operate in the practice of ZCL, they can achieve it more easily.

Did Jesus advocate a ZC lifestyle? He saw no value in building up wealth. He said, “It is easier for a camel to pass through the eye of a needle than a rich man to enter heaven”. He said “Consider the lilies of the field, how they grow. They toil not, nor do they spin: and yet I say into you that even Solomon in all his glory was not arrayed like one of these.”

Thoreau:

Thoreau deliberately lived a life of extreme frugality. He wrote Walden, the quintessential book about frugal and independent living. His life was important, influential and inspiring though he had no money, power or fame, or even many readers during his lifetime. He is an icon. His humble 10 x 14 cottage at Walden has been rebuilt and visited by millions of acolytes. I will revisit his words and ideas many times in this book. Reading his books, I feel like I am looking through a keyhole into another kind of life. A keyhole I will try to use to open a door to that life.

Van Gogh:

Consider the life of Van Gogh from a ZCL perspective. He lived in extreme poverty, spending much of the little money he obtained on paint and canvas. He sold almost none of them in his lifetime. Think of how much poorer the world would be if he had given up on painting to earn money doing some squalid low wage job. Instead, he lived almost zero cost, and painted. Today he is considered the epitome of artists, and his paintings are considered the epitome of art, and worth many millions.

Mahatma Gandhi:

He lived in frugal simplicity while leading India to independence. Among his many goals he wanted the people of India to spin cloth at home to replace imported cloth. He believed a simple machine could be invented that would perform this task as efficiently as any factory. His ideas on economics have been ignored or forgotten, but the social/economic disruptions of the global economy make them more relevant than ever.

A contemporary inspiration:

Ed Viesturs in his 2006 autobiography, ***No Shortcut to the Top*** practiced a ZCL lifestyle to afford to pursue his mountain climbing passion. He shared a house with eight others paying $75 a month each, sleeping in bunk beds. Ed wrote "I tried to be really frugal. I'd go to the grocery store, pick up a jar of peanut butter and then realize, nope-can't afford it this week. So I'd buy Top Ramen (noodles) instead, ...six packages for a dollar." This while attending The University of Washington, every day lifting weights, running five to seven miles, and climbing on weekends. Ed has extraordinary physical abilities, but his lifestyle suggests that exercise is more important to good health than fine points of diet. What does exercise cost? **NOTHING**.

His mountain climbing exploits are interesting, but most interesting (from a ZCL perspective), is how he managed to pursue them with very little money. He had no car, but biked and took buses to get around town and found climbers with cars who needed partners to get to the mountains. He writes, "...I got a funky pair of old ski goggles, army surplus wool pants and sweaters. My rain jacket was a yellow bicycle poncho... My foot wear was a used pair of Habeler leather boots. I thought I could get away without a sleeping pad, just lay in my bag on the ground, but one autumn night I learned you can't just economize like that - it's too cold. I made some of my own gear, and I patched the holes in the seat and knees of my pants with fabric from other cast off clothes."

Extreme frugality to pursue the goals you care about. That is the essence of ZCL.

The best part of any sport, game or challenge like mountain climbing must be the hot shower in the hotel when it is all over, where you can relax and be taken care of. But living ZCL you don't get that. Month after month you must take care of yourself; making it, after a while harder than any other challenging sport including the most difficult mountain climb. The climb ends one way or another, but ZCL is constant. It may grind you down. You might experience "grinding poverty" a trite term in the long literature about poverty that may become all-too-real for you. You must find ways to take a vacation from it, from living zero cost, perhaps by living a conventional life for a while. A vacation for you might be to live the way most other folks do when they are not on vacation. Such an experience might send you back to ZCL with renewed enthusiasm and appreciation for it. (There are free or almost free recreations and vacations described later in the book).

More Inspiring Lives:

In this book we will learn from the lives of folks, some almost unknown who have plenty to teach that can be applied to ZCL. Some of them have clever, even astonishing ideas, designs and methods I will examine later in the book.

Jack London in ***The Road*** describes his life as a hobo riding the rails in late 19th century America.

George Orwell in ***Down and Out in Paris and London*** describes his life of impoverished misery in pre World War 2 Europe.

Chris McCandless who lived without concerns for money and died in the Alaskan wilderness is memorialized by Ken Krakouer in his book ***Into the Wild***. Had he lived, I believe Chris would have written a fascinating book of his own.

Ken Kifer was an extreme long distance bike traveler and advocate of Thoreau.

Ken Neumeyer describes self-sufficient seasteading in his book ***Sailing the Farm***.

Harlan Hubbard drifted down the Ohio and Mississippi Rivers on a snug shantyboat he built of scrap materials - detailed in his book ***Shantyboat.***

Annie Hill crossed the world's oceans on a seemingly absurdly low income -described in her book ***Voyaging on a Small Income***.

Lin and Larry Pardey like Annie Hill voyaged the world on very little money and wrote about it in magazine articles and books such as ***The Self Sufficient Sailor.***

Hunza: A society in Northern Pakistan who could have inspired Shangri –la.

Dick Proennke: Practitioner of total independence in the Alaskan wilderness.

Mike Oehler: Designer/builder of underground houses at miniscule cost.

Ianto Evans: Designer/builder of houses and heating systems dirt cheap, because they are built of dirt.

Thomas Elpel: Expert in the use of the resources of wild nature to live.

And many others.

Some, like London and Orwell are famous and some are barely known, but destined, I suspect to be inspirations to many folks in the future.

1.4 HOW?

How can zero cost living be achieved?

Admission of ignorance is the beginning of all true knowledge said Socrates. To that I add; experiencing poverty is the beginning of all real wealth. To know how to solve poverty, to know what is really needed, you must live it.

ZCL requires knowledge and skills that might take years to gather. It takes time and practice to learn how to build and run a solar greenhouse, to make clothes, to bake a good loaf of bread, to repair a car, to maintain good health. I spent years living with a small income while buying horribly expensive private medical insurance that made my savings dwindle before I cancelled it and started living a truly healthy lifestyle and using available free or income based health services. (But I still recommend catastrophic health insurance - if you can afford it - to protect you from being financially wiped out by a major medical emergency).

Americans once were the champions of frugality. “A penny saved is a penny earned,” wrote Ben Franklin. (I know, I used this quote in the Foreword to this book, but it’s too good, I can’t resist using it again). The parsimonious Yankee was a legend. Later generations have grown up without the skills and abilities to live at very low cost. Most people cannot sew or repair their own clothes, (or even sew on a button), fix their cars, or milk a cow (let alone keep one). It’s not their fault. Cars are not designed to be easy to fix. Cheap imported clothes make it more convenient to buy new rather than repair the old, and farm animals are no longer permitted in urban environments. So folks are reduced to dependence by laws and markets and must therefore earn and then spend. That’s fine if you’ve a good high paying job with a future. But for many people, even most, this is not the case and they will be condemned to dead end low wage jobs, possibly for the rest of their lives.

As in the examples mentioned above, ZCL can be achieved by making and doing things that cost little or nothing to build and operate such as owner built solar greenhouses, zero energy use houses, efficient cars and alternatives to cars. Chapters 2 through 6 go into the details.

To achieve ZCL you must practice thrift, and not ordinary thrift, but **extreme thrift**. If you attempt ZCL and are not thrifty, you may end up in a life of drudgery, misery and grinding poverty like billions of poor folks around the world. Chapter 2 examines the concept of extreme thrift in detail. And - the second pillar of ZCL, you must build a **personal economy** that can provide all of your basic necessities of life (food shelter, clothing, etc.) as described in more detail on page 23.

In this book I won't attempt to teach **every** detail of the skills needed for ZCL. I'll reference other books that do that. Healthy eating, gardening, carpentry, and car repair are examples of these skills. I will, however discuss these skills with **some** detail and consider their potential for reducing living expenses.

Construct a life in which every aspect takes the option that costs little or nothing and ultimately you may live for free - achieve zero cost living. In the next chapters I will examine what life would be like living zero cost.

And would it be a bad life? No indeed, it could be a very good life, a much better life perhaps than a life spending masses of money and slaving to get it. It could be a life with no boss, no deadlines, no stress, no commute thru traffic jams, no daily grind of tedious work. It could be a life as part of a real community, a life among valued and valuable folk who share skills and abilities, an enriched and expanded life.

But these are only introductory remarks, "teasers" they are called in the writing industry. Shortly I will get to the "meat and potatoes" of zero cost living.

Have I achieved ZCL? Only twice, for a few months each time. Can I achieve it again? Probably. Can you? Possibly. It's difficult, very difficult, but not impossible, far from impossible. For a single person, it may be rather easy, like Thoreau. For a family, it may be a struggle.

The ideas suggested here are limited by my personal experience and research so some ideas may be left out or merely mentioned. Advertising signs on cars for example, can compensate for car expenses but are outside of my experience.

Some of the methods described in this book are only ideas, suggestions, or concepts that have never been tried. In some cases, new inventions and advances in technology are needed to make a particular ZCL method possible.

Some of the ideas in this book might seem obvious. But what is obvious to one reader may not be to another and therefore I have kept obvious ideas in the book

What this book is not. It is not ultimately, about sponging off others, although some help might be needed and welcome from time to time. Rather it is a book about how to unburden others - parents or children, friends, neighbors, the community, government, and the environment. It is about achieving secure economic independence. It is not about being cheap at the expense of others, not about taking advantage of others, and not about using others; because they'll resent it and you'll be on their X list. If folks help you, you need to help them back, if you want to get any help in the future. You can pay them back even if you have no money, perhaps with your time by providing a service, or by giving them things you grew, made or foraged.

1.5 PERSONAL ECONOMY

The second pillar of ZCL after **extreme thrift** is creation of a '**personal economy**' described in detail in chapters 3 through 6. Your personal economy or **P.E.** is analogous to your **personal computer** or **'P.C'**. The P.C. wrenched computers out of the hands of big companies with their mainframe computers and put them into the hands of almost everyone. Creating a P.E. could put production of your basic economic needs (food, shelter, clothing, etc.) into your own hands and make it unnecessary for you to buy most or all of the products foisted upon you by big business.

P.E. more precisely defined: I define your P.E. as assemblies of knowledge, books, instructions, web sites, skills, materials, tools, supplies, equipment, systems, facilities, buildings, land, anything and everything required to meet all of your basic needs. These needs include food, health care, shelter, utilities, mobility, miscellaneous, and recreation. Your P.E. may also include a business producing things or services you can trade sell for the things you can't produce in your P.E. And, a P.E might include investments in stocks or bank savings that produce dividend or interest income.

Your P.E. fully developed should allow you to provide for, produce all or almost all of your basic needs without having to buy anything - another words, live Zero Cost. Thus your business earnings and/or invested $ can be modest.

You may create your P.E. yourself gradually, over time building your own house (and car - see chapter 6), or with more money to start with have your P.E. built for you more quickly.

Some of the old pioneers went into the wilderness with an axe and a few other tools and built what I would define as rather complete and sophisticated personal economies as I describe more in chapter 8. Conceivably you could emulate them if you acquired the considerable array of skills needed.

1.6 ATTITUDE

Fundamental to the practice of ZCL, or anything else, even before knowledge, is attitude. Attitude is the key to success. A bad attitude can defeat you from the beginning. You can attempt ZCL with dread expecting misery and deprivation, or as a great challenge. In this book I am not going to get sidetracked into a psychological treatise on motivation. Diving right in to ZCL and attempting some techniques might give you more chance for success than passive introspection and contemplation of motivational discourses.

Look upon living ZCL as a great experience, a fascinating challenge, even a game, a really marvelous game. A reality show ought to be made out of it. Some former hobos who rode the rails out of necessity earlier in their lives go back to it for a vacation because of the novelty and excitement of it. Walk out the door of your home with nothing, and then survive, even live comfortably, and travel, and see the world.

Living off the land might be a great sport of the future, a sport to be learned by study and imitation of Native Americans, pioneers, and hobos. Most fascinating, it is, how they survived, even thrived; finding food and fuel on the land and water and living in simple shelters, or none.

Climbing to the top of the highest mountains can be an expensive, mindless, pointless, dangerous, even deadly sport. But, hiking and living in the mountains you may get fresh air, exercise, beautiful views, forgeable food; an all around healthy agreeable life. This attitude may apply to the rat race of contemporary life as well. Trying to climb to the top of the corporate heap may only get you bad health and feelings of defeat and failure for the overwhelming majority of folks who don't make it to the top, who spend their working lives as small cogs in corporate machines. Life outside of corporate hierarchies may be vastly more satisfying for you.

1.7 WILL ZCL SIMPLIFY YOUR LIFE? Can you achieve ZCL by simplifying your life?

In Walden, Thoreau wrote "simplify, simplify, simplify ". Well, that is hard to do these days, isn't it? It has become difficult to simplify, very difficult. I wish it could be simple to simplify again, like it was in Thoreau's day. Or was it?

Difficulties of simplifying: Imagine the misadventures of a Thoreau imitator: The house he builds is crooked, leaky and cold. His fireplace is smoky and dangerous and burns down his house. Animals eat his bean field. His neighbors are surly and hostile. His meager possessions are stolen or vandalized. Somehow Thoreau avoided any of these misfortunes. Yet any of them could have happened. He knew how to build a house and a fireplace, protect a bean field for animals, and keep on good terms with his neighbors. These are not trivial or easily learned abilities and most jobs today require less. So even in Thoreau's day, simplifying was not so simple.

An in fact, and paradoxically, today, the lives of many folks have been simplified to the extreme. You work at a service or factory job you can learn in a few minutes or hours and you buy everything else you need. No need to do anything except that job. Of course, living this way, living zero cost or even low cost is almost impossible.

So, rather than simplifying life, ZCL only increases complexity. Now you may not merely go to the store to get food, but must plan a year ahead to plant it, grow it, harvest it, preserve it, store it, and process it. Really, an extensive array of knowledge, skills, tools and facilities are required to do these things. Therefore, rather than expect simplification by attempting to live ZC, you must expect complexity, and you must figure out how to manage it.

Now, to further convolute the problem; consider this: To manage the complexity that is ZCL you must simplify wherever possible.

To live ZC you must be competent at many things, But those things must not be too complicated or the knowledge skills, and effort required becomes too much for one or a few people to master. Therefore the individual components or systems must be as simple as possible to master: cars must be easy to fix, gardens easy to grow, food easy to prepare. A technology of simplification must be developed or in many cases rediscovered in the lifestyles of the past, and revived.

To live ZC you must be a generalist.

We live in a society of specialization. Most career advisors would have you specialize in some field. That's great if you have talent and can get paid for it (unlike poor Van Gogh).

If not, then you may be better off if you diversify your abilities. Better because then you can practice a ZC lifestyle. You must learn skills, buy tools equipment, land and facilities that reduce or eliminate your cost of living expenses thereby establishing for yourself a secure economic circumstance.

Being a generalist is good and necessary for ZCL. Most folks specialize and want it that way and don't think or want to think about anything else. You need to be a jack-of-all-trades. But if you try to to make or do everything, these many diverse tasks must not be too complicated or difficult to do yourself.

If you are skilled or even talented in a field or two, they can be a source of income, of a surplus to cover expenses you can't eliminate: expenses like taxes and some insurance.

Medical care might seem to be beyond the capabilities of a ZCL practitioner. "Physician cure thyself" states an ancient admonition. But in medicine specialists abound so even a physician may find it impractical to cure him/herself. Nevertheless ZCL practices including exercise and diet may help - preventing diseases or reducing their severity and cutting down costs when medical help is needed.

Technology for ZCL requires extreme simplification and clarification. Modern technology unfortunately continually gets more complicated and difficult for the homeowner to fix (or even comprehend) unless s/he is a specialist. Needed is technology that goes in the opposite direction. Cars need to be clarified and simplified so folks might maintain, repair and possibly even build one in their garage. Also, appliances; refrigerators, washing machines, heating systems etcetera could use simplification so they could be serviced by the owner. Computers and the web could sometimes help with information on how to maintain technology, but the needed information is all-to often not online. Extensive online detailed illustrated pages on how to fix stuff might help. But computers, software, and the web itself have become more complex and incomprehensible so you must become a specialist, become a computer geek and devote a lot of time to it to use it effectively. The computer world itself needs to be simplified.

The world is not designed to be practical for ZCL. Complexity seems to be designed into everything - making it hard for you to learn, understand and practice the skills necessary for you to take care of yourself - thus making you dependent on professionals, businesses, government, corporations, lawyers, the medical establishment, dentists, plumbers, carpenters, automobile mechanics, the list is long. To live ZCL a big part of the task is to untangle your life from these dependencies.

In this book I will take you on a journey, an odyssey - or rather a reverse odyssey since Odysseus started with everything and lost everything along the way, (but got it all back at the end; oops, I gave it away). You begin with nothing; not knowledge, not skills, not a clue as to what to do. While spending very little money you end with a healthy, comfortable lifestyle.

1.8 CIRCUMSTANCES:

There are, in my estimation, a range of circumstances you may be in at the beginning of your attempt to achieve Zero Cost Living. At one end of this range you are destitute, you have little or no money, and at the other end you have money or can get money to build stuff such as an energy efficient house that will let you reduce or eliminate living costs. I will investigate both and stages in between. I will discuss circumstance from destitution to self-sufficiency. You may begin the process of achieving ZCL at any stage along the way that your economic status allows.

In **chapter 3: Homeless** I will explore living zero cost without a permanent home. This may be because you have no other choice; you are destitute and homeless. Or you may live homeless by choice, practicing a zero cost nomadic lifestyle so that you can travel and explore the world with little or no money. Or perhaps, you want to stay in one community, (though homeless), because you want to get to know it well, at your leisure, at little expense.

In **chapter 4: Seasteading** I will look at floating homesteading, sometimes called seasteading; living in the water whether on ocean, lake, river, or canal. A floating home has the advantage, of course, that it can be moved. Living on the water is very common in other countries, notably China, and is increasingly common here. In some ways, seasteading amounts to living on very cheap waterfront property.

In **chapter 5: Homesteading** I'll examine homesteading to live almost zero cost. You save money, then buy land to homestead; or you get permission to homestead on land owned by another, like Thoreau at Walden. Also, you have some assets, income from a job, business, gift, grant, inheritance or other source; that you can use towards developing your site.

In **chapter 6: Comfortable Living** I'll investigate achieving ZCL with more assets, $50,000 - $100,000 or more saved, invested, and in home equity, tools, and equipment. These funds might have been accumulated through a lifetime of savings, a profitable investment, a company buyout, or other source. Of course, living at or near zero cost a large percentage of a regular income whether from a job, social security, savings interest, inheritance, etc. can be reinvested against inflation, future medical bills, or perhaps to pay for vacations or hobbies. Or, income flow may be spent to further reduce livings costs, perhaps to less than zero, another words, delivering you a profit and thus more income flow.

It would be a very good idea to learn and practice skills needed to live at each ZC circumstance before actually attempting it. Attempting to live homeless without any preparation could be disastrous. Living out of a car, seasteading, homesteading, all will go better if you practice necessary techniques ahead of time. The appropriate chapters will consider the skills in detail that you want to have.

It may be possible for you to progress from one circumstance to another, from homelessness to homesteading to a comfortable living by practicing ZCL methods because you may save and apply whatever money you obtain to advancing your Zero Cost Lifestyle and building up your Personal Economy instead of wasting your money, as usually happens; on all the useless junk and distractions of contemporary culture. ***

"Being poor, I made myself rich by making my needs few."
Thoreau

Chapter 2: EXTREME THRIFT

Contents: **page**

INTRODUCTION

How can Zero Cost Living be achieved? The key way is by practicing thrift, and not the ordinary kinds of thrift you may read about in books, magazines, web sites, and see on TV. These media have thousands of tips for saving money or time, but they do not apply thrift in the efficient, thorough and systematic manner I call extreme thrift.

The key to the realization of ZCL is the application of extreme thrift to all of the essential requirements for a comfortable life. Some of these essentials of comfort include being healthy, dry, warm, clean, adequately fed, safe, and to put it simply: happy. You can spend millions and live in profligate luxury and still not achieve these goals.

In this chapter I will describe techniques of extreme thrift to achieve ZCL that are applicable to all of the four kinds of circumstances described at the end of chapter one: homeless, seasteading, homesteading, and comfortable living. These circumstances are explored in detail in chapters 3 thru 6.

Because it is so central to Zero Cost Living, here I will consider the meaning of the ideas of thrift and extreme thrift in some detail:

2.1 WHAT IS EXTREME THRIFT?

Before considering the meaning of extreme thrift. It is instructive to consider first the meaning of thrift.

What is thrift really? Thrift is thrift, right? Thrift is saving money by doing economical things. You know what it means, right? Or do you?

When you attempt ZCL; the practice of thrift can become more complicated. Certain practices that seem thrifty can end up costing you a lot of time, money or effort.

Thrift and frugal as defined in the Dictionary:

Webster's Dictionary definition paraphrased: Thrift comes from the word thrive originally the condition of thriving. Thrift means economical management; economy, frugality. 'Thrifty' means practicing thrift; provident; economical industry and clever management of one's money or resources, usually so as to result in some savings. Frugal stresses the idea of saving and suggests spending which excludes any luxury or lavishness and provides only the simplest fare, dress, etc.

Frugality verses Thrift:

In this book I use the terms frugality and thrift as synonyms. Frugal sounds dull, even tedious. Thrifty sounds clever, perhaps even inventive. So in this discussion I will stick with the term 'thrift'.

Ordinary thrift or simple thrift - as I call it - may be insufficient to achieve ZCL because thrift can be practiced inefficiently, costing you too much time, money, effort, or energy relative to the benefits or savings you realize.

To achieve ZCL, thrift must be practiced with efficiency, practiced with a kind of thrift I like to call extreme thrift.

So what is extreme thrift?

'Extreme thrift' is thrift practiced in an efficient, planned, voluntary, systematic, manner to obtain every basic human need while spending little or no money, or the least amount of money possible. Some folks might go to extreme lengths to avoid spending any money at all (and I am one), even though they may consume more time energy and money than can possibly be saved. That is inefficient thrift. Example: driving around to garage sales using up a lot of time and gas in the hope of saving a few dollars on a needed item. (One way garage sale hunting can be made efficient however, is by if doing it while on a trip for another purpose: making that trip on a garage sale day – usually Friday and Saturday - leaving early and looking for garage sales on your way).

Extreme thrift is best achieved if it is intentional thrift - thrift practiced intentionally based on plans and deliberate methods - as opposed to involuntary thrift practiced under the gun of necessity - thrift practiced because people have no choice - the situation of billons of poor people in the world. Thrift practiced involuntarily can be very difficult to practice with efficiency. It can become 'hard thrift'.

Hard Thrift:

The antithesis of extreme thrift is thrift practiced with inefficiency; inefficient thrift - which I like to call hard thrift. Hard thrift means the time and effort required to do a thing is so great and the gain or savings so small that the time/effort is not worth the trouble. If an individual living his life with thrift (perhaps out of necessity) finds his efforts are all hard thrift s/he will soon want to get out of his way of life altogether in frustration, and will at the first opportunity. It was the fate of many a hardscrabble farmer. His thrifty lifestyle degenerated into grinding poverty, a life of incessant toil and little to show for it. Hard thrift, a life of grinding poverty I believe, may be the not so secret driver behind many a life of crime, the concealed fear of many a thief, drug dealer, and ponzi schemer.

How thrift can become hard.

Thrift may not be practiced with efficiency for a host of reasons. A few general reasons include: no tools, wrong tools, no equipment, bad equipment, unsuitable materials, lack of skills, lack of creativity, lack of inventiveness, lack of technology, unsuitable circumstances such as climate. Specific examples of inefficient thrift: Gardening without well prepared fertile soil. Attempting car repair without adequate tools or skills on a car that is hard to fix. Buying an old car that break down often and has high repair costs. Installing a solar heating system that is too small and/or inefficient in a climate that has insufficient sun in winter, or a wind energy system where average wind speed is low.

Thrift can become a pain, until you just want to forget about it. The 19th century self-sufficient farm folks, thrifty by necessity, had to work long hard hours to have the basic necessities of living. Plus s/he had a heavy burden of things to worry about: bad weather, crop failure, sickness or injury of human and beast. Farmers will say: 'I don't need to try the usual kinds of gambling, farming is gambling enough'. Many a thrifty overworked farmer eagerly quit farming at the first opportunity, tired of the tedious dull hard endless hours of work required. The hard work set men and women to dreaming of other lives. Most ended up with factory job, (not much of an improvement over farming as described - to give one example - in the novel ***The Jungle*** by Upton Sinclair).

Because thrift can be hard, the allure of the Industrial Economy is not all at fault for folk's failure to live with thrift today. The difficulty of thrift undermines many, even most attempts at it, without much help from the Industrial Economy. They'll take care of you, (but you may be stuck doing their dirty work). It is simply easier to take a job, buy everything else, and forget about all those involved, complicated thrifty practices. Submit and relax. And, anyway; maybe you can get one of the few good jobs.

Today, people still attempt self-sufficient farming, often with an idealized unrealistic conception of what it demands.

You could become entangled into a life of hard thrift if you try to be totally self sufficient; making your clothes from yarn from your own sheep, weaving cloth, making shoes from hides, tools and furniture from trees, raising livestock, chickens, cows, pigs, bees for honey and candle wax, making butter, cheese, and soap. Some sources say you'll end up working 15-hour days for what amounts to 40 cents an hour. You may become bitter as well as poor. Many a poor hardscrabble farmer did.

Modern technology may undermine thrifty practices. Horses were and still can be efficiently thrifty, both for farming and transportation as amply proven by the wise Amish. Horses appear to make farming take more time. Most farmers use tractors, but then they have to grow more just to pay for them, plow, plant, cultivate and harvest more fields, and work long hours again after all, despite their 'labor saving device'.

Today, modern knowledge and technology properly applied might help us practice efficient thrift. The old Russian Anarchist Peter Kropotkin believed rural electrification would result in widespread local production of things and distribution and dissolution of large factories because, he believed, it ought to make home and small scale production more efficient and possible using electric tools to make furniture, toys, housing components such as framing lumber, siding and trim, - and all of the things of wood and metal that once were made with hand tools taking much time and human energy. Sadly it didn't happen. Instead, the old wood and metal working skills were abandoned and lost and factories remain as large scale as ever. It was too easy to take the tedious but quickly learned factory job. Home and local production may be practical today if folks relearned old skills and technology - helped by the Internet.

Plenty of thrifty advice may be found in magazines and web sites. Much of this advice describes many little thrifts, small economies. We practice small economies while ignoring big economies. "Penny wise and pound foolish" said perfectly by Ben Franklin.

Small economies may help, but the biggest savings are projects that result in big savings, big cost cuts; housing costs, mortgage elimination; car, utilities, food, and health care savings. From the perspective of 'extreme thrift' a lot of advice on thrift is just not practical unless carefully reconsidered, as I will throughout this book.

A Dilemma:

At the beginning of your attempt to live ZC you may quickly encounter a dilemma: Having a low paying job makes it worthwhile for you to practice thrift - to save every hard earned penny possible. But you may have to work long hours at your low paying job to earn enough money to live, leaving no time or energy for thrift. To be thrifty you need to have some time to devote to it and you need money to buy tools and systems and learn skills to practice thrift with efficiency.

Many folks in low paying no future jobs waste their money quickly thus putting them back at square one. Folks with low paying jobs may be seen doing un-thrifty things; eating at fast food or conventional restaurants, drinking, drugs, gambling, keeping cell phones, driving gas wasting vehicles, living in drafty badly insulated houses.

How do you escape this dilemma? You must practice extreme thrift. You must practice thrift with efficiency. How do you do that? The rest of this book is devoted to the problem.

2.2 THRIFTY TECHNIQUES:

How can you achieve extreme thrift? As mentioned before, more detailed discussions of techniques are made in later chapters, but here I will introduce some general methods with examples of each.

Here is a list of techniques to help you think about how you might practice extreme thrift.

Combine systems in ways that allow each to be used with more efficiency:

Example: Carry a bike in or on your car all the time. Park and use your bike to continue your task whenever possible. A problem arises when a bike is carried on the outside of a car. The bike may cause increased wind resistance, especially at high speeds and your car may get lower miles-per-gallon. In the future, cars or bikes or both need to be modified to solve this problem.

Make or buy things that are easy to repair and maintain.

Example: Design and build or modify your car to be easy to fix. Modern mass produced cars are hard to fix and therefore require professional help - thus making it hard to practice extreme thrift if you own one.

Example: Design and build your own house or modify your existing house to be easy to build, repair, maintain, heat and cool.

Make, build, buy things that save you money continuously. Build systems you only have to pay for once and then pay you back over and over

Example: Build your own house to be energy conserving and solar heated from the start. Build your house with most windows facing south – which may not be any more expensive than conventional construction. A window facing south can be as efficient as any solar panel at a fraction of the cost.

On an existing house make use of energy conserving techniques.

Example: insulating window shutters. Folks rarely use these. Windows loose a lot of heat, even the best are not very efficient; but it is practical to build insulating shutters to be closed at night or in cloudy weather (or all winter on north facing windows).

One method to build window shutters cheaply: buy polyethylene or 'blueboard' and cut to fit each window opening. To be effective the perimeter of the shutter must be as airtight as possible so use duct tape around the perimeter to create a lip all around that touches the window frame - using tape folded back on itself. To build insulating shutters almost free you can use layers of cardboard duct taped around the edges. (But you will have to buy duct tape).

Practice preventive maintenance in everything. Develop good habits: keeping teeth clean, exercising, eating right, keeping up with car maintenance.

Make thrifty activities your recreation. Examples: gardening, sewing, foraging for wild food (as the mushroom hunters, the 'mycophagists' do).

Multi-task. many a housewife and househusband knows this one. Clean while something is cooking. Combine trip purposes when driving around town.

Get things that last. Tools, materials, rugged clothes. Example: denim clothes. Example: cars with bodies that don't rust - made of fiberglass as in the Corvette or plastics as in the Saturn.

Create or buy things that have multiple advantages. Things that are durable, maintenance free or low maintenance, and/or easy to fix and maintain, and cheap (or even free) to operate all at the same time. Example: the bicycle.

Design so the component of an item that wears out can be easily replaced rather than design a longer lasting item that you can't repair. Example: Shoe sole: buy or make double sole shoes with a replaceable outer sole.

Make systems serve multiple functions. Example: A south-facing porch that can be enclosed to become a solar heated room or greenhouse in winter, and returned to a porch in summer.

Set up mostly automatic processes: Example: A garden automatic watering system using hoses, pipes, timers, and perhaps rain water collection and cisterns.

Batch: (Here used as a verb). Make stuff in large batches to save time and effort.

Example: Make bread dough loaves for two weeks or more all at one time, keep them frozen and take one out to rise and bake as needed.

2.2.1 Alternatives to spending money.

Everywhere, all around us is stuff, lots of stuff that still costs nothing, even in our highly commercialized age. Enough, I contend, to live almost zero cost. The key to ZCL is to find, make, grow, repair and substitute stuff that costs nothing for stuff that costs money. You only need to learn how. Why buy stuff and miss the fun of adapting and using free stuff. Be aware though: these methods may easily slip into inefficient thrift, and so not be worth the trouble. You must try to practice them with extreme thrift, with efficiency.

(I apologize for the excessive use of the word 'stuff' but it seems to be the word that best fits the huge diverse array of 'stuff' I am considering here. George Carlin would approve – I believe – and if you have seen his famous comedy monologue on 'stuff' you might agree with me. Stuff encompasses the meanings of the words items, materials, things, possessions, equipment, tools, food, shelter, clothing, and anything else you need to survive, build, and move towards ZCL).

Don't buy anything except as a last resort. Do everything possible to avoid buying. You must have **Attitude**. You must look at buying with contempt; develop a healthy contempt for buying stuff. More detail on alternatives to buying will be considered in later chapters.

"The vegetable garden was of the greatest importance. Out of it came not only all of the vegetables for the summer, but for the winter as well, for Maria would have considered it a disgrace to have bought food of any sort." Louis Broomfield: ***The Farm.***

Here is a checklist to get you thinking about techniques you can use to avoid buying anything, or if you must buy, spending the least amount possible.

Warning: Some of these methods, practiced with inefficiency can degenerate into hard thrift.

Beg: Especially, if you are living in a state of homeless destitution you must not be too proud to beg - to ask for help from strangers - when you need it: whether for food, shelter, or transportation to a place you must go (such as a public shelter on a cold night).

Chapter 3 discusses homeless living in detail.

Ask for help: Simply asking for help from relatives, friends, or acquaintances may get you the assistance you need.

Ask for stuff: Sometimes stuff is to be had simply by asking around, by letting folks know you need it. Vast quantities of stuff exist in attics, garages, and closets that people can't or won't sell, are unwilling to throw out or give to a charity but may be willing to give to you if you just ask.

Use Charity: Private charities such as Gleaners can give you immediate food with no paperwork. Gleaners may be found in many cities across the U.S. The Salvation Army can give you all kinds of help. Go to a library, get on one of the computers you can use for free, ask for help from the librarian if you need it and type in 'charities' in the search engine to find more help. To find gleaners locations type in ***www.gcfb.org.***

If you are destitute, don't be too proud to use every handout you can get when beginning to attempt ZCL. Use any money you obtain to buy tools and equipment and learn skills that can help you live ZC and eventually free you from the need for charity.

Free stuff: Check for free items on the web sites craigslist and freecycle. Some churches collect and give away things; usually things people couldn't sell at garage sales but don't want to throw out.

Government: Get it through welfare or government: But keep as an objective ultimately not depending on government handouts. They can undermine reaching true independence and ZCL.

Use free public places: parks, libraries, museums as places to hang out, rest relax, think, research, learn. Some museums are always free, and some have free days - usually during a weekday, and some are donation only - you need not donate. You must be presentable –not look like a homeless destitute or libraries/museums may show you the door. Chapter 3 considers this problem in more detail.

Go to free events: Go to free or donation requested (but optional) events and activities: Examples: every community seems to have its special festival with free entertainments and events: music festivals, cherry festivals, with parades, shows, games, displays etc. Public supported orchestras give free concerts-in-the-park in the summer. Libraries have free speakers and presentations. See free historical reenactments and encampments: Medieval, Colonial, American Revolution and Civil War, and hundreds of others. You can find information on these in newspapers, web sites, chambers of commerce, and local government offices.

Squat: Means to live on land or in a building you don't officially own. Widespread in 3rd world countries, seldom tried in the U.S. Squatting in abandoned homes has been tried in some American inner cites by organizations such as ACORN (Association of Community Organizations for Reform Now).

Forage: Foraging is a fundamental method of Zero Cost Living whether you are in the city or countryside, homeless or homesteading, nomadic or settled. Primitivists sometimes called "abos" short for aborigines (but not necessarily aboriginal natives) have the goal of going into the wilderness with just their bare hands and the clothes on their backs, and surviving - as a recreation and a sport. (read Elpel, Allen). They try to use only stuff found in nature. But living ZC no self-imposed restrictions need apply. In addition to natural resources, there are all kinds of things out there you can use from dumpsters, abandoned houses, vacant lots, junkyards, construction sites, etc. These can make your life easier. America is rich in trash.

How to forage: Efficient foraging

One method: Carry a bike in or on your car (on a bike carrier). Park and use your bike to continue foraging whenever possible, thus saving gas and getting a better view at a slower speed than a car can provide.

Where to forage: alley ways, vacant lots, 'back lots' behind industries, along roads on trash days, along railroad tracks, service drives behind commercial storefronts, construction sites, abandoned industrial sites. Everywhere you go may have something forageable.

Think as you travel around and keep you're eyes open. Remember where to find stuff to get it later. Keep a notebook handy in pocket or car to record finds to get later. Currently I know where I can find lumber, apples, firewood, bricks, blocks, wood chips, stones, free clothes and bread. In the 3rd world most trash is used. We throw away too much. You are doing the world a service.

When to forage: Trash days. Find out (from your local government or garbage collection company) when big item days are scheduled. Find out when local colleges or universities end their school years. Student throw out heaps of stuff, especially furniture.

The book ***Going Green: True tales from gleaner, scavengers and dumpster divers*** edited by Laura Prichett (University of Oklahoma Press 2009) may help you make efficient, successful foraging expeditions.

The hurricane Katrina was a disaster for the victims, but a bonanza for a ZCL practitioner, not by stealing, but by foraging and recycling damaged stuff, especially construction materials as houses were torn down and rebuilt.

And, a ZCLer would cringe watching homes torn down on the television show ***Extreme Makeover: Home Edition***, seeing all that perfectly good lumber smashed and broken as the old house is demolished.

Construction Sites:

Useful stuff may be gathered from construction and building tear down sites. Ask a worker on a site if you can go through the scrap lumber pile, or gather broken bricks, drywall, etc. They'll likely say yes. Useful stuff might include broken bricks, concrete chunks, drywall scraps, lumber scraps, sawdust, oriented strand board (osb) and plywood scraps, pallets, vinyl scraps, and nails. Later chapters will describe the uses that can be made of this stuff.

To efficiently find sites to forage, get lists of permits issued for building construction, remodeling and demolition from county and/or municipal building departments.

Salvage old buildings: Offer to tear down old buildings for a lower fee than demolition contractors charge and save the materials. (You may have to take a building down using hand tools to save materials, and the work might be too much for you. This is where you need friends that think like you).

Get stuff when it is available and store it. Construction goes in cycles. Years of new construction may be followed by years of little or none. At many sites you will likely be the only person recycling this stuff, (unless ZCL becomes widely practiced). Trade or give it away whatever you can't use. Find ways to keep it neatly. Keep your homestead orderly when storing foraged materials: Keep like items together in neat piles on the edges of your land to reduce messy appearance. Diverse things jumbled together disturb the eye.

Dumpster diving is one of the most valuable methods of foraging. If you ask permission, the owner might have to say no because if you are hurt he could be sued. So, don't ask permission, just go for it. And if you are challenged, you will most likely be shoed away, thus the owner is absolved of responsibility for any injury you receive.

Sometimes, if you are seen, the owner believes you are putting stuff into his dumpster when he tells you to leave. If you explain your true intention, he may not mind you taking stuff out. If the owner still objects, perhaps you can go back later when the owner (or person who rented the dumpster) is not around. I personally consider it an honorable and valuable activity to make use of stuff destined for the landfill.

You can forage while doing something else if you keep a 'foraging' attitude on your mind, perhaps as you travel to some appointment or event. Make and keep a list handy of stuff you need or will need in the future so you'll have an eye out for it as you forage or as you go about other activities.

Hoard or stockpile:

A lot of the things you come across while foraging or salvaging you will have no immediate use for but you may want to save and stockpile them anyway. On too many occasions items I left because I could not imagine a use for them at the time, I discovered a use for later. Examples: barrels, bricks, furniture, clothes, scrap metal. And items you can't use you may trade.

Hoarding can have bad connotations; selfishly keeping stuff other people need or can use. Here I emphasize the positive side of it: keeping stuff until you need it. Stuff that would ordinarily be thrown away, stuff that no one else can make any use of, but you can. As you forage you need places to keep stuff until it can be put to use, or to keep it until you find a use for it. Living ZCL lots of storage space will be needed. The barns and sheds of the old farms were full of stuff.

Repair stuff: Great quantities of broken stuff are thrown away or given away every day. Sometimes it is only slightly broken.

People don't have the time to fool around fixing an item so they just buy a new one. But, living ZC, you may have the time. It would be a great help to ZCL if more things were made easy to repair.

Improvise, Adapt, Substitute: are key ZCL techniques. Improvisation, can mean finding or making workable substitutes for all of the necessary stuff for life.

Discussion: Use what you have, use found materials, or use what is free or widely available. Make it up as you go, or use what you can make. Often clever, even brilliant things may be created by the serious application of improvisation.

Examples: many more are suggested throughout this book:

Seed starting containers: Replace commercial seed trays made of cheap brittle plastic with plastic containers food is sold in..

Old tires: can be made into tire sandals. See the website of Thomas Elpel at ***www.hollowtop.com/sandals.htm***. to learn how.

Drywall scraps: The gypsum in drywall can improve garden soil, especially clay soil. Get it from construction sites. Smash the scraps into little pieces and let the rain and sun work on it.

We need a new field of study: 'Improvisational design' and engineering. Making use of available junk: Imagine ways to improvise using diverse kinds of new stuff and composites of new and ancient stuff put together:

Example: Build a complete car using junkyard parts combined with off the shelf components (including perhaps items from a building supply store). The book ***Build Your Own Sports Car for as Little as L250*** ($465 U.S.) by Ron Champion shows how it might be possible.

Another example: Build a hydroponic solar greenhouse using, as much as possible, recycled lumber, trays, cups, pipes, etc.

See the book ***Shelters Sheds and Shanties*** by D.C.Beard. Most of the structures in this book are fascinating improvisations using local natural materials.

Stories of survival often have fascinating examples of improvisation: utensils, bowls, weapons tools, stone tools including knives using flintknapping (tools using flint as in the stone age A wooden spoon can be made using a coal from your fire to burn the 'hollow' into the wood.

Make/build it: The biggest savings in this book are realized by the use of this idea. And, if you make it or build it yourself you can probably fix it.

Design It right: When you build stuff; design it to make it easy to build, repair and operate using free or almost free materials if possible. In this book are design ideas for houses, greenhouses, farms, cars and boats that apply these design concepts.

Grow it: Gardening benefits you in multiple ways: exercise, organic food at a fraction of the cost of store bought, and uses for foraged materials as compost, mulch, and structures. And, solar greenhouses can make it possible for you to grow high yields of food and fuel in a small area. You can practice efficient high intensity farming without the endless backbreaking labor of the old time farms.

Do without it. Live so you don't need it. The Amish live without electricity by choice and conviction. (They are convinced it undermines their independence, and they are probably right). When they buy a house they rip out the electrical system.

Wait for it: Sometimes, the thing you need will just come your way, fall into your lap as it were, if you keep an eye out for it. I've had this happen many times.

Trade for it: A young man began with a paper clip and by a series of trades arranged through the web ended up with a house. The web site ***oneredpaperclip.com*** describes the entire process. Though not likely to happen very often, revealed here are the possibilities that trade can accomplish. Start thinking about what you have to trade or can get to trade, of what you need, of who has what you need, and try to make some trades. Be creative. Bedsides things, you can also trade services, your skills and your time.

Exchange stuff: One example: Some folks exchange houses as a way to get free vacations. If you have a comfortable house (as described in chapter 6) in an interesting location, you many be able to do this. A web search will reveal folks that do.

Share: Share it in common ownership: An underutilized method in our society.

Borrow: Ask around, borrow if possible. Read Thoreau's commentary on the axe he borrowed when he built his cabin on Walden Pond. He makes borrowing seem respectable, even honorable.

Make Friends: Build a network of helping friends and neighbors you can share, and trade with, borrow from, get advice, get physical help, etcetera. Be sure to help them in return.

Steal it: When, if ever? Theft costs others, if not you so I do not regard it as a ZCL method - strictly defined. Stealing, you may not learn skills, make, or do things that help you take care of yourself. Usually, in fact almost always, you won't need to steal if you try every method in this list first. If you are starving (and are not stealing from other starving people), who am I to tell you what to do. Stealing –and its negative effects on a ZC life - in the form of petty theft - is discussed more in later chapters.

Study, learn and practice: Careful study may sometimes reveal ways to do something without spending $ that ordinarily would cost you. There are countless teachers, web sites, magazines – including old magazines out there that can teach you skills and techniques applicable to extreme thrift. Retirees, with a lifetime of learning thrifty techniques can be goldmines of knowledge. Seek them out!

2.2.2 Health and Food:

Keeping your health is a huge, possibly the largest step you can take towards achieving extreme thrift, and Zero Cost Living. What if you were rich but ruined your health to get it? I would call it a bad bargain. T. Boone Pickens wrote, in his book ***The First Billion is the Hardest*** , "No amount of money success, or fame can raise a body from a bed or turn fat into muscle. .... Only constant and aggressive exercise can keep a human being young and fit."

Health is usually the highest cost these days - whether for insurance or for service paid out of pocket. It is heavily affected by diet and lifestyle.

"…you shall eat the plants of the field. In the sweat of your face you shall eat your bread…." said God in Genesis chapter 3 as he cast Adam and Eve out of Eden. A Biblical fable, maybe but the proof of it seems to be built into the human body. We all need exercise to be healthy.

Since you must get plenty of exercise to be healthy, why not do useful things with all that effort. Rather than doing boring and tedious exercise routines, perhaps even joining a health club costing $ (heaven forbid) or practicing useless sports, why not work on useful tasks that are likely to be more interesting than exercise. For example, the 5,000 steps or 3 miles a day recommended as a minimum for good health could be used to take care of an extensive garden or forage a wide area for wild food. Imagine how much of the physical work of the world would be accomplished if more of wasted human energy was put to useful tasks.

In the healthiest cultures people walk everywhere, many miles a day and the optimum is something like 10 miles a day. Wrote John Robbins in his book ***Healthy at 100:*** "Certainly part of the secret to the exceptionally healthy aging found in Abkhasia Vilcabamba, Hunza, and Okinawa is the extraordinary amount of regular exercise built into the routines of daily life." (Page 161). He notes that in Hunza, in the mountains of northern Pakistan, there were no roads until recent years and people walked everywhere. And, they used no money until 1965. Since its introduction along with roads and development their health has deteriorated. I will consider the significance of these startling facts in more detail later in this book.

Food

You must eat for health, not for pleasure to realize extreme thrift. Food may too easily become another of the many addictions foisted upon you by society. The result will be bad health in the form of obesity, diabetes, and a host of other expensive ailments. You can get enough healthy food very cheap and often free, and possibly entirely free without charity. But by all means use charity when you must.

It is possible to eat for $150 per person a year while still buying many items. Purchases: canned evaporated milk, no packaged items, no soda, alcohol, cookies, bakery goods, use no prepared goods like pizza or paper products except toilet paper. Buy fresh garden veggies canned and frozen. Get chicken at one dollar a pound. Buy 50 lb bags of staples like wheat and beans. Garden and can your harvest. I will consider the problem of food in detail in the next chapters.

2.2.3 Minimizing cost when you must buy:

What not to buy:

If you must buy, don't buy the wrong things. Buying the wrong things - the opposite of thrift - is buying that results in built-in rising costs: an expensive high maintenance car or boat, a huge energy wasting house, expensive things for show that can be damaged or stolen. Don't buy these things that eat your dollars in the first place.

What to buy:

Get stuff that lasts:

In your mind, divide everything for sale in the world in two. On one side put everything permanent: Things you can use over and over: knowledge, tools, durable clothes, wash cloths, and some that (ordinarily) never wear out: land, rocks, mud. These are the things you want to acquire. On the other side put all the things that are temporary, wear out and depreciate in value or are quickly used up: cars, food, electronic gizmos, non-rechargeable batteries, paper towels. These are the things you want to reduce or eliminate from your purchases.

Permanent items like real estate can be purchased and paid off, and you never need pay anything again (except for taxes). Once you have paid for land, it is available to you forever. You can stand on it as many times as you want, or even lay down on it and take a nap, and it is never consumed. A solar greenhouse once it is built and paid for can be used season after season - increasing your garden yield. It pays therefore to make as many of your purchases as possible be of the permanent kind and not the temporary kind.

When you buy:

Shop around, including the internet for everything. And/or use your telephone to shop thus saving much gas and time. Between the four auto parts stores in my town, the prices can vary widely, which can quickly be determined by a few calls.

Don't ever buy at "Party Stores" or convenience stores. You'll never get the best price. Stores in odd places, off the beaten path, away from the retail districts in towns, or out of town, are more likely to be cheaper, as long as you don't have to use much more gas to get there. Furthermore, don't buy from places with fancy showrooms and elaborate displays. And certainly not where the salesmen are after you as soon as you walk in the door. The cost of the sales force will be in the price you pay for anything you buy. YOU will be paying for their commission. On the other hand, find a place where the sales people know about the products they sell. In most chain stores the employees are hired for the lowest wage possible and not for their knowledge, and know little or nothing about the products.

Look for sales, going out of business sales, overstock sales.

And try not to buy heavily advertised products. They will cost more to cover the cost of all that advertising.

Make an effort to check how an item was made and by who. I for one, and probably you too, don't want products made by child labor, made in conditions of virtual slavery, or products that ruin the environment.

Buy bulk, it's cheaper that way. And, buying in bulk can result in fewer trips. You will need to make arrangements for storage and preservation - a problem to be considered in the home you purchase or build – which I will discuss more in later chapters.

Buy wholesale: Find wholesalers who will sell to the public. Many do. Check the phone book or company web site. Sometimes they will sell items only in large quantities. Perhaps you can trade or sell extra amounts of items or store them for later use.

Buy local if possible to help the local economy and thus help your own economic situation. Buy at farmers markets.

Get reciprocity: if you buy, the seller must agree to buy something from you. (We should have made this idea our policy in our dealings with China).

Buy basic raw stuff: unprocessed food, building materials.

Buy food only after calculating the price per pound. Learn the price per pound and keep a small notebook listing prices at various stores in your areas.

Buy in-season fruits and vegetables when they are cheapest and learn methods to keep them.

Keep all receipts: a purchase might not work, or not suit your needs, or you may be able to use an item and then return it.

Keep track of purchases (as you save your receipts): In my life, I find it amazing the number of things I find out later I didn't need to buy, that were of no use or less use than expected, and I suspect it's true of your life too.

Review and reconsider all of your purchases. Later, I sometimes discover ways I could have obtained or accomplished something cheaper; or for free. For example, in the case of car repairs; I've watched mechanics work on my car, reviewed books on how to do it, bought tools, and found I can do many repairs myself for a fraction of the cost of professional help.

Debt, and mortgage:

Can taking on debt ever be a reasonable technique of extreme thrift**?** Using a credit card or taking on a mortgage for example? Yes and no.

No: Why not: Debt can increase your cost of living. Most debt is taken on for the wrong reasons: trophy house, new car, more junk. A trophy house, for example rather than a practical house can resulting higher expenses all around (unless you can sell it for more to a bigger fool).

Yes if the expense results in saving or income greater than the expense of paying interest on the debt. Especially, borrowing to buy land can be justifiable if it is cheap enough, (though strangely, banks won't lend you money to buy land). Land payments – including property taxes may be less – much less than rent.

You can live on land, perhaps in a tent or vehicle or shed temporarily thus-saving rent so you can use the money to build a house, perhaps with "sweat equity" meaning building it yourself. Thomas Elpel did it and describes how in his book ***Living Homes.***

As you pay off your land, you build up equity (a percentage of ownership) until someday you have no payment and own it 'free and clear' another words without a mortgage. Unfortunately, you still have to pay property taxes.

On your own land you can grow your own food. You can relax at your ease. It can be a great stress reliever. Perhaps a family ought to buy their children land rather than a college education.

It is possible to imagine a 'turn-key' homestead that you buy with a mortgage, and produces on site enough income to cover the mortgage payments, and perhaps even enough to let you live 'zero cost'. Such a homestead might include built in sources of income like an apartment to rent out, solar greenhouses producing foods to eat and sell, and solar cells producing electricity for your homestead and a surplus to sell back to your electric utility. Of course you are left with the job of maintaining your homestead, but maybe the endless backbreaking work of the old time farms would not be necessary. I will pursue this idea in detail in chapters 5 and 6.

2.2.4 **Limits** of the methods presented in this book

Some methods that might save money are not included in this book. For example:

Water saving: valuable in a dry climate, or a seasonally dry climate.

Hunting: practiced efficiently, the savings in food and material (such as buckskin for clothes) might exceed the cost in time and equipment.

Every formula for a household product is not included in this book. A few are included. Many books with these formulas already exist, some listed in the references of this book.

The web site **http://0costliving.com** expands on the ideas presented in this book.

2.3 COST OF THRIFT:

Almost always, the techniques listed above have a cost. This cost might be in time, money, effort, or all three: To live ZC you want to minimize the dollar costs, but not let time and effort/energy costs get too high in the process.

In ***Doing Nothing*** by Tom Lutz, he wrote "I lived with some friends on a Midwestern farm, a commune, trying to live on nothing so I could do next to nothing. Somehow I ended up working all the time anyway." Read pages 41 through 46 for the rest of this true story.

2. 3.1 Time use:

To live ZC, you may not have the time to do all the things you have to do, or to learn all the skills required.

In practicing ZCL, more and more time may be needed to save fewer and fewer $ 'diminishing returns' to use economic jargon. Example: A fire may be started with a match, with flint and steel, or using a bow-drill. Each technique is progressively more difficult and time consuming. You must think ahead and plan ahead and multitask, more like earlier times in history.

As described earlier, and writing from experience many a method to save $ or avoid an expenditure may end up costing you more, may become hard thrift:

Examples:

An old used car: Can have high repair costs.

An old house: May have high maintenance, heating, and utility costs.

Motorcycle: May be less safe, when sharing the road with cars, and have high insurance costs.

Old technologies may require constant maintenance. Made of wood, iron, steel, organic cloth, hemp rope, etc. and require: painting, oiling, careful covering, tarring rope. Example of bad old technology: Old wooden sailboats. Good example: Traditional

Japanese homes. They leave framing and finish wood unpainted but well protected from water by wide roof overhangs.

2.3.2 Cost Analysis: Cost of thrift in detail:

Thrift costs in time, money, and/or requires skills so you must invest time to learn these skills. You can spend more money and less time and skill, or less money and increasing time and skill to achieve extreme thrift.

Here is a chart showing what bread might cost considering the "time use" dilemma, each step towards ZCL may cost or more time and less money. You must choose the option that suits your economic circumstance.

Bread Economics - Cost per loaf:

Method:	Total Cost:	Time use:	$ in savings:
Buy bread	$2	15 minutes	$ 40
Make bread	25 cents	12 minutes	$ 5
Grow grain	26 cents	18 minutes	$ 5.20
Forage grain	0 cents	4 hours	$ 0
Charity	0	1 minute	$ 0

Chart discussion:

Buy bread: Time at an $8 an hour job - about 15 minute to earn $2 for the loaf. About $40 must be saved – requiring 6 hours to earn – if interest income from a bank pays for the loaf at 5% interest not counting inflation, more if the interest rate is lower or inflation higher.

Make bread: Time at an $8 an hour job - about 2 minutes to earn 25 cents to buy the ingredients. Add 10 minutes = time to mix ingredients and put the bread in a bread machine. Rising time is not counted. You can do other thing while the bread is rising. If you knead the bread by hand add about 10 minutes. $5.00 must be in savings - requiring 40 minute to earn if you use interest income to buy the ingredients.

Grow grain: Growing and processing grain in small amounts may be too expensive and time consuming for most folks and might qualify as inefficient thrift. See the detailed discussion at the end of this chapter where I estimate 6 minutes of farming time per loaf for a small grain field. Relative to a small operation, conventional farmers can grow grain for low land, labor, seed, and fertilizer costs.

Forage grain: Foraging for grain is extremely expensive in time, but possible as Elpel describes in his book ***Participating in Nature***. Though no cost is listed, a percentage of the cost for suitable clothes, shoes, collecting bag or container, water bottle, food consumed while foraging, etc. could be added.

Charity: Though it costs you nothing, charity does cost others and therefore is not a ZCL method as I define it. You may need to take charity on occasion, but to live ZC I believe you must work to move away from dependence and towards taking care of yourself.

Time, Knowledge, and the Cost of Thrift:

Everything costs something whether in time or money, or knowledge/skills that must be acquired. Actually, knowledge/skills and money can be acquired with time, so really time is the true cost of everything. Thrift sometimes costs a lot of time and a little money; and may require knowledge and skills that vary from none to extensive and sophisticated.

You can't learn everything. You can't remember everything you learn. And you must be thrifty in learning skills and knowledge. In the internet you can get lost researching web sites about frugality. There are thousands of page of advice. You can't possibly follow it all.

Time is the most limited resource of your life. Time is not replaceable. Time is the real, fundamental cost of everything. Don't waste it.

Making bad thrift good: Attitude, skills, knowledge, technology, invention, improvisation, and plain cleverness can make it possible to turn hard, inefficient, 'bad' thrift into 'good' thrift.

For example, making products out of raw grain, – bread, pasta, etcetera can be a difficult time consuming process and doing it with efficiency requires skill and good equipment. A class or two on it, or a job in a bakery (or a lot of practice) would be extremely valuable for achieving ZCL.

Another example: It is possible to make useful things out of waste, trash, and otherwise useless materials: Most trash, I believe, can be turned into something useful. The question is, is it worth your time and energy. The answer is, it depends on whether you can gather and make waste materials useful in an efficient manner, another words, with 'efficient thrift'.

Example of re-using waste that may not be worthwhile - may be inefficient thrift: Making special trips gathering waste materials (such as compost and mulch for an organic garden) may not be worth the gas and time, and cost required.

Example of re-using a waste that may be worthwhile - may be efficient thrift: While doing other tasks such as shopping or going to work - gather waste materials. Allow extra time during your trip for foraging.

The list of 'thrifty techniques' near the beginning of this chapter serves as a general guide to techniques for 'making bad thrift good'. More methods in greater detail are presented in later chapters.

2.3.3 Ladder of costs:

Like the bread example presented above, for every cost, a 'cost ladder' may be constructed with a series of 'rungs' rising from making it entirely yourself of free or waste materials to buying something outright – and paying full retail cost. At each rung of this ladder your $ cost goes down, but you time expenditure may go up. And for each item a point - or rung may be reached where the cost savings is not worth your time.

More examples of ladders of thrift: descending:

Soup: 4th rung: Buying a can, opening, and heating it up. 3rd rung: buying the raw ingredients and throwing them together. 2rd rung: growing the ingredients for your soup. 1st rung: foraging the ingredients in the wild.

Book: 6th rung: buy a new hardcover book. 5th rung: buy a paperback. 4th rung: buy the book used. 3rd rung: buy a CD with the book on it and read it on your home computer. 2nd rung: get the book or CD from the library. 1st rung: get the book on the internet (if available, but many books are) and read it on your home or a library computer.

Each rung costs more, the lowest may cost you almost nothing except your time. (Though the library costs taxpayers – you may be a taxpayer if you own real estate or rent in the community that finances the library. Or if you buy stuff in the community, sales tax revenue may go towards the library – or the property taxes businesses pay may go towards the library). Trying to live ZCL, the top rungs of the cost ladder may be tipsy and unstable. You may become financially unstable buying things you don't need to buy.

Another ladder: transportation: **ascending** the ladder: 1.walk. 2. bike. 3. moped. 4.motorcycle. 5. bus. 6. small old car. 7. larger old car. 8. new car. 9. new sports utility vehicle. 10. Hummer. 11. motor home.

Determining the best rung of the ladder to practice from a ZCL perspective depends on how much time and money you have. Homeless and destitute you'll want to say on the low rungs. Living in a comfortable homestead with money in savings you may be able to splurge a little.

As you read this book, consider carefully whether a specific ZCL method is really worth the trouble it requires – given your particular circumstance.

Climbing down a ladder of cost, going from a conventional lifestyle to a thrifty lifestyle can result in what I call a '**cascade of savings**'

2.3.4 Cascade of Savings:

By living with extreme thrift you may have to spend only a fraction of your income from your job for your living expenses. If you earn more than you spend, invest it to further lower your living costs until, like a house of cards your structure of costs collapses. A cascade of savings results in a collapse of expenses as saving on one expense enables another and that allows several more, and so on until you approach ZCL. For example, if you can pay off your mortgage, (or avoid having one by building your own house) the money you don't have to spend for a mortgage might be used to make your house more energy efficient - cutting heating and cooling costs, and the money saved from that used to create a solar heated hydroponic greenhouse cutting food cost - and so on.

To achieve absolute ZCL, supplying some of your needs may require extensive and expensive options often using technologies used long ago and/or abandoned as inconvenient. For example, to keep food longer before the refrigerator folks used the icebox, the ice room, the cold cellar, drying food, fermenting milk (as yogurt or kefir). Using old and/or abandoned and inconvenient technologies, you could get trapped into inefficient or 'hard' thrift. However, modern technology, updating of techniques using modern knowledge, or relearning old skills may make these methods practical and efficient again.

There are expenses you just can't get rid of completely such as property taxes and so to live ZC you must stockpile some dollars in savings or investments that provide interest or dividends (where the return may be small or risky) or earn money from a job or business. Chapters 5 and 6 discuss this more. The more costs you can reduce or eliminate, the fewer dollars you'll need to save, invest, or earn.

2.3.5 Investment:

This book is not another investment book. There are thousands of those already.

What should you invest in - where should you put your money from the perspective of extreme thrift? "A penny saved is a penny earned." wrote Old Ben, but saved $ are eaten by inflation You may try investing, to get a higher return on your money, but investments have risk (Read the book ***A Random Walk Down Wall Street*** by Burton Malkiel to see just how irrational the stock market can be). Much bad free advice is out there, free advice. Good advice costs $, the more $ the better the advice. Only the wealthy can afford the best advice, and therefore profit the most from it. Ironic isn't it.

Secure that penny saved by investing it to cut your cost of living - resulting in more savings. From a ZCL perspective, savings are equivalent to income - as Ben said.

Here, I advocate investing in tools, equipment, facilitates, materials, information and learning skills applicable to ZCL that eliminate the need to spend dollars. Invest in ways that drive your living costs down such as a solar heating system for your house, greenhouses, garden tools, and food processing equipment. Consider taking this step: Don't buy products; buy equipment that makes the product for you: a bread machine, a yogurt maker, a sewing machine and sewing classes. Don't pay to get the car fixed, buy tools to fix the car and fix it yourself.

If you get unexpected dollars from a company buyout, inheritance, or perhaps from a stock market/real estate windfall invest it to realize ZCL, don't blow it on a trophy house, kitchen remodeling, new appliances, plasma TV, vacation, a new car or whatever wasteful junk advertisers throw at you.

Through step after step you can gradually drive down costs until like a house of collapsing cards one item affects another and the whole edifice of expenses collapses in a 'cascade of savings'.

2.3.6 COLA: Cost of Living:

COLA is an acronym for 'cost of living'. COLA expenses include food, clothing, utility bills, housing costs, transportation costs; all of the necessities required to maintain a comfortable but not extravagant lifestyle. Conventional economics would have you believe COLA is fixed, or going up due to inflation. Thus social security recipients, public employees, labor unions ask for COLA raises to keep up with inflation. But is COLA really fixed or rising? It is possible to invest in systems that reduce or eliminate many, even most of your COLA expenses.

A lot of nonsense has been written about poverty, about living on a low income. The reality is it is possible to live on a very low income and be perfectly healthy and comfortable, if you practice efficient thrift, if you live using extreme thrift and build your 'personal economy'.

2.3.7 Real Cost in ZCL Terms:

Practicing a ZCL lifestyle you try to avoid buying whenever possible, but when you must buy you need \$. So you must raise \$ whether by a job, business, or more ZCL methods (which can sometimes cross into 'hard thrift'). Or you can save money in the bank for the interest income or invest it (perhaps in dividend paying stocks). If you pay for things with interest or dividend income the real cost of purchases that depreciate in value (like a car) and purchases that get used up or consumed (like food and gas) is the money that you must save or invest to earn enough interest or dividend income to buy these things, not their purchase price. Why?

From a ZCL perspective, the amount of savings necessary to pay for things depends on the interest rate or dividend your saved money can earn. For example, a one-dollar candy bar, living ZC really cost \$20 because that is how much money you must save at 5% interest or dividend return per year - to pay for the bar.

But wait, inflation has the effect of continually eroding the value of a dollar. The U.S. dollar is now worth less than one cent in 1846 dollars, the year Thoreau lived at Walden. So cost of the candy bar is increasing each year. The purchasing power of the \$20 saved to cover the cost of the candy bar is continually eroding, so an additional amount must be saved each year and added to the $20 to cover the increased cost of the candy bar. The average rate of inflation in recent years has been 2 or 3%, so using an average of 2.5% the cost of a $1 candy bar increases by about 2.5 cents each year after inflation is figured in. To cover this 2.5-cent annual increase more money must be put into savings each year: at 5% return, 50 cents more each year. But where is that 50 cents coming from? To add 50 cents to savings each year, even more money must be added to saving in the first year. At 5% return, $10 more must be added to savings so the full cost of a candy bar becomes over $30.

Consider an annual cost of living of $10,000. Using the method of cost adjusted for inflation that was used for the candy bar, $300,000 must be saved to cover an annual living cost of $10,000.

You can quickly see that any step you take that reduces your annual cost of living can have a great impact on the amount you must have in savings.

Using the same methodology again, a million dollars in savings earning a 5% interest rate with inflation at 2.5% yields an income of only $33,000 a year. Thus, you may have only $33,000 a year to live on if you are a millionaire. So, even a millionaire may need to consider some ZCL methods.

Maybe you believe you can get more than a 5% return on your money. Then you must put your money somewhere else other than a bank CD (Certificate of Deposit), and your risks go up. The stock market, commodity trading, starting a business, even real estate in recent years have considerable risk

From personal experience, stocks are volatile, too often pure gambling. Much time for research is needed and still, too many unknowns exist, along with unexpected events and irrational valuations. Investors too often really don't have a clue as to the worth of a stock. A herd mentality prevails, you try to be first in some herd trend, or stampede is a good analogy, and first to get out of the herd before it runs over a cliff.

Rather than invest in the stock market or inflation eaten savings, it may be far safer to invest in tools, equipment, facilities, and learning skills that lower your living costs.

Revisiting the candy bar example: What if you were to make a candy bar. It is possible to do it at home. On the surface it's not worth it, saving say 95 cents for a lot of effort. But what if you made 100, one years supply and it cost you only a few pennies a bar. After all what is in it? Sugar, cocoa, some oil. So you save 95 x 100 or $95 a year. Living ZC, you would have to have $3,000 in the bank to buy all of your own candy bars. Making your own, to cover the $5 cost you only need $150 in the bank. (One source for making chocolate: ***Enlightened Chocolate*** by Camilla V. Saulsbury).

You can make 100 candy bars in a few hours. A few hours work to save $95 and avoid keeping $3000 in the bank begins to look like extreme thrift.

The same for pop or breakfast cereal or ice cream, or thousands of other products. Of course these foods are not even necessities, not even healthy. You could buy none and save all of the time and cost.

A more serious example: building your own house. You use your money to buy tools and materials, and your time practicing skills. That can be a far better use of your time and money than investing it. You might take 1 or 2 years to build a house and save $100,000 of the cost. Not a bad annual income. Skills you learn you can use to get a job or start a business. And when you are done (if you didn't borrow $ to build) you have a house you can live in mortgage free forever.

A house or land usually does not depreciate, except in a falling real estate market, which happened very rarely and usually, declines modestly, (except recently). And, a house and land is not consumed even though you constantly use it. It is the best kind of asset to have.

But a house needs maintenance and repair to keep its value, and utilities are a major real ongoing cost. So you must design your house to be inexpensive and easy to maintain and repair

And you can use money you save by avoiding rent to reduce utility costs - such as homemade solar panels for home heating.

Another excellent use of saved money: A solar greenhouse: A greenhouse only costs once – when you build it, is not destroyed every year, is not consumed and can increase your yield of produce – verses a conventional garden - year after year. Thus your food costs – and gardening costs - may be reduced year after year.

Zero Cost Living: Counting your real income:

From a ZCL perspective when you count up your real income the costs and expenditures that you avoid through your thrifty practices should be added in.

Dollars that you do not have to spend because of the way you live equals income. (A penny saved is a penny earned).

If you own your house free and clear and pay no mortgage or rent the dollars you save are not recorded or reflected in your income, under ordinary income accounting. If you pay rent or mortgage you must earn the dollars to pay these costs and these dollars are included in your income. In fact, owning your home saves you $10,000 or more a year in interest or rent payments. Your real income is higher by that amount.

Similarly, if you can walk everywhere or bike and own no car you can save the $2,000 a year (if you fix it yourself) a used car might cost you; or the $5,000 cost of a new car per year. Again the economy and your income reflect no evidence of this under ordinary economics. But accounting in ZCL terms, your income is higher by $2,000 or more per year.

At the typical service economy wage that is a lot of hours of labor - car and house savings together = $12,000 or about 12 months work after taxes. Therefore, if your service economy job pays you $12,000 a year, and you own your house without a mortgage and need no car then your income really is $12,000 plus $12,000 = $24,000 a year or effectively doubled.

2.3.8 The Wheat-field: Thrift gone awry.

Sometimes, doing a thing that seems thrifty is not thrifty at all. To show how complex and convoluted calculations of what is really thrifty and contributes to ZCL and what is not, I have made the following analysis of the cost and savings of growing your own wheat:

In ***Walden***, Thoreau had his bean-field. Here I will consider the costs and savings of your own wheat-field.

If the basic food of one person for one year were consumed primarily as wheat products what would be the cost? (This would not be healthy, but I want to determine from a theoretical perspective - if this would be thrifty. Perhaps you could trade wheat you don't use for other food). To get sufficient calories: one person needs about 3,000 food calories a day (or a less if you're keeping your weight down) or 1 million calories are needed per person per year. (By convention one 'food' calorie equals one kilocalorie or 1,000 'conventional' energy calories.) Wheat provides about 1,600 calories per pound depending on how it is processed and cooked.

2,400 calories are provided by about 1 1/2 pounds of wheat products a day. Assuming non-wheat products (goodies) provide about 600 calories a day, in 365 days an individual requires 550 pounds of wheat.

What is the cost of wheat in the form of bread bought at the store? One 24 ounce loaf (containing one pound of flour and a half pound of other ingredients in a standard 24 ounce loaf) contains about 1600 calories and 1½ loaves a day would have to be consumed to get 2400 calories a day - costing $2 a loaf and $3 a day for 365 days would cost $1,095 a year for 547 loaves of bread. Bought in part as pasta, cereal, cookies, cake, pies, etc. the cost would be much higher, easily $2,000 a year.

Wheat could be bought in 25-pound bags for about 40 cents a pound, thus 550 pounds used in a year would cost about $220. You would need the skill and equipment to process all of this wheat into the myriad of products ordinarily bought at the store: bread, pasta, pancakes, crackers, etc. etc. But it is quite possible to do. One more step might be to buy wheat berries and a countertop grain mill and grind them into flour yourself. These could be easier to keep than flour and would cost $15 per 50 pound bag and $165 for 550 pounds saving an additional $55 a year.

Living zero cost, $220 per year would require $4,400 invested at 5% interest – and an additional $2,200 to cover average annual inflation of 2½% per year.

The biggest advance towards ZCL and the most savings is realized by taking the steps already considered above - buying raw wheat and processing it; but you could go further. You could grow your own wheat, cutting costs further. Then what could you expect to spend? (Again, theoretically eating primarily wheat products). To grow 550 pounds of wheat you would require about 7,000 square feet or 1/6 of an acre of good land that you prepared, fertilized well, watered if necessary, and kept control of pests and diseases. (Estimate based on 75 pounds per 1,000 square feet as described in ***Back Home*** magazine issue 36 page 28 'Homegrown Bread' by Darryl Goodman). About 50 pounds of seed would be needed for this enterprise costing you - $15 a for 50 pound bag. You may spend perhaps $15.00 more for various fertilizers. For the $30 you need to buy your seed and fertilizer you would require $900 in the bank. You may be able to forage free fertilizer, or grow fertilizing crops (such as nitrogen fixing legumes) on you wheat field on some years eliminating fertilizer costs. And, you may be able to save some of your seed each year to replant. So you may begin to see how it is possible to live almost zero cost. You are faced with the tasks of preparing the field, planting, fertilizing, watering if needed, controlling weeds, pests, and diseases, cutting, threshing, winnowing, and storing. Growing your own begins to look like hard thrift.

And there are other costs to consider.

Land Cost: Unfortunately, land costs must still be considered. How can these be determined? Cost to purchase or rent your land, and property taxes are extremely variable. Here, I show how I would calculate these costs: A parcel of land may cost a few thousand or tens of thousands. I would assign only the cost of the 7,000 square feet used for this experiment to the cost, whatever percentage of your total land area that is. If you have 1/2 acre, that's about 33% of your land area. So, on a $10,000 lot, your 10,000 wheat-field costs $3,300. Land usually is yours forever once you get it, so you need only buy it once. The land cost, on an annual basis I estimate to be equal to the net interest you could have earned if $3,300 was saved/invested in the bank at 2 1/2% a year after inflation or $82.50 a year. (If you sell your land someday you may make more than you paid - reducing your land cost to 0 or less).

Property Taxes: I will assign property taxes on your wheat field based on the value of the land you use for it ($3,300 as estimated above). So your property taxes at 50% valuation of $3,300 (standard practice) or $1,650 and $20 per thousand dollars of value (the tax rate in my township of a house and land – vacant land is more) would be $33.

Total Cost: $30 +82.50 + $33 = $145.50 for 547 loaves of bread or $0.26 each. Cost for your labor has not been considered in this calculation. You save a total of $74.50 ($220 minus $145.50) by growing your own verses buying 25-pound bags of wheat. Your savings/earnings is low relative to the time/labor you invest. I estimate 60 hours (or about 6 minutes per loaf for 547 loaves) to prepare and harvest the grain field.
Efficient practices might cut the hours down.

As I said before; the greatest savings for the least time and effort is to buy wheat flour or wheat berries in bulk and process them yourself. Growing your own grain begins to look like hard thrift, inefficient thrift, the savings small compared to the time and energy required and you may begin to see why the old time farmers gave up and took factory jobs.

Many a frontiersman, trapper, prospector, and shipmaster bought supplies consisting mostly of flour, sugar, salt pork, and salt each year and hunted, foraged or traded for variety in his diet. Relying on a diet of these basics is neither healthy nor recommended but shows what is possible.

You could regard the time and energy needed to grow your wheat as healthful and useful exercise or recreation (so no health club membership or expensive sports are needed) rather than inefficient use of time and effort.

Small scale modernized wheat-harvesting equipment – if cheap enough - suitable for the home gardener might ease the processing burden. Such equipment would have to be invented.

If grain could be grown hydroponically in solar heated greenhouses, perhaps more savings in time, energy, land cost, and property taxes could be achieved. Theoretically hydroponics increases crop yield per area by 5 times so instead of a need for 7,000 square feet of growing area per person, only 1,400 square feet would be required. To my knowledge it has never been tried.

The estimates presented above for seed, fertilizer, land, and property tax costs make possible an estimate of the savings possible using a solar greenhouse of 1,400 square feet for grain production. Cost for seed and fertilizer might be the same. Costs for land and property taxes I estimate at 5 times less. Costs to build and operate the greenhouse/hydroponic system must be added in. The greenhouse, containers, pipes, water pump, and heating system (if you have one) cost once over many years. Electricity to run the pump would be continuous. Heating fuel would be seasonal. I estimate $2,000 to build the system (using scrap materials where possible) and 20-year life of the system or $100 a year, and $0 heating fuel cost (using free scrap wood for fuel burned occasionally early and late in the season – no winter heat). Electricity I estimate at $25 a year to run a small pump.

So total costs would be $30 + $8.25 + $3.30 + $100 + $25 = $166.55

For 547 loaves of bread the cost per loaf would = $0.31, - more than the field grown wheat (at 26 cents). However, costs for building and electricity could be reduced – by using foraged materials to build the greenhouse for example.

The best use of a greenhouse may be for greens production. 1,400 square feet of solar greenhouse growing lettuce hydroponically might produce 10 pounds per square foot - worth $1 a pound in the open market – or $14,000 worth of product. Rather than try to grow wheat yourself, you may want to use some of the $ earned growing lettuce to buy wheat flour or wheat berries.

Inflation verse deflation:

As I wrote this chapter, paradoxically the economy entered a period of deflation in energy and housing costs. I believe deflation is a short-term phenomenon only, and over the long term, the 2 ½ annual average trend of inflation of will gradually reassert itself. Therefore, over the long term the calculations made in this chapter should remain valid.

VIGNETTE:

Sunday morning. I chop wood, splitting another log, and another and another to add to the huge mound piled up in the yard. I know from last winter the drafty old farmhouse will need a lot of firewood to stay warm. An hour later I'm tired and sweaty and the pile a little larger, and I'm out of logs. I need a lot more. Where will I get them? I quit, rest a minute, then begin to work on my garden - an overgrown patch of weeds, trying to relieve my beans, carrots, and cabbage from their encircling besiegers.

Afternoon. I intend to go for a drive, explore the countryside and visit a friend. My car won't start. It cranks over but won't fire. I nearly run the battery down cranking it. I study the engine, pull wires and tubes, put them back, trying to diagnose the problem on the fly. Bad gas, fouled plugs, a failed sensor in the spider web of sensors in the fuel injection system. WHAT IS IT?! Even if I knew the problem, how can I get parts? The parts shop is 20 miles away. Too bad I'm on bad terms with the neighbors – letting the yard become a mess, borrowing of tools I only returned when I needed another one. I wish I could ask for their help or a ride. Ask a friend? Because I moved out here, the nearest one lives 30 miles away. I've already asked him for too much. He won't be a friend any more at this rate.

I kick the car. It feels no pain. My foot hurts. I dread the cost of a tow and professional repair. My bank account is empty, my credit cards are almost maxed out. I can't do what I planned today. At least I'll save on gas.

My rent is overdue. This house in the country is too expensive for my feebly paying job 40 miles away. I rented it because I hoped to get away from the city, experience a little country life, garden and heat with wood to save money. But after long hours at low pay six days a week; and the long commute to work I have little time here except to sleep, and Sundays.

If I can't get the car fixed by tomorrow, I can't get to work, I'll lose my job, (I've missed work before, I've been warned), soon be evicted, soon be homeless. Homeless, and winter coming on. I shiver in the warm autumn air. I whine, "Why does everything I do go wrong?" I wallow in self-pity a while, then get a grip on myself. Could I hitchhike and walk 40 miles to work, or at least to the auto parts store. If I left this afternoon maybe I can make it in a few hours. Where will I sleep tonight, on the streets? I contemplate another option. Abandon this place, my car, my garden, and my woodpile and maybe my stupid job. I'll lose my rent security deposit. I hate to do that. I am healthy (at least) and can start over, maybe trying another way. I'm lucky, really. I don't own this house. I can walk away from it. And I won't miss my junk car either.

***

CHAPTER 3: HOMELESS

Contents: **page**

Introduction:

The thought of living homeless may invoke horror in some people. Really it is all psychological. We notice wandering vagabonds on the streets, see Katrina victims massed in filthy stadiums, read about the dispossessed Okies as described in John Steinbecks' book ***Grapes of Wrath*** - and as a result we recoil from the idea of living homeless with dread. People make big decisions in their lives out of fear of it. Young beautiful women marry ugly old rich men. People work their lives out at dead end, unhealthy, sickening jobs in dirty factories and little office cubicles doing the same rote task over and over, throwing their lives away. They buy homes with mortgages that take 30 years of their lives to pay.

But some folks live homeless by choice as a low-cost, even zero cost recreation/vacation. Really, homelessness is what you make of it. People go camping, becoming temporarily homeless, for fun. The fact is; sleeping out under the stars in good summer weather can be downright pleasant.

Some folks live homeless by choice as a low-cost, even zero cost recreation/vacation. One example: folks who call themselves 'primitivists' or 'abos' (short for aborigines). As a (very) challenging sport, they walk into wilderness with nothing but the clothes on their back - and attempt to survive, or even achieve a degree of comfort.

And, homelessness can be healthy. Exercise is healthy. Being homeless, you'll likely get plenty of it. Exercise is the key to health, and exercise can cost nothing. Food and diet are important, but secondary. (As mentioned in the introduction, Ed Viesturs - American climber of 14 mountains over 28,000 feet - ate a diet of ramen noodles and peanut butter, while daily biking 18 miles and climbing mount Rainer as a guide, while remaining in robust health). Living outdoors for a month during the benign climate of summer would do many Americans a great deal of good. Here is a prescription for overweight people who want to loose weight: live homeless and on the road for a while.

I believe we all have a lot to learn about homelessness – including (especially) the homeless. Many, most people living homeless do not know how to deal with it. And, people who study homelessness to find ways to alleviate the problem – such as academics and policy makers do not know what to do either. Research, field research is needed. There are skills and knowledge that need to be discovered that are not in any book or web site.

I believe there are people out there who are expert at it (who would be called 'profs' or professionals by Jack London). It would be very worthwhile to seek out and learn from these folks.

I have experienced 6 months of living homeless. I cannot claim to be an expert on it, but here are my views. I'm not saying they are the only way or even the best way. Others folks out there have more extensive experience. Examples: read ***The Road*** by Jack London, read ***Down and Out in Paris and London*** by George Orwell, see web sites like: ***www.thehomelessguy.blogspot.com*** or use a web search engine like ***google*** to find many more.

My Experiences:

I lived homeless in Canada and Michigan in summer, Louisiana and Florida in winter. I wouldn't want to reverse it. Anyone homeless should move with the seasons, I believe. I carried a small tent but frequently slept in the car. For car ventilation in warm weather – screens over open car windows are absolutely necessary. A car quickly becomes too hot and damp without them. Have at least two screened windows – one on each side of the car, for cross ventilation. A screen may be duct taped to a window opening, or attached to a frame that is shaped to fit the window opening. In Canada, at some locations, mosquitoes beat against those screens like rain all night.

In Florida:

In the winter of 1972 I drove from Michigan to New Orleans, (and later to Florida). I lived in a tent in a public campground outside New Orleans – driving into the city to explore it. The temperature was in the 60's (degrees f) during the day and never got below 45 f at night, making tent camping comfortable. The cool temperatures kept down bugs. Then I drove to central Florida At very low cost, I rented a spot in a private campground that provided bathrooms and showers. I took a hotel job in nearby Disney World but I continued camping to avoid apartment rent and save money. (Later I rented an apartment – but then my savings evaporated).

In Canada:

In 1984 I drove and took a ferry to an area I was interested in exploring – Manitoulin Island in Georgian Bay, Ontario. I was out of money soon after I got there. To conserve gas, I drove just a few miles a day. Using the car as my base, I explored the island mostly on foot, hiking and foraging for food every day. I occasionally visited the local library. For shelter, sometimes I slept in the car, sometimes set up a tent. There actually was a free campground, but noisy motorcycles at all hours of the night disturbed my rest. Also, nobody, except users cleaned up the trash. Better, I found, to find a camping spot by an unused dead end dirt road in the extensive untrammeled wild places on the island. Sometimes I parked and slept outside of remote empty farmhouses – dozens of these were scattered across the island. (I left the farmhouses alone). I tried sleeping in public parks – the police ordered me to leave.

I dreamed of exploring beautiful Georgian Bay in a sailboat or canoe. Someday I'll go back.

YOUR CIRCUMSTANCE:

Your circumstance, as you read this chapter could be: you are homeless and destitute or near destitute. Within this circumstance you may fit one of these situations:

Situation A: You are destitute without preparation or money. You are likely to be in big trouble, terribly vulnerable to predators in human form, to the weather, to disease, and to a host of other dangers and difficulties. I have not lived homeless without preparation, so I will have to rely on the experiences and writings of others.

Situation B: You have time and a little money to develop skills, and make preparations. Maybe you are facing eviction or job loss, but you have time to prepare. Perhaps you are intentionally leaving home to live low or zero cost. Far better to be in situation B if you are near destitute, to "be prepared", as the Boy Scout motto says. My periods of living homeless have always been undertaken after preparation, and always were intentional.

Plan and study, get books, perhaps commit parts of them to memory, develop skills, gather equipment, and get some money in reserve, perhaps a few hundred dollars.

Why would anybody intentionally live homeless? As mentioned above, it can serve as a low-cost/zero cost recreation. For example you can travel, and have some great adventures free of the usual obstacle to travel: little or no money. Some folks, who were hobos in their past but are now more affluent enjoy it so much they leave their homes and ride the rails as a vacation. The web site ***www.Thespoon.com/trainhop*** is a great example.

Unfavorable Circumstances:

It would be a bad situation if you had to suddenly live homeless without any experience. It would be a very, very good idea to practice the skills you might need to live homeless before you actually do it; skills like keeping warm and dry, getting water and food, and keeping clean. Backpack camping trips might help. If not that, a crash course in survival with someone who knows how might help, rather than learning by hard experience. Thomas Elpel's books and DVDs may be of great value to you. But they are not cheap to buy or widely available, unfortunately. Some libraries might have them or could get them for you through an inter-library lending service.

Personal economy while homeless:

Creating your own personal economy while homeless and possibly nomadic – whether prepared or unprepared is difficult, but possible I believe. It is a great challenge. You will need attitude, knowledge, skill, cleverness and daring. You can carry or keep only limited tools, supplies, equipment. You can't build facilities you can count on as being permanent, (as you can in other circumstances such as homesteading described in chapter 5). Since you have less stuff, less 'hardware' you must rely more on skills and knowledge to survive. To achieve a degree of comfort you need to be proficient at it, what Jack London in his book ***The Road*** would call a 'Prof' or professional.

3.1 UNPREPARED: Homeless and destitute without preparation.

Here I will consider situation A:

You are destitute and homeless with no preparation, possibly not even a warning. Perhaps you've lost your home, been thrown out, evicted, or run away (possibly with good reason). Maybe you've gone bankrupt, made a bad investment, been robbed or cheated. Or, a natural or manmade disaster has claimed your assets. That was the fate of thousands after hurricane Katrina. You have lost everything. You may even be in debt for student loans, or medical bills. You've asked for, maybe gotten help from friends, relatives, everyone you know. Or perhaps you don't want help. You are really on your own. You are homeless, faced with living out of doors, on the street, or even in the wilderness. Perhaps you have only the clothes on your back and those in poor condition or not suitable for the weather.

The gulf between the homeless and folks with homes is huge and seldom bridged. You will not be a friend or companion to people with homes. They are not going to invite you home for dinner. They are not going to offer you a bed to sleep in. They will always worry that you will ask too much of them or steal from them or take up too much of their time and energy, or try to move in or otherwise become a burden.

3.1.1 LIVING HOMELESS IN THE CITY

You may be tempted to head for the countryside or even the wilderness and I will consider this option later in this chapter.

But, unless you have necessary skills, stay in the city for now where help is available. Just keep in mind that the city can be a dangerous place. Predatory people, as dangerous as any animal predators in the wilderness live there, looking for vulnerable people like you to rob and use.

A big problem for you is avoiding these predators, thieves and the places they frequent. Try not to look homeless. Study and practice the rules of behavior advocated by the ***Guardian Angels***. This organization of unarmed citizen vigilantes (good vigilantes in this case) have determined ways to behave that make you an unappealing target to thieves and sexual predators. And, read and study carefully the book ***Predators: Who they are and how to stop them*** by Cooper, King and McHoes.

Becoming suddenly homeless and destitute, your situation is not unlike being a survivor of a plane crash or shipwreck, except other people are nearby, even all around you. You can ask for help. If you're in or near a city you can beg. Folks panhandling are common in the big cities, and you can do it too. It might seem strange and desperate and humbling to your pride. But you're asking for dollars for food and necessities, and not using it for drugs and booze as so many panhandlers are. You are going to use whatever money you get wisely and effectively, right? Don't suffer, don't be too proud to ask for help when you really need it. You can get sick or injured, get too hot and thirty and suffer from heat stroke in summer, get too cold and suffer hypothermia in winter.

It would be a good idea to find out immediately, when you become suddenly homeless the locations of public shelters. Better still, know the locations before you are homeless. They should be able to tell you or find out for you at local libraries and city government offices, or ask folks on the street who appear to be living homeless. If you can; get on the internet (possibly at a library) or, someone such as the reference librarian could look them up for you. These web sites lists most of the homeless shelters and soup kitchens in the country: ***http;//4homeless hypermart.net/soup kitchens.html.*** and ***http://artistshelpingchildren.org/shelters.html*** Or you or your helper could use the web search engine 'google' to search, typing in 'homeless shelters' or 'community shelter'.

In the public shelters you can warm up, get water and food and a place to sleep, but you must endure their idiosyncrasies. Town shelter may have lots of possibly annoying and inconvenient rules such as: you must be in by 7 PM.

George Orwell in ***Down and Out in Paris and London*** describes his experience living this way. Orwell and his traveling friends preferred sneaking into barns and haystacks in the country to sleep – rather than endure the poorhouses in the cities of England.

It would be best to make some preparations if you intend, or are forced to spend a night on the streets. If you can, do these things. Get a weather report, water bottle, adequate clothes, blankets, food snacks. Have some kind of rain gear, even if only plastic bags. In colder weather find abandoned houses and buildings that can protect you from wind rain or snow. Find walls that block the wind. Get under bridges and viaducts when it rains. "Any port in a storm" sailors say.

If you can, get a portable shelter. A camouflage tube tent would be very useful. Tent stakes are not needed, your body weight holds it down once you are inside. You can set it up and take it down in an instant. Look for vacant lots, parks, any patch of green to set it up. Set it up it after nightfall and it its much easier not to be noticed and possibly forced to leave.

Living this way, you may feel helpless, hopeless and miserable at times. But, compare your situation to Mountain Climbers on Everest as described by John Krakouer in his book ***Into Thin Air.*** They endured dangerously thin air, sudden blizzards with 100 mile an hour winds, pitiful tiny tents, and only the supplies they could carry on their back. You are in way better circumstances. And they did it by choice. And, in India, some small children live on the streets; sleep on the concrete of the train station floors while masses of commuters flow around them. How much better off are you? Consider, if you have health and strength and possibly youth, you have a lot going for you.

Temptations: Hanging out in the big cities, living off of handouts and shelters, you have a big problem, what to do with your time. You might become bored with life and be tempted by drinking, drugs, prostitution, crime, gangs. In big cities are human predators. Thieves, pimps, drug dealers. You could become their victim or a predator yourself. Not out of malice but out of necessity. The temptation is great. Why not steal from someone who has plenty when you are destitute? I've felt it. Sure you can survive off handouts, but you'll feel the desire to get a little more. A cell phone or jewelry perhaps. And people around you seem to have stuff for the taking; purses, wallets, personal items. Resist the temptation. Apart from getting caught and going to jail or injuring someone or getting injured, you are less likely to develop the abilities you need to take care of yourself.

A pamphlet exists entitled "***An appeal to the homeless. Self sufficiency through shoplifting***" by Lone Wolf and Prometheus (pseudonyms). It describes how to shoplift. I've never done it and can't recommend it. No doubt web sites exist that elaborate on this idea, but I haven't looked for them. I can only say that if you are freezing and steal a coat, or starving and steal food, who am I to tell you don't do it.

The fact is, living by begging and charity and possibly petty theft is tedious and feels demeaning. It grinds you down. You want to take care of yourself, even though you have no money.

In big cities you are surrounded by vast buildings where thousands of people sit all day at desks 'working'. And you are surrounded by vast powerful institutions that dwarf the power of medieval kings and control every aspect of life around them. You are not part of their world. You will always feel like you are on the outside of everything, left out of everything, looking in. For all these reasons, better to get out of the big cities as soon as possible, as soon as you have the skills to live a more rural existence.

Far better, perhaps to flee into the countryside than endure the horrors of the public places folks were directed to after hurricane Katrina

And, Thoreau favored the environs of a small town; Concord, Massachusetts as a home base.

Smaller towns may be better than the large cities to be homeless. They may be less crowded, with more places to have a hidden camp, and there may be few or no other homeless people. You may not be ignored or remain anonymous if that's what you want. In the more open and friendly atmosphere of a small town strangers might try to talk to you. But, if you need help you may be able to get it more easily. They may not have a public shelter, but churches and the friendlier atmosphere may open doors for you.

Best to go south for the winter. The government ought to offer any homeless person a free trip south in the fall.

Even in the south it can get cold in winter, however so you must find ways to keep warm.

3.1.2 BASIC SURVIVAL METHODS:

Becoming suddenly homeless and destitute without preparation, and with almost nothing, you need a crash course in survival. To learn as you go is difficult. Here is a crash course:

Other books I will refer to do a better job than I can do here in explaining the fine points of survival. But for those without access to these books I will summarize some techniques here.

You want to stay warm, dry, hydrated, fed, clean, healthy, mobile and organized.

Stuff you want to get: extra clothes, water, food, cleaning supplies, backpack.

It is amazing how little you really need.

Warm: Clothes

In the north in winter, if that's where you are, you must stay warm. Hypothermia can make you sick or kill you quickly. Do these things: Create a dead air space around your body. Insulation is "dead" or still air. You can wear layers of clothes, anything you can find, or stuff whatever you can get into your clothes. Get sweat pants and sweat shirts to wear as an outer layer to make this easier as Thomas Elpel does on his jaunts into the wilderness. If he gets cold he stuffs his sweat clothes with leaves and dry grass, varying the amount to suit the weather. In the city wadded up plastic bags and newspapers will work.

Getting wet can ruin the insulation value of any material. A warm coat or layers of clothes, upon becoming wet will suck the heat from your body. Wet will really make you cold. Wind and wind chill multiply the danger. A rain poncho or even a $3 blue poly tarp or a piece of plastic or a garbage bag can keep you dry.

Plastic bags may be obtained at stores for the asking. You will want big ones.

Over your head and clothes plastic bags can serve as a rain hat and coat. Plastic grocery bags over your socks can keep your feet dry even if your shoes get wet. If you have no socks, any piece of cloth wrapped around your foot can serve as a sock. A large handkerchief, a small towel, a T-shirt or the arms of a cut up flannel shirt can work.

Wool is the poor mans Gore Tex: Wool wicks away body moisture and keeps some of your body warmth even when wet. So get wool clothes when you can.

A winter coat may be made out of a wool blanket with a slit in the middle so you can slide it over your head. Then wrap strips of cloth, leather, cord around your torso to secure the sides.

If you can get them, put on layers of clothes.

Thoreau wrote. "Often the poor man is not so cold and hungry as he is dirty and ragged and gross. It is partly his taste, and not merely his misfortune. If you give him money, we will perhaps buy more rags with it. I was wont to pity the clumsy Irish laborers who cut ice on the pond, in such mean and ragged clothes, while I shivered in my more tidy and somewhat more fashionable garments, till, one bitter cold day, one who had slipped into the water came to my house to warm him, and I saw him strip off three pairs of pants and two pairs of stockings ere he got down to the skin, though they were dirty and ragged enough, it is true, and he could afford to refuse the *extra* garments which I offered him, he had so many *intra* ones. This ducking was the very thing he needed. Then I began to pity myself, and I saw that it would be a greater charity to bestow on me a flannel shirt than a whole slop-shop on him." ***Walden***, page 56.

You can get decent clothes at places (such as churches) that give away clothes for free. (Americans have heaps of good unwanted clothes cluttering up their closets – which they donate or throw away – clothes that are too much trouble to sell). For a few dollars you can get good clothes at Salvation Army stores, garage sales, and resale shops.

Shoes: If your old shoes are falling apart wrap several layers of duct tape around them to keep them together a little longer.

How to avoid looking homeless, and why. Sometimes it doesn't matter, sometimes you don't care, and sometimes if seeking help you want to look homeless.

If you're begging, you may do better looking ragged and perhaps a little disheveled.

You will want presentable clothes when you don't want to look homeless – such as when you go to the library. Have rough clothes for daily wear, but keep a set of clean, and not tattered clothes in your backpack or perhaps in a locker, that you can change into when you don't want to look homeless.

When you want to "fit in" to society and not be looked at with disgust, loathing, pity, it would be good if you could keep even your day clothes (and yourself) clean and presentable while homeless, but this takes some skill and practice as I'll discuss below under 'Hygiene'. The ability to sew would be a great help and a skill well worth practicing before living homeless. Also good – have something to sleep in other than your day clothes. Slept in clothes soon get a slept in look. But now, you're faced with the problem of having a private place to change when you get up and go to bed. So, you need a secret or hidden place to camp or hang out, which I'll discuss more under 'Camping'.

Avoiding looking shabby:

With a little practice you can cut your own hair- and make it look presentable. I discovered this when a drunken barber cut my hair - making an uneven mess of the hair on the back of my head. I fixed it myself using two mirrors, one in front of me and one behind.

The mirror behind me showed the view of the back of my head and the mirror in front of me showed me the view in the mirror behind me. With the mirrors I was able to see and even out the crooked cuts on the back of my head.

Hydrated: Water

Water is the second thing that can kill you quickly. You can go only a few hours in comfort without it. No soldier in war goes anywhere without his canteen. You need one gallon of drinking water per day on the average. In heat and deserts and strenuous activities, or when sick, perhaps with diarrhea, you may need much more. Use pop bottles for water bottles. Get them and keep them. A water (or pop) bottle carrier would be very useful. Many types exist, some latch on your belt, some include a strap that goes around your waist or shoulder. You could make your own with some twine (perhaps from Home Depot twine folks use to tie up their lumber, available free outside the stores). You can make a sort of basket with twine wrapped around and under a bottle, tied with square knots or "half hitches". (I'm not going into detail on this. Just experiment and you'll get it to work). With some leather strips (for the fashion conscious homeless) you might make an elegant one. Some small types of bottles will fit into your pockets, but create a bulge and may chafe as you walk.

Water can kill you two ways, through a simple lack of it, or through pathogen or chemical contamination in it. Oh for the days when Native Americans or pioneers could safely drink from any lake or stream they encountered.

Water purification: You can kill germs with a little bleach, 1/8 teaspoon (equal to 8 drops) per gallon mixed into the water. An eyedropper can be used to measure out drops. If the water is cloudy you should double the dose, or let the water stand until the sediment settles to the bottom and the water is clear. Pour the clear water into a clean container and then treat it. You can get rid of the chlorine taste by letting the water stand for a few hours, or by pouring it from one container to another a few times. Or, use hydrogen peroxide, 1/8 teaspoon per gallon, again letting the water stand or agitating it to dissolve out the peroxide. Or purify water by bringing it to a boiling for at least a minute. A hobo stove (described below) can do this with some efficiency. You can get portable filters used for camping that clean water, but of course this costs money you don't have. Or you may make or buy a still. A solar still operates for free when the sun shines. They are common (and can be expensive) on ocean voyaging small sailboats. You can make one from a piece of plastic, a bowl, a cup, and a stone. The dirty (or salty) water goes in the bowl. The plastic goes over the top, taped or tied or to the bowl. The stone is set in the middle of the plastic so the plastic slopes evenly to the middle. The water heats up and condenses on the underside (bowl side) of the plastic. The clean distilled water then runs down the slope on the underside of the plastic to a spot beneath the stone and drips. A cup in the middle of the bowl collects the dripping distilled water.

A sheet of plastic draped across a shallow hole in the ground may collect distilled water from the soil. Secure the edges of the sheet with sticks or rocks.

Why drink pop? It costs money. Water is available free everywhere. The sugar in pop can make you thirstier. Water quenches your thirst better. The acidity of pop ruins your teeth. Water cleans your teeth.

Food:

As long as you have water you can live for weeks. You can live weeks, perhaps a month with no food. Men lost on the ocean have done it. On example: John Caldwell describes his experience in his book ***Desperate Voyage***. He went 24 days without food of any kind and 25 days before that with only a few morsels of food and food substitutes like his wallet and (don't try this!) engine oil. Of course, this was starvation, not fasting and he almost died. Nevertheless, a little fasting can be healthy for you. Some health books such as ***Prescriptions for Nutritional Health*** by James and Phyllis Balch recommend fasting three days a month (and twice a year for as long as ten days - with juices and under the supervision of a doctor) giving "all your organs a rest".

Begging. If you ask for money folks may think you will to use it for drugs or alcohol. But if you beg outside a fast food restaurant, and ask each customer if s/he will buy you a hamburger (like Wimpy from the old Popeye cartoons), you may get all you can eat rather easily, since there is no ambiguity about what you require.

Gleaners: Gleaners community food banks exist in many places. The web site ***www.gcfb.org*** lists them all. Go to the local library to get this list. Look for food you can prepare while camping out. Find the location of the local gleaners, go there, fill your backpack. Find a place to camp out within a few miles so you can revisit when your food runs out.

Another food source: a County Human Services food distribution center often located in the County Seat (the city where county government offices are). As with gleaners, camp within a few miles.

Churches: Some churches really practice Christian charity, and by asking may provide you with food. Some have weekly dinners - you could be invited. It would be polite (but not required) to go to the church religious service.

Learn to identify and prepare edible weeds and flowers. They can tide you over, perhaps when traveling between cites.

Edible flowers: Raid neighborhood or park flowerbeds for food.
Violets
Marigolds
Johnny jump ups
Pansies
Nasturtiums,
Daylilies: all parts may be eaten. Or they can be deep fried.
Tulips
Lavender

Flowering Herbs:
Cilantro
Chives
Basil
Mint

Edible weeds: Here are a few edible common urban and rural weeds: there are many more.
Lambs quarter also called goose foot or wild spinach: use as a salad green or cook like spinach.
Solomon's seal: young shoots.
Wild onions
Amaranth
Dandelion greens: the smaller the better.
Plantain
Haw- wild apple
Berries- raspberries, black berries, strawberries mulberries from trees.

Acorns: white oak acorns can be eaten raw, roasted or ground into flour.
May apple
Sumac berries: mashed and soaked for a lemonade-like drink
Wild grapes: mashed and soaked for a tart drink.
Grape leaves: the smaller the better.

Books such as ***Stalking the Wild Asparagus*** by Euell Gibbons and ***Botany in a Day*** by Thomas Elpel identify edible weeds and how to prepare them.

Both of these authors foraged for food as a recreation, a pleasure - regularly gathering full meals on foraging expeditions. I don't see this method as regular, year round source of food, but in season, when temporarily short of food, (perhaps while traveling) it could tide you over.

Pesticides, herbicides and air pollution might be on plants you forage, so wash them first. Or, eat them after a rain. Rain is initially dirty as it washes dust and pollutants out of the air, but as it continues, rain and the air and plants it washes become cleaner.

Free after season food source:

Pumpkins on the day after Halloween become worthless. Visit any place that sold them and they'll probably give you all you want. The seeds, after drying are edible, even tasty with a little salt. Or they can be boiled for 10 minutes, then coated with oil and baked for 30 or 40 minutes at 300 degrees - stir every 10 minutes. The whole pumpkins can be baked, like any squash but the strong taste will probably keep you from eating more than one a season – unless you are really hungry. Or mash it up and add sugar and cinnamon to make pumpkin pie filling.

Clean and healthy: supplies and methods:

Health:

Remember in a medical emergency: hospital emergency rooms are required by law to help you even if you can't pay. Go there if you must.

Hygiene: Keeping clean is a very difficult problem while living homeless. If you can stay clean and presentable, you can go to lots of places and hang out where otherwise you might be shut out.

Paper towel (or toilet paper) substitutes: Crinkle and wad up newspaper or phone book pages as much as possible, the more you do the softer and more absorbent it will get. Or – long before use - soak a lot of pages and let them dry out. They will become crinkly and more absorbent. You will still have to crinkle and wad up the pages to make them softer.

Washing and keeping clean.

Living homeless or on the road you can get dirty, sweaty, and smelly; and may seldom have access to a shower, bathtub, or laundry.

Washing yourself: It is possible to wash your whole body with 2 gallons of water - one gallon if you are careful. Essentially in a bowel, you first wash with ½ to one gallon of soapy water, then use the other ½ to one gallon for a clean water rinse. You need a deep pan or plastic bowel (able to hold 1 or 2 gallons), a gallon jug, (perhaps an empty milk jug), washcloth, towel and soap - either bar or liquid. You can do it at any water source including a pond, river, or even a shallow hand dug well. (But you'll have to preheat the water if you want it warm). You can do this at any bathroom sink - perhaps at a public restroom - ideally in one where you can lock the door so you can take all of your clothes off with privacy.

I prefer to put water in my own bowl rather than use a public sink. For privacy you could do it in a stall, getting water from the sink for your bowl and moving to the stall. To avoid making several trips to the sink (naked and wet) fill your gallon jug using the sink to take into the stall with you. (Your gallon jug and bowl will not fit in the sink so you may have to use the somewhat tedious method of getting a cup that fits under the sink faucet and repeatedly refilling it to dump in your jug).

Bathing Steps: First you put warm soapy water in the bowl, a half-gallon to a gallon. Dip your hair in the soapy water and swish it around for several minutes. Pour out the water, refill with fresh water and get the soap out of your hair by swishing it around in this water. If your hair is really dirty do this twice but I have always found once is enough. (Better to keep your hair short to be easier to clean). Add a little more soap, wet the wash cloth and rub the soapy washcloth all over your body. Or, use a soap bar. The idea is to get a layer of soap all over your body, especially underarms and between legs. (Don't use the washcloth between you butt - this areas is especially dirty. Use toilet paper or a paper towels for this area for washing, rinsing and drying). Wring out the washcloth. Empty the dirty water, refill with fresh water, wet the washcloth and rub all over to remove the soap, wringing out the washcloth several times. Try to avoid making a wet mess all around you (just for the sake of the people that clean public restrooms. Out in the woods this doesn't matter). You will feel clean and refreshed after this process.

Washing clothes. One method - hang them up dirty on a line outdoors. Let the rain and sun clean them. I've done it. It works. Spots won't come out unless you pre-treat them by rubbing with soap or use spot remover - which cost money. Baking soda, possibly followed by vinegar, which are very cheap, may work. Don't wear white, or light colored clothes - so stains don't show up as much.

Dishes and utensils: let them soak in water for a while, or leave them out in rain and sun like clothes.

A cheap disinfectant that kills everything: distilled vinegar followed by hydrogen peroxide. Both are extremely cheap. Better than antibacterial soaps and sprays. Get two spray bottles, one for vinegar one for hydrogen peroxide.

Zinc oxide: skin protector and healer. It is the basic ingredient in baby diaper rash ointments, and cheaper than the ointment.

The book ***How I Lived Seven Years without Electricity and Running Water*** by Esther Holmes goes into more detail on methods to keep clean. For example: She describes homemade sweat lodges of sticks, tarps, and carpet scraps. In a backwoods camp this could be practical for you. Of course, where possible, there is jumping into a lake or stream, clothed or not.

Mobile: Backpack

Get a backpack. Your stuff in plastic bags in a grocery cart marks you as homeless and restricts your mobility. Ideally, acquire a decent backpack such as a student might carry before you become homeless, and you'll look less like a homeless vagabond.

A lot of perfectly good backpacks - except for tears, worn bottom liners or non-working zippers - are thrown away or given away. If you can make repairs they can be made useful again. Consider buttons or laces (shoelaces) in place of zippers. Stitch in material behind tears or a worn bottom. You might start a new fashion trend (like torn jeans).

Two other options for backpacks, incredibly cheap but possibly more obvious marks of homelessness and therefore more suitable for a rural or wilderness existence are described by Thomas

Elpel in his book ***Participating in Nature.*** He made a backpack out of two old cloth cement sacks, and out of a blanket folded and tied together with ropes or cloth strips for straps. And he describes how you can make a blanket roll - your stuff rolled up inside, the ends tied together and carried over your shoulder. I prefer a blanket roll to a pack. It is more comfortable than a pack because there are no straps digging into your shoulders, but it is hotter in warm weather.

3.1.3 MORE SURVIVAL TECHNIQUES:

You want to quickly build up the skills and knowledge you need to survive if you are suddenly homeless and destitute. Books on survival explaining how to keep warm, start a fire, sew a button, purify water, etc. are relevant. Examples include ***Book of Survival*** by Anthony Greenbank 1967 Harper and Row.

Psychology:

Mountain climbers live virtually homeless for weeks or months out of choice and in the worst weather imaginable. Books by Ken Krakauer, Bob Viesturs, and many others explain how (and try to explain why). Really your homeless experience can't possibly as miserable as theirs is by choice. The difference though, is their experience will end. Probably the best part of mountain climbing is the hot shower at the hotel at the end of the trek. No hotel shower awaits you. Living homeless, your experience is not going to end when you choose, perhaps not for years. That really makes living homeless in destitution more difficult than any mountain climb, or any sport for that matter. But consider, it only makes the challenge greater. Many people have climbed Annapurna and survived. And a third of those who attempted it have died. But how many have lived homeless for any length of time. It is an easier sport perhaps; to live and die suddenly on the most dangerous mountain on Earth than to endure living homeless for an extended period of time. Again and again, it's all in the attitude you take.

With enough money, plenty of oxygen and a good guide perhaps almost anyone could climb Mt. Everest. It makes it meaningless, except as a good hike and exercise. You could do the same thing at home for free. The challenge would be for someone with no money, eating the cheapest food or foraged food and using homemade equipment to make it to the top of Everest.

It may help to think of yourself as living outdoors, instead of being homeless. Your home is a place or places in the vast area outside of ordinary homes.

Shelter:

Today, a homeless man cannot erect a tent or start a fire on public land in the city without violating laws prohibiting camping. (So, by law, he is made poorer than even the poorest prehistoric man or Native American).

So you must find a hiding place to sleep, build a concealed shelter (such as the scout shelter described later in this chapter) or have a temporary shelter you can set up at night and take down with the dawn - or go to a public shelter.

Even worse, in many places, it is against the law to sleep in a public place, or in a vehicle overnight in a public parking lot.

In the summer, in most cities you can comfortably sleep outdoors on many nights in your clothes, (if you have a good hiding place). Bugs are not a problem, usually – all the concrete, mowed lawns and drainage systems provide few breeding places for mosquitoes. If your hiding place is not roofed, keep plastic sheets or bags handy in case of rain.

A discussion of hiding places to sleep is worth a whole chapter. I leave it to you. Just realize – there are a lot of places you can lie down and (usually) no one will bother you. Drunks regularly sleep on the sidewalks or in alleys. (But stay away from them).

In colder and wetter weather make up a 'blanket roll' – wool is best - stays warm even if damp, and mosquitoes can't bite thru it. Lie down and roll up in it. Many a soldier has done this through an entire campaign. You need a ground cloth underneath, (a piece of plastic) and another piece of waterproof material you can throw on top if it rains. Don't wrap up in waterproof material or moisture from your body will be trapped and make your bedroll wet. Wool (cheap) or Gore-Tex (expensive) breathe a little and wick the moisture away.

A step beyond the blanket roll is the **'tube tent'** - which allows better air circulation and reduced build up of moisture from you body into the blanket - so you may stay warmer. You can easily set it up after dark and take it down before dawn. You can make it out of a cheap blue polytarp (a couple of dollars at a hardware store), a piece of ***tyvek*** or canvas, or even a sheet of plastic. Set it up after dark in an overgrown corner of a park or vacant lot and you may pass the night undisturbed. Several methods will work to hold the tube open. At the simplest, a rope or stick or two passed longitudinally through your tube hold up your roof/ceiling. Build a small teepee at each end to rest your longitudinal sticks on or rest them (or tie your rope) to a convenient shrub or tree. When you crawl in, your body weight holds the floor down so no stakes need be put in the ground – or use rocks or sticks on the inside to hold the edges down.

If the ends are closed off in cold or wet weather a tube tent can be greatly improved. Close off the ends with any scrap of material you can find - plastic, cloth, canvas, tyvek, carpet scraps, etc. Use clothes pins, safety pins, sewn seams, sewn in buttons and slots, lacing (like a shoe) etc. to hold the end material in place.

Tube tents are described on these websites: (and many others):

www.netbackpacking.com/camping without a tent.

www.equipped.com –how to be equipped to survive.

www.beprepared.com –tube tent and rope $3.95

The **tarp shelter** is a step beyond the tube tent. Light a fire on the downwind side to get some reflected heat into your shelter. The web site ***www.equipped.com/tarp shelters/htm*** containing the article ***Tarp Shelters: An Introduction*** by David B. Macpherson provides an excellent and thorough explanation of how make tarp shelters in various configuration. I especially like the 'Adirondack wind shed'. A 'hobo stove' described below can proved you with a small concealed fire (but requires frequent refueling).

Light canvas works well, whether for a tube tent or tarp, (though it is an old fashioned material). It breathes, letting your body moisture out, yet the fibers swell up and keep you dry when it rains. Don't touch your canvas roof /walls when wet or you will get dripped on.

Perhaps the simplest and cheapest, most versatile, yet most comfortable tent accommodation would be this combination - blue poly tarp rain fly overhead, a canvas or ***tyvek*** tube tent beneath with material to enclose the ends if cold or windy, screening or mosquito netting to enclose the ends on warm nights, wool blankets, plastic sheet ground cloth. Use leaves, straw, pine needles, old carpet etc. underneath as a mattress.

As the weather worsens, you should seek out protected places to camp. Any wall in the path of a wind that is chilling you can serve as a windbreak. A wall with openings - like a fence with slats or (or a line of thick bushes) can be more effective than a solid wall – because less turbulence may be generated just behind the wall.

Under bridges is a vagabond favorite. You can be out of sight with a waterproof roof over your head.

Living in a cardboard box is an old joke but can keep you warm, wrap you box in plastic to protect it against moisture and be sure to provide some ventilation to remove body moisture.

Abandoned houses or buildings: pitch your tent inside. Or create a small well-insulated space in a small room or in part of a larger room. See the 'body heated space' discussion in this book in chapter 5 'Homesteading'. Old blankets, curtains, cloth of any kind, old mattresses, cardboard scraps, even piles of leaves can all be used. You need not have standing headroom. Leaves, grass, wadded up newspaper stuffed into plastic shopping bags - the bags then tied up - can make an excellent insulating and draft sealing material. It is very vulnerable to fire, however, so don't smoke, use candles, oil lanterns or campfires near this type of insulation.

In the winter, in cold climates, without adequate shelter you could die from hypothermia - excessive cooling of your body temperature if you get too cold on a cold night out. You need to seek a homeless shelter. If you wave down passing police, they might direct you or even give you a ride to a shelter.

These web sites list public shelters in the United States.

www.shelterforthehomeless.org.

www.homelessshelterdirectory.org

www.artistshelpingchildren.org/shelter.htm

http://homelesshypermart.net

or google 'homeless shelters' for more web sites and locations.

Besides hanging out in homeless shelters, here are places you could go in cold weather to warm up. Go to a hospital waiting rooms or any really big waiting room and pretend to be waiting – while you warm up. And of course there are indoor shopping malls. Or, go into an office building and wander the halls. Walk slowly through like you have business there. Don't just stand around. Go to a laundry, and very slowly wash or dry a few cloths (the manager might kick you out if you just sit around).

University: I highly recommend University towns as homeless hangouts. Libraries are open 24-7. There are endless classroom halls you can amble through, and large classes you can sit in on without being noticed. (And maybe learn something). You must try to look like you belong, try to look like you are a student. University gyms are open all night and if requiring a card swipe to get in, you could slip in when somebody goes out. You might attend numerous free or cheap activities including art events, concerts, movies, sporting events, etc. You can hang out in the (usually) crowded bars on weekends - buying one drink and sipping it for hours.

As recommended earlier, the best idea of all is to take a seasonal trip south before the worst of winter hits. Hike, hitchhike, bike, or stow away on a boat going south – but get there and your life through winter will be a whole lot easier.

Shelter is discussed in more detail under 'Living in the Wilderness' near the end of this chapter and in chapter 5.

Storage: You can live without a house but you may get tired of lugging all of your stuff around in a backpack. A backpack works for a few basics: snacks, extra clothes, and if kept light is not too intrusive or mark you as homeless. You may want a cache, a storage place to keep all of the stuff you don't need now. If you have good winter clothes, you need a safe place to store them in summer. Plus you may want a place to keep extra food, tools, etc. If you can afford the few dollars, get a locker available at airports, bus stations, train stations. (Recall the locker where Susan (Madonna) kept her stuff in the movie ***Desperately Seeking Susan***). In a locker you can keep your stuff with some security. For valuables or serous amounts of money you may want a safety deposit box at a bank.

Urban Camp:

If you stay in an area for an extended period - weeks or months, you will want/need an urban camp - a place to cache food, supplies, and personal stuff, a place to prepare food and relax in safety and comfort where no one will bother you. Another words, a place most people call home, that for most folks consists of a house or apartment but in your case is an encampment. It feels good to have a place you can call home even if it is temporary and out of doors. If you look carefully, occasionally you might find a place that can serve as your 'home' for a while. Like places to sleep this topic is worthy of a whole chapter. It is an art requiring skill and experience. Here I will just introduce the problem.

Ideal places are hard to find, but they exist: Criteria: Look for places where no one else goes (ideally where no one has been for years), where your access routes can be kept concealed or effectively blocked, and where you can come and go without being noticed. (Animals are experts at this). Examples:

1. The old hobo favorite, along railroad tracks but back a little from the tracks in brush/trees on vacant land or behind abandoned building. In the right location you can leave your camp, walk onto the tracks, (keeping your trail as faint as possible - like a deer trail) and not be noticed.

2. Along freeways - back in the brush along the fence line or beyond on adjacent land. Motorists passing at high speed will not notice you. Sure, it's noisy, so get some cotton or earplugs. Bike paths, almost never used were built along some freeways. Get a bike and you have a fast way to get to and from your camp.

3. A good location might be a neighborhood with abandoned or vacant building, alleyways and overgrown or fenced backyard. You use the backyard and alley to come and go. You might use a back room or two of a vacant house - accessed through the back door (or perhaps a window) from the back yard, (front door closed up and not used - nailed shut, locked, etc). The back yard should be enclosed by high wooden fencing (or perhaps tall hedges) or otherwise not visible to neighbors. Access the alley from the backyard through a tall gate you can close, lock or wedge shut from the inside when you are there. Ideally you should have a way to view the alley (such as a hole in your tall gate) to see if anyone is in it before entering. You wait for them to move on before leaving. If you are in your alley and about to enter your abode - and someone else is in the alley and will see you go in, pass by your gate and come back later. Thus you can come and go without giving away your home site.

4. Camp in rarely (or never) visited odd corners of public land– city or county parkland, or state or federal forestland – or overgrown vacant lots; again where the site is hidden, the access route is concealed or can be blocked, and you can come and go without being noticed.

Mentioned earlier but worth repeating, camp within a reasonable hike to Gleaners or County Human Services Agency food distribution center to replenish your food supplies.

Urban camping techniques: This subject is worthy of another book. Here are two examples.

1. Find several campsites and move between them so you don't spend every night at one camp which may make your trails in and out get too well worn, make your campsite looked lived in, and make your camp subject to discovery.

If you camp in a place where people might occasionally come by - as is the case in many campsites in or near urban areas – it would be a good idea to keep your camp so that if somebody were to stumble across it while you weren't there they would not realize that anybody was camping there. So, anything you leave there must be well hidden, in a thicket perhaps, under leaves or logs, or in a carefully covered hole in the ground. (See, I told you this is an art). In a vacant building hiding your more valuable stuff may be a good idea too. Try the attic, basement or perhaps in the garage rafters.

If you are at your campsite (camping in a place where you are not supposed to be camping) and someone discovers you; well, you may have to move rather suddenly. Another reason to have alternative places to go.

2. Hike and camp for an entire season along one of the national trails like the North Country Trail or Appalachian Trail. You needn't hike the whole trail, but might merely travel up and down a section of it – perhaps along your favorite part. As far as other folks you meet along the trail are concerned you are a hiker/camper along the trail, not a homeless vagabond.

Starting a fire:

Matches: Possibly you can get free matches by asking for them or merely taking a few at the counter at motels or restaurants. But today - with smoking less common or banned - free matches are more difficult to get. Sometimes, people have trouble starting a fire even with matches. People rely on lighter fluid and 'starter sticks'. (I've even seen people using propane burners to start wood fires).

Matches or a lighter can be so necessary for survival (to ward off hypothermia and cook food) and the alternatives take so much skill and practice that, in a desperate situation - with absolutely no money on a cold night and no one willing to help you - you might consider stealing them. (Someday when you have money pay the store back and thank them). Better in the long run, however, to learn the alternatives.

To get your fire going successfully you must get material burning gradually in stages from dry tinder to leaves, paper and pine needles to twigs to small sticks to larger sticks to logs. You must not add big sticks until smaller sticks are burning well, and you must add them so as to not put out what is already burning. You need to practice this.

Fire starting tinder: You need tinder. Get dryer lint. Carry it in a small waterproof bottle or tin. Or get the inner bark of a dead tree such as cedar, aspen or cottonwood by stripping off the bark and rubbing off (and collecting) the material underneath with your fingers or a stick.

Hobo stove: The hobo stove makes a small fire that burns hot and steady using only a few small dry twigs, sticks, or pinecones for fuel - because of the 'chimney effect' of the can. (You will have to steadily add fuel). Possibly most importantly; unlike an open fire, which must be larger and could show a long distance, the hobo stove may hide the flame - if you are in a place where you don't want to be discovered. If dry sticks are used there shouldn't be much smoke

To make a hobo stove: Start with a coffee can or equivalent with the top cut out. Turn it over and around the sides of that end, (using a can opener or even a nail) make a series of holes (so smoke can escape). Cut a door about 4 inches square at the base (the open end) to insert fuel and to allow air to the fire.

ILLUSTRATION # 1 - below shows a hobo stove design. A web search, typing in 'hobo stove' will turn up many more designs.

ILLUSTRATION # 1: HOBO STOVE.

Cooking:

People make a big deal out of cooking, but all it really is, is applying heat to food to make it more palatable.

Thomas Elpel in his book ***Participating in Nature*** describes 'ash cakes' made by simply placing a mass of dough (not too wet or sticky) on the medium hot coals of a fire. They can be thick or thin, and use any kind of flour. Spear them with a stick to turn them and get them out. The outside will be black with ash. Brush off the ash and eat. His book describes other simple cooking methods using devices such as a stone oven and steam pit.

Raw potatoes - simply placed in an open fire also cook well. With a hobo stove and can or pan to cook in you can efficiently cook a wide variety of food.

Bugs

Having just discussed keeping clean, now I will consider deliberately not keeping clean. Mosquitoes can be a big, big problem, especially outside the city. You must find ways to stop them: As Native Americans knew: you've got to get smelly, greasy and dirty to keep them off naturally. Smoke from the fire, sweat, a little cooking grease can work. Of course then you're not socially presentable. And, you'll have to learn to live not perfectly clean. It does not feel comfortable, at first. Frequent bathing was uncommon until modern times - arriving with the advent of running water in the home. How did they do it?

I have not tried it, but lemon balm, a wild herb; may serve as a natural mosquito repellant. Crush it between your fingers and rub it on your skin.

Hats with mosquito netting can be purchased for a few dollars at stores selling camping supplies. Plastic screen door material may be sewn or duct taped into the ends or openings of a tent you made yourself. Or throw the screening over yourself to sleep.

Stealing:

For a ZCL perspective theft should be attempted only if absolutely necessary for survival. In the Spartan training regime, (not the football team) the ancient youth were forced to live homeless with nothing - to toughen them. One Spartan hero was a youth who stole a live fox that tore out his guts when he refused to reveal it and be caught. Of course the Spartans gradually went extinct as fewer and fewer passed their standards and survived to become hoplite soldiers. In general theft undermines thrift. If you succeed you give up skills to take care of yourself, if you fail and are caught you're in jail. Sure you're living zero cost in jail, but without freedom. Jail will give you a horrible and debilitating feeling - cut off from the real world and set among masses of predators.

I can't imagine most thieves having the desire, will, or skills, necessary to live ZC or the ability to learn. (Any thieves reading this - prove me wrong).

Foraging:

Foraging was discussed in chapter two. Here are a few more ideas. (Foraging for food is mentioned here, but described more elsewhere in this chapter).

Beyond foraging for food, our society is replete with useful stuff that is not used, underused, or thrown away. Through study and skills, creativity and plain cleverness you can take advantage of free stuff available for the taking lying around everywhere.

Efficient, productive successful foraging requires a mindset. You must develop an attitude and an eye for the potentially useful. The average product life of many things and materials is only a few minutes. If you can't use this stuff (you're homeless right, you have no use for a TV or appliance) you still might stockpile items to trade or sell later.

Where to look: Here are a few examples. (Many more examples are peppered throughout this book).

.• Trophy house subdivisions: Go through on trash days –especially on warm spring days when garages and storage spaces are cleaned out. Affluent neighborhoods throw away a lot of useful items: bicycles, furniture, CD and DVD players, televisions, appliances, etc.

• College/university student housing areas: Forage them at the end of the school year (in May/June). Students throw away heaps of stuff they can't take home for the summer: furniture, appliances, TVs etc.

• Forage on trash day in any area – you won't get as much useful stuff per mile traveled as in the first two examples, but may find scrap lumber, carpet scraps, paint, coffee cans, etc.

• Garage sales: Go on Fridays and Saturdays (and increasingly on Thursdays) in warm weather. Garage sales may be advertised in local newspaper classifieds and (much more common today) online (on weekdays use the library to research these sources and make a list). For efficiency, try to visit subdivision sales and sales at churches, schools, and community organizations (like veterans groups) where a lot of stuff may be offered. Arrive near the end of day - 4 or 5 o'clock - and you may be able to bargain, buy at reduced cost – or get things free.

- Dumpster diving was discussed in chapter 2: I have found dumpsters at construction and building remodeling sites to be the most productive, finding lumber, plastic sheeting, ***Tyvek*** scraps (useful for tents) furniture, bricks (worth 70 cents a piece new), blocks.
- Foraging along railroad tracks: (including adjacent property): besides things along the tracks, walking tracks offers views into adjacent properties such as abandoned industrial sites, vacant lots, junk yards, etcetera. Much of the decaying industry of rust belt America is located along railroad tracks. (Don't let the scrap material companies cart it all away for new Chinese industries). A few useful things I have found: scrap metal of all kinds, railroad spikes (useful as tent stakes, as tools such as chisels to clean up bricks, etc), steel barrels, plastic barrels, tires (for tire shoes), old cast aside railroad ties, bricks, blocks, stone, apple trees, berry bushes, edible weeds.
- Alleyways: Look in the backyards of abandoned buildings and in vacant lots: You may find fruit trees, berry bushes, volunteer vegetables in old overgrown gardens, edible weeds
- Fast food restaurants are good for cups, plastic utensils, napkins, salt, pepper, cream, mustard, ketchup, relish, sauces: Arby sauce, Taco Bell sauce, etcetera.

Keep a list of items you need. Over time, build up a list of places where you can find them.

Mobility: is covered in detail later in this chapter under 'Living on the Road'.

Biking:

Used bikes can be got for a few dollars, and even free put out with the garbage. Even a crummy bike will multiply your mobility and load carrying ability. In the Vietnam war bikes carrying hundreds of pounds each were pushed through narrow jungle trails to supply the Viet Cong/North Vietnamese army.

Recreation and Entertainment

Living homeless, with little or no money; you may be faced with long days and nights of merely surviving, of no opportunity to indulge in recreation, entertainment, or the 'finer' things in life. If you can stay reasonably clean and neat you can visit libraries and museums. Learn to appreciate reading. Museums, the bigger the better, may request a donation at the entrance but often it is not required.

Library:

If you are destitute and filthy, and look homeless, it may be hard to walk into a library; librarians and visitors frowning at you. Possibly you'll be asked to leave. But, a Library is a wonderful place. Warm, dry, bathrooms, entertainment in the form of books and magazines, internet connected computer work stations - but you must be clean and presentable, a real problem when you're homeless. And at night you must leave. In university towns are huge libraries open virtually all the time. Students may spend all night studying. University libraries may be vast - with many rooms and floors. You can move around,, almost get lost in them. You can get away with sleeping - head down on a table, possibly in one of the small private study booths - as many students do in the midst of their studies. Plus they may have useful books on survival. University of Michigan Graduate Library has a dusty section of these books buried in basement shelves. You may stay there many hours and study undisturbed, and probably not see another person the whole time. Study booths, little rooms with doors, a little larger than a phone booth line the outside of the stacks. Bathrooms are nearby. You could live there for days, if you look like a student and "study", and can stay reasonably clean and presentable. If you are identified as a homeless vagrant though, you will be made to leave. You must try to look like you are a student.

The article ***Homeless Living: A Week in a Library*** by Venus Lee describes how a student named Dolce Wang spent a week inside a university Library trying to emulate the experience of a poor college student. (Do a net search for it).

3.1.4 **RAISING $** while homeless.

You may be able to live for a while without a penny in your pocket. Nevertheless, I'm sure you will find it very useful to have a few dollars as a cushion against adversity - to buy food when nothing can be found for free, a bus ticket south in the fall, or perhaps a small extravagance. And, you may want to accumulate $ towards buying land and homesteading or buying a boat and seasteading.

Charity:

The county office of your State Human (or Social) Services agencies can provide emergency assistance. They will have to document your need before giving you money – you may need personal I.D (like a drivers license), social security card or number, proof of income and assets, etc. Phone books will usually list the address and phone number of the agency serving your area. Also, web sites with your state name followed by the tag ***.gov*** such as ***Michigan.gov*** will list locations and phone numbers of these agency offices under '**department of social services**'. When visiting to get food, you could fill out the paperwork needed for assistance. And they can provide emergency shelter. (usually at high cost to the government - $90 a day for an apartment). So your survival problems can be temporarily solved. (But you are not living Zero Cost, only loading your cost of living onto others).

Begging, discussed a little elsewhere may raise you some dollars. Some beggars are rumored to make a decent living by skillful practice of this art. (It is an art). I have not tried it. A web search may turn up the sites of folks who can give useful advice about it.

Selling Stuff:

Beyond begging, being able to give something or sell something to folks for their money could work. The old depression era scheme of selling apples or pencils on the street corner comes to mind. Or you could offer a service – cleaning, lawn care, etc. (At this point some people might think of prostitution, and sadly, many, many desperate people - from the miserable beginnings of poverty in history - have gone this route. If you try a little, I believe you can always find a better solution than this. In my opinion, the easy money of it, and the damage it does to your pride will undermine the determination, willpower, and strength of character you need to advance towards ZCL.

Selling drugs: The idea of growing, producing, selling drugs to raise money might come to mind. It is resort of many destitute people. A small high value - high risk product, that can get you a lot of money fast if you can get away with it, and stay alive. I can almost understand the appeal it has for destitute/homeless folks with no money and no apparent future. Like prostitution, (with which it seems always to be linked) the easy money and loss of pride involved; and also the loss of your freedom (whether as an addict or a pawn in a drug gang) make it the antithesis of ZCL.

Job: You may be able to get jobs through a temporary employment agency. Merely showing up at their office looking fit and ready to work may get you jobs. You will need documentation such as personal I.D. and social security number. You may need a home address and phone number. This you may be able to obtain through your County Social Services Agency. You could get a post office box and put that number down. (Or you could 'lie' putting down fake numbers or numbers were you don't really live). Millions of undocumented or fake documented illegal aliens are given jobs in this country every year. You should be able to find something.

Business: Beyond selling something on street corners, there must be other businesses homeless folks could start. I don't have experience at it, or solutions. It is a difficult and interesting problem worthy of research. I believe some folks out there must have started in desperate straits and succeeded, and could help/instruct others on what really works. I hope to pursue this topic through the web site **http://0costliving.com.**

3.2 PREPARED:

Now I will consider situation B: You have knowledge and skills. Better, by far, to have these; even though you have little else before living homeless in destitution. Train yourself ahead of the experience. Perhaps take short trips to practice these methods, first overnight and then longer. Now you may decide to try living homeless and Zero Cost by choice and not necessity.

Survival skills are especially necessary before going out on the road or living in the country and essential before living in the wilderness.

Knowledge:

You may not be destitute as you read this, but you can think about how you would live if you became destitute. It could happen to anyone, perhaps. And thinking about it ahead of time may help you to deal with it if it happens.

Living homeless and destitute, and striving to live Zero Cost you may feel your life is going nowhere. You are accomplishing nothing. Your family and relatives may complain. But if economic freedom and making your time your own is important to you then you can perhaps do what you really want to do, not what others compel you to do. Perhaps you can learn a new skill, attend college, or create a new invention that helps people to become more independent and makes ZCL more possible, (there are plenty of inventions that reduce people to dependence) or even write a better book than this one. You could push the concept of ZCL to new extremes.

You could, should I believe, use your time living homeless to study and practice the skills you need to live better even though homeless. And, work to get, make or find better equipment. Jack London at the tender age of 18 became a "prof" (a professional in the jargon of hobos) a master at living homeless as describe in his book ***The Road.***

ZCL is an ongoing research project with plenty to learn, invent and discover. We can learn from a diversity of sources: archaeology can reveal ancient technologies, written histories describe how people lived, museums display useful artifacts. The lifestyles of Native Americans, surviving primitive cultures, even the Amish, can teach us plenty. One thing they have in common; living as they did you must look farther ahead than the next shopping trip. They live and lived with the seasons and so had to plan as much as a year ahead.

SUPPLIES and EQUIPMENT

These are the 14 items of essential equipment for living outdoors.

Food and water	Sunblock, sunglasses
Clothes	Signaling device
Matches	Pocket knife
Fire starter: tinder	Emergency shelter
Maps	First aid kit
Compass	Toilet paper and towel
Flashlight	Backpack or haversack

There are substitutes for all of these items and with skills you could theoretically, go into the wild with nothing and survive. Some have done it and I'll discuss it more at the end of this chapter. Some folks do this intentionally.

Primitivists or survivalists sometimes called "abos" short for "aborigines" attempt to walk into the wild with nothing but the clothes on their backs and survive. They consider it a fascinating, challenging and useful recreation, sport or game. Jim Allen, for example, in his book ***Sleep Close to the Fire*** describes his experiences and methods of primitive living. And, books by Thomas

Elpel and his videos ***The Art of Nothing*** describe more of these methods.

Now, consider each of these items in detail, and possible substitutes.

Survival kit and substitutes:

Food: Cooking pot or pan: a stone heated over a fire dropped into a bag, soup cans, possibly found, to cook or boil water in.

Basic food to carry: flour, oatmeal, rice, beans, instant potatoes, powdered milk, raisins, bouillon, baking soda, salt, pepper, cinnamon, other spices From Elpel's book ***Participating in Nature.***

Wild food guides, Gibbons, Elpel, others

Fishing line: twine Fishhooks; bits of bent wire

Water: Solar still: 6' of plastic tubing plastic sheet, metal cup: to distill water to make it clean for drinking.

Water purification method: boil water using a hobo stove to efficiently deliver the heat of a small fire to the water.

Clothes: Rain gear: Large plastic garbage bags; free where folks throw them out after recycling pop bottles at supermarkets

Shoes: Elpel has a web site ***www.hollowtop.com*** where, in an excerpt from his book he explains how to make your own from sections of old tires, worn over homemade moccasins.

Matches: were discussed earlier. In place of matches primitivists may use a firebow and string, steel and flint, magnifying glass, or even broken pop bottle glass as a magnifying glass. These methods are worth knowing by anyone living homeless or out of doors, but require skill and practice.

Fie starter: Starting a fire and tinder was discussed earlier.

Maps: Find a library that has internet access. Print out copies of the maps you need. If the library has actual maps (fewer do today) scan them to make copies. Usually libraries charge 10 cents a page.

Compass: If you don't have a compass, like ancient mariners, use the sun during the day, the North Star at night. If cloudy, more moss grows on the north side of trees and rocks in forests.

Flashlight: use a burning stick from campfire, candle, lantern (hundreds of designs for these exist). Small hand held baked clay or ceramic oil lamps served as the flashlights of ancient folks.

Sunblock: Zinc oxide from a drug store smeared and rubbed into the skin. Natural sunblock – mud caked onto your face and body where exposed. In general, rely on shade, hat, neckerchief, clothes, parasol (homemade like Robinson Crusoe), and/or a mask of cloth to block

the sun. Recall that natives of the Sahara desert clothe their faces and bodies in turbans and long lightweight robes.
Sunglasses: In sunny weather in snow country you can get snow blindness from the glare. If you have no snow goggles or dark glasses, make a cloth, leather, or bark mask with horizontal slits in middle. Also, ashes rubbed under your eyes can cut glare.
Signaling devices: Plastic whistle, bright or shiny objects laid out in the sun, sun reflecting devices- piece of glass or metal, fire at night, smoky fire in the day. Morse Code would be well worth learning – in your backpack carry a piece of paper (in a waterproof plastic bag) with Morse Code letters listed. Memorize the list during slow times at camp or while hiking/biking. Practice to keep your memory fresh. Assuming you are lost in the wilderness and this is your only book, here is Morse Code: **A · – B – · · · C– · – · D – · · E · F · · – · G – – · H · · · · I · · J · – – – K – · – L· – · · M – – N – · O – – – P · – – · Q – – · – R · – · S · · · T – U · · – V · · · – W · – – X – · · – Y – · – – Z – – · · 1 · – – – – 2 · · – – – 3 · · · – – 4 · · · · – 5 · · · · · 6 – · · · · 7 – – · · · 8 – – – · · 9 – – – – · 0 – – – – –**
Pocket knife: alternatives - sharp rocks, metal can lid, broken shard of glass.
Emergency shelters: discussed elsewhere in this chapter.
First aid kit: ideally should include instruction book, various bandages, gauze pad, adhesive tape, soap, antiseptic, needle and thread, scissors, tweezers, safety pins, splint, safety glasses, nonlatex gloves, mouth barrier device for rescue breathing CPR (from ***The Boy Scout Handbook***). Substitutes for these items would be an interesting study I will have to leave to another book.
Toilet paper: smooth rocks, moss, leaves, straw, handful of grass, wadded up paper phone book, catalog, or newspaper), corn cobs, sponge soaked in salt water on a stick, (Ancient Rome used the sponge/stick method).
Towel: Use a spare shirt. Flannel works well.
Backpack or haversack: Homemade ones were described earlier. The website ***www.Backpacking.net*** has designs for homemade outdoor equipment including backpacks, tents, and cooking devices.

And items not so essential but for important for health and comfort, and substitutes for these items:
Tooth brush: twig as toothpick. Slit the ends of a stick into "tines" to make a brush.
Tooth paste: baking soda and salt.

Lip balm: vaseline, mucilaginous plants such as plantain crushed in your fingers.

Soap: Soap may be obtained from a common wild plant - useful for hand and body cleaning. Common name: 'Bouncing bet' or 'Soapwort'. Latin name: Saponaria officinalis. It grows about 18 inches tall with pinkish-white flower petals when in bloom. Leaves are opposite on the stem. It is very widespread in the eastern U.S. (writes Jim Allen in his book ***Sleep Close to the Fire***). Crush the leaves and stem to bring out the soap. The plant is good in the spring summer and fall, but dried out and useless in winter.

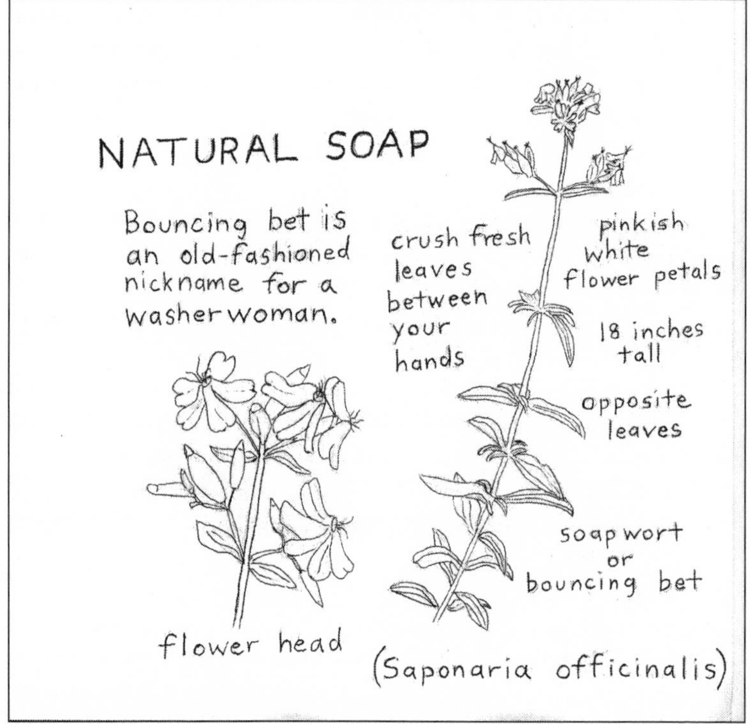

ILLUSTRATION # 2: SOAPWORT

Bug repellant: Lemon balm is a natural mosquito and horsefly repellant. It is an herb that can be found growing wild in woods and fields. Crush it and rub it on bare skin and clothes.

Knife, fork spoon: sharp stones, forked twigs, carved and hollowed out sticks.

Cup: reused plastic containers. Or you could emulated Diogenes the Cynic. He destroyed the single wooden bowl he possessed on seeing a peasant boy drink from the hollow of his hands.

Hat: Pirate like, tie a large handkerchief around your head. Have a plastic garbage bag in your pocket for a rain hat, and tuck it under your handkerchief if you're concerned about appearance (or over if you're not).

Really, Robinson Crusoe had it easy. He salvaged the stores of his wrecked ship; weapons, gunpowder, food, clothes, lumber, rope, etc. He had an entire island all to himself; an island boasting a warm climate, no large predators, a convenient cave for shelter, and an abundance of wild food. Alexander Selkirk, on whom Stevenson based his story wrote that he looked back at his four-year sojourn on Juan Fernandez Island (off Chile) with nostalgia. Loneliness was his only real problem.

3.2.1 LIVING ON THE ROAD

Staying in one place while living homeless (or even with a home) can become tedious, monotonous, boring. Travel, now that can be adventure. But you need money, preferably lots of money to travel, right? Maybe not. Living homeless and on the road can be a low-cost, even zero cost recreation or vacation.

Once, two maiden ladies invited Jack London, begging door to door, to a 'set down' breakfast at their table, a very rare and treasured occurrence for a hobo. Upon telling the ladies a pack of lies about his life and circumstances in exchange for breakfast, Jack London wrote "My coming to sit at their table was their adventure, and adventure is beyond price anyway." **'Pictures'** from ***The Road.*** Keep in mind, Jacks words "…adventure is beyond price…"

Sadly, today begging door to door for food like Jack London did is not practical. If you go up to someone's door asking for food they'll probably call the police who will then pick you up. It just isn't done anymore. People don't expect it. They'll think you are casing their place for a break in. The police may take you to a homeless shelter or perhaps the jail where you'll get food and shelter, but it most places in today's society you will not be permitted to beg door to door.

But you can be a nomadic gypsy vagabond. Sounds romantic and adventurous. And it can be, a little, as long as you know how, and don't do it too long. Why stay in the north in winter, or in the south in the summer? If you are a gypsy vagabond, you can go wherever you want to. Even walking at say 15 miles a day, you can go from the cold north to the sunny southland in maybe 60 days. Riding a bike at 50 or even 100 miles a day you could make it in 10 or 20 days. Riding a raft down the Mississippi in maybe a month. Move with the season to the comfortable climate. On the way, you can eat from the bounty of the land, if you've learned to forage.

Besides begging, or instead of begging, you can try travel foraging.

TRAVEL FORAGING:

What is it? As you travel keep on the lookout for things you can use. On foot, by bike, in a car, or even on a boat drifting down a river as Harlan Hubbard did. It is a mind set, an attitude, as you travel look at anything and everything with the thought of the use you can make of it. It could be a great game, foraging as you travel.

Walking and foraging:

Walking can be slow and tedious and you can't carry much when you find something. So easier might be:

Bike foraging.

Without a doubt the ideal method and tool for foraging is the bicycle. Bike foraging uses no fuel, is relaxing, provides exercise, and is an interesting challenge.

Biking you may explore 60 miles a day at a moderate speed with an open, unobstructed view of your surroundings. For large items, you may have to go back later with the car. It is easy to stop and conceal the bike for exploring sensitive places in foot: trespassing, perhaps on a field, forest or junkyard.

I can imagine a game based on bike foraging. The winner comes back with the best or most useful items. Or, perhaps each contestant makes a list of forage-able stuff as s/he travels to be judged on his return.

For bike foraging, a good thing to have is a bike trailer. These are rarely available used and expensive to buy, unfortunately. You might try making your own. The web site http://biketrailerblog.com lists a dozen sites that explain how. A skilled dedicated ZCL practitioner might build one for free of foraged/recycled parts.

Bike foraging your way south in the autumn, and north in the spring, (as mentioned above) may be the cheapest and most practical way to travel with the seasons.

Car foraging.

A car on the road moves too fast to get a good look at forage-able stuff. You've got to pay attention to the road and traffic, and not be distracted (like cell phone users).

A car is useful for going to yard/garage sales but gas cost can quickly eats up any savings. You can easily end up spending more on gas than the value of anything you find Car foraging and garage sale hunting may most efficiently be done while going somewhere for another purpose like shopping or a medical appointment.

A good method I use is to drive to car to a likely area, park the car and walk forage or carry a bike in (or on) the car and bike forage to look the area over at a practical speed. Then, when you've got all you can carry, return to your car with found stuff to drop it off and go again. You can drive the car to pick up large items. You haven't wasted gas looking for it.

Motorcycle:

I have not tried foraging on a motorcycle. It may work well, or like a car, you may find yourself going too fast for good foraging. Your view may be better than a car, and your gas mileage better. Like a bike, a motorcycle has limited capacity to carry what you find.

TRAVEL LIVING:

Walking:

You have a backpack, well stocked with food, you have water bottles, good extra clothes, and a tent. The world is at your doorstep to wander and explore. The Australians call it a walkabout.

Mountain climbing near the top of Everest Ed Viesturs had to breathe 15 times before taking a single step. You have it easier.

Thoreau wrote in ***Walden:***

'One man said to me, "I wonder that you do not lay up money; you love to travel; you might take the cars and go to Fitchburg to-day and see the country." But I am wiser that that. I have learned that the swiftest traveler is he that goes afoot. I say to my friend, suppose we try who will get there first. The distance is thirty miles; the fare ninety cents. That is almost a day's wages. I remember when wages were sixty cents a day for laborers on this very road. Well, I start now on foot, and get there before night: I have traveled at that rate by the week together. You will in the meanwhile have earned your fare, and arrive there some time to-morrow, or possibly this evening, if you are lucky enough to get a job in season. Instead of going to Fitchburg, you will be working here the greater part of the day. And so if the railroad reached round the world, I think that I should keep ahead of you: and as for seeing the country and getting experience of that kind, I should have to cut your acquaintance altogether.' 'Economy', page 40.

In ***A Walk Across America***, the author, Peter Jenkins set out in October 1973 down the Appalachian Trail. Though not his intention, his journey suggests homeless hikers could make seasonal migrations to the warm southland in the fall and back north in the spring using the Trail.

You're living like a one-man army on the march, poorly supplied and foraging for some food, going to gleaners when all else fails. Poor you may be, but this is your country too. Go out and make use of it.

Bicycling:

Perhaps you have a bike. A bike is one of the most useful of all inventions for ZCL. You gain tremendous speed and range and load carrying ability over walking. You can use the over-extensive American road system for free. No license or insurance are required to ride a bike anywhere. And the cost is minimal. Walking you may travel perhaps 15 miles a day, on a bike 60 miles a day average over months (or much further for a few days) is possible as Ken Kifer describes in his web site ***kenkifer.com*** Ken Kifer made epic journeys by bicycle through the United States and Canada. In his web site he describes his journeys and methods with profuse detail. It makes you feel you are with him, and makes you feel you could do it too. A recent very useful book is ***Art of Cycling*** by Robert Hurst.

Motorcycling:

The old movie ***Easy Rider*** idealized motorcycle touring. I have no experience at it. Motorcycles are expensive when large and new. They are dangerous among automobiles. Nevertheless, they may be practical for cheap touring. They may be inexpensive and easy to repair relative to a car, and get good gas mileage. They could carry a substantial amount of equipment for camping, and be easy to hide when you want to set up a hidden camp.

Small simple motorbikes may be a good option. They can be cheap to buy. Possibly, you could even travel on a moped, with pedals that could be used in the event of an engine breakdown. Take rural less traveled routes at a slow pace. Possibly stay on dirt roads. Such routes may be safer, with less traffic. It is amazing how far you can go in a few hours for the cost of a little gas. The passing scene, which you see up close at low speed can be interesting and so the time passes quickly - not-at-all like the tedium of the freeway. You really get to see the country. Group riding might be another good idea - you can enjoy the pleasure of shared adventures - and it may be safer than lone riding.

Considering the advantages and the appeal I've never seen fleets of mopeds or even a lone motorbike festooned with packs and compact camping gear cruising the country. Perhaps it is more common in other countries.

Inventions needed; a motorbike with equipment designed specifically for travel camping. Equipment example: A tent using the motorbike as part of the tent structure, and covering the bike to protect it.

Disadvantages of motorcycles and motorbikes verses the bicycle: not much exercise, greater cost, gas and oil needed, polluting, more complex, harder to repair, insurance and license required. (People don't buy insurance for bicycles; yet ride them on streets regularly).

Living out of a car, van or motorhome:

If you have a car, you have an asset: but also all the expenses that go with it.

See ***Car Living Your Way*** by A.J. Haim and ***10 Consecutive Years Living in Cars*** by Craig Roberts subtitled: ***Living, Traveling, Camping, Attending College, and Performing Surveillance in Cars – and loving it.***

Craig Roberts book has extensive detailed tips on car living. I'll summarize a few here. So no one knows he is living inside, he tints the side and rear windows and puts a sunshade behind the windshield. In the city, he rarely gets into and out of his car at the place he parks to sleep. He has means to use the toilet onboard. For cold weather, he wraps the interior of the car behind the drivers seat with 6 inches or more of high-density pink upholstery foam. He places a blanket/curtain just behind the front seats for insulation and privacy. Body heat keeps the space warm. He removes the back seat and sometimes the front passenger seat in small cars to get adequate sleeping space. In hot weather he lays on a low cot set up in the car to let air circulate around him. Along with car vents open and windows open a crack, he uses tiny 12-volt brush-less dc fans. He is able to shower using two one-gallon jugs of water. **ILLUSTRATION # 3 below diagrams car modifications recommended to make it suitable to live in.**

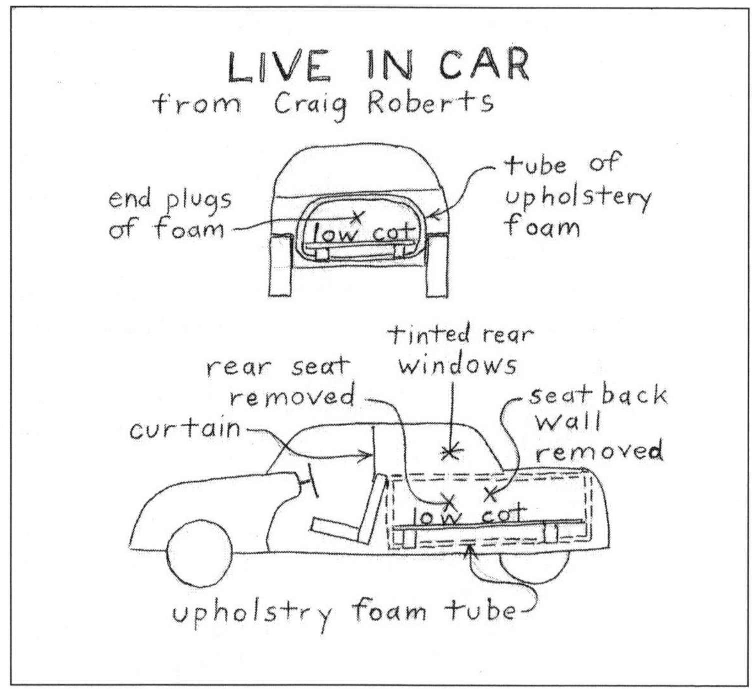

ILLUSTRATION # 3: LIVE IN CAR

Roberts attended college for years while living in a car stating: he "enjoys minimal expenses, extreme privacy, helpful campus police, highly productive people/environment, safe on campus living, fine athletic and swimming facilities, nice showering facilities, inexpensive quality health care, ... inexpensive student health insurance, etc. Also see ***Mobile Homeless: One woman's account of living on the streets of San Francisco in her camper-truck.*** by Cynthia Johnston San Francisco Chronicle March 2, 2003. Forced to leave her comfortable apartment and suffering from cancer treatments she bought a rusty 1972 pickup truck with a cab over camper for $650. She didn't have much but she considered herself to be a step above living on the streets. She had many problems including finding places to park for extended periods, alcoholics and junkies in the places she could park, and no money or skill to keep her old vehicle working. There were two to 3 thousand vehicularly housed people in San Francisco in 2003 according to the Chronicle.

Places to park: To park and sleep without causing or getting into trouble, you must carefully pick places to park. Roberts book gives extensive and detailed consideration of how and where to park. I'll summarize a few of his ideas here: **Avoid these locations:** single family residential areas. Areas where children are: playgrounds schools, day care centers, etc. Near police stations. **Park at these locations:** large all night business parking lots, university campus parking lots, on the street or in parking lots where two or more diverse land uses exist close together: apartments, offices, retail stores, restaurants, casinos, hotels. Hospital parking areas, freeway rest areas, rural public and private vacant land.

Places to park a car in the country while living out of it: abandoned gravel pits and farms, the ends of dead end roads. Ends where nobody lives.

If you have no food, or means to get it, park near a Gleaners food bank or other free food source like a County Human Services food distribution center. Park close enough so you can go back without driving - perhaps a mile or two away.

Look for rural two lane roads with wide rights of ways and lots of tree, brush and weed growth along the right of way. Try to park well away from the road among the trees and weeds. Possibly camouflage your car a little. You may be able to conceal a car and camp for weeks. You may be little noticed and if you are, perhaps by police, merely told to move along.

Also, this type of road is a good route to travel on foot or by bicycle usually having wide shoulders. Usually, there is not a lot of traffic. If you have no car, you can easily duck into the adjacent woods along the right of way and camp unnoticed. These roads can serve as your own vast, many miles long personal camping ground.

The luxury of a car: It can carry a lot of stuff (look for the gross weight sticker) perhaps 1,000 pounds. That is a lot of food, water, and gear. Place storage bins where the removed seats were

Getting camping stuff together: what you'll need. Stuff to have along: Tent, screening, cooking gear, water jugs, solar shower.

A tent is good if you have a spot. Otherwise, as is the case in or near a city, it may not be practical and you will have to sleep in the car.

Modifying a car to live out of it is an interesting problem. It is essential to have enough room to lay full length. I've done it without being able to and it is an irritating discomfort not to be able to stretch your legs out. Take out the passenger seat and rear seat and place a bed there. Hang a cover above the bed so you may sleep below and not be noticed by someone looking in the car.

Mosquito/bug screening for car windows. Another vital item in summer: tape it on. Without it you'll swelter or be bitten by bugs. Both bad choices. At a home supply or hardware store you can buy a roll of plastic screen used for repairing screen doors for a few dollars. Cut it to fit and duct tape it all the way around the windows you intend to keep open.

Curtains and means to hang them are essential for privacy.

Rent a post office box to receive mail.

A wireless lap top computer could give you access to the net from your car.

You will want to have auto repair skills and tools.

If driven gently even an ailing vehicle may be kept going for many miles. For example: In the case of a cylinder out, accelerate slowly, avoid freeways, keep the strains on the engine low (keep r.p.m. low).

Van: Compared to living out of a car a van can provide luxurious space, comfort and privacy. Usually gas mileage is worse. One way to get around this problem - don't drive around much. Park at a carefully selected location and stay there, perhaps for days or weeks. Eventually you may have to move. Scout out suitable new locations before you move so you can avoid driving around wasting gas when you move. When you drive, to save gas, keep your speed down and accelerate slowly.

A van towing a trailer, even a small trailer will give you extravagant space and capacious storage. You will find it easy to get to things like food, clothes, camping gear, and tent. The van interior need not be filled with stuff piled on top of other stuff. With your van free of all of your gear you might sleep and hang out in it and dispense with a tent.

Motorhome: Old used motorhomes often with low miles on their odometers are widely available cheap - for a few thousand dollars or less. Whether they run is another question. Just sitting around can be hard on vehicles. If you go to RV Parks you will not be able to live low cost. And their gas mileage will soon use up your money if you drive them around much. But if you have a place to park one for long period, or perhaps permanently, for free or modest cost, then that's not a problem. Now you are at the luxury end of homelessness, perhaps not even qualifying as homeless though you have no 'house'.

Consider the advantages from a ZCL perspective. If you don't own the property where you park, you pay no property taxes, a great savings. Or, if you own the property you pay taxes only on the land, since you have no house. Of course owning land, you are far from homeless and destitute. I have more to say on living ZC on land you own or can use in chapter 5 'Homesteading'.

Trailer: A trailer may work if you can find a place to park it. (Of course, if you have to move it, you are faced with the problem of getting a vehicle to move it). It may be cheaper to buy than a motor home, and have lower upkeep and maintenance costs. Esther Holmes describes her experience doing this in her book ***How I Lived Seven Years without Electricity and Running Water.*** Conceivably you could get a damaged trailer free or nearly free and fix it. You might even build your own, perhaps buying a flatbed trailer frame to begin with and building the upper 'home' frame yourself. See the web site ***www.tinytears.com*** for "teardrop" trailers, so named because of their shapes. These are small lightweight, easy to build trailers with sleeping space for two. The web site ***www.woodworkersworkshop.com*** - Free woodworking plans - Camper Trailers has numerous variations of the teardrop and other trailer designs. Also, see the book ***How to Build Campers and Trailers*** by John Gartner.

3.2.2 LIVING IN THE WILDERNESS:

I've only attempted living in the wilderness for short periods, and so will rely on several sources in this discussion.

It has psychological appeal unlike living homeless in the city. Urban folk sometimes dream of living in the wilderness as a means of escaping their restricted lives and so books about it are popular. Of course many, even most go to the wilderness in a motor home or stay in a well-equipped cabin. But here I am considering wilderness living almost Zero Cost and homeless.

You need to practice and develop certain skills to live in the wilderness.

Many of these techniques can be used in city, small town, farming, or rural region, not just in the wilderness.

The difference is huge between being thrown into the wilderness without preparation vs. having skills and time to make preparations. Primitivists do it and consider it to be the greatest sport of all. It is a great and admirable skill to deliberately walk into the wild with little more than the clothes on your back and make your way. Thomas Elpel takes an astonishingly short list of food and equipment on his wilderness jaunts.

For a challenge comparable to climbing Mount Everest, or any extreme sport try living in the wilderness with little or nothing for an extended period of time. Few have done it for more than a few days. And doing it destitute without equipment or practiced skills is a challenge that may cost you your life.

One example, well worth study is described in the book ***Into the Wild*** by Jon Krakauer 1996

The book is about the life and death of a young man named Chris McCandless. The book follows his wanderings from 1990 to 1992, as he lived an extremely low cost lifestyle. Then he went to Alaska, intending to live off the land, to practice what I would consider a Zero Cost Living existence. He lived 4 months in the bush North of Denali National Park from April 28 to August 18 1992. Writes Krakauer, "He tried to live entirely off the country and he tried to do it without bothering to master beforehand the full repertoire of crucial skills." He shot a moose and tried to smoke the meat to preserve it and failed and so it rotted. Krakauer writes, "easiest way to preserve meat in the bush is to slice it into thin strips and then air dry on a makeshift rack."

Chris' attempt to return to civilization was blocked by a river in flood that was frozen and passable when he went into the bush. Slowly starving, he ate wild potato seeds not listed as poisonous, the plant was plainly identified as non-toxic in a book he had entitled "***Tananaina Plantlore***". The roots are edible and the seeds were not listed as edible or toxic. He was poisoned by the seeds according to Krakauer who writes, "alkaloids in the seed coats in late summer … discourage animals from eating the seeds." Chris died, but there is plenty to learn applicable to ZCL from McCandless's life as revealed in Krakauers' book. To live ZC by foraging you must know what you are doing.

Mountain hiking and moderate climbing can be an almost free sport if you live near mountains. For the modest cost of a park permit you can hike, camp, and climb for weeks. Or you could try sneaking in. Mountainous areas - consisting of big chunks of public land are not easy to patrol. You could sneak in for free as Jon Krakauer did when he climbed the Devils Thumb as described in his book ***Eiger Dreams***.

From a ZCL perspective, mountain climbing is a useless, wasteful, possibly dangerous, and sometimes expensive sport. (Permit fees to climb in the Himalayas have made it a recreation for the wealthy). Another useless sport - walking around hitting little white balls into holes in the ground. Better to use all that effort in some productive activity.

Ed Viesturs, in his book ***No Shortcut to the Top*** describes a "Bamboo bivouac" he had to build to survive. Caught out on Mount Rainier in winter at night without equipment "I dug myself a snow cave. I didn't have a shovel so I used a pot lid. No sleeping bag or pad… All I had was a batch of bamboo willow wands" (used to mark trail in snow) "which I laid out as a mattress. Inside the cave it was about 25 degrees F. All I had for food was a single Snickers bar."

Dangerous sports are an anathema to ZCL. You could suffer a serious injury and have no way to pay for it. You could be financially wiped out. To live ZCL it's better to live carefully. Leave these sports to the wealthy and foolish.

SKILLS

Foraging in the Wild:

Once there was a lot of wild food out there free for the taking. Vikings called this land Vinland the Good and I believe it to be the best name ever given to this land. Lakes rivers and ocean coasts held abundant fish. The land was rich with game such as passenger pigeons, wild turkeys, and buffalo. Forage-able food such as wild grapes, chestnuts, groves of hazelnut trees were abundant. Books by pioneers such as ***Land of the Crooked Tree*** by Ulysses P. Hendrick describe what was once available.

Non-native pests, farming, over hunting and urban development destroyed vast quantities of forage-able wild and freely available foods. I believe most of the bounty of the past can and should be restored as described more in chapter 7: 'Society

Practicing ZCL". Bits have been restored, wild turkey, Canada geese. Whitetail deer are more abundant than ever. There is still a lot of wild food available.

Wild foods I have foraged in Michigan: mayapples, apples, raspberries, grapes, grape leaves, acorns, hickory nuts, lambs quarters, purslane.

"Grasses can also be eaten green, except that you only swallow the juice and spit the fiber out. Chewing on the tender grasses, and particularly the immature seed heads, is an excellent way to get a healthful and sustaining dose of vitamins and minerals. In fact many health enthusiast grow wheat and barley sprouts, and process them through a juicer. You do not have to do all that work, though, if you just graze on the tender grasses as you walk through the woods. **Grazing on grass is just the kind of health tonic that every person in this country desperately needs.** (my italics). Please note, however, that some grasses produce cyanide compounds as they wilt. This may be an evolutionary strategy to ward off foraging animals when the plants are already stressed from heat and drought." Elpel ***Botany in a Day*** page 163.

"I personally have fantasized all my life about being like the native scout, able to travel light and invisible, like the wind, living with nature with only my bare hands." Elpel, ***Participating in Nature*** page 16.

But even Elpel does not rely always and entirely on foraged wild foods. Here is his list of "Basic foods to take hiking and camping": oatmeal, rice, beans, instant potatoes, powdered milk, raisins, flour, bouillon, baking soda, salt, pepper, cinnamon.
(This list was presented on page 94 but is worth repeating). These items are very cheap and almost universally available.

In his book ***Participating in Nature*** Elpel describes how he cooks with these items, making concoctions such as "ash cakes".

Hunting, fishing and ZCL: As usually practiced today, as a sport, hunting and fishing may cost too much in time, and money relative to the value gained. Thousands of dollars may be spent on an expedition realizing a few pounds of meat. I am not a hunter or fisherman but I believe it should be possible to make hunting worth the trouble and expense if you practice it with efficiency. Wild fish and game can be very healthy compared to fish farm and feedlot grown meat - low in fat, low in pesticides, with abundant omega 3 fatty acids.

Campsite:

You need a camp, a place to process, use, and store stuff. An unusual example that worked very well was Harlan Hubbard's shantyboat. With his wife he drifted with the river, tying up each evening. On some days, or sometimes weeks he foraged inland from his shantyboat camp for food, firewood and "waste' materials left by the river in past floods. He processed and stored food and supplies aboard. He rarely spent any money.

Edward Romney in his book ***Living Well On Practically Nothing*** wrote: "The big secret is that the woods are empty of people except near rivers, waterfalls, high mountains, and natural attractions and during hunting season. Astonishingly empty! People climb 6,000 foot Mt. Washington, but never 7000 foot Mt. Eagle Rock or 1,800 foot North Pack Monandnock. Also, they are lazy, they will not go cross country. They must have a path. Any climbing or dense brush will stop them cold. Just like a wild bird, you must look to hiding in dense brush as your protection." His book has much more advice on picking a good campsite for ZCL.

Shelter:

You have it much easier than the high mountain climbers described earlier. In the north, in summer, the climate really is benign. You can sleep out in the open on many nights. You need mosquito netting you can throw over yourself, or a mosquito hat. Or get dirty and smelly with campfire smoke and salty sweat to keep them off.

As a shelter a tent, if well built, is not to be dismissed. Tents are used on the highest mountains as the only shelter of serious climbers, sometimes for days during blizzards. Uncomfortable perhaps, but they work. They stop the wind and keep out rain and snow. The web sites ***www.Backpacking.net*** shows some plans for tents. These require sewing and recommend you use good quality material that can be expensive.

A simple tarp of cheap material - thrown over a stick/ rope frame can keep you dry and block the wind. Tarp tents can be made from blue polytarps costing only a few dollars, scraps of ***Tyvek*** from a construction site that you may be able to get for free by asking, or even sheets of plastic. As cited earlier, the web site ***www.equipped.com/tarp shelters/htm*** describes how tarps may be set up for shelter.

For survival shelter concepts **see Illustration # 4** below:

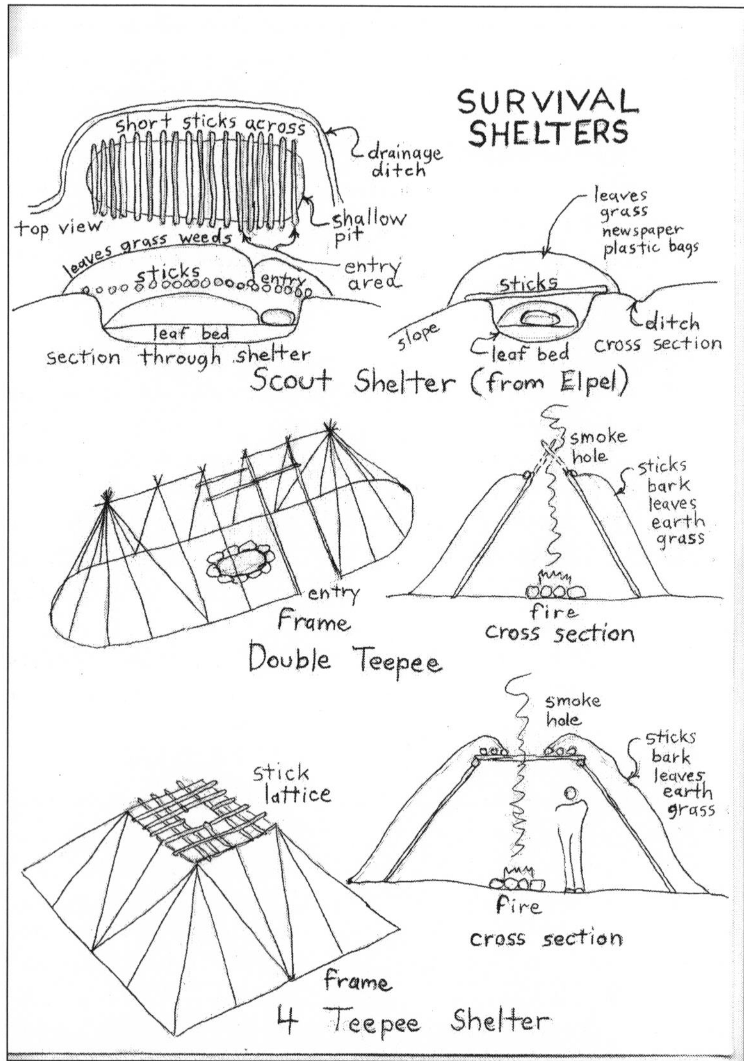

ILLUSTRATION # 4: SURVIVAL SHELTERS

Illustration 4 shows the construction of a scout shelter as described by Elpel in his book ***Participating in Nature***. This shelter can save your life by keeping you warm and dry if you have nothing, and are caught outdoors in bad weather. It can be made of foraged natural materials.

A teepee covered by bark is recommended by Brown in his book ***Sleep Close to the Fire.*** Bark, usually from downed trees is layered on working from bottom to top shingle style, making a shelter that is dry in the heaviest rain if made carefully. Sticks laid against the teepee frame before the bark is placed and more sticks laid over the bark help keep the bark in place. Illustration 4 shows modified teepee frames suitable for bark covering.

Either of these shelter types can serve as the basis for a 'debris hut' in which a lot of material is piled up inside and out as a cold weather survival shelter. Debris can include leaves, cut weeds, straw, grass, pine needles, newspapers, plastic bags, old clothes, anything that can trap air and form an insulating bulky, fluffy mass.

Skills and tools:

Fire starting: You need tinder. Carry a small bottle, perhaps a vitamin bottle or small tin can containing dryer lint, or get aspen cottonwood, or red cedar inner bark from a dead branch. Rub the inner bark between your fingers to make tinder.

Flint knapping: means making tools from flint, a stone that can be shaped to hold as sharp point. Allen in his book ***Sleep Close to the Fire*** described it in detail. Elpel in ***Participating in Nature*** describe glass and bone pointed arrows.

See the ***Art of Nothing*** by Thomas Elpel: a series of DVDs that may be ordered from the web site ***hollowtop.com:*** examples of topics:

Shelter: grass sleeping bag, debris shelter with hot rocks.

Fire: started with a soda pop bottle lens, cottonwood root bowdrill set

Water: boiling water in found bottles and cans.

Purifying water with aerobic oxygen

Food: cattail roots, rose hips, burdock, mustard greens, milkweed shoots, tree mushrooms, sweet cicely, wild sunflower, dwarf huckleberry, musk thistle stems, brook saxifrage, rose petals, wild onions.

Cooking: cooking on an upright stone slab

Tools: discoidal stone knives, digging sticks, foraging the nail knife, tin can knives, glass knapped knives, willow toothbrush, pine bark pot

Native American Skills

Study how native Americans lived and where they lived for what they can teach us. One example: They set up summer camps along the lake Michigan shoreline where wind off the lake keeps off mosquitoes. They stayed out of the inland woods in summer. They knew every source of wild foods and how to use and process them. They could build simple shelters in a few hours from nearby natural materials that would keep them warm and dry in the coldest weather.

Another example of how Native Americans lived and what they can teach us: The Atl-atl is a stick, an extension of your arm on the end of which you secure a large, long arrow. It has greater range and accuracy than a spear. It is much easier to make than a bow and arrow and so may be more practical than a spear or bow as a survival tool. Eskimos used it as recently as a century ago. According to archeologists, it was the hunting weapon of choice for 30,000 years before the advent of the bow and arrow a few thousand years ago. The atl-atl was used to hunt wooly mammoths. Arrowheads too small to be spear tips and too large to be arrows from bows have been found in their remains.

Again quoting Edward Romney from ***Living Well on Practically Nothing:*** "At best, living off the land is a full time, 12 hour a day job just getting food, and you'll still be losing weight. For all their great hunting skills, American Indians suffered from famines and starved." A prescription for modern overweight Americans perhaps?

He wrote: "The survival lifestyle cost nothing for shelter, utilities, and taxes. You will get your meat by killing animals and fish, but you will probably need staples: flour, shortening, oatmeal, dried peas, beans, sugar, and powdered milk as well as soap, Zippo lighter fluid, bug powder, ammunition, and antiseptic. These provisions will cost you about $300 a year for two persons if you must buy them all. But most of the food items are available from government surplus food programs."

One thing for sure, living homeless will make you appreciate the simple things; make you appreciate a home, any home no matter how humble (as the song goes) and make you realize what matters in life.

You need not live ZCL in homeless destitution indefinitely. With a source of income and/or some assets you may progress to seasteading or homesteading - circumstances described in the next chapters. Then your life may become more comfortable.

3.2.3 INTO THE GREAT NORTH:

A ZCL option that can be a great adventure, like seasteading described in the next chapter, is journeying whether by hiking, horseback, canoe, bicycle, or automobile into the Great Northern regions of the world. Circling the Globe is a vast almost empty region where folks could travel and/or live with minimal taxes or expenses if they know how to live. The fact is, in the Eastern United States, if you have some skills, it wouldn't cost much to buy and equip a canoe and, with or without companions head for the North. In the West you might ride a horse North.

Inspirations: These are a few I have read. There are many more.

Richmond P. Hobson: ***Grass Beyond the Mountains: The true story of the discovery of the last great cattle frontier on the North American Continent***

Eric and Pam Morse: ***Freshwater Saga***

Alan Kesselheim: ***Water and Sky***

Richmond Hobson went into the wilderness of British Columbia by horseback in the 1930s, as part of an effort that discovered and opened up previously unknown grasslands to cattle ranching. He learned how to deal with the intense cold of winter and the hordes of insects in summer, all of it a great wild adventure.

Eric Morse spent every summer of his life exploring the waterways of Canada getting to know dozens of canoe routes.

Alan Kesselheim and his wife canoed into the Great North of Alberta, Saskatchewan and the Northwest Territories (now called Nunavik) stayed through the winter then canoed further north the next summer.

***

CHAPTER 4: SEASTEADING:

Contents: **page:**

4.1 INTRODUCTION:

What is Seasteading? Seasteading means living on the water in a harbor, along a canal or river, on a lake or bay or other protected water, or on the open ocean.

Reading, study, and conversations, have convinced me that seasteading can be an eminently practical and economical way of life. This chapter is an introduction to the concept. Before attempting seasteading you need to study and practice navigation, seamanship, boat handling, living aboard, keeping and preparing food, etcetera.

In fact, study of seasteading methods is enormously useful and instructive to anyone attempting ZCL in any circumstance, (even though you may never live on the water); because amazing things can be done in boats that may be only 30 feet in length and have less space than the smallest apartment. If seasteaders can do that, (sometimes on a rolling sea), how much easier would it be with an actual house and land that is stable and unmoving.

I confess I have never attempted seasteading. The nearest I have come to seasteading to is live and cruise aboard small sailboats for a few days at a time. So, my commentary here relies more on the writings of others, rather than on personal experience. If you plan to seastead, or just want to study seasteading, read some or all of the books that I list here and you will be well informed:

INSPIRATIONS:

Shantyboat by Harlan Hubbard.

The Self Sufficient Sailor and other books by Lin and Larry Parday

Voyaging on a Small Income and other books by Annie and Pete Hill.

One Hand for Yourself One for the Ship and other books by Tristan Jones.

Sailing the Farm by Ken Neumeyer.

Living off the Sea by Bonnie O"Boyle

Sensible Cruising: The Thoreau Approach by Don Casey & Lew Hackler

The Simplistic Sailboat by Dan Hookham

Seasteading by Jerome FitzGerald

WHY SEASTEAD?

• **Incredibly cheap travel:** You can travel 100 miles a day or more, day after day for zero cost. The wind is free. Sailing is, in my opinion, cheaper, safer, more forgiving, and more comfortable than any other method of travel, (certainly safer than travel on land by car).

• **Extremely low cost living is possible:** You can stay in a protected anchorage for weeks, months, and years on your own anchor (not a marina slip or mooring that costs $) and spend almost no money. You can avoid rent, a mortgage, property taxes, and owning an automobile (with all of its associated costs).

• **Follow the seasons**: Sail with the seasons to a more pleasant climate and avoid heating and air conditioning costs.

• **Independence and self-sufficiency**: Generate your own electricity with solar cells or a small windmill of the type made for a sailboat. Use your boat as a platform for fishing and foraging along coasts and islands to get food for free. Grow or make food onboard such as sprouts, yogurt, cheese, bread and pasta as Ken Neumeyer describes in his book ***Sailing the Farm.*** Building your own personal economy based on a boat may be quite possible.

• **Save the environment:** By seasteading, you can remove some of your contribution to the burden humanity imposes upon the crowded land. Done right, seasteading ought to be non-polluting.
• **Long vacation:** You could take a low cost (or even zero cost) vacation for weeks, months, or years from usual life (and from your homestead - if you build one as described in chapters 5 and 6).
• **Challenge:** Getting most of what you need to live by seasteading could be more intriguing and challenging than any game, hobby, sport, entertainment, or recreation imaginable.
• **High adventure:** (at very low cost). You can explore remote wilderness, strange cities, dark jungles, exotic islands, intriguing rivers and canals, the untrammeled ends of the earth. The mind boggles at the possibilities.

4.2 SEASTEADING: WHERE?

In ***Sailing the Farm***, Ken Neumeyer writes "Why possess land when there are millions of acres on the seacoast of the world that nobody will contest your using. .... You just have to have means to live and a shelter that can be easily moved. .... Spend your money on tools, not land that in many places is already free." (page 13)

To that Harland Hubbard might add: millions of acres along rivers.

Ken writes, "You may eventually wish to settle on a deserted beachfront somewhere to build a base of some sort, or to get off the boat awhile. For this there are several tools and materials that could make survival much more comfortable…" (page 17).

You do not need to cross any oceans or take any risks; seacoasts, lakes and rivers provide vast areas where you might seastead. Ken writes, " A hundred thousand miles of practically deserted seacoast along the Alaskan and Canadian shoreline are absolutely teeming with salmon, seaweed and wild foods of all kinds. There are some areas where there may not be another human soul for a hundred miles. The reason why this vast region, so rich in natural resources, is so thinly settled is that people have not yet learned to adapt themselves to its sometimes-harsh environment. With a boat you could live in these less populated areas in the summer, and then sail south with the geese in the fall…"(page 3).

In a warm climate it is possible to live aboard year round but in the summer heat why not go north to cooler weather, and when the North gets cold why stick around and freeze.

With a shallow draft flat bottom boat you can anchor over tidal flats. When the tide goes out vast spaces are suddenly yours to explore and forage for a few hours. Or you can sail along beaches, the endless sand beaches of the Great Lakes for example, and with the right kind of boat, run your boat up on shore whenever wind and waves are calm.

. You will want to avoid cold damp climates such as the Pacific Northwest in winter. Jerome FitzGerald lives aboard and cruises there year round however, relying on a well-insulated boat with a carefully designed heating system using diesel fuel. Nevertheless, in midwinter, he mentions thoughts of going south.

In the Eastern United States, before winter strikes, sail to Florida along the Atlantic coast, or motor down the inland Waterway, (but that will cost you fuel). In the shallow waters of the Florida Keys, you can sail, fish, forage, and anchor for the night at will. If you feel bold and adventurous cross, the Gulf Stream to the Bahamas where more warm islands and shallow water beckon. Or, seastead among the backwater bayous and rivers of the Deep South near the Gulf of Mexico. Winter there is agreeable to most refugees from the North, though not as warm as South Florida, but neither is it so crowded.

Maybe, drop anchor or tie up to shore in a flood plain along a river where, when the river is not in spring flood, you can live ashore for a summer of foraging and gardening as Harlan Hubbard did. Consider buying land in a flood plain - it may be inexpensive. You won't be building a house on it (except maybe a shed). Locate close to a town so that you can hike, bike or boat there.

The Great Lakes are rarely used by seasteaders. It is a vast region; beautiful, with long empty coastlines in the north and thousands of uninhabited islands. Try it in the summer, but be gone by November when the temperature difference between air and lake water is at its greatest, and wind, storms, and lake effect snow are at their worst. In the future, I believe, many thousands of seasteading folk will make the Great Lakes their summer homes.

Your boat is mobile, no car needed if you locate where you can take advantage of your boat's mobility. Locate for a while where you can sail, or take your dinghy to a nearby town for supplies, company, library, post office, etc. Harlan Hubbard for example, occasionally tied up his raft to the riverbank where he could take a short hike over the levees to a town.

Regions that have numerous islands, fjords, bayous, canals, river deltas, or chains of lakes are, I believe, especially well suited for seasteading. They may have countless protected, quiet, safe waterways you can explore or anchor in as you please - where you can go ashore, maybe tie up to a tree to hike and forage.

A sailboat is a multipurpose machine that can be used to forage for food and materials. For example:

You can fish from the boat while sailing. You can shorten sail to the mainsail only, sail on a close reach (at an angle into the wind), drag a trolling line, and in this way fish at a near perfect trolling speed. On a close reach with a correct set of sail - mainsail only set and other sails lowered, and the main sheet pulled in tight (so the mainsail is pulled in close to the centerline of the boat) many boats will sail themselves at an angle to windward (at an angle into the winds) without a hand on the tiller.

If your boat is shallow draft with a flat bottom and centerboard and the waves are small, you can forage the land by grounding on a sandy beach. The shores of the Great Lakes, Florida and Gulf of Mexico have thousands of miles of suitable sandy beaches. Alternatively, with a boat of sufficiently shallow draft - 3 or 4 feet - you can anchor in water shallow enough to wade ashore. And, you can get into small, shallow well-protected harbors. Along rivers, you can sometimes tie up to a tree, as Harlan Hubbard did along the Ohio and Mississippi.

You needn't cross an ocean; you just need quiet and free places to "drop your hook" as the old sailors say when they drop anchor. You might spend an entire summer without spending a dime.

If you tire of life on the water and want to live on land for a while, you can find remote sites up rivers, on lakes, or perhaps on uninhabited islands. You can look for and settle at a place that is seasonally flooded (so no one can live there or build there permanently), and stay there for the season of low water. When the water rises, leave. If a flood comes early, you are secure - your home floats on any flood. In many ways a boat is better than a house.

In Georgian Bay, which is part of Lake Ontario in Canada, there are a hundred thousand islands, most uninhabited. Claim one for a summer. Water is no problem. In most of the enormous Bay you are surrounded by clean fresh water. For food there are fish. Wild blueberries grow everywhere in the region in season - July and August. You can even set up a temporary garden/greenhouse on your chosen island.

And more thousands of islands exist along the Pacific Ocean shore from Seattle to Alaska and beyond to the Aleutians.

In the Caribbean, there are countless desert islands that have no fresh water supply. Put a solar powered desalination system aboard your boat, set it up on an empty island and plant a garden, using your system to make fresh water for you and a garden.

Have some dollars saved and/or invested and earning interest or dividend income and you have almost unlimited flexibility and freedom as described by Annie Hill in her book ***Voyaging on a Small Income***.

On your boat you might carry a tent or better, something more than a tent. I will discuss this more in the chapter on ‘Homesteading’, but even a modest shed is vastly superior to the best tent as a comfortable shelter. Carry on board tools, materials, and components to build a little house you can use for a season on shore. Disassemble the components and put them back aboard at seasons end

Desert nomads carry tents and all of their possessions on camels to seasonal encampments and pastures, following desert rains. Mongolian nomads use pack animals to carry light, simple, and warm moveable homes called yurts. You could be a seagoing version of these nomads, but carry on you boat many times the weight and bulk that a nomad carries with pack animals.

Tools: axe and saw, hammer and chisels, sharpening stone.

Materials for windows: polycarbonate sheets, screening, clear plastic sheeting.

Materials for roofs: tar paper, black plastic.

Components: metal brackets, nails, screws, window and door latches.

Shelters of the Native Americans: wigwam, teepee, long house, are instructive of what is possible.

Transitioning to Seasteading - Possible steps:

There are a series of steps you might take to get ready for a life on the water. Look for a small town with a good harbor – large and well protected from wind and waves –a harbor of sufficient size to allow boats to anchor out - away from shore but still safe in the harbor (thus avoiding marina fees). For a cheap place to live, look for a town bypassed by commerce and a little run down – a town that is not a tourist haven, and not a hangout of the wealthy. Suitable towns exist along the coast of the Gulf of Mexico both coasts of Canada, along the Mississippi River, and on the Great Lakes In Michigan on Lake Huron for example, towns like Algonac, Harbor Beach, and Oscoda fit these recommendations. (In some regions notably New England - in fact most of the east and west coasts of the U.S. protected harbor space has all been dedicated to floating moorings you must pay for. These moorings are cheaper than a marina dock, however).

Find a place to live within walking distance of the harbor area. Rent a cheap house, or buy one and settle there while you buy and prepare your boat. Sell your house when you go, or rent it out for some income.

Look for a boat suitable for seasteading. Use the internet. Visit local boatyards and marinas. Boats abandoned in a marina with marina fees owed may be bought cheaply. Cheap sailboats are especially plentiful on the Great lakes.

If your boat is anchored out, you will need a small dinghy to get to your boat. You may be able to keep your dinghy on the beach or (since it is small) for a small fee at a marina up on the shore (not tied to a dock). A dinghy that looks cheap, beat up, and (apparently) crudely built is less likely to be stolen. Nevertheless, you want a dinghy that is strong and lightweight. Phil Bolger designed several suitable dinghies such as 'shoebox' and 'brick'. The web site ***www.ace.net.au.Bolger Books on the Net*** describes these and other boats that might be useful to a seasteader.

If you are on the ocean you could keep your boat on the tidal flats that dry out or become too shallow for bigger boats when the tide goes out. Your boat must be of a type that allows it to settle upright when the tidal flats go shallow or dry out – by having a shallow draft, or a flat bottom and a centerboard, or a double keel upright when the tide goes out. (common in many English boats) or you must attach poles to each side of a full keel boat that keep her propped up.

4.3 BOATS: Boat size and type:

For full headroom and adequate space for seasteading a boat typically must be about 30 feet long minimum. A 35 foot boat would be about the maximum – to keep down cost, for ease of handling and to make it possible to have a boat with shallow draft.

A shallow draft boat with a centerboard is ideal. Boats that have a shallow draft can be anchored in shallow water. With the centerboard pulled up, some can be run aground. You could cruise along the endless beaches of the Great Lakes for example and, when wind and waves were right, run your boat ashore to beach comb or camp - costing you nothing for the privilege. Don't try this directly in front of cottages or a public swimming beach - but many miles of shore exist where no one will be disturbed by your presence.

For travel downriver, your boat could be a simple raft like the one Harlan Hubbard built on the banks of the Ohio River using recycled and scrap materials. And, a raft will work if you don't intend to travel much, settling in a backwater bayou for example. For more mobility, including upriver travel when conditions are right, I recommend a sailboat. On the Nile River, cargo-hauling sailboats called feluccas drift downriver (to the north) with the current, and sail upriver with the prevailing wind from the north. On the Mississippi you might do the same, (reversing the direction) drifting south on the current with the sails down, sailing upriver with the prevailing summer wind that usually blows from the southwest.

Old fiberglass sailboats are widely available and can be bought for little money. Fiberglass is generally almost indestructible, repairable, and adaptable. Modify a boat to suit your purposes – for example replace a deep keel with a shallow draft keel and centerboard or a new 'wing' keel - (a shallow keel with short wings resembling whale flukes at the base).

Boats have living spaces that are compact, tightly fitted, and purely functional with miniaturized appliances, multipurpose fixtures such as bed/seats with drawers under, and moveable fixtures like folding tables. Boat living spaces are smaller than you would ever dream of living in, on land. A 30-foot boat with a 10-foot beam may have 250 square feet inside and 250 more on deck. It is a space smaller than most apartments and much smaller than the smallest urban lot. Harlan Hubbard's boat was 24 foot length x 10 foot beam with a 16 x 10 cabin. Annie Hills' boat is 34 foot length x 10 foot beam.

Chinese Junks are designed for the purpose of living aboard. They are perfectly suited for seasteading. They are cheap and safe by design. Junks are almost unsinkable because their hulls are divided into numerous bulkheads. If one compartment is holed or leaks, the other compartments will keep the boat afloat. They have flat bottoms allowing sailing and anchoring in shallow water close to shore – and travel up rivers and canals.

A Junk sail rig (a form of the standing lugsail) can be extremely low cost as Annie Hill explains in her book ***Voyaging on a Small Income.*** Though not as efficient to windward as a 'modern' Marconi rig (such as you see on most sailboats today) you can get decent sailing performance from the junk rig. You can make your own junk style sails and rigging at low cost because cheap and simple fittings and inexpensive sailcloth of canvas or plastic polytarps can be used and you do not need to be highly skilled at sewing or sail making,

Modify the mast to allow quick and easy lowering and securing on deck. On the sailing boats of Holland this is common so they may pass through canals and under the numerous bridges. For ways to do this see the article **'Tabernacles and Hinged Mast Steps'** beginning on page 58 in the magazine ***Small Boat Journal*** - January 1989 issue.

Some of the seasteading books listed above recommend no motor; the Pardays, the Hills, FitzGerald. You save a bundle of cost and trouble. You have to learn how to handle a boat without a motor, for example rowing or sculling (as the Pardays do). A boat under thirty feet can usually be rowed or sculled in calm wind and water – as in entering a harbor. If you are caught directly downwind from a harbor entrance without a motor you might have to anchor, or sail back and forth, or go elsewhere until the wind changes. If offered or available, you might submit to the indignity of a tow, but the seasteaders listed above never did.

If you add an outboard motor, an outboard motor well with a lockable lid in your boat is a very good thing to have. Instead of hanging your outboard off the stern it is placed in a 'box' or well set in from the stern where it is not visible to covetous eyes. It is protected from theft, vandalism, damage and weather. An outboard motor in a well is almost like an inboard but with the advantage of being removable for service and repair.

See **illustration 5** on page 123 for an example of a sailboat suitable for seasteading.

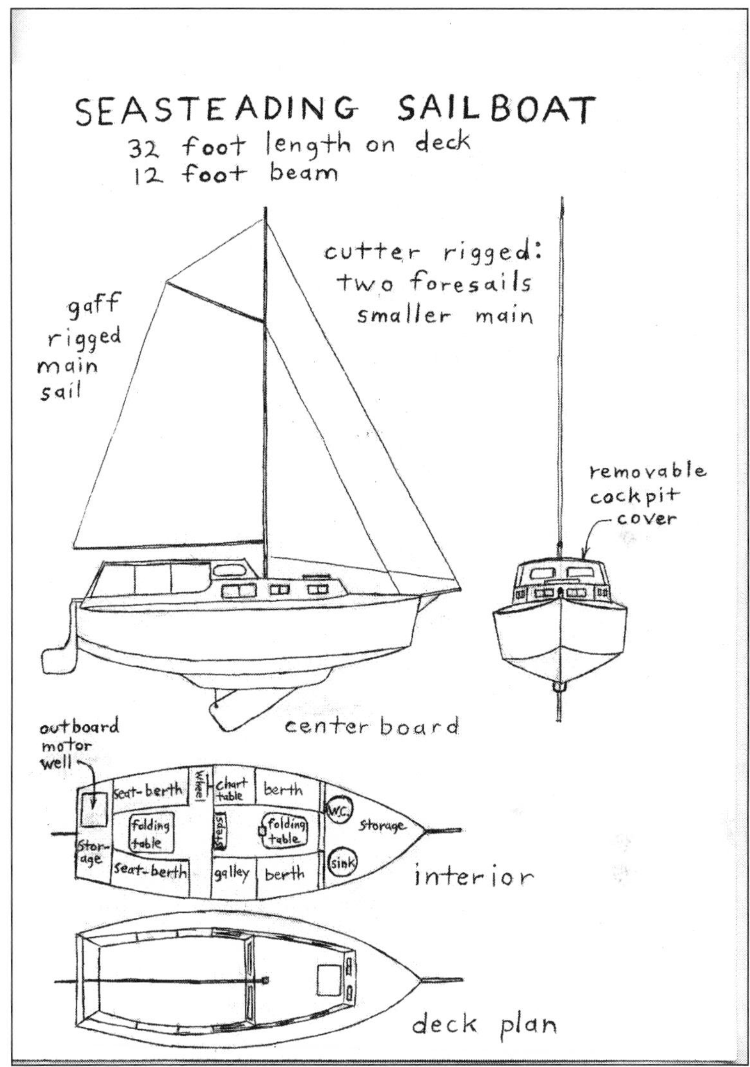

ILLUSTRATION # 5: SEASTEADING SAILBOAT

4.4 LIVING ABOARD: HOW?

How many thousands live on boats today in the United States? It has never been researched. How do they live? It is a subject worthy of more study.

A sailboat can be a mobile **personal economy**, a neat package, combining house, mobility and maybe a business in one structure. With sails and oars you can be free of the cost of fuel for mobility. Owning no land you avoid property taxes. You can sidestep a host of problems you encounter homesteading on the land.

Living on the water, you might be called (perhaps behind your back) a boat bum, which sounds bad or a seasteader, which sounds better. Certainly, money is not the criteria. The Pardays and Hills voyaged with little money, yet they can hardly be classified as boat bums. The Hubbards, on their homemade raft were not labeled boat bums. What is the difference? Mostly, I believe in comes down to whether you ever take your boat anywhere, or most importantly, whether you boat looks like you could take it on a voyage – in other words, shipshape. If your boat looks like a floating junkyard, (unless well hidden in a backwater) you may be assigned bum status. If your boat looks trim, clean, orderly, and ready to take to the sea you may be considered an intrepid seasteader. Is avoiding the boat bum label important? It could be, possibly making it easer for you to be accepted by the local community.

4.4.1 EQUIPMENT:

Below is a list of things you might want for seasteading. The list is not complete or thoroughly discussed. (The books listed above are thorough). It is presented here it to give you an idea of what might be required. As you can see the list is extensive and many items are not cheap if purchased new at retail prices. However there are usually inexpensive alternatives – used or homemade.

You may be able to get along without some items. For example: you may not need GPS if you learn celestial navigation. The book ***Airborne*** by William F. Buckley Jr. provides an excellent explanation of celestial navigation.

If you never intend to cross an ocean, perhaps always staying in sight of land you might get along without use of celestial navigation (and its attendant books, tables and equipment). But then you should have good coastal navigation charts, compass, and binoculars and know how to use them.

1. **Navigation:**
   Compass, sextant, binoculars, GPS.
   Charts, maps, books, pencils paper, divider (looks like a protractor), parallel ruler.
   Radio: batteries charged with solar cells.

Watch: for determining your speed (without GPS) and for celestial navigation.
Sounding line: to test water depth in an anchorage. A depth sounder is an expensive luxury if your boat is shallow draft.
Oil lamps, candles, flashlights if you have no electrical system, (or if your electrical system goes out).
Self-steering system: The book ***Self-Steering for Sailing Craft*** by John S. Letcher, Jr. describes cheap simple homemade systems.

2. **Safety:**
   cell phone or CB radio batteries and/or charger
   life preservers
   rubber dinghy
   medical kit
   rope or wire lifelines and harness
   anchors- two minimum, more would be better of different sizes and types for different kinds of 'holding ground' – mud, sand, rocky, etc.
3. **Propulsion:**
   oars: instead of an engine or if the engine goes out.
   sculling oar: a long single oar used off the stern of a boat.
   long pole: for 'poling the boat' in shallow water.
   extra sails: such as a 'Genoa' jib used in light winds.
   outboard: cheaper to buy, easier to repair than an inboard – you can take it ashore to get it fixed.
   spare parts for your motor.
   fuel, oil, and lube
4. **Tools:**
   boat repair
   rope and wire repair
   sail repair
   engine repair
5. **Materials and supplies:**
   extra wood, copper, pipes, metal brackets
   fiberglass repair: tape, matting, resin
   extra spars to replace or 'jury rig' broken spars
   spare blocks, cleats, screws, bolts, and fittings
   extra wire, rope, thread, string
   spare sail cloth.
   fuel for heater and /or cooker: wood, coal, charcoal, alchohol, etc.

6. Food related

matches
stove: alcohol, kerosene, or propane
charcoal and charcoal grille
coolers
portable water closet
water and containers or water tank
cooking equipment, pressure cooker, pots, pans, teapot, baking dishes,
thermometer, can opener.
utensils: knives, forks, spoons, ladle, spatula, etc.
cleaning items: dish soap, washcloths, towels, wash tubs, drying rack
seed sprouter
yogurt maker
food dryer
canning equipment

7. Clothes and bedding

swimming
raingear
everyday
cool/cold weather
warm/hot weather
dress up
sleeping

9. Bath

soap, shampoo
towels
balms and creams
nail clippers
toothpaste and brush
bug repellant

10. Heating , cooling, and comfort

cabin heater: wood, coal, charcoal, diesel, alcohol, kerosene, or propane stove.
electric heater to be used if/when you have shore power.
electric fans to be used if/when you have shore power.
canopies, tarps and awnings for shade.
bimini: small shade canopy for the cockpit.
Insect screening for windows, hatches, and around the cockpit (to be used under a shade canopy or bimini).

11. **Ashore:** items you might want when going ashore:
    tent
    backpack, day pack, fanny pack
    hiking shoes
    bicycle
    canteen or water bottles and bottle carriers.
    sleeping bag
12. **Recreation and miscellaneous**
    laptop computer
    books - especially how-to books.
    games
    sports equipment:
    tools, materials, equipment. for an on-board business.

Discussion of the list: Nautical equipment is too often expensive, or if cheap, not of good quality and not long lasting in a marine environment of sun, wind, waves and sometimes salt water.

To keep costs down you may have to look for used items, substitute, make your own and try all of the other methods described in chapter 2. It would help to start getting things together early, long before abandoning the land. Then you can shop at leisure, look for bargains. Looking for deals on marine equipment is a whole science by itself. These methods are explained in the books listed earlier.

Not all of the items listed above are essential. Some are merely nice to have. It depends on your voyaging plans.

Consider the experiences of Dan Hookham as described in his book ***The Simplistic Sailboat***. Dan and family lived on a homebuilt houseboat in Seattle. Though it was his dream, it proved impractical to easily take voyaging. So he built a 24-foot simple sailboat for $600 and took his wife and little daughter on months long summer cruises through the San Juan Islands. Sailing and rowing just a few miles a day from island to island, they spent practically no money. His equipment was cheap and minimal. His book reveals one way anyone could take low cost vacations.

If you stick to coasts and rivers, and go south in winter, you can cut back on this list. Harlan Hubbard floated down the Mississippi without most of the equipment on this list. By going south in the winter, or always staying in a warm climate you could eliminate the need for heating equipment, fuel and winter clothes.

And, you don't need an engine with all its attendant demands. Lin and Larry Parday never had an engine in their 24-foot sailboat as they cruised the world. Annie and Matt Hill cruised without an engine for years, before adding a small outboard motor.

4.4.2 METHODS:

Below is a summary of a few of the methods described in the books listed earlier. Get and read these books to learn a host of techniques applicable to ZCL in any circumstance.

Heat:

A boat can easily be heated with a tiny on board wood, charcoal, or coal burning stove with a small chimney through the cabin top called a charley noble. The fire danger is considerable on an all-wood boat – the wood, oiled to preserve it may be quite flammable. On a fiberglass boat the danger may be less, but interior elements – curtains, upholstery, wooden bulkheads, are still burnable. Also, the cabin must have adequate ventilation or an outside air intake must feed air directly to the fire, or oxygen can become depleted. Wood to heat may be obtained by beachcombing or foraging ashore. A tiny shipboard stove burns only small sticks, not logs.

If you intend to stay in a place through cold, or cool seasons, consider roofing over the deck with a temporary greenhouse. Through a hot season, or in a hot climate add a sunshade covering most of your boat. By doing so you could almost double your comfortable living space - make your place a two-story 'house'.

Electricity:

Most of the sailors referenced above do not use electricity, relying instead on oil lamps, various cooking fuels (kerosene, alcohol, propane), and a host of tools and devices from the pre-electric age. The Pardays thoroughly discuss the use and usefulness of oil lamps in their book ***The Self Sufficient Sailor***.

If you must have electricity you can buy solar cell arrays or small windmills made for boats. These windmills are hoisted up the mast or stays (the rope or wires holding up the mast). These systems will provide enough power to charge small batteries, run a few lights and a laptop computer, and keep a cell phone charged, but not much more. They are expensive. A large and extremely expensive system would be required to keep batteries (a lot of batteries) charged up to run a refrigerator.

On sunny days, solar cookers, solar water heater, solar shower, might work well on a boat. Web sites such as ***builditsolar.com*** and books such as the ***Carbon Free Home*** describe theses devices, including making them yourself.

If you plug into shore power for an extended period, then you might install a complete array of electric appliances on your boat. For example, a small electric heater or mini heat pump would be practical in a cold climate. In the small cabin space of a boat they would not be expensive to run. The problems of heating with a wood-burning stove listed above could be avoided. To get shore power you usually have to buy docking space (called a 'slip') at a marina with associated costs. If you stay at a marina during the 'off' season your slip costs may be lower. I can't recommend staying in the North in winter, but in the spring and fall, most marinas are empty even though there are many days of good weather.

Refrigeration:

None of the sailors referenced above used refrigerators or freezers. Without an engine they had no means to charge batteries to keep the refrigerator running. They did not keep food cold or frozen except what could be kept in ice in a cooler for a short time. Annie Hill in her book works out in detail a cornucopia of food possibilities without refrigeration. Recall, before refrigeration humanity worked out ways to keep food: drying, smoking, salting, pickling, fermenting, canning, preserving, root cellars, winter ice stored for summer use, etcetera. These ancient methods are worthy of careful study and use in any situation where you are attempting ZCL. Research these methods on your own. Annie Hill's book is especially thorough and detailed on this subject.

Tristan Jones in ***One hand for Yourself One for the Ship*** writes about refrigeration on page 77 "In my opinion anyone who sets off on a four-year cruise with one will return home an expert in refrigeration repairs, but he won't know much about the places he has been to. Freeze dried food does not need a fridge."

Even with an engine, the complexity and costs of refrigeration are considerable. You may have to run the engine as a generator to charge batteries every day even while in port – causing noise, smell, pollution, wear, and breakdowns. If your engine fails your refrigerated food may spoil. The sailing books of wealthy folks like William F. Buckley Jr. describe breakdowns at sea, delays in port, frustration, anger, and misery as they struggle to get all of the systems in their big boats fixed and keep them running in remote ports where professionals are few, high priced and not very competent. It makes for (unintentional) humorous reading as they whine about the incompetence and greed of the 'lower classes' they need to fix their boats.

Phone:

You can get an emergency cell phone for free, (as mentioned elsewhere in this book). Do a web search for 'free 911 cell phone' fill out their forms and they will send it to you postage free. Out on the water, if an emergency arises a cell phone can be a life saver- if you are in range. The other method is to maintain a CB emergency radio onboard. You will need means to recharge the cell phone or CB batteries, maybe with a small onboard solar cell array.

Internet wireless:

In the right location, you may access the Internet from your boat through a 'wireless system' becoming increasingly common in the world. In some places it may be free for basic service. (Companies make their money when folks upgrade service). I leave it to you to look into it.

Food:

Jerome FitzGerald in his book ***Seasteading*** writes " **. . .** people in an active environment eat the equivalent of ½ pound dried food per meal as a base; that is ½ lb pasta, rice, flour, lentils, beans, whatever." " . . .a pound and a half per day. . ." Basic food for one person for one year, would weight 550 pounds. If purchased as wheat at 40 cents a pound it would cost $220 a year. FitzGerald estimates a half pound of other food he labels "goodies" would be consumed to complete a diet - equaling another 180+ pounds a year.

Tristan Jones estimates one person needs about 5 pounds a day of food of all kinds (including the water to make dried beans edible).

Harlan Hubbard seldom bought food. He settled ashore in the summer along the Mississippi river to grow a garden, forage for food and build up his onboard larder by canning and preserving food. When he traveled downriver he frequently tied up ashore to forage the countryside.

Ken Neumeyer in his book quoted earlier describes a cornucopia of food sources that may be found by foraging the sea or along remote seacoasts.

Water:

Voyaging on saltwater, you must carry adequate water supply on board or carry desalinization devices which can be as simple as a solar still – a plastic sheet suspended over a cup with a small weight in the middle – fresh water collects on the underside of the plastic, runs to the middle and falls into the cup.

Also, you can collect rainwater from deck, sails or a suspended tarp. Rain has saved many a thirsty sailor. (Air pollution has made it unclean however even over the ocean so purification or boiling might be a good idea).

Inland waters sadly are mostly too polluted to drink today. (Imagine, at one times Native Americans and Pioneers could safely drink the water from any lake or stream they came across).

On the Great Lakes 30 miles offshore the water is still clean, cleaner than municipal water – except in bays, off big rivers or near shipping lanes. You can still drink it directly from the lake, a humbling and wonderful experience. That vast empty expanse is still almost as it was and has been since the ice ages. Would that more places on Earth were so. This water contains no municipal additives such as fluorine or chlorine. And sun, wind, and waves break down and render harmless many of the chemicals permeating the world today.

So, if you're living on the Great Lakes, take a sail offshore once in a while to replenish your water tanks. No marina hose and municipal supply needed. None of the hassle of going ashore with bottles or jugs. Fresh, clean water can be a problem for seasteaders on the salty oceans, or at most other places on earth, due to human pollution but not on the Great lakes.

Mobility on land: Keep a folding bike or moped on board.

Clothes: If you go south in the winter to a cold climate you won't need as many. Another reason to move with the seasons.

Recreation: When you are seasteading, your boat is your recreation, you live on it live with it, and your whole circumstance can be endlessly fascinating and entertaining as revealed in the stories told in the books listed above.

Vacation from the boat: Nevertheless sometimes you may need a vacation from the water. A desire to spend time in massive mountains, endless forests or simple unmoving dirt might grow in you. Time to take your bike ashore and maybe take a long trip like Ken Kifer. Or sail to a region of high mountains such as the Pacific Northwest, or immense wilderness like the Lake

Superior Shores. Hike into the wilderness from your boat, using it as a mobile base. You might begin looking for a place to homestead, maybe in some remote location accessible only by boat – an uninhabited island in Georgian Bay, British Columbia, or the Bahamas.

Raising $:

You could use your boat as a base, a moveable base, for gathering free stuff and/or for saleable. Your boat can function as a mini 'tramp steamer', or 'tramp sailer'. You could carry items that are small, valuable and saleable – tools, DVD's laptops, computer software, jewelry, watches, electrical equipment, etc. Your boat could be both a home and business in one. Entire families live on the canal boats of Europe and the Junks of China and so could people here. Of course, they carry heavy cargo, and the boats are far larger and more costly than any seasteading boat. But for small, high value items, your boat could work.

The books listed above say a lot more about businesses you can run from your boat.

4.4.3 COSTS:

Boating is expensive, but seasteading can be very cheap if you virtually abandon the land and have no car, no land, no house, and therefore no property taxes. After purchase of your boat and equipment, you expenses can become extremely low. As Annie Hill points out, while voyaging you can't spend any money.

Some seasteaders have even abandoned engines and electricity; relying on sails, oars, oils lamps and tiny marine coal or wood stoves. They still manage to live in ease and comfort. You don't even need expensive modern sailcloth sails. The Hills used a Chinese style 'junk rig' with sail of cheap cotton - practical on a rig of this type. The frugal Chinese have been using the Junk rig – and refining it to reduce the cost for a thousand years. Even, sails of cheap blue poly-tarp could work as described in the website ***'www.the cheap pages'.***

Also, although most folks living on boats in America do so, you do not need to live on your boat at a marina. You can anchor for free away from the shore in places that are protected from wind and waves. Look for anchorages away from other boat traffic, and noise and disturbances from shore (like lights and traffic).

Jerome FitzGerald in his book ***Seasteading*** gives this advice He writes: “As of 2005 most cruising material suggests that 1000 dollars a month is perhaps the basic low end of the cost of cruising for a couple.” “ . . . . by going simple, and by going without an engine – and having the skills to get along comfortably without it, which you can indeed do - this cost can easily be cut in half. I have cruised comfortably on four hundred dollars a month in the United States and Canada and did not feel burdened by this. I know others who live more primitively and get by on less, but at some point living really cheap seems to me to be more work, not less, than an occasional job.”

One of the skills he recommends learning is sailmaking. “ . . . one can save two third the cost of sails by building them by oneself.”

Cost Estimate:

Boat: - modest old fiberglass sailboat	$20,000
Equipment (very approximate)	10,000
Saved $ to cover expenses (as Annie Hill did)	20,000
	$50,000

Notes: I’ve seen old fiberglass sailboats about 30 feet long with standing headroom – suitable for living aboard for as little as $10,000 in the Seattle area and on the Great Lakes.

Fitzgerald believes you’ll need to spend about one dollar a pound to buy a suitable boat and another dollar a pound to fully equip it – without an engine. He believes about 28 feet and 7,000 pounds boat weight is the minimum for a seasteading sailboat.

It could cost much less to get a boat. Get a damaged boat with a fiberglass hull and patch it. Rebuild the interior using foraged scraps of wood, (driftwood?). Re-rig mast and sails (Annie Hill style) to a cheap simple Junk rig.

Boats of suitable design have been partly built in apartments. The frames, small parts, and crossbeams, for a 28-foot Wharram catamaran were built in an apartment. Then the boat hulls were each built and finished, one at a time, in a tiny backyard. Then, the two hulls and crossbeams were carried separately to the launching site and assembled together there.

I believe seasteading may be the only way possible to have assets of less than $3,000 and therefore keep you eligible for Medicare, and still live without taking welfare and with a measure of self-sufficiency. You boat would be modest, perhaps well under 30 feet with a basic toilet and full headroom over only part of the cabin. Harlan Hubbard's' homemade shantyboat; a very comfortable boat, fully equipped at today's prices probably would qualify.

VIGNETTE:

He woke up. He had slept here for the last time. He had paid rent for the last time. This was the last day he could live here without paying another month of rent. He looked around. The place was empty except for his backpack, sleeping bag and mattress. He rolled up the bag, grabbed his backpack and walked out the door. He left the mattress and house key. Outside, he looked at an American flag on a pole in a neighbor's yard, noting the strength and direction of the wind.

His old car sat in the driveway, rusty but reliable. It was sold but not delivered yet. He drove to the buyer's house and collected $1,000 for the car, money that would significantly augment his cash reserves. He had the new owner drop him off at the harbor beach as part of the deal.

As the morning mist dissipated over the lake he could see his boat lying quiet at anchor. 'Phoenix' he had named her. Phoenix because he had rebuilt her from a fire damaged hulk (as the Phoenix bird was reborn from ashes) that he got for a pittance. Her interior had been ruined, but her fiberglass hull had withstood the flames.

His dinghy was pulled up on the beach and turned upside down. It looked like an old and decrepit box, built to look that way so people left it alone, (or occasionally used it as seat while beachcombing). He easily turned it over; it was built strong but light. The oars were wedged under the seat. He pulled them out and laid them on the seat where they were handy. He wedged his backpack and bedroll under the seat, took off his shoes and tossed them in to the dingy. He pushed it into the lake, waded in after, and climbed aboard, reveling in the funny feeling of floating again. He rowed out, tied the dingy to the stern of Phoenix, climbed gingerly aboard over the stern rail. No need for a bath in cold harbor water.

The Phoenix had no engine to avoid the need to fuel and maintain the metal beast. He would have to sail out of the harbor.

But the wind was right! He made sure before he left his apartment. (If the wind was wrong, he'd have to stay in the harbor until it turned).

He removed the sail covers, and made sure the halyards were not tangled where they ran up the mast. Pulling on the anchor line he hauled his little ship forward until he was directly over her anchor and, pulling hard broke it free of the bottom and hauled it aboard. She was adrift in the light wind. Quickly he hauled on the main halyard, raising her mainsail and, gaining a little speed in the morning zephyr, he maneuvered deftly out of the harbor. His ties to civilization were broken. He was the king of his own mobile country.

He reveled in the skills and knowledge he had accumulated for this adventure. He knew how to fish from her as he sailed, and where there were uninhabited islands and shores good for foraging for food and firewood - like Harlan Hubbard. And he could prepare food on board from a few cheap ingredients – sprouts from seeds, yogurt from dry milk powder, bread or pasta from a 50-pound sack of flour. He seldom bought food.

A vast new world, that to him at that moment felt infinite lay before him: all the navigable rivers, lakes, seas, and oceans to the ends of the earth.

Through the summer he foraged the Great Lakes, troll fishing for walleye, perch, bass, sheepshead, crappie, carp, and catfish from his boat under reduced sail. In Georgian Bay, to forage the land, he frequently and carefully maneuvered his boat into little rock edged harbors on uninhabited islands. He harvested a plethora of wild blueberries. He made blueberry bread, blueberry muffins, blueberry pancakes. He made blueberry-flavored drinks, dinners of blueberries mashed into the batter of pan-fried fish, and pemmican of berries mashed into a paste of dried fish.

He rowed up granite cliff edged fjords, where the wind cut out, using slow easy strokes on long oars.

He sailed to Port Severn, the entrance to the Trent - Severn canal system of Canada, went ashore and walked along the canal. Like a Dutch boat, Phoenix had a mast that was easy for him to take down. Next year, he thought, he would lower the mast and explore the canal. Somehow he would have to get a small outboard motor

In the early fall with cool weather he knew the bugs in the north declined so he sailed to Sault Ste. Marie and through the locks and on in to cold Lake Superior, exploring along the lake coast of Canada. Granite cliffs lined the shores, massive and beautiful.

A desire gradually came over him to take some time off the boat, to take a vacation from the water. He explored up Nipigon Bay on the north shore of Lake Superior. Occasional cottages were tucked along the shore. He found a secure anchorage, protected from wind and waves from any direction where no cottages were nearby. Rowing his dinghy near a rocky beach, he put on old shoes, climbed out carrying his good hiking shoes, waded through stony water towing the dingy, and carefully hauled it up onto the rocky shore – thus saving the bottom. Walking, he discovered a path, then a rough gravel road though a land of endless evergreen trees, white granite rocks and rare evidence of human occupation – a few cottages and gravel roads near the shore, nothing inland. Used to the rolling lake, he felt strange on the stable land. Smell of pine, spruce, and cedar, perfumed the air. He was thankful that the crisp autumn air was dry and free of mosquitoes or black flies. He explored for miles.

On the way back, a quarter mile from his anchorage, deep in the woods off of a barely passable road he found a weathered 'for 'sale' sign on a patch of rock strewn woods. The site was warm and quiet, protected from cold winds by rocky hills to the north and west.

Back on board, he consulted his maps. There was a town to the west a few miles away by boat but many miles away by road. Sailing to the town, using a public phone, calling the barely legible number on the sign, arranging to visit the owner, negotiating with firm resolve, he was able to buy the lot for a price that took only part of his cash reserve. (They met at the only bank in town to convert his cash into Canadian money). He bought saws, axes, and sharpening tools. Sailing home, going ashore again, he cut a few logs on his site, began to build a cabin. He didn't make much progress.

The air was chilly. He was determined to stay in the north a little longer, try to get his cabin a little further along. He had not intended to stay in the north this late in the season. His winter coat was threadbare. He had expected to go where the coat wouldn't be needed. He wore layers of his old cloths under his coat, trying to stay warm. (He was warm enough while working but quickly began shivering when he took a rest).

He wished he had studied and practiced making clothes. (Sure he could repair a sail, but clothes were different). He decided to sail to town again to see if he could find some affordable warm clothes. In town again, right near the waterfront he came across an interesting store. He went in. Clothes of hide, pelt, and fur hung on one side. Things made of wood: furniture, toys, lined the other. The shop smelled of pine and cedar and oiled leather.

A girl wearing buckskin spoke to him.

"Can I help you?" He couldn't decide which were more beautiful, her or her clothes.

"Nice duds." He said.

Thanks."

"I'm just looking."

"Well," she said, "everything in here was made locally. It's all we sell".

"Just work here?" he asked, amazed at his own nosiness.

"No, I help make clothes, I made what I'm wearing."

"Good work." he said.

She looked at his ragged coat, saw him eyeing the parkas, said, "You won't be cold in one of those. They're more than warm enough for the winter here. This is the warm south to the people that wear them. They're made in the Inuit style - of caribou hide, with the hair on the inside - warm in the coldest weather."

Finding the price tag, he blanched.

She saw his reaction. "Those take a lot of hand labor to make," she said.

He looked at fur-lined moccasins, this time hiding his surprise. He wondered if he could afford anything in the shop.

"You a tourist?" she asked. "It's way past tourist season. You can't be. You don't live around here. I know everybody. Just passing through?"

"I just bought some property outside of town."

"Staying for the winter?"

"Well I don't have a cabin built yet."

"Staying in town, then?"

Phoenix bobbed in view of the shop window.

He pointed at his boat. "I live there".

"Oh," she said.

He wanted to tell her he intended to sail south in a few days.

But he didn't.

She said, "Well, if you're staying around, there's a class in making these clothes. Mother teaches it - with my help.. Maybe, you could afford a class. If you could make your own, just pay for the raw materials, you might be able to afford a parka, boots, moccasins, everything."

"What's the class cost?"

"Not too much. You can earn it back you know".

What do you mean?"

Well, even though our clothes are expensive, we can't keep up with orders. We can always use more people to prepare hides, and sew. But you won't earn much at first, because they take a long time to make, especially for a new worker.

"I can sew a little. I repair my own sails, taught myself. I don't know if it's anything like sewing parkas.

"It's not just sewing", she said.

She asked him to him feel the material, saying. "Preparing caribou hide, or buckskin to be soft and supple and durable is a long process involving at lot of handwork. These clothes are expensive, but when you count all the labor we don't make a lot of money.

"We make most of our sales on the internet, mostly to folks who must have plenty of money. In money terms we are kind of poor around here, but we wear clothes only the rich can buy.

She asked "What will you do over the winter, got any plans?"

"Well, I….."

"If you're staying, think about it. We work hard all winter, catch up on orders, but we have a lot of fun, too."

"I can't stand the winter," he said. She stopped talking to him and turned away.

But he said, "I'll think about it. Maybe I can meet you later, talk about it more."

To his surprise she said, "Well, maybe I could meet you after work, in the coffee shop just down the road. It's the only one in town. Unless you're busy."

They were the only customers in the coffee shop. They sat in the front booth by the window with a view of the harbor and bobbing Phoenix.

"Nice boat," she said.

"Thanks, built her or rather rebuilt her myself".

"Good work," she said.

What else do you do?" He said.

"Oh, I look for, I like to gather edible food and healing plants from the forests -and prepare them."

"Other than blueberries?"

" Other than blueberries." she said.

At that moment he couldn't tell her he intended to sail south to the Chicago ship canal, then to the Mississippi, then drift down like Huck Finn and Harlan Hubbard to the warm south.

He wished he could ask her to come with him. But she hardly knew him, (and he hardly knew her). He knew she would say no, maybe even stop talking to him.

That was the problem with seasteading. You were rootless; freer than a bird, but with no stable nest.

He said, "next summer I want to explore the North".

"Sounds interesting," she said.

She said she was half Native American. She had learned from her parents - Cree mother and Canuck father. She said she knew how to lives in the northern wilderness. She talked of endless forests, caribou and moose, wild geese by the millions and fish teeming in cold waters. And, she described vast wild rivers flowing through almost uninhabited wilderness.

She named a few of them: "Kenogai, Mattagami, Missinaibe, and Attawapiskat". The names rolled off her tongue as if they tasted sweet.

"And Hudson Bay. You've got to see Hudson Bay" she said. "I've got relatives even as far as Hudson Bay."

He imagined it to be vast cold, and remote beyond imagining. She said. "When my family goes to visit my Cree relatives, maybe you could go with us. We go by canoe, live off the land on the way."

Her words made him remember a book by Tristan Jones, The Incredible Journey about how he crossed South America with a 22 foot sailboat named Sea Dart. The boat was hauled by truck into the Andes, sailed across Lake Titicaca, hauled by rail out of the Andes, manually dragged where the railroad ended, and towed by wading through the Chaco swamps to the Paraguay/Parana Rivers. He imagined a Tristan Jones like journey of his own. If he could get her over the Canadian Shield, maybe he could take his sailboat down to Hudson Bay on one of those rivers. The Canadian railroad crossed the Mattagami. Maybe he could move her there by rail and launch at the crossing.

But he feared the northern winter. He intended to try his northern voyage next summer. He thought about asking her to go south with him. “You ever see the south?” he said.

As if she could read his mind she said, “You think I’m the kind of girl that runs off with the first sailor she meets?”

“What? I didn’t mean any anything”.

She said “I can’t abandon my family, my home, my job, my way of life just because another place is always warm. For me, this place is warm.”

She assured him winter could be a good time in the north.

She said, “Most of the cottages around here are empty in the colds seasons. Some owners would be happy to rent if they could. You could rent one for practically nothing.”

Phoenix, in view of the window bobbed, beckoning, calling “Lets go. It’s warm in the south”.

When he left the coffee shop, the wind felt colder than ever. If he lingered too long he would not be able to leave until next spring, or try sailing in the worst possible season - in November when the giant lake freighter Edmond Fitzgerald went down. What if his relationship with this girl didn’t work out? He’d be stuck here. He had no way to live here through the winter – yet. How strong were his feelings? How strong were hers?

He wanted to see her again. He feared the cold. He couldn’t decide what to do.

***

CHAPTER 5: HOMESTEADING

Contents: **page:**

INTRODUCTION

Wandering may be fun for a while, but eventually becomes tedious. Tedious, constantly camping out, living off charity or foraging, moving on down the road. A desire to settle down begins to grow in the wanderer. Harlan Hubbard spent two years drifting down the Ohio and Mississippi rivers as described in his book ***Shantyboat***, but, finally he had enough of movement, no matter how pleasant; and settled down beside the river at Payne Hollow, Kentucky. He wrote his second book called ***Payne Hollow*** about it. He stayed beside the river on his own immovable land. He felt the need for a base, a permanent place to build, grow things and relax.

To return to a home after wandering can be as satisfying an experience as leaving. My experience: In the 1980's I built a shed on 10 acres where I lived for half a summer, (no building permit, easy to take down if discovered). I became bored and in August I left my homestead to wander Canada. After a month of interesting travels, often with no money, I returned. Leaving and exploring was fun, but returning was even more pleasant. In sedate repose I reveled in the familiarity and security of my "Old Homestead".

A nomadic existence for an extended time may not be very healthy or low cost. Even nomads settle in carefully chosen places for long periods before moving on. And, for a wanderer, a homestead can be like insurance or a refuge if something goes wrong on the road such as sickness or injury.

Apparently some Native Americans didn't have the need for a permanent homestead. They moved their camps with the seasons. Perhaps the whole area of their tribal land felt like home. It is a feeling alien to most of us, who crave permanent settlement with precise lot lines, possibly because we have no tribe and no tribal land to share. A tribe must be like an extended, a widely extended family working together to survive.

Personal economy and homesteading: Compared to a homeless, nomadic or even seasteading existence, homesteading makes it easy to create your personal economy. You have space to store stuff you forage, you have space for greenhouses, gardens, etc. You have a place to relax, take it easy, and practice and perfect skills. You can build or modify your house to be what you really need for ZCL. Your land may contain useful resources: trees, sand, clay, stones for a house of natural materials. You have sunlight and space to put collectors for heat, cooking, light, and electricity.

College vs. Homesteading: College may be overrated. Many young people who expect to gain a life of privilege and ease because of college may be disappointed, especially in a bad economy or as high tech jobs are outsourced and sent offshore. The costs for college have gone way up. The jobs graduates get may pay much less than they expect. They may be left with huge debts and be unable to pay them off. An alternative plan might be; build a homestead, achieve financial security, and then go to college.

"Humbly he never saw that within himself lay the greatest and surest means of acquiring an education. He never saw that his own passionate curiosity about everything in the world and his own hunger for knowledge was a better means than all sorts of professors and academics." Louis Broomfield, ***The Farm.***

In early America as we all know so well; there was no welfare, no social security, no corporations, no factory jobs. Homesteading was the way to economic security, usually the only way. I believe the job insecurity endemic to the present era may again make homesteading, for many folks, the way to economic security.

Thoreau's Homestead: Thoreau was not very thrifty:

Even though Thoreau was perhaps the greatest advocate and practitioner of thrift and frugality in America; from the standpoint of Zero Cost Living, he was not very thrifty. Thoreau, in his book Walden practiced a lifestyle readers may consider very low cost, if not zero cost. But, his seemingly frugal lifestyle is more a demonstration of the decline in the value of the dollar through inflation than evidence of his frugality. Remember that he lived and wrote by Walden Pond in the 1840s when U.S. dollars were worth 100 times or more what they are worth today. So the 25 dollars he started with, seemingly a modest amount equals perhaps $2500 today and the cabin he built for $28.12, would be $2812 today, not cheap for an 10 x 14 cabin with no electricity or plumbing. The land he was permitted to use for free. His annual living expenses as summarized in the first chapter of his book ***Walden*** reveals his not so cheap tastes, as even he admits. $8.74 for food = $874 today at least. And, $62 dollars or $6200 today was the total for his annual expenses including the $28 to build his house, $14.72 farm expenses, $8.41 clothes and 2.00 for oil. His earnings, $36.78 or $3678 left him $25 or $2500 today in expenses not covered by earnings, almost the same amount he started with. So he did live zero cost, albeit he had to earn $23.44 by growing 7 miles (the length of the rows in his 2 ½ acre field) of beans - and earn $13.34 by day labor. For one adult $6200 in expenses for a year seems high from a ZCL perspective considering that he had no utility bills, car, insurance payments, or any of the costs of modern life. He finished the year with empty pockets but to his credit he owed no one a penny, and "... bedside the leisure, and independence and health thus secured, a comfortable house for me as long as I chose to occupy it." He built more than a house, he created a very basic but viable personal economy. Living ZCL today, and adjusting for inflation you would be doing well to do as well as Thoreau did. But perhaps, you can do even better.

Building zero cost:

Is it possible to build a homestead and spend no money? Perhaps, if you could get a site for free, as Thoreau did at Walden. Then, if you were determined to buy nothing, you would have to borrow, make or scavenge up tools. Thoreau borrowed an axe to begin his homestead at Walden. And, you would need to hunt, fish, farm or forage for food, activities that would take away from time needed to build. So homesteading with no money might be very difficult; a great, a huge challenge, like an unclimbed mountain. In fact hardly anybody has done it in modern times. Some skilled and destitute pioneers started with almost nothing and succeeded in building homesteads as their biographies reveal. The Homestead Act of the U.S. government gave 160 acres of land for free to anyone who settled it for 5 years.

One man who did it in the 1950's for almost zero cost was Dick Proenneke as described in his book ***One Man's Wilderness*** and a video about him entitled ***Alone in the Wilderness.*** He homesteaded at Twin Lakes, Alaska, near the south coast. His is an inspiring example of homesteading. He had a great attitude, not at all worried or intimidated by the circumstances he placed himself into, but triumphing over them. He lived there 30 years.

Another book I recommend is ***Living Well on Practically Nothing*** by Edward H. Romney - a very useful and instructive book. Some of his methods are similar to methods suggested in this book. My book was written before I discovered his book, so similar ideas are coincidental and may reflect the soundness of both of our methods.

In the year 2005, a young man did a series of trades beginning with a paper clip and ending up with a house. (See the web site: ***oneredpaperclip.blogspot.com***). I believe this was more of a stunt than a practical method of homesteading, although trading is certainly a key ZCL method.

Can you live zero cost after building a homestead? Almost, but if you own land and a house you will be stuck with property taxes and possibly house insurance and utility bills. I'll discuss ways to minimize these later.

5.1 STEPS to Homesteading:

These are possible steps to homesteading if you are starting out fresh, or starting out again after a failure in some other enterprise; want to try homesteading and want to avoid or minimize any period of homelessness.

Beginning destitute. If possible, live with your parents or relatives, work and save to build up dollars. Or, share an apartment with friends.

Things you can do towards ZCL with little or no money while you are living at home or in an apartment: Get books, magazines and surf web sites. For example read back issues of the monthly magazines ***The Mother Earth News*** and ***Back Home.*** These are available at some libraries. Visit garage sales and flea markets looking for used books and tools. Get basic how-to books on gardening, irrigation systems, canning, sprouting, cooking, construction, bike or car repair, etcetera – like books listed in the appendix of this book. Begin to accumulate basic tools.

Practice skills and methods: learn to prepare food, to use tools, to work with wood. Study home construction and gardening.

If you are not bound for college, or not going any time soon, you must educate yourself. Read, study, practice skills and you can become well educated without getting a college diploma. You can concentrate your studies as you please – you can focus on learning subject matter applicable to ZCL.

If you have the time and money, go to community college or adult education at high school where some courses are applicable to college credit. You could meet capable and interesting people who share your interests. Take fun classes, but be sure to take practical classes. Practical classes such as welding or carpentry can be surprisingly interesting.

Should you attempt ZCL alone or with others? Ideally, live and work with others. Find or create a network of folks with similar goals and interests. However you may not find this practical. You may be too much of an individualist. You may have difficulty working with others. You may lose flexibility to do what you think is your next best step towards ZCL.

But friends and allies are worth many (often small) sacrifices. They can be sources of information, keys to ZC living not considered in this book. You can trade, or borrow, or share with them. Together, you could purchase better tools and get better prices for things by buying in bulk and dividing it up - than you could alone. Together, you may be able to get a larger and better property for homesteading. They can make ZCL easier, more interesting, and fun.

Raising and keeping $ to begin homesteading:

Most folks won't have to start out in their journey to ZCL from a state of destitution. Most will have a little money from inheritance or a gift, personal items of value, savings, investments, social security income or a steady but perhaps low paying job. You may have a few thousand to tens of thousands in assets. Don't squander and waste your precious resources on a car, apartment, mortgage, big screen TV or other things that eat your time and money. Use your saved dollars to buy tools, materials and non-perishable supplies. Find places to keep what you gather, perhaps at a relative's or friend's home in a basement or garage corner, or in a shed, or under a tarp in an out of the way place. And, begin to look for a permanent site to build your homestead.

The old prospectors would call their saved money their 'grubstake', money to buy supplies to live on until they 'hit pay-dirt', struck it rich or went 'bust' and had to go back to work to build up a new grubstake. Your 'pay-dirt' will not be gold, but a comfortable homestead as described in chapter 6. Don't go 'bust' on the way by wasting your money on the tempting cornucopia of useless junk thrust in your face by modern society.

Job:

Probably you will need to get a job to build up savings. Hopefully you will get a job with a future and decent earnings. However this is becoming increasingly unlikely. For all too many folks today it will not even be an option. More likely you'll be stuck in the miserable new jobs in the 'service' industry earning full time take home maybe $7 or $8 an hour and $14,000 a year, seemingly not enough to build up much savings towards homesteading.

You are in a trap. You may have to work long hours to pay for rent or mortgage, insurance, car payments, gasoline, taxes, etc. (I believe half or more of the problem of building a homestead is getting the legions of leeches - sucking your money - out of your pockets).

And the 'skills ' you may learn at many jobs are of no use for homesteading. Try to get a job in construction, or farming, or even as a cook where you can learn skills you can use outside of your job.

Ways to find time and save $ even if you have a low wage service industry job:

1. Find a job near where you live, or move close to your workplace so you can walk or bike there. Avoid owning a car if possible.

2. Live at home or with relatives, or share a cheap apartment with friends – the more the better.

3. Escape apartment rent altogether: Find ways to live rent free or for very low rent. Then your money can go towards ZCL. One option: As described in chapter 3, live in a trailer, van, or motor home. Find free places to park. Don't drive around much, or at all, if possible. Cancel your vehicle insurance if you're not driving it around. Another option - as described in chapter 4, try living on a boat.

4. Don't waste your money on frivolities. Find cheap or free recreations and entertainments. Look for free concerts, find out when movies theaters offer lower cost tickets, rent a DVD or check one for free from a library. Take up reading as a recreation - library books cost you nothing.

5. Take advantage of whatever charity and government assistance you can get at the beginning of your attempt at homesteading - to help you save money and preserve your 'capital', your 'grubstake'- your saved dollars. The pay in many new service industry jobs is so low that you may still be eligible for food stamp assistance while working full time. Be sure to check this out by asking at your local social services agency.

6. Avoid buying retail and avoid buying new things. The U.S. is full of good unwanted and unneeded stuff. Begin gathering it early. Stockpile tools, lumber, windows, doors, everything you'll need to build a house. Look for things that will last. Things that are old might be good - because they have already lasted a long time.

In the beginning, your situation may be crowded and uncomfortable with few or none of life's amenities. The knowledge that your sojourn will end - and the more frugal you are, the sooner it will end - should help keep you going. Consider, millions of students live this way while attending college, and after graduation remember them as the best days of their lives.

As you build up your savings, and then your homestead, take yourself off charity and government handouts, and gradually take care of yourself and your family as you reduce or eliminate your costs of living, and trade or sell any surplus you produce for $ to buy what you can't produce yourself.

Look for co-housing and co-operative groups to join. Or join with friends to create a co-op to pool resources. Look for and buy land together. I can't emphasize enough the importance of learning and practicing co-operative behavior, and creating or joining co-operative enterprises. For many people it is the key to success in achieving ZCL.

Try to join or start a co-op or co-housing group aiming at producing things, not just socializing and sharing. So join one with plans for workplaces and businesses, not just houses.

More on Traps:

The stock market: Avoid it. Investing in it is too much like gambling. Read ***A Random Walk Down Wall Street*** by Burton Malkiel for a dose of cold water if you imagine that you can beat the market. Unless you get good advice, and many of us don't, you may loose your money. I lost the first $1,000 I earned - money earned at $1.60 an hour - in the stock market. Somebody is buying or holding all those stocks that go down. Better and safer to invest in yourself, in your education, in learning skills and buying tools.

Car:

Avoid owning a car if possible. The automobile takes your money and the costs associated with using it are high, and rising. Most people are trapped into using cars because the layout of cities makes alternatives inconvenient and expensive. Look for towns where you can get around without a car, where you can walk, bike or take mass transit.

If you have an expensive or newer car or a used car with some equity in it, more value in it than you owe, sell it to get some cash. Sell your car and you've dumped a huge cost burden. Now you can really save money. You can save $2,000 a year or more and avoid all the dissipation the automobile makes possible. Ideally, begin a lifestyle not requiring a car. It is possible. I'll say more on this later. Look for a job within walking or biking distance of your home.

If you insist on having one, get a cheap car you can fix yourself. You've learned how, right? No? Better not to have a car. Repairs made by professionals – cooling system or oil leak, brake job, tune up, exhaust system replacement will eat your money fast. A bad transmission, a blown engine, accident damage costing thousands for repair - could destroy your savings.

If you must own a car, possibly you can live out of your car thus saving rent. The book ***10 Consecutive Years Living in Cars*** by Craig Roberts tells how.

Mortgage:

I felt no sense of peaceful repose in a house on which I owed a mortgage (or in a apartment where I owed rent). When you make a mortgage payment, most of the money may go to the interest charge on your mortgage. You may realize little or no build up of equity in your home. A mortgage may work if a high percentage of your payment goes to principle, but that is seldom the case today. Consider buying a modest house, or a house requiring a lot of work – that you can obtain at a low enough price so much of your money goes to 'the principal' and you can quickly pay it off.

Rent:

Renting a home or apartment, or paying lot rent for a mobile home site are like having a thief permanently in your pocket. You pay another to own the house or apartment you live in. Let me restate this for clarity: Your landlord takes your rent money and pays off the mortgage on the property - building up equity (and increasing wealth) in it. You do not build up any equity in the property you pay for. As a tenant you may think you don't pay property taxes, but the reality is you pay property taxes even when renting - you pay them through your rent.

More reasons not to get an apartment: In an apartment or condo you may not have enough to do so you'll be out running around spending $. And, your opportunities for physical activities may be limited.

More Traps:

Bad health, medical costs, physical disabilities, mental illness, drugs, alcohol, expensive useless sports or hobbies, plain laziness, assorted personal weaknesses (like gambling), and a thousand other causes can thwart your attempt to homestead. Some can be avoided, some you may be able to work around and some you'll have to face head on, maybe going to therapy groups like Alcoholics Anonymous. I believe, for example that a ZCL homestead might be built that is suitable for folks in wheelchairs by techniques such as carefully designed raised bed greenhouses and modified tools. Full consideration of these problems would take another book. I intend to give more consideration to these problems in the web site **http://0costliving.com**.

Ladder of Assets:

If you avoid all of the traps, keep expenses down, and retain your income in the form of savings, productive, useful assets such as tools, and equity in real estate you may be able to construct a 'ladder' of assets that will make it possible for you to climb out of homelessness, poverty and destitution as described in chapter 3 and achieve a comfortable living as described in chapter 6.

5.2 LOCATION:

Choose your location for homesteading very carefully. Try to optimize your location, get the best possible site you can find that meets the criteria suggested below.

Location Options:

Small Towns: Consider first locating in small towns beyond commuting distance to major cities where land and houses are cheaper. Locate where work, shopping, farmers market to buy and sell stuff, library, post office and recreation are nearby, within walking or biking distance. Try to find a site near a small town but outside public sewer and water utility system - to avoid these annoying costs. Instead, you will have a well and septic system. Possibly, you will find a site in the adjacent township.

University Towns: Smaller college and university towns may also be good, but more expensive. University towns may be more interesting, especially if they are an integral part of their community. (You might be able to attend large classes unnoticed. Or, try asking the instructor if you can 'audit' the class meaning no official attendance record, homework or grades, and no tuition fee). There will be many clubs and organizations, good cultural and recreational facilitates, and fine libraries.

Big City: The more prosperous parts of big cities (not the so called 'ghetto') are expensive. Plenty of money eating entertainments, distractions and temptations exist. You may find it hard to save any money.

There may not be suitable places to do ZCL things - garden, build greenhouses, store materials. Nevertheless, energetic folks with clever ideas might attempt it. They might covert old factories, lofts, rooftops, vacant lots to homes and greenhouse gardens.

Inner City: Land and houses may be cheap but you pay a price to live there anyway in the form of safety and security problems. You may have no peace due to crime, gangs, drugs. Public services - libraries, schools, police, mass transit, etc. may be poor.

Suburbs: They are too spread out - were made for the convenience of cars, and therefore you'll have to maintain one. They usually are not bike or pedestrian friendly. They may have zoning laws and ordinances limiting home businesses, require conformist standards for lawn and yard appearance, and building size and setback requirements that make ZCL homesteading difficult.

Suburbs were originally created between city and country to realize the advantages of both. People wanted to live near the city for close proximity to jobs, shopping, urban entertainments, and use of good roads, freeways and mass transit. They wanted to live in the country for nature, beauty, peace, quiet, fresh air, green space, and rural recreations. As suburbs grew to become vast metropolitan regions they spoiled the advantages of both - becoming tedious, monotonous, traffic choked, suburban sprawl so familiar to us all.

Rural: The first place most folks think of when choosing a homesteading location is rural. But rural homesteading may not be the best ZCL location. Like the suburbs, you are likely to need a car or truck to go anywhere. For example the book: ***How I Lived Seven Years Without Electricity and Running Water*** by Esther Holmes describes how she had frequent need of a vehicle to get water, go shopping, get to work, and perform all the errands of daily life. The attendant cost of maintaining a vehicle may eliminate any savings realized from a rural location. If you can live without a car, you can make a giant step towards ZCL.

Amish Country: Locating where the Amish have settled may be a good way to live rural without a car. The Amish use horses and horse drawn vehicles to get around and so could you. Horses (and wagons, buggies, carriages) on the roads are more common, accepted, expected and automobile traffic is light, making travel using horses use a practical alternative to the automobile. (Would that there were more such places in America).

Take note: The Amish do not live in isolated rural locations. They locate near small towns, and within easy horse traveling distance of each other – a whole community interspersed among 'English' (non Amish) farms - within an area of a few square miles.

Wilderness: As in rural and suburban locations the need for a car in a wilderness area may increase the difficulty of living ZC. Without a car you may find it difficult to go anywhere. You may find yourself living in isolation.

The book ***How to Live in the Woods for Pennies a Day*** by Bradford Angier describes wilderness living methods, but doesn't say anything about the problem of access or cost of a vehicle.

An interesting challenge could be living in wilderness without a car. Dick Proenneke relied on his canoe to reach his homestead. A canoe could be used to access a homestead location among wild rivers and chains of lakes in Minnesota, Alaska, and The Canadian Shield region of Canada. Alternatively, a boat might be used to reach a homestead located among the islands and isolated coasts of the Great Lakes and the Pacific Northwest.

Ideal Location: After consideration of all possible locations, I believe the best location for ZCL would meet these criteria:

1. Near a small town with complete basic services where a car is not needed, land and homes are cheap; tools, seeds, lumber, and help are readily available, and opportunities to forage and recycle exist.
2. In a region where Amish or folks with similar ideas such as the Mennonites have settled.
3. Within a reasonable distance (maybe 50 miles) to a big city and its suburbs – so you can make occasional trips there for entertainment, cultural events, market for produce, major hospitals. A bus, or rail line from your town to the big city would be ideal. Big cities/suburbs generate enormous waste streams and foraging opportunities such as materials from buildings torn down or remodeled. (A truck, perhaps borrowed would be required to pick up any heavy/bulky items).
4. A university within 30 miles - close enough to visit or attend for educational, cultural, and entertainment opportunities. As with big city access, a bus or rail line to the university would be ideal.
5. Within a reasonable distance (maybe 50 miles) to wilderness - state or national forests useful for vacations, hiking, foraging for wild food.

As you explore for locations, if the distance is reasonable, I believe you should try to walk or bike to new towns to thoroughly explore them. If you drive there, get out and walk or bike (carry a bike on your car). In this way you can get to know an area intimately. And, walking/biking around a town will reveal how suitable it is for these modes of transportation.

As you explore the town talk to people. Be honest. Tell them what you are doing. You may get great advice, maybe a tip on an especially good property bargain.

Look first near where you live now. Look in out of the way places. Look for a small or medium size town beyond a big city and its suburbs. Cheap land and houses may be found in or near small towns in economically stagnant or declining regions; but check crime rates (look at government statistics on the internet) – in some regions that have suffered long economic decline - they may be high. Avoid them. Look for land outside the town limits (to avoid city sewer and water bills) but close enough so a vehicle is not needed to get to town.

You may have to make a long and careful search. Once you have chosen a town, try living there a while to get to know the place. Try to share an apartment - the more roommates the better - to save money. Get a job, any job to learn more about your town and to build up savings. Don't buy property and begin a homestead you may live in for the rest of your life until you are sure you like your community.

Despite everything I just wrote, these criteria are not sacrosanct. It may be possible to live ZC in many places.

Now step back with me a moment and survey ZCL location prospects from a continental perspective. Think of yourself as a hunter looking for good hunting ground –in this case a region especially suitable for ZCL. Look for out of the way places. Is there wild country near where you might homestead? Land to hike, forage and explore. Is cheap land available? What about the Climate?

Climate:

Cold: Is there abundant wood – for firewood or lots of sun good for a solar heating system? Cloudy regions may have plenty of wood as in the Pacific Northwest. Cold dry regions may have few trees but plenty of sun in winter as in the Great Plains.

Hot and humid: You can build a house cooled by natural means suitable for living in Florida and the Gulf Coast.

Wet: You don't mind damp cloudy weather: Try the Coastal Pacific Northwest.

Dry: Is water available onsite or nearby? Desert sand with a source of water can be made rich farmland and grow several crops a year using the 'Mittlieder' methods. See the web site: ***www.mitleidermethodgardening@yahoogroups.com***

Seasonal Migration: Semi-nomadic lifestyle.

Does a region you favor seem to have one bad season, and another that is fabulous: One option - be a nomad.

In the far north you can get cheap land, even free land. I like to think of it as the great Northern frontier. Consider building a seasonal habitation you can leave for the long winter. Build and live accordingly. Build so the house can be left for long periods without worry with features such as lockable outside shutters on windows. South of the permafrost are vast coniferous forests and in the east is the Canadian Shield. You will be bothered by blackflies and mosquitoes. Read the book ***Water and Sky*** by Alan Kesselheim for an understanding of this region.

The road network may be primitive or nonexistent so you may need a 4 wheel drive sports utility vehicles – with its associated costs to get to your homestead. Better if like Dick Proenneke and Alan Kesselheim you choose a site you can get to with a canoe.

Go south in the winter. Find a small town in the southern U.S. where expenses may be low. Own and maintain two properties and a means to travel between them. Birds do it. Ancient nomadic peoples had winter and summer hunting grounds. Possibly, go by boat between your properties.

Seasonal migration may be economically justified by the longer growing season and low heating costs of the South. Migrating can give you a refreshing change of scenery and climate. Possible winter places: the deep south, north Florida, Southern Appalachia, New Mexico, Arizona, Texas, or even the mountains of Mexico.

5.3 LAND

Property criteria: What is the minimum land area needed and what property characteristics should you look for, for a ZCL homestead? I will consider these questions next.

Land area needed:

Thoreau lived on 11 acres of land. He planted 2 1/2 acres of beans. He had to hoe seven miles of furrows, as described in Walden.

His footprint on the land was not small. In those days of small population and free land in the west perhaps it did not matter. Today, with higher lands costs and the pressures of population, it matters more. A very small footprint on the land may be possible while living ZC. In chapter 6, 'Comfortable Living' I will discuss in detail the design, layout and construction of a 'solar farm' on a half acre. A half-acre, the size of some city lots and many suburban lots should be adequate for homesteading ZCL.

Land Criteria:

Drainage: Does the land drain adequately after a rain or spring thaw. A percolation test, called a 'perk test' is used to determine if a property drains. You can hire a professional to do this, perhaps along with a soil test to determine how 'firm' or suitable the land is for building. You can perform your own test by digging a hole, pouring in water to the top, and with a watch and yardstick timing how long it take to go down a foot. If it is down a foot in one hour drainage is good. If is down an inch or two or not at all, drainage is poor. If you decide to buy the site and build anyway, (because the land is cheap), you may require engineered footings and no basement (wiping out any savings on the lot purchase).

Sunlight: If you have too many trees you'll have to clear some off to have sites for garden, and greenhouse, and solar devices.

Hillside: In a climate with a cold winter, a south sloping hillside would be ideal - cold wind will be blocked by the hill to the north and the south facing slope will receive extra sunlight..

Seclusion and privacy: so you can be undisturbed, and not disturb neighbors with your somewhat unusual activities.

Quiet: for your own peace of mind. Away from freeways, busy roads, railroads, industry, fire stations, retail businesses.

Healthy and Clean: Away from, and not downwind of industry or commercial farming and animal feedlot operations that can generate odor, noise, pesticides, and pollution of air and water – including underground water.

Public Land: Near federal, state or local public land you can use to pursue outdoor recreations and forage for wild plants.

Zoning: Look at Zoning laws and subdivision ordinances affecting the site to determine their hostility or friendliness to homesteading kinds of activities. Avoid areas with strict laws on building design and placement, lawn appearance, and permitted land uses. You may be prohibited from doing some of the things you want to do for homesteading.

Buying Land:

Build up enough cash for a down payment on a vacant lot. Offer 80% of the asking price. You may get it from an anxious buyer. (I paid 80% or near 80% from every land parcel I ever bought). Vacant lots are usually sold for cash but you might try to get a land contract where you pay the owner off over time, no bank involved. Have a real estate lawyer review all of the paperwork. Try to get terms than let most of your payments go to principle, not interest so get as low an interest rate as possible. Usually the interest rate on a land contract is a little higher than a mortgage.

If bought on land contract, you don't really own the land until it is paid off and you own it 'free and clear' with a 'warranty deed'. Ask the permission of the owner before doing any work on the site. The owner likely will allow you to make improvements even though he technically still owns it. After all, if you default - stop making payments; he gets it back with any improvement you made.

Also, consider joining with others to buy land. Then divide it up, incorporate as a condominium (with some space shared and some private) or keep it in all in common. It may be much cheaper – per person to buy this way.

Shelter:

After living homeless or on the road for a long time; when you are tired of it, and bored with it, and exhausted with the challenges of it, there is nothing like owning a piece of land that you can live on and nobody can legally kick you off. You may have to park an old van to live in and store things in at first. You may be building your place up for years.

Once you have land, live on the land any way you can to save rent money. Then, when you get a job, any job, even the lowest paying job, you can build up dollars to improve it. Live cheap as described in chapter 3 - live like a homeless person - to save more money. One option: create a concealed scout shelter as described in chapter 3 on homeless living – possible if your land is wooded or overgrown. If neighbors notice you, you may need to explain what you are doing there - tell them you are the owner, camping out temporarily and will soon be building - essentially the truth.

Tent: Thomas Elpel in his book ***Living Homes*** describes how he lived in a tent on his land for many months until the house he was building was far enough along to move into - although far from finished. Various improvements can make a tent more comfortable such as a wooden floor of foraged pallets and plywood or an inner liner possibly packed with straw or leaves between the walls. Tent design for long term living - possibly making your own - is an interesting topic worthy of another chapter or future book. (A web search could turn up useful ideas. I leave it to you).

If you set up a tent, you might want to build a lockable bin or shed for some security for your possessions. Keep the shed hidden if possible. Don't keep your most valuable items there though because it still could be broken into. Building laws may not require a permit for a shed smaller than a certain square feet - perhaps 120 square feet or 12 x 10 feet. Option: Have a hidden locked 'cache', a water proof bin buried in the ground - an old cooler perhaps - for valuables.

Trailer: You may have to leave the trailer wheels in place. Zoning sometimes requires that a trailer parked on a site really be moveable - not be a permanent building. Thus it can qualify as a recreational vehicle. Check zoning at your township or country government before you buy the lot if you intend to do this. To preserve the tires: support the trailer underneath to take the weight off the tires, and cover the tires against the sun. Sunlight ages tires. You may be able to buy cheaply or get free an old or damaged trailer you can fix up. Smell carefully and look for rot and mice damage before you attempt this.

Van: Consider parking a car or van on your site to live in. If zoning permits it, possibly get a non-working van or truck and have it towed there for a solid shelter. Cost could be next to nothing, perhaps free from folks wanting it off their property.

Garage: Build a garage on the site. Park a van inside to live in. You may be able to build a pole barn type garage for a couple of thousand dollars - or less by doing the work yourself. The floor of a pole barn need not be concrete since it is support by poles set in the ground, and therefore can be cheap, simple sand and gravel. You could get creative with the floor, using recycled bricks, or carpet remnants over plastic laid directly on the ground.

Shed: Build a 'storage' shed to live in. Put up privacy fencing to hide it and conceal the fact that you are living in it. If overgrown vegetation exists on the site, leave it in place to hide your shed. More on this in the next few pages.

Greenhouse: A solar greenhouses as described on page 188 might serve as temporary shelters. A pit type, low to the ground could be easy to conceal. And, plants or thermal storage devices (such as barrels or concrete blocks) in the front (south facing) half of your greenhouse could conceal your living arrangement in the back half.

5.4 HOUSE:

Pioneer cabins were small, and you are a pioneer. All of the cabins Lincoln lived in his youth were tiny, only a few hundred square feet. If you would avoid a mortgage, as I highly recommend, build a small house. The minimum size in many zoning/building codes is 900 square feet for areas zoned for small lots of 12,000 to 22,000 (1/2 acre) square feet. For larger lots, 1/2 acre or more 1000 square feet may be the minimum.

To get around this consider building a shed to temporarily inhabit while gradually building a house that meets the building code requirement. You will not be permitted to live there under the zoning ordinance. But if you are discreet you likely won't be disturbed. Are the authorities going to not permit you to camp on your land or live in a shed on it, therefore condemning you to homelessness? Tell the authorities you are building a garden or tool shed. A 10 x 12 shed can be built without even a building permit under many zoning/building ordinances as long it is within yard setbacks. Setbacks are the area around the edges of your lot where you are not supposed to put a building, often 40 feet in front and 10 feet on the sides and rear. Is 10 x 12 feet large enough to live in? Thoreau's cabin was 10 x 14 feet.

On a large acreage it may be possible to hide a small shelter and avoid building codes. I lived in a simple solar heated shed on 10 acres I owned in the Thumb of Michigan for most of a spring and summer. The shed was far more roomy and comfortable than any tent. It was not legal or concealed and the building inspector eventually required that I take it down. But it worked, and I believe I could have built a concealed shelter in the back of the property and lived there indefinitely.

Property taxes: As the owner of land you'll have to pay property taxes on it – and under a land contract where you don't own the land yet - the buyer usually pays the property tax. But taxes will be low on undeveloped land and in remote places.

'Squatting' on land you don't own is an ancient practice whether on public or private land. But sooner or later you'll likely be discovered and must move on. Idea: design a moveable – take apart version of the building described below that can be moved if/when you are discovered.

What is it like, living in a shed or basic house? If you have been homeless or living in a tent, a shed is way beyond a tent in comfort, even if it is primitive. If you have been homeless and now you are in your own 'house' (no matter how modest), on your own land and no one can kick you off, the feeling is marvelous.

The sheds and the small houses described below would be best designed so you can easily expand - add on later to make a larger more comfortable house perhaps 1000 square feet to conform to local zoning laws.

Early History of shelter:

In the beginning man was cold and wet and in the dark, and was hopelessly vulnerable to attack whether from animals or other men. He could fight cave bears and other men for the luxury of huddling in cold dark damp smelly caves.

Man discovered fire. In the cave with fire Man was warm, Man had light, Man could cook BUT,

Caves were few and sometimes far from the best hunting grounds and when man took fire outside the cave and built a campfire his back was cold, and the wind blew the smoke around so man was sometimes suffocated by smoke and forced to move from his comfortable spot by the fire. And, wild beasts & other men could sneak up on him in the dark and attack him from behind.

Man learned to use an element of the cave away from the cave - the wall; natural at first, later built up of sticks, logs, stones, hides, etc. The wind off his back, the smoke didn't blow around as much, the heat of his fire was contained, he was warmer, and he was more secure from attack from behind.

Man still got wet. To stay dry he invented the tent, a wall sloped inward of sticks and hides, grass, or bark When he built a tent on top of a wall, and a tent topped wall all around his fire, (leaving a smoke hole in the center); his head was dry, the smoke went up through the hole in the top (most of the time), and, the wall made his shelter defensible against attack.

This shelter, with fire enclosed within must have been a fabulous luxury to early men, better than a cave and the beginning of all houses. The house, perhaps, was the greatest invention of all time. Man could live in ease and comfort wherever he wanted warm, dry, secure, and able to see by firelight so s/he could work, rest, think and (eventually) read and write.

Three $500 Houses:

How about a $500 dollar house? Is it possible? Yes. Here, I will discuss three types I have discovered over the years.

Mike Oehler: underground house
Ianto Evans: cob cottages made of straw and mud.
Ben Gleason: straw bale house.

Mike Oehler's House: He dug, literally, a hole in the ground to live in. But what a hole! His $50 house under 200 square feet is small and crude but adequate. His $500 house, an expansion (to 500 square feet) of the $50 house seems spacious, even luxurious. Inside a rectangular flat floored hole cut into a hillside; he builds using a system he calls "P.S.P."; posts, shoring (horizontal boards to hold back the dirt) and plastic polyethylene sheets to protect the posts and shoring from direct contact with the earth and thus rotting. Plastic, out of contact with sunlight can last indefinitely underground. He cut trees on his land for posts and shoring. The post bases, buried at the bottom of his "hole" he charred over a fire or coated with preservative. More round logs from his land served as his roof rafters and roof shoring. Plastic and then earth went on top of his roof. Rugs over plastic over bare earth served as his floor. He used no concrete in his underground house.

Ianto Evan's House: Ianto built a cob cottage on which he says he spent $500, making extensive use of recycled doors, windows, and lumber. The walls are of 'cob' and old English word for a lump of straw and clay. So, the walls cost almost nothing except labor, lots of labor. Oehler did lots of digging and earth moving by hand to make his hole. Evans did lots of digging and earth moving as he built up thick walls of cob. In a shallow pit he mixed straw, sand and clay together, worked it to proper consistency by treading it with bare feet, made football size lumps of cob with his hands, and tossed the cobs up to helpers on the walls to be placed. Evan's ***The Cob Cottage Company*** and web site of the same name give more information. He teaches classes on building with cob.

Ben Gleason's House: is a house of stacked straw bales built in Old Saybrook, Connecticut and called the 'Hay House'. Built in 1974 for $500, the way it was built it would not cost any more today. It is the oldest straw bale house in the Northeastern U.S. It is a much more basic house than what you will see in books about straw bale houses, which have conventional foundations. The foundation is of cement-stabilized earth – a small amount of cement mixed with the earth already under the house - after the topsoil was removed. A sheet of plastic was laid over this foundation upon which a 12 x 20 foot rectangle of poor quality and therefore cheap straw bales was built up, with reused lumber frames around recycled doors and windows and a light frame gable roof over. Two lofts were built in for sleeping and storage. Shingles were made of split cedar using logs from a nearby swamp. The floor is of boards and plywood over the plastic ground cover with carpet scraps on top. Doors and windows were framed as the bales were stacked up. The bales were plastered over with a sand/clay mix made from soil on the site - smeared into bale surfaces, making them almost fireproof because the bales are sealed from the air which fire needs to burn. Plastered straw bale walls are far superior to framed walls because fire cannot get oxygen in the dense mud sealed straw bale walls. Straw bale walls amount to walls with massively thick insulation without using industrial materials.

The house has been occupied continuously up to the present (2008) and remains in good condition, a remarkable and unexpected outcome since the builder intended it to last 5 years, maybe. The current owner, David Brown lives virtually ZC, with no electricity or indoor plumbing, water from a hand pumped well, and food from an organic garden.

It is hard to say which of these houses is more remarkable. Perhaps a homesteader could build a house combining methods from all three.

Here are some more concepts on cheap shelter; not complete plans but concepts to stimulate your imagination.

Other Earth based houses: The Viking built houses with walls 6 feet thick of turf: grass rectangles cut and piled up, with a frame and turf or thatch roof over. The Scots had their "blackhouses" of similar construction. The book ***Earth Structures and Construction in Scotland*** by Bruce Walker and Chris McGregor 1996 describes dozens of interesting structures.

In the 1970's dozens, perhaps hundreds of self-sufficient house schemes were thought up by hippy architects and budding environmentalists. Some of these schemes may be seen in old publications such as the ***Whole Earth Catalog***, ***Resurgence, Radical Technology***, ***The Integral Urban House***, and many others. They are still instructive and useful. University libraries, used book stores, or web searches may turn up copies you can borrow or buy.

Trailers: Park a trailer or several trailers on your land. Check the legality first. You may be limited to one and it may have to be truly moveable so the wheels will have to be left on all the time. (Mobile homes usually have theirs removed).

Source of trailers: get used or build your own. (Books and web sites describe how, I leave the search to you). Look for damaged trailers

Consider, if allowed, parking several trailers arranged in a rectangle and making a covered or even enclosed courtyard between them for a cheap, spacious, but still moveable home. Such an arrangement is perhaps, especially suitable for the North in summer and the Deep South year round.

Mobile Home: Used and damaged mobile homes, traded in for newer models may be found parked in the back lots of mobile home sales centers. They are destined to be bulldozed and taken to the dump, and may be available for the cost of moving. They may be wind, water or fire damaged. Check for smell, they may not be salvageable. With a little luck, for modest cost, and possibly requiring of replacement of windows, doors, interior paneling, siding and insulation you may get a decent shelter.

If windows are intact, to save heating costs and reduce drafts, improve the cheap windows of old mobile homes by making insulated shutters to cover them during cold weather. Use sheets of insulating pink or "blue board" styrofoam. If you have no money, use layered sheet of cardboard and plastic held with duct tape (You can afford duct tape can't you?)

Some newer units have 2x6 walls. Try to get one of these for lower heating and cooling costs.

Build on to you mobile home a 'greenshed'; an enclosed attached porch on the sunny south side. On sunny winter days open the door between your greenshed and your mobile home and let free solar heat pour in. Another method for heat - build air type solar collectors on the roof of your mobile home. Commercially built panels may be expensive and too heavy for a mobile home roof. Homemade panels may be cheap and lightweight as described in the book ***The Carbon Free Home*** by Stephen and Rebekah Hren. Compared to a conventional house, a mobile home roof may be easily accessible by ladder.

Another way to get cheap solar heat: Make the skirt on the south side of your mobile home of clear or translucent plastic, and insulate inside the skirt on the other three sides. On a sunny day solar energy can flood the space under your mobile home and warm it up. Vents in the floor could tap into that heat. Close and insulate these vents at night and on cloudy days.

In my opinion, Mobile Home Parks are unfair to residents. Residents can never own the land they live on. Lot rent never goes away. I believe residents should be able to purchase their lots or, together, have a way to purchase the whole mobile home park – perhaps owning it under laws used for condominiums. Needed are laws and public or private agencies dedicated to helping residents obtain ownership of the land their mobile homes sit on.

Log Cabin: No discussion of homesteading would be complete without inclusion of the log cabin. Many books exist describing different ways to build with logs such as ***How to Live in the Woods on Pennies a Day*** by Bradford Angier, ***Living Homes*** by Thomas Elpel, ***Shelters, Shacks and Shanties*** (an old boy scout oriented book) by D.C. Beard.

Now for my thoughts and suggestions on it. A lot of unused logs are around these days. Dead ash trees, elm trees, land being cleared for subdivisions and roads, etc. And, if you can learn to use short pieces and crooked pieces, as I'll discuss in a moment, you have unlimited abundance.

Two methods of log construction have been used in America, the French method called 'Post-de-terre' and the familiar, English (really Scandinavian) method of horizontally laid logs with interlocking corners. Post-de-terre means post in the ground and is simply a house size stockade, with posts set 3 feet or so into the ground and a roof of poles covered with shakes on top of the stockade.

In horizontally laid logs, the ends may be interlocked by any of dozens of methods. A problem with all of these methods is the shaped log ends are exposed to water and weather and may decay rather quickly.

Thomas Elpel, as described in his book ***Living Homes*** avoided all of this, interlocking his horizontally laid logs by drilling vertical holes and driving rebar from log to log, thus avoiding shaping the log ends to fit. As you may imagine this was heavy and slow work; moving the massive logs onto the walls, drilling holes clear through these logs, and driving 4 foot or longer lengths of rebar through the holes with a sledgehammer.

Logs are large, heavy, and hard to move requiring cranes and other heavy equipment. Or, as the pioneer's did, requiring block and tackle and possibly oxen or horses and skills long gone from America - skills described in beautifully sketch illustrated books by Eric Sloane such as ***Museum of Early American Tools.***

Post-de-terre has the advantage that the logs used are modest, perhaps 10 or 12 feet long. But their bases, depending on the soil they are set in, may rot after a few years.

The first English settlers in America built the familiar-to-them wattle and daub method of construction. This method is visible and obvious in Tudor buildings with their exposed frames. A frame of heavy posts is built first, and then in-filled with a lattice of sticks covered with a straw/clay mix like cob, but with much thinner walls. It has the advantage of making irregularly shaped wood useful for construction. In England wood had become scarce and expensive, so every part of a tree was put to use.

Stackwood, or cordwood construction has the advantage of using short, firewood size logs stacked into walls just like firewood, but walls are massively thick and a lot of wood is used up in construction. The method requires a lot of cutting and manual labor (as all these methods do). Stackwood has the advantage of being within the skills of most owner builders.

Log Cabin using short logs: Given the problems and disadvantages of all of these methods, I propose, therefore, a new type of log cabin that is a cross between these types. Basically I propose building a rough frame of peeled logs, and then infilling between the frames using any of several methods: wattle and daub, short logs whether vertical or horizontal, or short pieces of 2 x 4 and plywood, or other material. The frame of a substantial cabin could be built using no log over 12 feet long and rafters of poles not over 14 feet long.

In conventional log cabins the doors and windows are cut in after the logs are built up, but it means moving heavy logs that you then cut in place to short lengths between windows and doors - a waste of effort. Better to frame openings as you go, and make use of short pieces to infill the walls between doors and windows. Thus, short logs, easy to carry or drag can be used throughout the cabin.

Also good: use ordinary nails and brackets to connect logs rather than massive connections such as rebar or notched ends. This might be achieved by using simple two hole or four hole rectangular brackets thin enough to bend a little to bridge over irregularities between logs. No tight fit would be required between logs - spaces between logs can be sealed or chinked with smaller sticks, stones, clay/straw mix, oakum, sphagnum moss (in the far north), or even plastic. Bradford Angier in ***How to Live in the Woods for Pennies a Day*** wrote: "...drive lines of nails upright in the cracks for anchors." and "The toughest and most harmonizing chinking I've ever seen, in Hudson Hope, was made by mixing sawdust and melted sheet glue." By not requiring exact fit, it is possible to use natural logs and sticks requiring minimal cutting, shaping and milling.

Some walls may be in-filled with wattle and daub to make use of irregular sticks.

In fact, a cabin could be built using mostly materials that are discarded, usually burned, or left to rot in the woods.

Some folks waste many hours a day doing puzzles, even 3d puzzles. Wattle and daub - and the short log construction method in general - is a 3d puzzle with a practical result. Problems you will need to solve to build with short logs: reducing the labor intensity of the method, making it look neat, and developing a systematic method to attach logs to each other.

See **ILLUSTRATIONS # 6 and** 7 below for basic house design ideas:

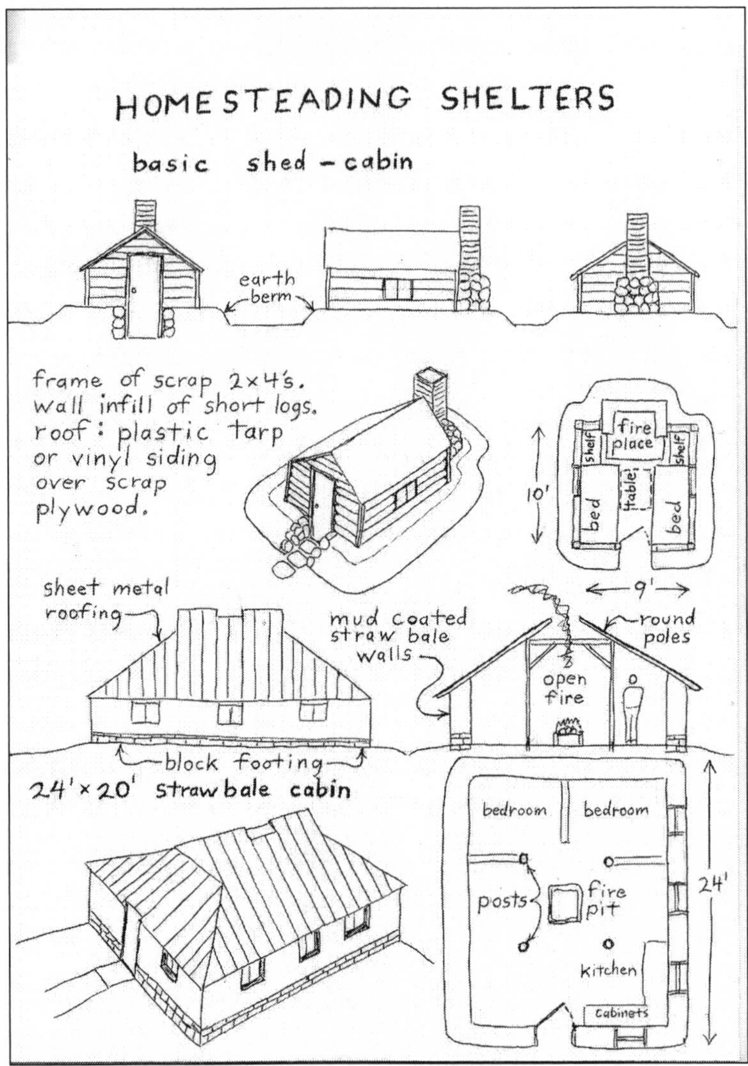

ILLUSTRATION # 6: BASIC SHELTERS: A rocket stove could replace the fireplace or open fire pit shown in these designs.

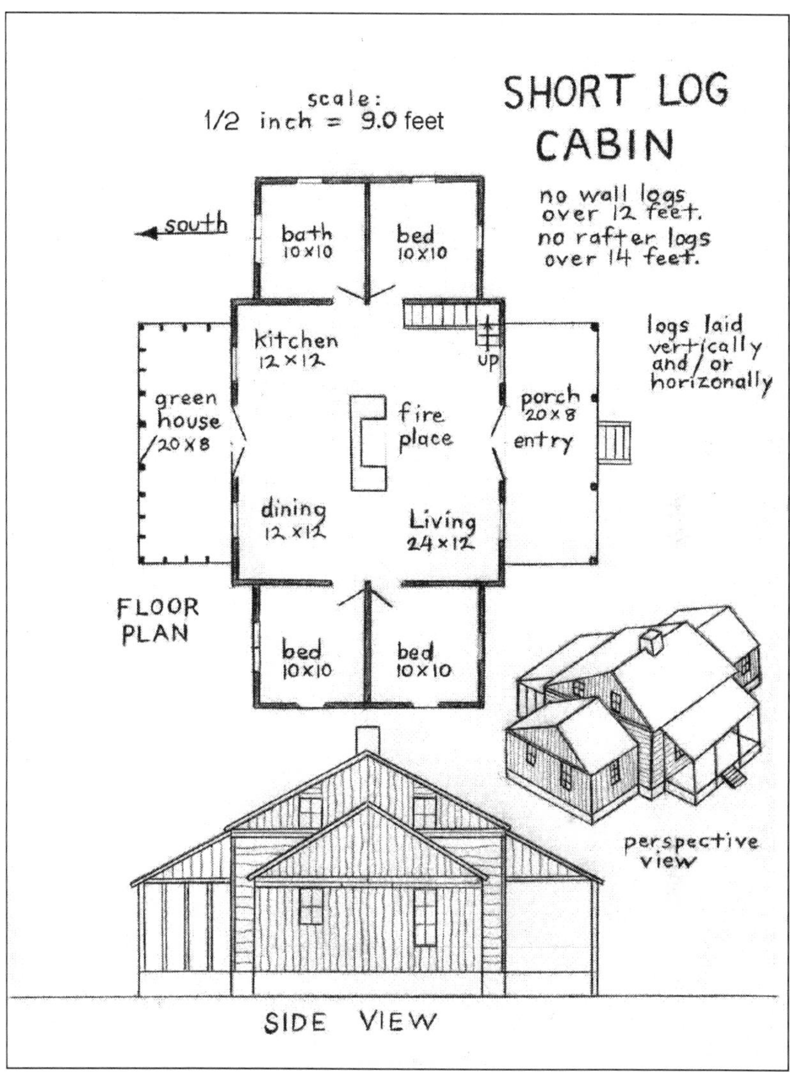

ILLUSTRATION # 7: CABIN USING SHORT LOGS.

Note: This cabin is expandable. Build the core first; then add the greenhouse, porch and wings as circumstances permit. Also note, the core is equivalent in size to a standard two car garage and not much more difficult to build (except I recommend a crawl space or basement and the roof raised on knee-walls to serve as a second floor).

Body-heated space:

What is a body-heated space? It is a shack, shed, vehicle, boat or a room in a house that is small enough and well insulated enough that the heat given off by one person will keep it warm.

Precursors: Curtained beds of the 18th century (like Scrooge), and the Dutch beds that were built like cabinets with closeable shutters. The natives of the Arctic usually have tiny houses where large families live as described in the book ***Water and Sky*** by Alan Kesselheim. The Inuit igloo also illustrates the concept though these maintain a temperature that is much colder than we want.

A book on car living referenced in chapter 3 describes compact enclosed heavily insulated space in the back of a car or van that can be body-heated even in very cold conditions. The book ***How I Lived 10 Consecutive Years in Cars*** by Craig Roberts is proof of the practicality of the concept of body-heated space.

A space could be designed, either as a stand-alone structure or part of a larger house or building that could be heated by the energy generated from the human body.

How to design a body heated living space: Using heat loss estimates based on the book ***Natural Solar Architecture*** by David Wright.

One person can generate about 500 Btu (British thermal units, a measurement of heat) per hour and 12,000 Btu per day. For short periods such as during heavy exercise you could generate up to 1,500 Btu per hour.

Method 1: Create a body-heated space as a 'stand-alone' structure by building a **'DOUBLE ENVELOPE'** shelter. Build an **inner envelope** as a 12 x 10 x 8 foot well insulated space then surround it with an **outer envelope -** a larger space that is 'tied' to the ground and able to pick up the 55 degree f constant heat of the earth thus remaining at that temperature. Heat given up by the ground into the air within the outer envelope keeps the outer envelope at 55 f. The illustration on page 171 shows a possible design for a 'stand-alone' body heated shelter.

An **inner envelope** of 10 x 12 x 8 feet has 600 sq ft. of envelope in the walls, floor, and roof. Insulate the 10 x 12 foot space to R20 (equal to 6" thick fiberglass insulated walls).

Calculations:

Formula: using Btu (this may look complicated but is just simple multiplication):

U x A x T x H = heating need per day in Btu.

R20 insulated walls have a 'U' value of about .05

U= heat loss through the envelope in Btu per hour per square foot of area per degree of temperature difference between inside (interior envelope air) and outside air (exterior envelope air).

U = 0.5 Btu heat loss per hour.

A = Area = 600 sq feet of exterior area

T = Temperature difference = 10 Fahrenheit, 65 degrees inside, (within the interior envelope) 55 degrees outside of the interior space (within the exterior envelope).

H or hours per day = 24 hours.

U x A x T x H = heating need per day in Btu.

.05 x 600 x 10 x 24 = 7,200 Btu/day. So the human body, producing 12,00 But per day could heat this space **......**

EXCEPT:

Cold air will infiltrate your shelter through cracks and when you open the door or widows. It is possible to reduce infiltration to a very low level by wrapping the inside in sheets of plastic, with carefully sealed joints where sheets meet; as if you are in a huge plastic bag. But you must breathe, and moisture will build up in your shelter so you dare not make it too tight. About one air change per hour would seem to be optimal because the internal volume of this body-heated space is 12 x 10 x 8 = 960 cubic feet and one person requires 900 cubic feet of breathing air in an hour.

Now you must consider the heat loss due to air infiltration from cracks and openings in the shelter - and for adequate breathing air. Infiltration per hour = 1.0 or one air change per hour. Calculations: Air heat capacity = .018 Btu/ft3/F. 960 cubic feet at 10 F temperature difference between indoors and out .018 x 960 = 17.28 x 10 (temperature difference) = 172.8 x 24 hours = 4,147 Btu per day.

7,200 + 4,147 = 11,347 Btu per day are needed to heat a 10 x 12 foot shelter. As I mentioned the body can produce about 12,000 Btu per day so a space heated by the human body would seem to be possible based on these calculations.

The inner envelope obtains fresh air from the outer envelope, air warmed (by the outer envelope) to 55 f. The outer envelope obtains fresh air from the out-of-doors – and then warms the outside air to 55 f before it enters the inner envelope.

If you have electricity, get a small backup electric heater to warm the place quickly when you first come in on a cold day, then turn it off and your body heat should maintain a comfortable temperature. Or, when you first arrive, exercise to heat up your house thus making your body kick out more Btu than it does at rest.

Ways to improve your shelter:

Add a dog, cat or roommate for more Btu. Of course you'll need more breathing air with more people so you must increase air infiltration, perhaps by leaving a window open a crack.

Add a rocket stove or very small barrel stove. In a small space even a small stove will quickly draw all of the oxygen out of your space. So, you must have a place that is drafty enough to draw plenty of outside air or, better - have a pipe that feeds outside air directly to the stove.

Add an "air lock" entry - possibly through an attached greenhouse to keep heat from being dumped out of your house every time you open the door.

Add a 6 x 12 lean-to greenhouse to your shed 16 x 12 = 192 square feet total area of house plus greenhouse.

Calculations for an added greenhouse: sunny winter day solar gain from 8 x 12 glazing area of 96 square feet equals about 1000 Btu per day per square feet = 96,000 Btu on a sunny day, - more than enough to heat your space. On a cloudy day solar energy gain might be about 1/3 as much or 32,000 Btu. But much of this, perhaps half will be lost through the greenhouse structure leaving half to be added to the shelter total or at a minimum 16,000 Btu per day on a cloudy day and 48,000 Btu on a sunny day.

Illustrations 8 and 9 below show how a body heated space and homesteading shelter could be designed.

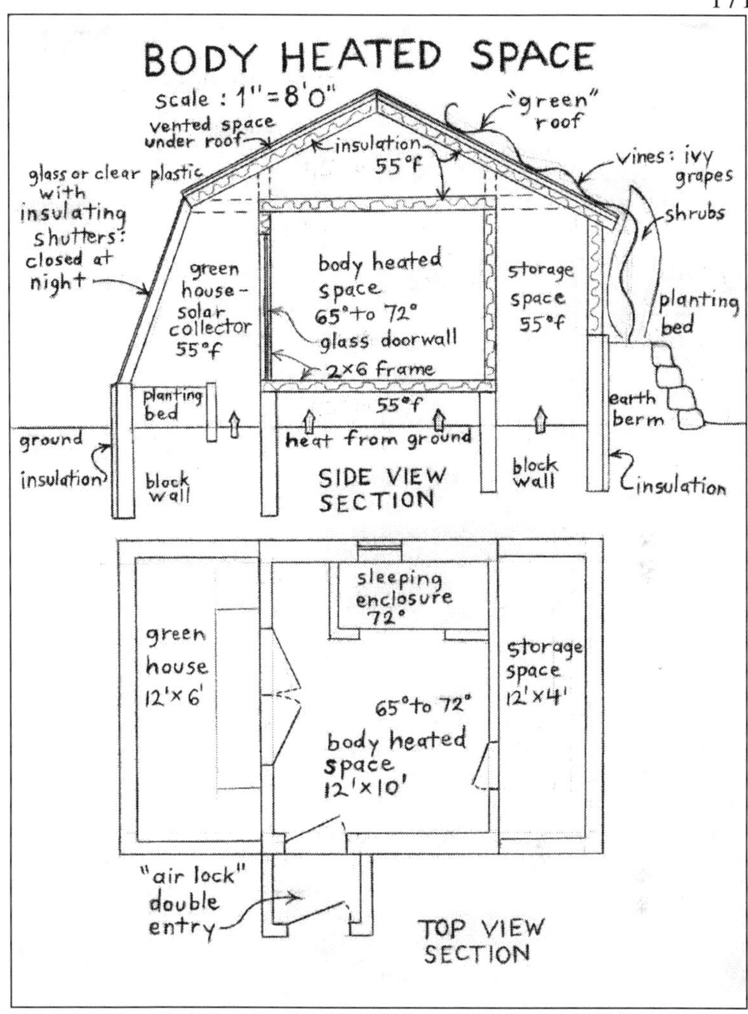

ILLUSTRATION # 8: BODY HEATED SHELTER.

This illustration shows one possible design solution for a shelter heated primarily by the heat output of the occupant estimated at 12,000 Btu per day. The suggested 'green roof' of vines such as grapes and ivy growing over a steel roof –the screw heads holding the steel serving as anchor points for the vines. A green roof of this design could be very lightweight and low cost compared to the heavy earth covered schemes presented in usual green roof proposals.

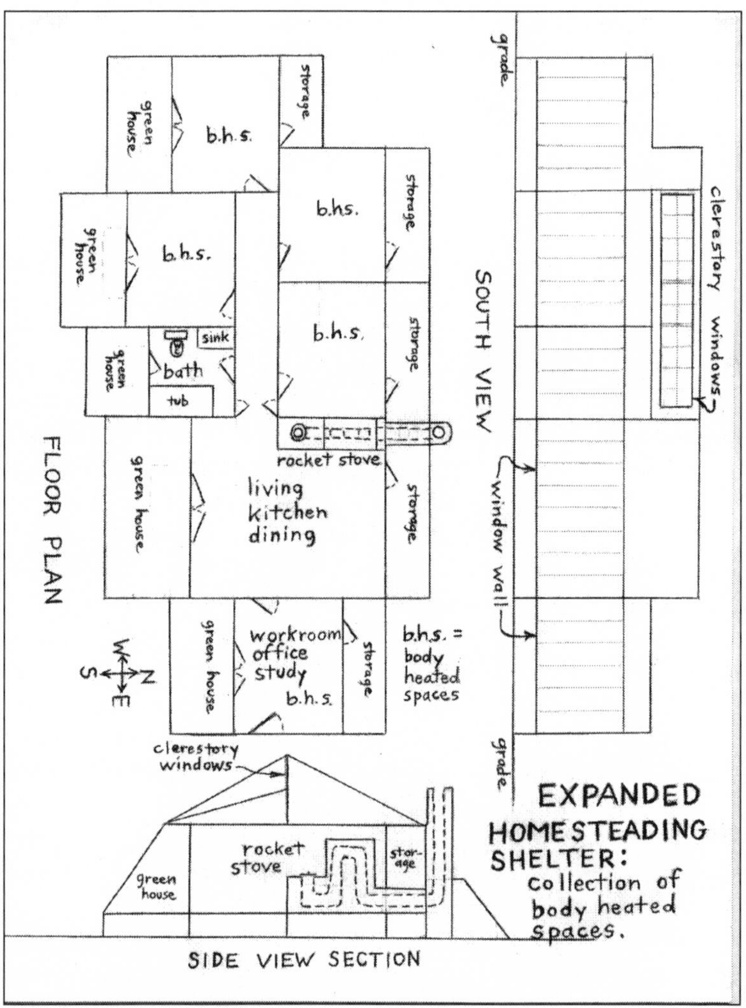

ILLUSTRATION # 9:
EXPANDED HOMESTEADING SHELTER
– using a collection of body heated spaces.

In the scheme in illustration # 9 a rocket stove is used to heat the large 'common' space. However if all of the occupants –say 4 were to occupy the common space at one time their combined heat about 2,000 Btu per hour could keep the space warm. Heat from cooking, lights, and appliances could also help warm the space.

Method 2: within a house or building: Create a well insulated space - a 10 x 12 x 8 foot room (I call it a 'cocoon room'). A space of this size is adequate for one person to live in, I believe. Bathroom and kitchen would be located outside of this space. They would be heated only when used – possibly with a small electric heater or 'mini' heat pump if you have electricity. A small kitchen could be heated in the process of cooking, and by heat given off from the coils of a refrigerator.

From personal experience (for south-eastern Michigan) an unheated house may remain at 45 degrees F through a winter. This occur because the house interior picks up heat from the ground through the basement floor into the basement and then from the basement to the upper floor. (The ground 6 feet below the surface maintains a temperature of about 55 degrees). Insulating the exterior walls of the basement above grade and to a depth of four feet or more would facilitate heat gain from the ground. (The basement walls of my house were not insulated).

Modifying an Old House:

I believe it is much easier to have a ZCL suitable house by building new - if you build it yourself. However cheap old houses can be found that might be worth modifying. A few years ago this was less of an option. How things have changed! But even during the housing boom cheap houses could be found in and near small towns beyond metropolitan areas. They still can. In Michigan, old houses in rural towns may be bought for $45,000 or less. You may be far from big city jobs, shopping and entertainment but your cost of living can be lower.

What to look for: Look for the worst house in a good but not expensive neighborhood. Your neighbors will thank you for improving it.

Look for a backyard on the south side of the house that is not shaded in winter (no pine trees or tall buildings for example).

Get an adequately sized lot if possible –1/2 acre would be ideal.

What to avoid: houses with foundation damage, flood prone areas, high crime areas, noise (a location near a freeway can be noisy), smells from industry or farm operations (such as a livestock feedlot), nearby industry.

If you are living on a low income, to save money (possibly to pay down your mortgage quickly) consider living without phone, car, electricity, or air conditioning. No law requires you to have any of them.

Living without these you are practically homesteading like a pioneer. The Amish do it. They rely on a wood-burning stove in an oversize kitchen for cooking, house heat, and hot water. They don't have indoor plumbing either - relying on a hand pump and cistern, outhouse, and hand washing of clothes.

If your house is on city water, you will still have water pressure even without electricity. With a well, you will need electricity for the pump or else install an Amish style hand pump system.

Build a 'body-heated room' or two in your house- as described earlier. Why heat a whole house, especially at night. My experience: As an experiment I spent a winter in Michigan with the heat turned off in my house. The whole house never dropped below 45 degrees f. In the bedroom an electric heater was used to boost the temperature upon entering the room - then turned off. The room would stay at 55 degrees. The bed area was enclosed in curtains - above and all around and stayed at 70 degrees f when I occupied it. No heavy blankets were needed. A bathroom directly accessible from your cocoon room would be a very good idea.

The book ***The Carbon Free Home*** by Stephen and Rebekah Hren describe a host of projects to modify an existing house to be 'carbon free' – projects that also happen to save you money, reduce you living cost and move you towards ZCL if implemented with diligence. Projects include improving house insulation, window insulation, solar panels, photovoltaic system, solar water heater, outdoor solar shower, heating and cooking with wood, composting toilet, rain barrel water collection, edible landscaping, transportation options and much more. Some of their projects can be owner built using recycled materials.

Paying Minimal Taxes:

To keep your property taxes to a minimum consider these methods:

Locate in a neighborhood or community where property tax rates are low. A good choice might be a township surrounding but outside the limits of a city. Service may be less, but so are taxes.

Close proximity to the city may let you take advantage of certain city services and amenities without living there.

Keep your lot or land area modest; ½ acre as recommended above.

Build or buy a small simple house without ostentation. Avoid use of expensive landscaping, architectural features, appliances, materials, and fixtures. I'm not saying make your place look shoddy, but make it look modest, unassuming, and practical, not for show.

Design so you have unfinished and unheated extra space such as attic or raised basement that you can finish later, and provide a place store things outside of the heated envelope of the house. These spaces may be taxed at a lower rate, your house square footage for tax purposes is based on heated space.

Make improvements after the building inspector has gone. One example: an extra bathroom. Another example: Adding a large window in a window well to make a basement space useable for other purposes such as a bedroom - without being noticeable from the outside.

5.5 UTILITIES:

Heat: Alternative heating and cooling methods:

Heating with wood: Through efficient house design heating with wood can go from a tedious chore to an occasional pleasant exercise. The 5 to 10 chords of wood a conventional house might use in winter may be reduced to 1 chord or less. You will not have so much firewood to cut, haul and handle, and only a little at a time will be needed. No huge piles of wood will be required to last the winter.

Rocket stoves: May be built cheaply of old barrels, bricks, and dried mud. These are described by Ianto Evans in his booklet ***Rocket Stoves*** and on the web site ***aprovecho.net*** and ***aprovecho.org.*** Rocket stoves with flue pipes through thermal mass can store heat that can continue to radiate even after the fires goes out.

Solar Heat: Cheap homemade solar collectors may be built of 2 x 4s, plastic sheeting, cans, and/or black screening. See the web site ***builditsolar.com*** for examples.

Another method: Build solar greenhouses adjacent to your house and covering windows or doors. On sunny winter days open these windows or doors to let excess heat into the house. See the book ***The Food and Heat Producing Solar Greenhouse*** by Rick Fischer and Bill Yanda for more information.

Electricity: While homesteading you may dream of being independent with a windmill and solar cells, but these are expensive and require knowledge and skills if you do-it-yourself, or are expensive if you hire professionals. The reality of your economic situation is you may have to hook up to the utility company or go without electricity. Better to wait until you can accumulate skills and dollars as described in chapter 6 'Comfortable Living'. Small simple wind and solar cell systems exist that are easy to install, but they are expensive and provide only a few hundred watts of power. ***Real Good.com*** sells them.

Refrigeration:

Consider using no refrigerator. The Amish do not. If you have one, turned off it is still useful as a food storage cabinet. Annie Hill sailed (and continues to sail) the world without refrigerated food in her 34 foot sailboat. Her book describes how she buys, stores, keeps and uses food without the trouble of refrigeration. Chapter 4 'Seasteading' describes more about the techniques Hill and others use to eliminate the need for refrigeration.

Old time method of refrigeration: In cold climates in winter before electricity to homes, folks used a window box cooler: They would open a window, then build a wooden box that fits inside the lower half of the open window. A curtain was kept drawn over the opening. In winter, It kept milk better than an ice-box. The box was 12 or 15 inches deep, fit snugly into the window opening, and rested on the windowsill. See the book ***The Carbon Free Home*** for plans for a modern version.

Water:

Build a rain barrel water collection system for watering lawn and garden. See ***The Carbon Free Home*** for ideas.

If you have no electricity look into installing a hand pump well like the Amish.

Hot Water:

The pioneers continuously kept pots of water hung over their fireplace fires or on top of their wood burning stoves. They had to pump water, carry it to the fireplace/stove, and do all of the tasks necessary to keep the fire going. The time and effort to do this - compared to a modern system of pressurized pipes, electric pumps, and water heaters- may qualify as hard thrift and if possible, avoided.

A solar water heating system is one method to reduce the energy cost of a conventional system. The web site ***builditsolar.com*** and the book ***The Carbon Free Home*** describe several types of solar water heaters. The so called 'breadbox' or 'batch' type water heater is the simplest and least expensive type, but in a cold climate, must be shut down in winter or it will freeze up.

A compost pile has been used to heat water in at least one instance: Coils of pipe are placed within a mass of composting materials. Compost can generate heat at 140 degrees f or more. Source: ***builditsolar.com***

Sewage and Waste Disposal:

To reduce the load on your home septic tank system (if you have one) or municipal system consider building a 'grey' water disposal system. Grey water is waste water from your kitchen sink, bathtub and laundry. This water can be piped to a drain field where nature will break down any pollutants or used to water a garden or lawn.

All non-meat kitchen waste can be composted and used as garden fertilizer.

Meat waste, bones, etc. must be deeply buried to keep animals from digging it up.

Yard wastes - grass clippings, leaves, decayed wood, can be composted for garden fertilizer or used directly as mulch around plants.

Compost water closet verses a flush toilet: Compost gives human waste back to the land where it belongs, enriching the soil. It does not need to go to expensive water treatment systems or into our waterways causing algae bloom and making the water toxic to fish.. Refer to the books ***Goodbye to the Flush Toilet*** by Carol Hupping Stoner or ***The Humanure Handbook*** by Joseph Jenkins.

In pre-industrial cities, human waste or 'night soil' was removed at night to be taken to the land. I believe it should be used to enrich the soil again.

Paper waste can be burned in your wood stove or a barrel in the yard, or shredded for garden mulch.

With a composting system for human waste, a grey water system for waste water disposal, etcetera; a municipal sewer system, or septic tank system might seem superfluous. In most places, laws require you to have one or the other of these systems today. But they are not necessary. Fees to hook up to city sewers, and annual maintenance fees are expensive. Septic tanks and drain fields professionally installed can be even more expensive. NOT installing these systems can make homesteading less expensive and more practical. Consider looking for locations to homestead here you can do this. Where these systems are required, it would be good (from a ZCL perspective) for folks to lobby local governments to change laws.

Phone and Internet:

At the economic level of homesteading a phone can be a burden and an extravagant luxury. Probable cost $500 per year. Live without it. Consider having no phone and using a public pay phone or a friendly neighbor, or borrow a cell phone when you must make a call. Or, use e-mail and a library computer to contact people. If you have a job, while at work, use the phone there.

You can get a free cell phone for use in emergencies – it will call only 911 – through the web. Do a web search, typing in the words 'free cell phone'. On the web site you will have to fill out only your name and address. Postage to send it to you is free.

Internet access without a phone or internet connection in your homestead: (You can save $600 a year or more – the cost of phone and internet service to your home by doing this). Don't have your home computer hooked up to the internet. If you need a file or program, find a library with computers and T-1 connection (so it has fast internet) and the capability to download (or 'burn' is the term used) data to a CD/DVD. Take a CD/DVD to the library, (or your library may sell CD/DVDs), download to your CD/DVD and take it home to use on your home computer. Or you can buy a 'flash memory stick' for a few $ you plug into the USB port on your home computer and the library computer to move files.

If you intend to do this, it would be a good idea to live near a library with internet capability.

5.6 GARDEN AND GREENHOUSE:

The fact is gardening has never been easier or more productive. A host of simple methods some new, some old but revived and improved have been developed. Gone are the days of relentless toil to farm. 1/2 acre can produce a good living. In the book ***The Contrary Farmer*** by Gene Logsdon he writes: $238,000 was earned from a 1/2 acre salad farm in Berkley California named

'Kona Kai Farm'. Logsdons' source was ***New Farm*** magazine July/August 1990. More sources are presented in chapter 6.

Some methods that improve farming/ gardening:

Drip irrigation system: Waters plants at a steady controlled rate without much effort by the gardener except for installation of the system. It takes the work and worry of watering out of gardening.

Compost: Has multiple benefits: keeps moisture in the soil, controls weeds, adds nutrients to the soil as it decays, creates a microclimate at the plant roots as explained by dozens of organic gardening books such as ***Gardening Without Work*** by Ruth Stout.

Mittleider method: has been describe as a 'poor man's hydroponc system. It involves adding correct amounts of nutrients at the correct time - and a host of other methods as explained on the web site. ***www.mitleidermethodgardening@yahoogroups.com***

Plastics: black plastic laid between growing plants control weeds.

Trellises: uses vertical space and increases crop yield per square foot.

Raised planting beds: sometimes called the 'French intensive method'. Rather than rows, plants are planted close together in beds of 4 x 8 feet or longer. Plants may be covered in cold weather with a hoop type solar greenhouse and defended from animals with fences.

The book ***Jeff Ball's 60 Minute Vegetable Garden*** by Jeff Ball (who else?) goes into detail on these methods and many more. These methods save space and time and used together can produce 2 to 3 ½ pound of food per square foot. He uses raised beds, plastic tunnel covers, trellises, compost, succession planting, seedling starting indoors, drip irrigation, crop rotation, companion planting and more.

Watering System: An almost automatically watered garden may be possible (in a climate with adequate rainfall) with water fed to barrels, cistern, or pond from roof runoff from house, garage and greenhouses. From the barrels, pond, etc. run pipes to gardens and greenhouses - gravity fed where possible, or using a small electric pump.

Solar greenhouses: extend the growing season. They are detailed below.

Hydroponics:

Hydroponics food production within solar greenhouses by some results can increase yield by 5 times over open field production. A reasonably efficient garden might produce 2 pounds of produce per square foot per year. A hydroponic solar greenhouse might produce 10 pounds of produce per square foot per year.

Food needed for one year - estimate:

The **ENERGY CONTENT** of the food you eat (not the weight) as measured in 'calories' or 'Btu' determines the amount of food you need for one year.

To provide all of your own food yourself, growing beans I estimate you would need 670 square feet of greenhouse space - based on the energy content of beans and the solar energy conversion efficiency of beans to edible food. How do I come up with this number?

I will convert calories to Btu or British thermal units because it is easier for me to use this unit of energy for all calculations. One food calorie is actually 1000 ordinary calories or one kilocalorie (the dirty secret of the food industry). One Btu equals about 250 ordinary calories.

One person requires about 3000 food calories per day if eating for health and moderately active lifestyle. 3000 food calories equals 3,000,000 energy calories per day divided by 250 equals about 12,000 Btu per day. 12,000 Btu x 365 equals about 4.4 million Btu per year, (or 1.1 billion energy calories per year).

Note: diet experts suggest eating fewer calories for a longer life and better health through life – perhaps 2500 or only 2000 calories per day. See the web site ***Science Daily*** search articles on-aging. (Note: antioxidants to increase your lifespan are called into question by some science articles on this web site, but eating less has attained increasing validity) So here is a great way of practicing "extreme thrift": eat less food. And by eating less – enjoy improved health over your entire life - and extend your lifespan.

Field grown beans convert solar energy to food at an efficiency of 0.33% or 1/3 of 1 %. In a hydroponic solar greenhouse assume 5 times field-grown efficiency or 1.67%

Solar energy gain in the Midwest is averages about 450,000 Btu per square foot per year so a 1000 square foot greenhouse realizes 450 million Btu of solar energy. One percent of this amount is 4.5 million Btu. 1.67 percent equals 7.51 million Btu.

But you only need 4.4 million Btu of food energy per year so the greenhouse can be smaller than 1000 square feet - about 1/3 less or about 670 square feet.

Therefore a hydroponic greenhouse of 670 square feet growing beans might provide sufficient food for one person for one year.

Doing these calculations for corn, which is only 0.25% efficient or one fourth of one percent you come up with about 880 square feet.

Doing these calculations for wheat which is only about 0.1% efficient or one tenth of 1 percent you come up with about 2,200 square feet.

For spirulina Algae at 25% efficiency in converting solar energy to food only 88 square feet of solar greenhouse would be needed.

Another option: Grow food to sell:

Rather than try to grow enough food to meet the energy needs of your body (4.4 million Btu per year), a more efficient method might be to grow food to sell or exchange for food of higher energy content such as grain, beans, corn, or rice.

Food with low energy content such as lettuce or tomatoes can get a good price in the market - $1 per pound or more and twice that if 'organic'.

Growing garden produce to sell: If you grew food primarily to sell, 550 square feet of garden area could provide enough income to feed one person for a year. 550 square feet growing 2 pounds of produce per square foot equals 1,100 pounds of produce saleable for $1,100 non-organic or $2,200 organic, enough money to buy a one-year supply of high-energy content food such as grains or beans. As noted at the end of chapter 2 in the discussion of the **'The Wheatfield: Thrift gone awry'** (page 57) - one person may consume 1.5 loaves of bread per day to obtain the calories s/he needs – (equal to 2,400 food calories). 547 loaves of bread purchased over one year at $2.00 per loaf equals about $1,100.

But wait, as noted in the discussion on page 58 - $165 could buy enough wheat berries to make all of your bread for a year. Therefore you need grow only enough produce to earn $165 if you made all of your own bread products. Therefore a garden producing 2 pounds per square foot, and earning $2 per square foot – would need to be only 83 square feet in area to realize a $165 return.

This is a theoretical example. Few folks would care to live on a diet consisting primarily of bread. Thoreau relied on a diet consisting primarily of beans and rice. A complete (and healthy) diet should include a variety of high energy and low energy foods.

The fact is: you may realize a higher dollar value per square foot of garden area - and for your time - growing low energy food.

Herbs, spices and some other crops can realize a very high $ value per pound and per square foot of garden area: examples: Oregano, ginger, cayenne pepper, marjoram, turmeric, garlic, scallions, chives, cinnamon all sell for several times more per pound than vegetables.

Dark green salad crops you might grow for sale and for their health benefit: romaine, baby greens, arugula, kale, spinach, escarole, broccoli. Any of these crops you don't sell, and eat yourself, can benefit your health.

BUT ANOTHER STEP IS POSSIBLE:

A hydroponic solar heated green house could produce 5 times as much food per square foot as your garden or about 10 pounds per square foot per year. Therefore, 1100 pounds of produce worth $1,100 or more could be grown in an area of 110 square feet or 11 x 10 feet. 110 square feet - the size of an average bedroom. Not much space really.

This is a theoretical estimate. Actual production will depend on the design, efficiency, operation, management etc. of a solar greenhouse.

ONE FINAL STEP:

Rather than spend $1,100 or more on processed food such as bread you could buy basic high-energy foods and process them yourself. As noted above, $165 worth of wheat berries you make into various grain-based products could provide most of your food energy requirements for a year. Another option, slightly more expensive, would be beans. (Best would be a combination of high energy foods). SO, to be generous, $300 might be enough money to buy all of the food you need for a year, and at 10 pounds per square foot, you could produce 300 pounds of produce (and $300) from a hydroponic solar greenhouse of 30 square feet.

Now you may begin to see how folks in the poorest parts of the world can live on a few hundred dollars a year (and you can too). And perhaps you can do better, because they usually do not have hydroponic solar greenhouses. And you may begin to see how on a small parcel of land, in an apartment, or even on a boat you can live almost zero cost. (But you'll have to grow more and have a bigger greenhouse to cover rent, mortgage, car, etc. unless you eliminate these costs using methods suggested elsewhere in this book).

Solar Greenhouses:

As noted above, solar greenhouses can be a tremendous boost to your ability to produce a healthy abundant crop in a small area. I recommend having a number of greenhouses on your homestead.

Techniques and Advantages:

In general you can control the climate, the soil conditions and the pests - instead of relying on nature, on chance, thus reducing the gambling aspect of gardening.

Automatic watering is possible with a drip irrigation system to each greenhouse.

Sun protection is possible for plants that need it by placing shading materials over the roof frame in hot sunny weather: radishes, lettuce and plants that bolt in hot weather can benefit.

Rain water may be collected from the greenhouse roof and piped to barrels or cisterns. If the barrels are elevated a little above the planting bed level (but below the greenhouse roof level that feeds them the water) gravity can provide the 'power' for an automatic watering system. A toilet tank flush assembly could be adapted to serve as a water flow shut off system – to feed water to plants in a controlled manner.

Roof plastic or glazing may be removed when the weather is warm and to let plants to be watered directly by rain.

Protection from wildlife and pests is possible with fencing and screening on walls and roof, and a rubble/broken brick and block foundation to keep animals from digging in.

Evaporation control is possible in hot dry climates. Walls can keep hot dry winds from plants, overhead shading controls sunlight, and irrigation can be routed directly to plant roots.

Heating may be practical and inexpensive in cold weather using solar heat, thermal mass and insulated shutters closed at night. Supplemental heat may be used such as a rocket stove with flue pipes run beneath the planting beds as described by Ianto Evans in ***Rocket Stoves***. A mini heat pump may be efficient and practical if you have electric power to the greenhouse.

Thermal mass may be used to store heat from sunlight or a heating system to provide heat when these system are not operating. Water in barrels or any dense heavy material may serve - broken brick or concrete blocks, broken up concrete paving , etc.

Compost: around plants can help insulate the soil in cold weather and cool the soil in hot weather.

Compost pile heater for a greenhouse: a properly managed decaying compost pile can give off a lot of heat - reaching 180 degrees in the core. A large pile in a greenhouse might help heat it.

A small land area can grow a lot of produce. Very high yields per square foot are possible - 4 lbs or more. John Duckworth grew 8 pounds of lettuce per square foot – as described in his book ***Home Hydroponic System***.

A greenhouse may be built with only a rudimentary foundation: The foundation may consist of treated posts in the ground, or concrete block pillars to hold the frame off the ground with the space in between in-filled with rubble or concrete chunks below ground (to keep animals from digging in).

Recycled materials can be put to use in a plethora of ways.

Uses of recycled materials in a solar greenhouse: (Page 188 - discussing foraging, repeats this list adding more detail).

Pallets attached together can be used to build north, east and west walls.

Pallets sawed in half and tied together may serve as compost bins.

Short pieces of wood - usually throw away - may be used to build small greenhouses. Short pieces may be 'butt spliced' together when longer boards are needed for framing.

Scraps of OSB (oriented strand board) can be used as north facing greenhouse roof underlayment - and as sheathing on north, east and west facing greenhouse walls.

In-fill for planter areas: a compost of mixed sand, clay, leaves, grass, clippings, sawdust, rotted straw, chopped weeds, broken drywall bits, wood chips, kitchen waste, ashes (to provide potash) etc.

Chunks of concrete, broken bricks and blocks may serve as foundation in-fill, floor paving, and edges around planter boxes.

Sticks and poles are useful for trellises to hold up beans, tomatoes, cucumbers, squash, any climbing plants. I favor sticks used teepee or tripod fashion (tied at the top) so the base of the sticks are not buried in the ground where they rot.

Plastic bags stuffed with other bags and grass or weeds can be used as greenhouse wall insulation.

Plastic milk jugs filled with water can serve as thermal mass in a greenhouse. With their bottoms cut out they can become 'cloches'- covers over small plants in cold weather.

Old tires can become planter boxes, their black walls absorb sunlight and help keep the soil warm.

Tires, stacked, packed and encased with sand/clay can be used to build walls for a greenhouse, shed or even your house as exemplified by '***Earthships***'. Enter this word in a net search engine like Google to learn more.

Plastic barrels may be used to hold rainwater collected from the roof.

Greenhouse design considerations:

The danger of a large, tall solar greenhouse: In Ann Arbor wind got under a large A frame solar greenhouse when the ends were opened up and the structure, like a giant kite was lifted and destroyed. Best to keep your greenhouses low, perhaps 7 ft maximum, or build a pit greenhouse half sunk in the ground if possible. Have heavy anchoring walls to the north and west. And have several greenhouses to limit pest infestations.

Landscape timbers 8 feet long costing $3 each can be used as posts down the center of a greenhouse - supporting a ridgepole on which short rafters sit – with their other ends resting on short 2 foot or 4 foot outside walls.

Use brackets to attach framing component, and screws to allow easy assembly. Do not use toe-nailing (nailing through the end of a board into another board at an angle). Toe-nailing may create a weak joint. It is easier to attach light framing lumber with screws and brackets rather than nails - and easy to make changes.

End walls need framing. Doors will be needed in the end walls. The endwall and the frame of the door need to be secure, tied to the sidewalls with brackets and to the ground with stakes, or secured to the foundation using metal straps - or the door may wobble. Be creative!

Extreme method: center posts may be built up of shorter pieces butt jointed. Short pieces of scrap wood and pallets are plentiful and free.

Greenhouse costs verses earnings:

However much you forage borrow, improvise, etc; gardens, solar greenhouses, and other activities on your homestead are liable to cost you something:

Costs:

Consider, 1120 sq. ft. of greenhouse, perhaps in four 14x20 structures of 280 square feet each, costing \$2,000 each to build or \$8,000 total based on John Duckworth's cost per greenhouse. Using hydroponics they might produce \$32,000 per year (see below) a very decent income for a ZCL practitioner.

A greenhouse designed for the Mittleider method would cost about \$10 a square foot. A 1000 sq ft greenhouse x \$10 sq ft. = \$10,000 total cost.

Using recycled materials, you may be able to build a cheap hydroponic system. Duckworth required \$800 of PVC pipes per greenhouse. Milk jugs, glass jars and all the various containers thrown away by our society of might serve as substitutes. (Lots of tubs, tanks and pieces of pipe are need).

It may be possible to build a greenhouse of used, scrap, and recycled materials for \$100 or less. Now you may begin to see the usefulness of found and foraged stuff for gardens and greenhouses. They provide great ways to use many kinds of trash, garbage, waste, and improvised material. Another reason to have gardens and greenhouses.

Earnings: How much can you expect to earn?

Hydroponic: (from John Duckworth) He earned \$8,000 in a season using a greenhouse of 14 x 20 = 280 square feet. = \$28.57 per square foot.

Mittleider method: might realize half the earnings of a hydroponic system or \$4,000 in a greenhouse of 14 x 20 = 280 square feet = \$14.28 per square foot.

Intensively cultivated organic raised bed garden with hoop greenhouse covers in winter might grow 4 lbs of produce per square foot and earn, at a price of $2 per lb. for organic food perhaps $8 per square foot.

All of these methods avoid pesticides and save land.

Other greenhouses:

Hoophouse greenhouses are described by ***The Mother Earth News*** Feb.-Mar. in an article entitled **'*Low Cost Versatile Hoophouses*'** by George DeVault. 2003. A 14 x 96 foot, 1344 square foot hoophouse described in the article grew $2,500 of produce in a season or almost $2 a square foot. Hoop houses can be built for a few hundred dollars, or even less using foraged recycled materials. DeVault wrote, ... "from British Columbia to Russia I have seen serviceable hoophouses made from plastic water pipe and rebar, saplings and rusted bedsprings, fiberglass rods, electrical conduit, strips of old fire hose, scraps of plastic ironed together between sheets of newspaper ... and old car tires."

Pit greenhouse: dig a trench to walk in, perhaps 2 or 3 feet deep and 2 feet wide and the length of greenhouse, 12 feet or more long. Then build a low greenhouse around it. The greenhouse may be very low to the ground 4 or 5 feet above grade, just enough to allow headroom while walking in the trench. The walls may be very low, perhaps 3 feet on north and south sides. The thermal mass of the earth controls temperature swings at no cost. Thus the structure may be very inconspicuous, not noticed by neighbors or the building inspector or even subject to building codes. And, build earth berms on the north and west sides up to the eaves and let plants grow there for even less visibility and more thermal mass.

See the article ***Earth Sheltered Greenhouse*** by Mike Oehler in ***The Mother Earth News*** Feb-Mar 2004 issue 202 for more details and refinements.

A 'rocket stove' could provide backup heat as described by Ianto Evans in his book ***Rocket Stoves***.

The web site ***117builditsolar.com/projects/Sunspace/sunspaces.htm.*** lists dozens of books and websites where you can get plans for solar greenhouses. Some of the web sites have free plans. You can study these plans online or print them out. As you consider them think about ways you could use recycled materials in their construction and operation.

See **ILLUSTRATION # 10** below for greenhouse design ideas.

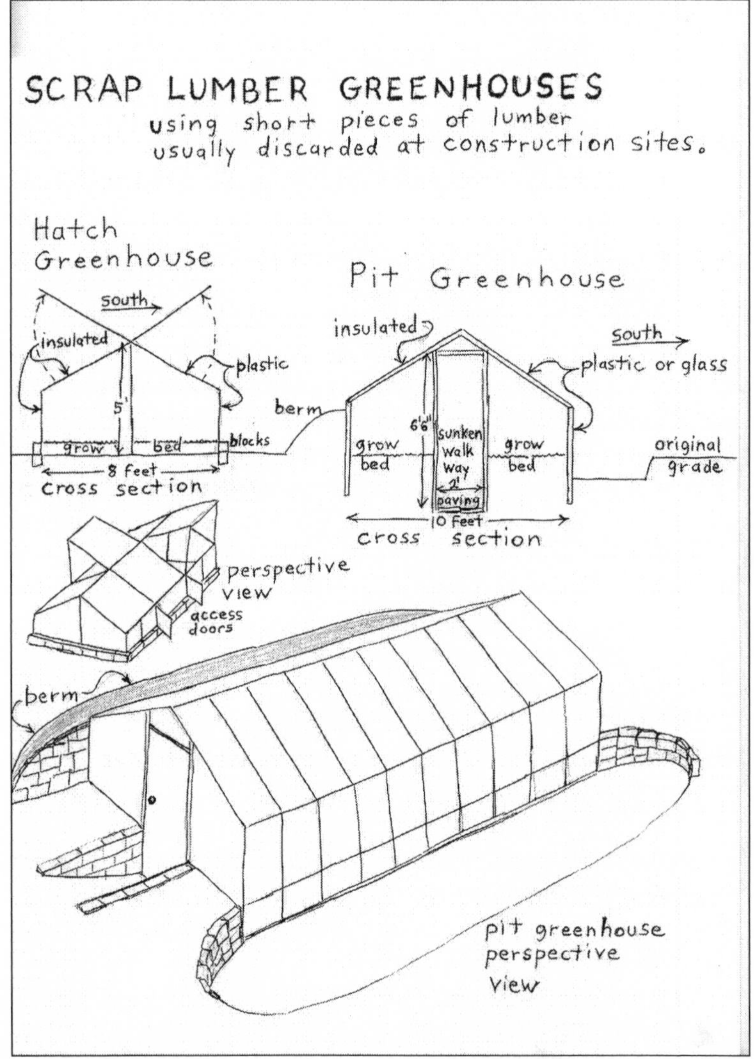

ILLUSTRATION # 10: Greenhouse Design Ideas.

FORAGING:

Foraging can be useful and productive enterprise while building a homestead. I will discuss foraging here because a garden and solar greenhouse can make use of a host of foraged materials.

When you own land, or have the use of land, you have a place to store things, so you can forage for diverse items. You have a place to keep them until needed. Organize them neatly: scrap lumber, logs, sticks, stones, gravel, sand. You must become a saver and a packrat. You will need lots of containers, shelves, storage bins, and space.

A homestead with a garden and greenhouse can make use of many kinds of materials you find while foraging:

Stick and poles become trellis structures or tripods for pole beans, tomatoes.

Chunks of concrete, brick, blocks and stones become planter box borders, greenhouse foundations, and garden paths.

Any organic waste: straw, leaves, sticks, kitchen scraps, grass clippings, can become compost.

Containers of many kinds: plastic, metal, cardboard etc. (usually thrown away) - can be used as seed starting pots and trays: laundry detergent measuring cups, left over PVC pipe sections, egg shell halves with the halves kept in egg cartons, toilet paper rolls cut in half with the ends taped up. Larger containers can be used as larger plant pots.

Pop bottles, turned upside down with their bottoms cut off and stuck in the soil can be filled with water periodically to slowly feed water to adjacent plants.

Scrap lumber can be used for greenhouse and/or planter box frames.

Pallets become greenhouse walls, compost bin walls, and wood stove fuel when cut up

Milk jugs may serve as outdoor seedling protectors and strawberry covers, can become clotches (plant covers in cold weather), thermal mass when filled with water, insulation when stuffed with leaves or grass, and plant containers in a low cost hydroponic system.

Drywall scraps made of gypsum may be used for the improvement of clay soil.

Old tires may serve as planter boxes.

Egg shells crushed and scattered around vegetable plants discourage slugs.

Plastic shopping bags of all kinds can be used as greenhouse insulation: wadded up as wall insulation or stuffed around door and window frames to stop drafts.

Other uses of foraged materials. A few examples:

Burnable waste of all kinds: scrap wood, sticks, deadwood, paper, etc. can be used in a wood burning stove. The ashes can provide potash for plants.

Metal cans: A coffee can may be used to make a 'hobo stove' as described in chapter 3. Lids may be used as cutting tools. Hundreds (or thousands) of cans painted black may be used as the collector surfaces of a solar heating system.

Glass jars, beer or pop bottles may be used to create windows in the walls of a 'cob' house. The bottles are laid in the walls as they are built so they let light in.

Office dumpsters: may be a source of paper. At Staples, or any copy center, there will be heaps of bad copies in the trash bins next to the copiers, the back sides of these pages will be good.

Golf courses: golf balls may be found in the rough. Worth 25 cents each or more.

Foraging, trespassing and petty thievery:

In general, from a moral perspective, I believe foraging can be a very good activity – recycling thrown out, wasted, surplus, unused or underused materials and resources. However; if, in your attempt to live zero cost you practice methods that cause others folks problems, higher costs, expenses, and more work you are not really practicing ZCL.

As you forage, you will quickly run up against a concern: when does foraging become trespassing and petty thievery? It is easy to drift over the line from picking up found items to petty thievery. I know, I've done it. Stuff left lying around unused and unwatched and easy to take unnoticed might be a temptation when you have little or no money. You will be torn between the laudable aspiration to make use off things otherwise wasted and the necessity of committing trespassing or possibly petty theft to get them.

Examples: cases

Railroad track foraging is trespassing on railroad property but you can find good stuff along tracks. Railroad spikes: really taking them is theft and trespassing - as is taking stones, which may undermine the rail sleepers (wooden crossties). But a spike or two has many uses: as a chisel to clean used bricks for example. The spikes labeled 'HC' for high carbon may be used to make tools, including knives. They can be honed to a sharp edge.

And, hiking along tracks can be a more pleasant way to get around than walking along roads. Also, tracks may provide a more direct route to a town.

I have never been challenged while walking along tracks, but it could happen.

Bicycles designed to ride on railroad tracks exist. A web search of the term "rail bike" will turn up relevant web sites. It is a marvelous way to travel. But as with hiking, you are trespassing on RR. property. Of course, the authorities will never approve this method of travel and will prosecute if they catch you.

Dumpster diving: You will be seldom challenged but it is trespassing and you could be injured doing it. If you ask, are given permission, and you are injured, you could sue. So, to protect themselves, if you ask the owner/renter/user must say no. So don't ask, but be careful. (Since you weren't given permission, if you are injured and try to sue, you may have trouble winning your case).

Never take lumber lying around construction sites. It may be needed. Consider taking something only if it is in the dumpster or the scrap pile. Ask if anyone is around. I've never been refused. On construction sites short scraps of lumber are abundant: 2 x 4s and OSB - usually in a scrap pile. Ask to search their pile of scrap wood and the workers will usually say go ahead. It is not their property (usually) and they just have to pick it up later and put it in the dumpster so it saves them work.

Theft of copper, steel, aluminum, brass, etc. for scrap metal is all-to common these days. It is the opposite of ZCL. Don't do it. (And turn in anyone you notice doing it). You are costing utilities, government, businesses, and society in general, many times the cost of any $ you receive at a scrap yard to repair/replace the damage you do.

Take downed trees on public land? No, (they are wildlife habitat and are important for forest health). Of course if I really needed firewood to keep warm and nothing else was available then perhaps, I would take some.

Bricks- some broken and all needing cleaning from a house that had burned down. What is the morality of taking them? No one was around to ask or to stop me. The site was due to be bulldozed and the bricks buried. I decided to go ahead and was never challenged, but I could have been prosecuted for trespassing and petty theft. Bricks cost 70 cents each new, (but some labor is required to clean old bricks).

Other materials from private or public property: compost, (leaves or grass clippings) stones, sticks, wild food. The do-unto-others rule may apply here. If you take a pile of leaves or grass thrown on public land (some folks do this) no harm seems to be done to anyone - you may even be helping to improve the appearance of public land. On the other hand, trespassing on someone else's property to take a pile of leaves without asking may be over the line - they may want it as compost and you could be prosecuted for trespassing. (Folks don't want strangers in their yards even if they're only taking leaves). This topic may be worth more discussion than I want to give it here. I may add it to my web site **http://Ocostliving.com.**

If you come across something lying around that you really need and it is clear that taking it will not cause anyone else any harm, and you truly have no other options I can't say don't take it. However, usually it is possible to find a free source that is not equivocal, where you can ask someone - thereby removing any doubt.

5.7 HEALTH:

Man must do physical work if he is to be healthy; including, I believe, psychological health. I don't like exercise, nor do many others. Exercise is tedious and boring. I want to do things that are mentally and physically stimulating. Needed are fun, interesting and useful physical activities Try to live so that exercise is part of the routine of your daily life. You may be able to accomplish several things at once: useful work, exercise, and health.

I know the Bible says something else, but I suspect the real reason Adam and Eve got thrown out of the Garden of Eden was because they were getting fat and lazy. Looking at Adam and Eve in the Garden, God might have seen them lounging about with nothing to do, their bodies becoming flabby, weak and unhealthy. Perhaps God commanded Adam and Eve to exercise, but their life was easy in the Garden with everything right at hand. They didn't see the point. They disobeyed God. They didn't exercise. Man and woman might have been kicked out of the Garden so they had to work to obtain, food, shelter, clothing; everything. Thus God forced the miscreants to get exercise (and perhaps for other reasons mentioned in the Bible).

Modern health books all reiterate the necessity of exercise for health. Two examples: prevention of heart disease as described by Dean Ornish in his books, or the prevention of cancer as described by David Servan-Schreiber in his book ***Anti-Cancer***.

The obsession with making everything effortless and easy in modern life is bad for health. Find ways to add exercise – as part of regular daily activities - back into life.

Examples of ways to add useful exercise into your life:

Walk or bike to work, or if too far away, park a half mile or more away from your work place and walk, or carry a bike on your car and bike.

Gardening is a natural aerobic exercise activity. Two things are accomplished in one task: healthy food (especially if grown organically) at nearly zero cost and exercise.

Work - you don't want to be too physical so it wears you out - the way the physical jobs of society all to often do. After 8 hours of hard physical labor or tedious work in a factory you're not fit to do much else except rest and so any actions to live ZC are put on hold. Needed, a job with a few hours of pleasant physical and mental work. Jobs ought to be designed around the physical, emotional and mental character of man, not man around the work. (See to book ***Economics as if People Mattered*** by E.F. Schumacher for a thorough discussion of this idea).

Subsistence hunting, as practiced using primitive methods is an example of 'work' that is physical, emotional, and intellectual. (requiring planning and technology). Modern, and ancient hunter-gatherers like Australian and Kalahari Bushmen do not work hard. But they do lots of walking foraging and tracking game - and get steady exercise preparing food. Usually, the way hunting is practiced in a modern society - as a sport; the cost is far more than the value of the food, and the exercise may consist of sitting in a blind reached with a 4 wheeler or a short walk from a car.

Building your own house is another example: It can be pleasant steady work if you pace yourself; stop, rest, take a walk on a pleasant day, and even take a nap once in a while. Keep the task and the design so you don't need skills that are hard to learn. So keep your house design simple.

Drug company products may treat only symptoms, leaving you sick. The medical establishment would have you believe only they and their drugs can cure diseases. But there exist incredibly inexpensive cures for many diseases.

Advertisements and TV shows Grays Anatomy, House, etc. would have you believe health is about brilliant doctors and gleaming hospitals. But it is mostly about diet and exercise and avoiding the chemicals spewed in to our environment by industrial civilization.

Cheap, even free cures: (Pages 220 thru 229 in chapter 6 goes into this topic in more detail).

Exercise helps cure a host of diseases:, high blood pressure, heart disease, digestion, obesity, etc.

The sun can prevent disease. Vitamin D is produced in the skin under sunlight. Adequate vitamin D can prevent rickets in children and osteoporosis in adults.

Sweating can be healthy- cleaning and detoxifying the body. A sauna or sweat lodge can be homemade, or try Thoreau's zero cost method to sweat - hoe seven miles of beans.

Cold cure: Branson's vitamin C crystals: ¼ teaspoon, (1,000 mg) every 20 minutes until bowels move. From ***Natural Cures "they" don't want you to know about*** and ***Natural Cures Revealed*** by Kevin Trudeau web site: ***www.naturalcures.com.***

Avoiding the dentist: Brush and floss twice a day. Avoid acidic foods such as pop, many juices, and citrus fruit or use a baking soda tooth rinse after (or even during) consumption. Cheap toothpaste: baking soda and salt. A toothpick and mouthwash also help clean teeth.

Use incredibly cheap readily available basic substances for most health care needs:

Mouthwash: 1 teaspoon of salt in 4 ounces of water

Bleach: Bleach is toxic. If added to water to kill germs, let the water sit to let the bleach dissipate.

Antibacterial stuff: soaps, creams, etc. create super bacteria, not recommended.

Vinegar and hydrogen peroxide kill about every germ and virus. Have two spray bottles with one substance in each - spray your table with one and wipe - then use the other.

For health care: go to and help support an income based clinic. An income based clinic may operate at a loss and need donations to survive. So donate $ or help with fundraising efforts.

Food and Health: Eat for health, not pleasure. Eat to prevent the two biggest diseases; heart disease and cancer, and a host of other ailments that may be prevented by diet and exercise.

5.8 FOOD

The healthiest foods are often cheap, simple, less processed; and easy to grow, prepare, process and preserve:

Foods requiring minimal or no processing to eat: raw fruit, vegetables, nuts.

Foods that are easy to make at home: sprouts, yogurt, dried fruit, dried meat.

Foods are easy to grow in a home garden: organically grown vegetables, berries, edible flowers.

Don't' make a big deal of tasks like cooking and eating, keep it practical. Not necessary are formal meals and/or fancy exotic foods looking pretty on the plate. Soup doesn't look like much but is simple, healthy and easy to make.

Healthy Cheap Foods:

Spices: oregano, cinnamon

Fruit in season: apples, all berries, grapes, grapefruit,

Grains: brown rice, oatmeal, wheat berries, whole-wheat flour, barley, buckwheat

Dairy: skim milk, nonfat yogurt, kefir, and cheese, eggs

Meat: turkey, chicken

Fish: canned wild caught salmon and mackerel

Vegetables: beans, tomatoes, carrots, broccoli, cauliflower, cucumbers onions, beans, mushrooms, sprouts

Anti Cancer Diet: Known to help prevent cancer.

Herbs and Spices: turmeric curcumin 4 to 8 grams a day, curry powder, garlic, ginger, black pepper, chili peppers, green tea.

Vegetables: soy, cooked tomatoes, onions

Cruciferous vegetables have powerful anticancer effects: cauliflower, kale, cabbage, broccoli, Brussels sprouts, kohlrabi, watercress, turnips.

Sprouting: sprouting seeds is like miniature gardening in your kitchen. It greatly increases the vitamin/food content of seeds. Get a clean glass jar, add seeds, add a little water (you don't want to drown the seeds) swish the water around so all of the seeds get wet, pour out the excess water (put cheesecloth over to the top of the jar to keep the seeds from running out with the water). Do this several times a day for two or three days –VOILA sprouted seeds. Seeds to Sprout: Alfalfa Lentils, Mung beans, Chickpeas, Green peas, Wheat berries, Rye, Triticale, Clover, Fenugreek, Mustard, Radish, Sesame, Sunflower, Adzuki beans.

As you can see, most of the foods on these lists can be grown in a home garden or greenhouse, and be processed in the home kitchen.

Money saving methods when buying food:

Buy bulk: 50-pound bags of flour, bushels of apples, cases of canned food etc.

Buy raw basic staples: dried beans, brown rice, potatoes, whole-wheat berries, and prepare them at home.

Buy in-season produce and can/preserve it at home: carrots, onions, sweet potatoes, all berries and cherries, apples, grapes, etc.

Buy in season locally grown produce: visit farmers markets, buy in bulk, shop around, and bargain before buying.

Buy the store brand or the 'no brand' product.

5.9 MISCELLANEOUS:

'Miscellaneous' things are most of the things you find in the various departments of 'department' stores, supermarkets and retail outlets: clothes, bedding, towels, kitchen, bath, household, hardware, appliances, electronics, media, yard and garden, and so on.

They try to make you an addict of their products, make you believe you must buy what they offer; that there are no alternatives. You must break these addictions, these chains. They get you to buy products that you must continually replace as they are used up, wear out, decay or become obsolete: fashions, cosmetics, computer software, etc. You must strive to replace these with products that are permanent and never need replacement, that you can make, repair yourself, or get repaired, possibly as part of a consumers/producers co-operative. This may require re-creation of entire technologies made "obsolete" by the corporations, objects made of wood, and stone, and workshop foraged iron and steel.

You may have reached a point where you don't even know there are alternatives to everything on the supermarket shelves. You must resist the advertising instilled urge, every time you want or need something, to run down to the mall to get it.

Go to supermarkets and stores and look at what they have and think of, and look for alternative for each item on their shelves and very often you'll find something somewhere that works. Welcome to the department store of zero cost living.

Departments:

Soft stuff: clothes, shoes, bedding, towels, etc.
Kitchen, bath, and cleaning
Household, tools and appliances
Yard and garden
Media
Recreation

(The full consideration of all of these items would take volumes so here I will provide a summary of some alternatives and sources for further study).

Soft: Clothes, shoes, bedding, towels, etc.

Clothes: Repair and recycle old clothes whenever possible. If you buy new clothes look for someone who makes them locally. New clothes are mostly foreign made and are either cheap, and wear out fast; or if good and durable - extremely expensive. Now, even LL Bean makes all of its clothes outside of the U.S.

The best clothes are durable repairable, simple cloths such as 19th century farmers wore and the Amish and Mennonites wear today. Long turned in cuffs can be modified for people of different leg lengths. Pants with suspenders allow them be wearable by people with different waist sizes.

Today, computerized sewing machines may make home production of clothes, bedding, curtains, etc. more practical than ever.

Shoes: As described in chapter 2 Thomas Elpel explains how to make tire shoes with moccasin liners on his web site: ***www.hollowtop.com/sandals.htm*** or in his book ***Design With Nature***. He describes them as the best footwear ever for hiking and camping.

Slippers: Worn instead of shoes around the house, keep dirt out of the house and can save wear on socks (when socks are worn around the house). You may want to make homemade 'sock saver' or sock substitute slippers of leather scraps or cloth that doesn't slip easily on bare floors. Lay your cloth out, put your foot on it, (your material must be larger than your foot all around), fold the cloth up around your foot, sew with thread or make holes as needed for string or strips of leather to tie the cloth up over your feet.

Kitchen, bath and cleaning:

Dish and utensil washing: Methods for efficient hand washing of dishes: Dump or scrape all non-meat leftovers into a compost bin. (Meat waste should be put in a plastic bag and put in the trash bin outside, and/or deeply buried later). Then pre-soak all dishes in hot soapy water for half-an-hour. It is the heat that kills germs, 120 degrees will scald your hands and kill most germs in 5 minutes. The soap congeals grease and perhaps makes germs and food particles slide off items. And soap may damage germs outer coating. Rinse in hot water and let dishes air dry in a drying rack, don't towel dry. Towels may merely add and smear around germs Do not wash, but simply rinse dishes that only have crumbs on them.

Another method: Label dishes and utensils with the users' name or keep them separate for each person - merely rinse and reuse over and over (to aviod sharing germs on the dishes/utensils in the dishwater, cleaning brushes and washcloths.

To reduce handling use moveable baskets or trays – (as used in restaurant dishwashing machines) - one tray with utensils, another with plates, etc. each tray and its contents moved from wash to rinse and then air dried.

Another method: Minimize the number of the dishes and utensils you have. In his book ***The Forgotten Arts and Crafts*** John Seymour wrote "…in days of old there was very little to wash. I saw houses in the west of Ireland in the early 1950s that contained practically no crockery at all. There would be a huge black kettle hanging over the fire, an equally big and black pot, chiefly for cooking potatoes, and a few wooden bowels. When cooked, the potatoes were placed in a shallow basket and perched on top of the cooking pot; the family would sit about on three-legged stools and eat with their fingers. And the food, I imagine, tasted none the worst for that." Page 238.

Soapmaking: Again in ***The Forgotten Arts and Crafts*** by John Seymour he writes: "The housewife would often clean her greasy dishes by rubbing ashes on them, for if you rub wood ash on greasy plates you make soap. To shift more stubborn dirt she would use sand or brick dust ..." Page 238

"Lye was made by allowing water to seep through wood ash, placed on top of a cloth on a lye dropper (a perforated tub), into a tub." "Grease and dirt ... were loosened by the alkaline solution and were therefore easier to remove." Page 276

To make soap with lye the housewife mixed one pint of lye with two pounds of clean, melted fat or oil, and simmered it gently for three hours, stirring frequently...". Animal or vegetable oil could be used. One pound of salt was added as the mixture cooled, fell to the bottom, and hardened the soap. Caustic soda can substitute for lye.

"Some people made lye and boiled the linen in that in the "buck wash". Page 277.

Warning: Making soap and some of these other items can be time consuming and begin to cross over into hard thrift. Making a large batch a few times a year with extra to sell or trade, and finding time saving techniques might make it worthwhile. Maybe someone could invent a soap-making machine.

Operating your homestead with no running water is possible. The Amish do it. But it can be extremely labor and time intensive. One book describing methods is ***How I Lived Seven Years without Electricity and Running Water*** by Esther Holmes.

Line drying clothes: verses a dryer saves wear on clothes and the considerable energy use of a clothes dryer.

Substitutes for store bought times: a few examples

Toothpaste: make up a paste of baking soda and rinse with salt water.

Paint brushes: Clothespins attached to cut up old sponges.

Fennel anti-dandruff treatment:. Steep one heaping tablespoon of fennel in boiling water. Wait until water is room temp and pour over hair.

Toilet paper: Thin paper thoroughly wadded up may serve as a substitute for toilet paper. Phone book paper, newspaper, catalog paper, adverting sheets may serve. Invention needed: a device that makes toilet paper out of scrap paper at home - that crumples the paper and removes ink (when necessary - perhaps by soaking it briefly and then letting it dry). Homemade toilet paper may save a family of four $50 a year or more.

Paper Towels: Replace paper towels with reusable clean rags: old cotton shirts work well. Like toilet paper, paper wadded up for softness can replace paper towels:

Writing paper: look in the trash cans at any printing business such as Staples: People discard hundreds of usually blank sheets of paper at these places every day.

Ideas from ***Clean and Green*** by Annie Berthold-Bond 1990:

Cheap and Natural Cleaning Ingredients:

White Vinegar: grease cutter, window cleaner, dissolves gummy buildups, dissolves minerals, dusting and furniture polish inhibits molds, air freshener.

Baking soda: (don't use baking soda containing aluminum) odor absorbing, abrasive, use ½ cup with boiling water as a drain cleaner, fabric softener, scouring powder silver polish.

Washing soda: ¼ cup as drain cleaner, cuts grease, cleans petroleum oils and dirt. May be used as laundry soap or with soap to soften water and improve the effectiveness of soap. Washing soda is caustic: wear gloves don't use on aluminum pans.

Linseed oil: furniture polish.

Olive oil: dusting aid.

Lemon oil: furniture polish.

Salt: may serve as an abrasive, mouthwash, gargle.

Borax: disinfects deodorizes, inhibits mold.

Chalk: non-abrasive cleaner and whitener.

Cream of tartar: cleans porcelain, metal.

Pumice: removes stains and polishes.

Sodium percarbonate: natural bleach for whites. It is made of washing soda and hydrogen peroxide.

Citrus lime, lemon, grapefruitjuice: cleaning, flea control.

Vegetable oil soap: coconut oil may serve as dishwashing soap.

Lanolin: sheep wool oil, leather cleaner.

Cornstarch: sprinkle dry on books to absorb mildew. Mix in water and rub on and off as a window cleaner.

Pure lime: (not chlorinated), absorbs moisture

Pure soap flakes: for dishwashing. Grate a bar of pure soap into a saucepan and simmer on low heat to melt before using.

Baking soda and vinegar: drain cleaner; pour in baking soda and then vinegar.

Tomato juice or paste: clean stained pots.

Rhubarb: clean stained pots.

Lemons: clean stained pots.

Household, Tools, Appliances, Furniture:

A surplus of used items exist in this society. They may be picked up for pennies on the dollar at garage sales, flea markets, resale shops, salvation army, habitat for humanity, or online on Craigslist online - or free on Freecycle, along the road on trash day, in dumpsters, or even free for the asking from friends and neighbors.

Tools: Look for used tools. The book ***A Museum of Early American Tools*** by Eric Sloane (and many others) describes how to use hundreds of rugged simple tools of the past. Old dull saws and other tools may be bought for almost nothing. Often they are merely thrown away. Learn to sharpen tools and you can put them back to work. Broken or cracked wooden handles can be replaced. Hammerheads, axe heads, and garden tools with broken or missing handles are common.

Appliances: An alternative to the dryer is, of course the clothes line and/or clothes drying rack. Store bought clothes racks may be cheap and breakable. Racks are easy to make at home of 1 x 2 boards in an A frame or scissors configuration.

Alternatives to the refrigerator are described on page.

A Rocket Stove may be used for cooking and heating water. It can be extremely cheap and relatively easy to build as described by Ianto Evans in his booklet ***Rocket Stoves***.

Furniture: Basic furniture may be built out of construction lumber and recycled building materials - 2 x 4s, pallets, plywood scraps, metal brackets, concrete blocks, etc. Using these materials it is possible to build very simple tables, chairs, bed frames, shelves, and desks. If you buy furniture, never buy new, and even used may be expensive. Most of my furniture cost me nothing. It was thrown out, put in dumpsters when people moved, broken (and easily repaired), given to me, or inherited from relatives. As better pieces came along I upgraded and traded or gave away my poorer quality pieces. Over time you may be able to accumulate better and better versions of all of the furniture you need, if you are patient.

Yard and Garden:

Plan your yard (if you are building new) or change your yard to keep the areas of grass small so you can easily cut them with a push mower, weed whacker or cord type electric mower. Let the corners of your yard go wild so you don't have to care for these areas at all. Wildlife will like it.

You can water your yard and garden with water collected from your roof if you install a rain barrel water collection system as described in the book ***The Carbon Free Home.***

You should have a compost pile. 'Garden and Greenhouse' starting on page 177 describe composting, mulching, using recycled waste, etc.

Media:

Look for technologies being phased out. Vast numbers of typewriters once costing hundreds of dollars are worthless and given away or thrown out.

Computers $2400 new may be bought for $50 after 6 years. TVs: used are cheap and plentiful as people replace them with big flat screen TVs.

VCRS have been replaced by DVDs. VCR players and videos are widely available or $1 or $.50 at garage sales, or even free. And even new DVD players are cheap now - $20. But DVDs themselves are not cheap today, although used ones are coming up for sale. Someday, as they are replaced by newer technology, they will be cheap.

Recreation:

Sports equipment: Never buy new. Used equipment is widely available. Search resale shops, flea markets, garage sales; also Craigslist, and Freecycle on the web.

Pets: Rescue an animal from the humane society to be your pet. You give a forlorn animal a good life and the fee you pay benefits their work. Or, look in local newspapers or search the web for animals offered for free.

Toys: Toys may be made out of cheap or free stuff of all kinds – taking only creativity and imagination.

The influences of media, stores, schools, and friends may undermine a child's interest in toys made out of cheap, free, and homemade stuff. But even children with heaps of store bought toys have fun with free stuff. Basic cheap/free toys children might play with for hours include sticks and logs, pieces of scrap lumber, cardboard boxes, cereal boxes, empty milk jugs, empty cans, old socks, sand in a box, scraps of paper, plastic containers, almost anything saved can be a toy. And, found items might serve as playthings: swivel chairs, exercise devices. Of course, be sure they won't hurt themselves on these things.

5.10 MOBILITY

Walking:

Walking has great advantages. Walking costs nothing; you can do it any time and is healthy. A half hour a day minimum walking is recommended in dozens of health books. Remember again - the Hunzas' of Pakistan and the natives of Vilcabamaba in Peru have no roads in most of their country, and therefore must walk everywhere, 10 miles in the course of their normal day, and enjoy long lives and excellent health. Great, would be to live in a place where you could walk every place you need to go. Sadly there are not many such places in modern society, but they do exist. Look for them and consider living there.

Biking:

The bike is one of the most fabulous inventions of all time. You can travel at 4 times walking speed with less effort than walking. A bike is easy to park, store, and repair. It is not difficult to carry around if necessary, like up stairs. It takes up little room in storage. It causes no pollution. Roadways for bikes may be narrow and cheap, and leave nature intact. A "Bike City" might be practical and is described in chapter 7.

A bike may quadruple the distance you can easily travel to work, shop or forage. You can go six miles instead of a mile and half in 30 minutes. In a city, with traffic lights and jams, a bike may travel faster than a car on the same route.

Bikes are made dangerous however, by automobiles. Bikes can go fast, too fast for car drivers to see or react to them, sometimes, so you must be careful, very careful. In the car you are in an armored chariot. On the bike your soft body is exposed to that armor.

I have gotten used bikes in good condition for $5 at garage sales and occasionally for free either as gifts from relatives who never used them or from neighbors who put them out with the trash.

A bike consistently used may save almost the entire annual cost of a car. Consider carefully the value of moving to a place where a car is not needed.

For a really cheap bike consider the 'Track Bike' used by bicycle messengers in New York City. It is cheap, simple, rugged, and efficient. It has one fixed gear, so there is no gear changing, no shift cables to freeze or get wet and dirty, and seize up.
It often has no brakes; the messengers have methods to stop without brakes – such as suddenly turning the front wheel sideways. Some bikes just have a front brake and you must slide back on your seat when you brake to keep the rear tires on the road and prevent you from rolling over the front. Track bikes are sometimes not even locked to save time when the messenger must make a fast delivery, but still, they are not stolen much because using them is such a challenge. If you could learn the skills of a bike messenger, you too could avail yourself of this cheapest form of bicycle.

Car:

I write this for those of you must have a car, who cannot arrange a lifestyle that doesn't require one.

A used car may cost about $2,000 a year for all expense if bought cheaply, you maintain and repair it yourself, can get cheap insurance, and you don't drive too many miles per year – thus not running up gasoline costs.

From a ZCL perspective: To pay for $2,000 per year of car expenses, $40,000 must be invested at 5% return after inflation whether as dividends or savings interest or capital appreciation. So your pre-inflation rate of return must be higher. Inflation eats about 2 or 3% of the value of your money per year so you must obtain a 7 or 8% return on your money, far higher than bank interest in the best of times.

A new car, need I say it, is completely out of the question living ZC:

A new car may cost $0.50 to $1.00 or more a mile for all costs including depreciation, gas, insurance, maintenance, repair, drivers license, plates etc. So, driven 10,000 miles, the car costs $5,000 to $10,000 - plus per year. From a ZCL perspective a whopping $100,000 to over $200,000 must be invested to cover this cost if the money earns a 5% after inflation, or an 8% return before inflation with inflation at 3%.

Really, from a ZCL perspective, owning a car is an enormous obstacle. First depreciation in the value of the car eats your money. Once depreciated, and the car is old and no longer loosing value then maintenance and repair cost may be high, and again, eats your money. Always, a car is big cost. Never is it a stable or appreciating asset - with one exception - an antique or classic car may hold or appreciate in value. But then you dare not drive it much for fear your precious investment will be damaged or break down on the road.

I will give a lot more consideration to the problem of car ownership for anyone attempting to live ZC in chapter 6 on 'Comfortable Living'.

5.11 RAISING $: while homesteading:

Work:

Look for jobs where you can learn, practice, and refine skills applicable to ZCL: organic gardening, cook, seamstress, bike repair, possibly even automobile repair. (Sadly, most service industry jobs teach little or nothing applicable to ZCL).

Look for a job that requires mental and physical activities. Unfortunately most jobs in this society are divided into desk sitting or continuous all day physical activity. A moderate amount of physical work can be a pleasure. Enough for health would be ideal, perhaps 3 or 4 hours of physical work per day. Work designed for people should be part mental and part physical.

In our increasingly service oriented economy, unfortunately you'll more likely be stuck in various 'service' jobs rather that an interesting or useful job with a future. If you get stuck in one of these all-to-common miserable and tedious jobs generated by our economic system consider, you'll soon be anxious to quit and thus inspired to attempt ZCL.

Businesses:

If you practice a ZC lifestyle, production of many of the things you need is moved back to the place of consumption - your home - and moved away from distant regions and centralized factories. You will make your house and yard units of production, not just consumption. You may be able to expand things you produce for home consumption a little or a lot to sell or trade - and start a business.

Home business: Why at home? Start-up and operating costs may be low. You may be able to undersell stores and possibly even imports. Failure may not result in a big loss. Running a business you may develop many more skills and abilities than you would as an employee in a job.

Type of business: Possible might be extension/expansion of activities you already do as part of ZCL. You can use faculties and resources already available. For example, surpluses generated from growing your own food such as organic produce.

Organic produce is, I believe a tremendous barely tapped source of income with a greenhouse/garden/small scale organic farm. Organic vegetables sell for twice as much as non-organic. Organic beans sell for $2.00 a pound vs. $1.00 for non-organic. A 1,000 square foot greenhouse growing 4 pounds of beans per square foot or 4,000 pounds of beans total selling for $2.00 pound = $8,000 a year. It could be set up for very modest cost and difficulty, yet make a considerable contribution to the income of someone living ZC. In fact, the high cost keeps many folks from buying organic who might otherwise prefer it. More, many more small-scale organic farms could reduce the cost of organics and thus expand the market, while still making a good profit for mini-organic farming operations.

Energy production: Put an array of solar cells on the roof of your house or garage and produce more electricity than you need - especially on sunny days and/or in sunny climates. Laws and technology exist that let you sell the surplus back to the electric company. You can make your electric meter run backwards!

Gather and cut up scrap wood and dead or downed wood for firewood to sell.

Woodworking: With woodworking equipment you can make wood items using scrap wood and downed trees. Objects now made of plastic were once made of wood. And, wood is still useful, even preferable for many tasks. Examples: furniture (of real wood, not the fake wood boards), spoons, wooden toys, boats. Craftsmen skilled in woodworking were once common. Locally made, high quality but inexpensive wood objects were once widely available and could be again. It might be possible to replace imported plastic toys with locally crafted wooden toys.

Vehicle repair and maintenance: If you create the facilities and develop the skills needed to maintain and repair your own car as described in chapter 6, you have the ability to work on other folk's vehicles. You can be selective in your clients perhaps specializing in certain makes or model that are easier to repair such as older cars. If you build your own car (also described in chapter 6), you could build more to sell.

If you have become dedicated to the bicycle as transportation in the process of living ZC, you could specialize in bike repair and maintenance. For your business, you could build a bike shed equipped with repair tools in your backyard, or dedicate a room in your basement, especially if you have a basement door to the outside.

With skill and sewing equipment you could produce clothes, bedding, curtains, towels, upholstery at home.

In the future I think there may be a dispersion of centralized manufacturing facilities as computers and robotics are improved. If knowledge, information, programs software can move around the world in an instant, many kinds of production operations need not be centralized. Someday, local, small-scale manufacturing, possibly even manufacturing at home, could be efficient and practical. Order your parts online from dozens of small parts makers, assemble your car in your garage, no factory required.

Someday we may experience the end of people working as employees of business. Centralized factory labor with ownership separated from the workers might be replaced by dispersed co-operatively owned enterprises.

The old anarchists of France and Russia such a Peter Kropotkin believed rural electrification would make possible the dispersion of manufacturing and industry across the country side and into the capabilities of small producers because every household and small business would have a source of cheap power and with electric tools could make much of the stuff made in centralized facilities. That didn't happen, but with the advent of the computer and the web, it may be more possible. We need to make computers get up, become active, grow arms and legs and do some work, as it were, rather than just sit there processing data.

Exhortation:

Van Gogh lived an almost ZC life. He made beautiful paintings he couldn't sell. Today, those paintings are worth hundreds of millions. Beautiful but of no practical use. Maybe there are too many aspiring Van Goghs. I'm not saying any artist should give up his art.

But some of you are not so talented or not able to sell your art to people who have heaps of excess money. Why not turn some of your artistry to practical arts, making stuff you and others can use, the better to cut back on Chinese imports. Sew a simple shirt. Make a soupspoon by the hot coal method. Repair a bike. Turn a pile of sticks into a pole bean trellis. This may not be worth hundreds of millions someday - and that happened too late for Van Gogh to benefit - and perhaps success will come too late for you too, but you can be warmly clothed and adequately fed at zero cost while waiting for it.

Practicing extreme thrift while homesteading: (Reiterating chapter 2):

Whenever you can, do things that get you double or multiple benefits because they can be efficient – save you time, money, and effort.

Examples:

More exercise equals better health equals lower health care costs. And doing something useful that is also exercise can multiply the benefits to you.

Organic Gardening: You can get the multiple benefits of exercise, organic food, fewer pesticides in your food, and use of recycled materials. Otherwise you may have to buy expensive organic food, drive to get it, and to get exercise go to a gym or health club for a fee.

Sauna: You could buy, build or visit a sauna. Or, like Thoreau hoeing his 2 ½ miles of bean field rows you could work up a sweat weeding beans thus avoiding use of any time or effort on a sauna - and getting food from your sweat.

Add an attached solar heated greenhouse to your house: It can extend the growing season thus providing vegetables during the off-season when produce is most expensive. Sell the surplus at high prices during the off-season for income.

Biking: As mentioned in chapter 2, foraging while biking is an efficient combination of activities. Biking rather than driving a car saves you gas and wear on the car, provides exercise, and can give you a more intimate knowledge of your community.

A combination of extremely thrifty methods to realize ZCL: On your own lot, build and live in a homemade solar greenhouse; with a rocket stove for backup heat; near a small town where you can walk everywhere. Grow surplus produce in your greenhouse to trade for food you don't grow – and to sell to pay for property taxes.

5.12 RECREATION and VACATIONS:

Homesteading, especially homesteading to live zero cost can be hard. Constant hard work, boredom and sameness can be a problem. You may feel like you are in a trap with no way out. The boring tedium of the daily grind of the old American farm culture was a major factor in its demise. Some farmers, unable or unwilling to leave livestock and crops in the care of others took no vacation in their entire lives. A major appeal of city life, and of our ruinous modern culture is that it can be interesting, fun, exciting. What is the answer to that? You will need recreations and vacations. Of course living ZCL you may build up savings if you have any kind of job at all and so be able to splurge a little.

When the game-like challenge of ZCL becomes tedious you may begin to dream of a life of profligate luxury. You may feel envy of the well moneyed no matter how unhealthy - restaurant steaks, candy bars, parties, mass entertainment. Being poor keeps you automatically from many of them. So you must find or create you own low cost, no cost recreations. Or, if you have extra money, possibly splurge a little: go on shopping binges, eat badly, drink till you are sick and you'll be cured. The pleasures of the rich are overrated.

Many recreations leave me with a feeling of emptiness, and dissatisfaction: amusement parks, movies, restaurant food, sporting events. After all the hoopla what use is it to me?

Don't you have to go to Disneyland or Las Vegas to gamble to have a great time? After initial equipment costs many recreations can cost nothing. Hiking is especially cheap and healthy as is 'ultralight' and primitive camping using minimum or homemade equipment.

How can ZCL be made exciting? How can you have fun and not spend any money? Consider first, most of your time is your own. You can try things the wealthy and busy wouldn't have the time to do. Not having money may actually expand the kinds of recreations you could try.

The idea of hopping a freight train and riding the rails is absolutely fascinating to me. But don't do it without a guide who has already done it. The book ***Hopping Freight Trains in America*** by Duffy Littlejohn (Sand River Press 1993) explains how as do web sites such as ***www.slackaction.com/hopping.html*** and ***www.Thespoon.com/trainhop***.

Thespoon website also introduces a new costless sport, "Urban Adventuring" defined as the "cheap thrill of going places where you don't belong." One adventure describes sneaking into the back areas of Disneyland.

Historical re-enactors recreate the Civil War, the World Wars, in fact just about any war or historical time period. The 'Society for Creative Anachronism' for example tries to recreate the Middle Ages.

Go to special events: political meetings or conventions related to a hobby or a sport. (A 'Zero Cost Living' convention someday, maybe?) You might attend an event as a concessionaire, a retailer of stuff you've made or grown on your homestead. You might make $ while enjoying time away from the homestead.

For travel cost savings go as a group in a bus or rented van. Or, join a co-op non-profit travel club such as 'Hostelling International U.S.A' (web site www.hiusa.org). Formerly 'American Youth Hostels' the organization runs 'hostels' – low cost dormitory style shelters for travelers at 80 U.S locations. State branches of the club organize trips, hikes, bike rides, etc.

Countless museums are free or request a donation (which you don't have to pay) to visit. Possibly you could volunteer to work at a place you'd enjoy visiting.

Try a 'stay at home vacation': You relax, stop your old routines, visit interesting local places, maybe even trying some "urban adventuring" as mentioned above. Some folks go on cruise or to a far away country and read a book. You could've read it at home. Eat in fancy restaurants? You could prepare a special meal at home too - for a tiny fraction of the cost.

Visit friends or relatives for a vacation. But you want to somehow reciprocate for their hospitality. Think about how. Possibly you can invite them to visit you. Of course, they may have to camp out or have a trailer to stay at your rough new homestead.

Try a house exchange, perhaps with another homesteader in a (to you) exotic location: You trade houses for a limited time. I've never done it, but understand there are networks of folks doing this.

When the pioneer farmers took a day or two off, they still made their time useful by going fishing, hunting, or "berrying". (as Laura Ingalls Wilder describes in her books.). Like them, you could undertake a long foraging expedition that also serves as a vacation. For example, go to northern Michigan when apples or cherries are in season; pick them yourself, pay a fraction of retail price and bring them home to eat, store, or sell.

"Picking wild berries was the best of our vagrant summer pleasures, the fruit sometimes abundant beyond belief." From ***Eighty Acres*** by Ron Jager.

Three almost free recreations are hiking, biking, and boating. More expensive recreations are often not so appealing. A ZCL vacation need not be a money spending binge but a change of location, a long bike tour like Ken Kifer, or a kayak, canoe or boating trip. Great low or no cost boating trips are described in the magazines '***Small Boat Journal***' (long out of print but available online) and '***Messing About in Boats***'.

Hiking:

In most areas of the country, places to hike exist near your home. A local hike can be just as healthy and enervating as a trip to a distant place. Long trips just to hike are not necessary. Going far away multiplies the cost for the activity.

But maybe you're bored with the local scenery? Certainly, different exotic scenery and surroundings are refreshing stimulating, enervating. Go there but avoid the expensive tourist traps. Jon Krakauer in his book ***Eiger Dreams*** describes impoverished East Europeans coming to climb Mount Blanc in southern France. They camped in the fields outside the expensive tourist town of Chamonix, brought their own food, used homemade equipment and seemed to get as much out of the experience as the well healed climbers.

Biking:

After hiking some distance, biking feels almost like you've taken to the air. It is easy to see why the Wright Brothers, avid bicyclists readily made the transition to flying, not bothering with the automobile at all.

Bike touring can let you go many miles at low cost. Ken Kifer made marathon bicycle tours of 3,000 and more miles throughout the Eastern United States and Canada. Starting from his Alabama home he averaged 60 miles a day and was on the road for two months. He spent by his accounting 2 cents a mile or a total of $150 on a trip for bicycle maintenance such as tires, brake pads, lube oil, etc.

Boating:

Yachting is expensive, has been made expensive but boating can be cheap, almost free. Not much is needed. How simple and cheap can a boat be? 12 to 16 feet and a few hundred dollars to build or buy used, a sail, oars, or paddles, a tent or canopy for a summer cruise and compared to hiking, you are living in unparalleled luxury. Sleep on board almost anywhere on water and no one will bother you. Or, uninhabited islands, empty shores can offer camping sites. Georgian Bay; part of Lake Ontario in Canada has 100,000 islands, many of them uninhabited or in the Georgian Bay National Park. Harlan Hubbard camped along the Ohio and Mississippi rivers.

A number of useful books describe how. One book is ***Roving in Open Boats*** by Ian Nicolson. Another book is ***The Simplistic Sailboat*** by Dan Hookham in which the author describes taking his family cruising /camping for a month in the San Juan Islands north of Seattle. He built his boat for $600.

For Harlan Hubbard, his life was his recreation as he drifted down the Ohio and Mississippi rivers over a two-year period (with frequent long stops). His book ***Shantyboat*** describes his journey.

Crew on sailboats. Racing sailboats sometimes look for volunteer crew. Look on marina bulletin boards, or talk to captains and crews. Another option; crew on "tall ships" such as the Niagara, a replica 18th century sailing ship on the Great Lakes. Sometimes these replicas of old ships advertise for volunteer sailors in harbor town newspapers or on their web sites.

VIGNETTE:

Setting out to live zero cost is a fascinating challenge. To me it feels almost like the opening gambit of a chess game, a chess game with life. My backpack is prepared. I am prepared. I've learned and studied and in my pack is a guide to edible wild plants. I have money saved from a fast food job I just quit with great pleasure. I've sold the car I foolishly got while in high school for more $.

I've practiced camping out to prepare. I put my backpack on, say goodbye to mom and dad and walk out the door. The whole world awaits and I am king of the world - utterly independent, as free as I will ever be. I feel as if everyone is applauding as I step out. But the applause is in my soul. This is a great adventure. I walk through a society of fools doing foolish things.

I walk through the tedious and boring suburbs. I follow railroad tracks because they are free of automobiles, their noise, danger and disturbance. To the countryside I go; and then on back trails and dirt roads. It is late spring. The bugs aren't out in force yet. Birds sing, flowers, scent the air. Young light-green leaves on trees wave in the gentle breeze.

I walk and camp until I reach a town that is compact enough so that cars are not needed to get around - a town I'll try to live ZCL in. A hundred years ago people went everywhere the way I do, walking on roads that in those days were blessedly free of automobiles. Weird, walking to the place I intend to live, instead of driving. It gives me a whole new, and fresh perspective. I note things I'd pay no attention to in a car. Places to sleep, to forage, to hang out, to relax.

I've scouted the town before. I've studied the town on the internet, know something about it, have a map in my pocket. I know I can live here without a car. I forage for some of my food, visit gleaners and the county human services agency for more food. I ask for help when needed and ask for and look for free stuff.

I sleep in a tent made of a tarp, use public restrooms in the library, town hall, and shopping mall. I have to move my campsite occasionally. Staying too long at one campsite draws unwanted attention to me, but I keep my eye out for a really great place.

I wander the town, dumpster diving, learning the trash days, live with growing skill on the streets. No one knows I am homeless.

I find a bike for free during my foraging. It is in bad shape but I learn to fix it by asking questions at a bike shop. After visiting the bike shop a few times and learning a lot, I am able to get a part time job there. When I am not using it, I keep my bike locked and whenever possible, concealed. Now my range is quadrupled. I can bike many miles out of town, hide the bike and hike. I take occasional longer trips costing almost nothing. I forage as I bike. I have learned from the writings of Ken Kifer who lived months on the road while biking and spending only a few dollars.

I become tired of sneaking in and out of hidden campsites near town. I would like to live indoors again. I look in the local newspaper and at advertisements on the web for people needing roommates.

I join a local food co-op. While young I learned to behave in ways necessary to get along in cooperative enterprises: courtesy, respect, patience, goodwill. Through the co-op I find a spot in an apartment shared with six friends. I am off the streets! But my living costs are still low because I share the cost of rent. I attend the local university on the sly. Colleges, I have learned are too clubby. But, universities are large and open, with large classes I can sneak into without being noticed. I've picked a school that has practical courses. I take courses that teach practical skills, with some philosophy thrown in. With occasional money (a windfall from my family) I actually pay for some courses. I find a group interested in appropriate technology and another group that forages for wild food as part of their studies in biology. Another class studies and recreates Native American skills. I start a group trying to attempt a co-housing community. Together we begin looking for a site.

During my search for a homesteading site, I meet a man and wife who built the most amazing things out of waste items and materials: used pallets, scrap metal, old lumber, logs and sticks, broken bricks and blocks, plastic bags and milk jugs, empty cans and bottles, anything and everything. Their house was made mostly of recycled materials. Their furniture was all thrown out broken items that they fixed themselves. Their car was an ancient jalopy – a mix of body styles and parts that nevertheless ran smoothly and efficiently. Their clothes were all homemade, not the latest fashion statements, but copies of long wearing, easy to make clothes of 19th century farmers. I learn a lot from them, more than I learn from university professors.

My co-housing group finds land close enough to town to bike there on a bike path converted from a railroad right of way. My group formally incorporates as a non-profit cooperatively owned company.

My group buys the property keeping ownership in common. On our land is a meadow surrounded by big trees, a beautiful place that we preserve. In the middle of our land we hand dig a well, sharing the work. One well will serve all of us, saving the cost and labor of creating many individual wells. By informal agreement we divide part of our land into half-acre sites but use our company as the legal owner.

We do not legally divide the land up because if we did, our local building and zoning department would require roads, paving, and expenditures to meet township subdivision regulations. We build no driveway into our home sites - we have trails in. For cars we concede a parking spot on the edge of one corner of our site.

I explore and study the half-acre site assigned to me by my co-op. Sometimes I camp out on there. I collect materials: compost, mulch, logs, blocks, bricks, storing it neatly on my site – for later use.

We deal with nature, neighbors and the authorities. My group fights the authorities about access roads for fire trucks they claim are necessary for safety. Neighbors fear we are building a 1960s style "hippie commune" with drugs and crime. We reassure them, help then out, gain their confidence. Nature deals us blows: bad weather, plant diseases. We work hard now to avoid creating homes and a community that require endless hard work in the future, to make the place eventually easy to keep and maintain.

Our community leaves half of the land wild. We work together to improve the other half, transplanting foraged perennial vegetables, berry bushes, and young fruit trees. Some, we buy, an investment for the future.

Winter is coming on. I hate to spend $ on rent and heat. I am given an old car, not running sitting in someone's back yard. Hooking it up to a friend's truck, I am able to tow it out, take it to my site, and park it in a well-hidden spot among the brush where no one can see me enter and leave. Now I have a weatherproof, lockable metal and glass structure. I fix up the interior to live in - layers of cardboard cut to fit and duct taped together. Masses of plastic bags stuffed over and under the dash serve as airtight insulation there. It becomes a warm, safe cocoon of a shelter. I have parked with the windshield facing south. On cold but sunny winter days I remove the insulation there and the sun warms the interior so much I must open windows a crack for fresh air. I build a tiny attached shed accessible from the rear passenger side door. Inside I install a portable toilet. Luxury!

In the spring, maybe I'll get the car running, then trade, sell it, or use it. But I cringe at all the expenses involved. Parts, labor time, title, plates, gasoline. I'll have to work long and hard for it, when in fact I can go everywhere in town without a car.

On days of good weather in winter and spring I build simple sheds, greenhouses, and garden beds. When summer comes, I start a business selling surplus fresh organic veggies that mature early in the season in my greenhouse - getting a high price. I use the university computer and a free web site to contact and inform folks about my business. I take orders and deliver locally on my bike – fitted with a used bike trailer to carry my produce. I write and sell articles to a local paper on ZCL methods. Then, with friends I start a local magazine on ZCL and distribute it free. To pay for it, I sell adds in the paper to local businesses. I promote the idea of a community wide ZCL economy devoted to local production of food, energy, materials, tools, clothes, etc.

On my half acre I build a tiny well-hidden shed to live in, earth bermed, half buried, clay walls among a thicket of bushes. I use the old car as a storage shed now.

Now I am well on the way to achieving the final phase of living zero cost, comfortable living; the subject of chapter 6.

***

CHAPTER 6: COMFORTABLE LIVING:

Contents: **page:**

Introduction:

If you are homesteading at Zero Cost, you may have grown tired of living in a shed or tiny house, of foraging and scrounging for everything, of squeezing every dollar you get. You are anxious to achieve the final phase of ZCL, living in ease, health and comfort. You need to turn your rough homestead in to a pleasant place to live. You are working to achieve the full realization of your '**personal economy**'.

6.1 CIRCUMSTANCE:

You have saved money from whatever source by living low cost while homesteading. Or, you don't need to homestead, but can go right into comfortable living at ZC because you have money from a job, business, investments, a windfall, or a company buyout; not millions, but tens or even hundreds of thousands of dollars. You don't have the money to live in luxury, but want or need to stretch your dollars as far as possible

Even though you have money you may want to practice many of the methods suggested for living in circumstances of homelessness, and homesteading to preserve the money you have.

The amount of money you have built up and have available may determine which route you try to reach comfortable living. With tens of thousands your best chance might be as part of a group or organization such as a co-operative or co-housing community. With hundreds of thousands you might live more or less independently. However you might live better, much better, even luxuriously as part of a co-operative or co-housing community whereas living in complete independence you will probably have a lower quality of life.

6.2 USING TIME AND MONEY EFFICIENTLY:

ZCL may eliminate all or almost all of your costs, but it will still require your time. In fact it can create a big time use problem. ZCL can take up all of your time. Pioneers and farmers worked dawn to dusk or more. Instead of comfortable living, you may end up with a life of tedious drudgery. Or you can spend more money to get convenience, which is the counterproductive usual method of "living" today.

In Chapter 2 I explored the practice of extreme thrift. Here I will explore extreme thrift applied to **comfortable** zero cost living.

As I said in Chapter 2, thrift can be efficient, or hard and so not really thrift at all. Here are some methods to avoid the pitfalls of attempting to be thrifty, and make efficient use of time and money while achieving comfortable living ZC.

Method one: Create effortless, almost automatic systems/equipment. Get devices/systems that work almost automatically such as a yogurt maker, seed sprouter, bread maker, solar collector, self-watering planting pots. Use piped systems vs. buckets and hoses to water gardens and greenhouses. Presoak dishes before washing.

A negative example: Burning wood for home heat requires a lot of time and effort. The old saying that it warms you 4 times is only too true. You must cut trees or gather deadwood, carry it home, cut it up and stack it, and bring it into the wood stove or furnace several times a day. Keeping the fire going properly takes more time and attention. And last, the ashes must be removed and disposed of. Better for comfortable living if you only burn wood occasionally, and build your house and heating system so this is possible. Then, maybe burning wood could become a pleasure and recreation instead of an example of hard thrift. I will detail how this may be achieved later in this chapter.

Method two: Get things that are easy to fix and maintain: Some examples:

House: Design it so it is easy to fix anything that may go wrong. A steep roof, for example may be difficult to climb on to fix a leak. Build it with long lasting low maintenance materials, a coated steel roof rather than wooden shakes, for example.

Furniture: Get simple rugged furniture that is practical, useful, can take abuse and is easy to clean. Replicas, perhaps homemade, of the rustic wooden furniture of the American pioneers and the 'craftsman' style furniture of the early 20th century are great examples.

Appliances: Some appliances are easy to repair by design, and many are not, but must be thrown away if they break: One example: Whirlpool built washing machines can be repaired by the homeowner. (Note: do not tip one over to look underneath. The gear lubrication will run out a small ventilation hole and can't be replaced. The outside case comes off easily with the machine upright). Other brands such as Maytag may require professional help.

Vehicles: Maintenance and repair are discussed in detail under 'mobility'. One example of a possible problem: If you own a van: access to parts of the engine is more difficult, sometimes much more difficult than opening the hood of a car or truck.

Method three: Combine functions: Do two or more things at once.

Combine practical activities with activities that also provide exercise and/or recreation. Examples: woodworking, framing a building, fishing, hunting, gardening, foraging, cutting and burning wood.

Many, even most recreations are useless, even harmful to your health, pocketbook, and the environment. Examples: watching TV, gambling, drinking, smoking, boating. (Don't think you can justify, from a ZCL perspective; getting a big boat with a powerful engine for fishing. The cost would be many time the gain).

Take vacations that are useful. Examples: Go north for apples and cherries, or forage for wild mushrooms in season. Visit garage sales and flea markets while vacationing.

Combine biking around town with foraging.

Method 4: Practice versatility whenever possible: Get things that have multiple uses: tools, furniture, vehicles, rooms in houses. For example, have a versatile vehicle that may be used to haul items (such as items found while foraging) on a car top carrier or tow a trailer. Older compact station wagons may be a good choice. Another example: the old time country kitchen was a multi-purpose room useful for ordinary cooking but also for canning, sprouting seeds, making yogurt, or just sitting around the table talking.

Method 5: Practice "being preventive" in all things: preventive maintenance, preventive medicine, preventive dentistry, etc. Ben Franklin wrote "A stitch in time saves nine." and the statement perfectly illustrates the concept. One example: practicing dental hygiene conscientiously can save you a bundle.

Method 6: Buy things that last: In your mind divide the world into two parts. On one side put items that don't last, that get used up, that wear out, that lose value, decay, becomes obsolete, may be stolen or lost. Examples: food, cars, most electrical devices, fashionable clothes, decorations, art work, don't buy this stuff. On the other side put things that last, keep their value, don't wear out, never become obsolete, are reusable, repairable, and is rarely stolen or lost. Examples: how-to-books, land, well-constructed buildings, durable clothes (work clothes) and quality tools, compost, rocks. Buy these things, (or better yet find them or make them for free).

Method 7: Practice safety in all things: Example, build or modify a house to be everything proof - fire, wind, rain, flood, accident, vandalism. Build or modify your car to be as safe as possible in an accident.

All of these methods will be considered in more detail the pages of this chapter.

6.3 HEALTH:

"The first wealth is health," wrote Emerson in ***The Conduct of Life***.

Better to be healthy and poor than sick and rich. And, if you were rich and sick you would spend all your money to be well, if necessary. Poor and sick is a very bad circumstance to be in however and so health must be the first priority of a ZCL lifestyle.

To maintain health for little or no cost is quite possible given the right behavior. Many people don't take care of themselves and have sedentary jobs. Look at all the smoking Americans and all the fat Americans and the chemical soup industry has made of our environment. But, diet and exercise might protect us even from some of the bad effects of pollution. So once again I'll state the obvious. To achieve comfortable ZCL you must not smoke, or drink to excess, you must get exercise, and you must eat a healthy diet:

A low cost small portion diet is the healthiest. The big eaters are fat and sick. Eating less actually extends the lives of animals in tests, and probably in man too.

Free health care: Here I don't mean a government program. I mean things that can cure you, or prevent you from getting sick and cost nothing. Nature; your own body and your immediate environment provide many, even most of the ingredients to cure or prevent diseases.

Fresh air: fresh air flowing in to your lungs from exercise is extremely beneficial to your health.

To clean the air in your house, crack a window occasionally. Fresh outside air is usually five or ten times cleaner than inside air, because we live with so many chemicals

Exercise: Has been proven in hundreds of studies to do nothing but good for your health in many ways such as improving blood flow, heart and muscle condition. Yoga techniques of stretching and breathing along with mental exercises like visualizations may be especially effective.

Sweating: Sweating helps clean and detoxify your body. Sweating while doing useful tasks can be more interesting than exercise. Wood cutting, gathering, carrying, and fire making has always been more interesting to me than time on a exercise machine. A sauna is another way to sweat. Far infrared light is the best for a sauna. A Native American sweat lodge is another option. You could build one yourself for little or no cost.

Sunlight: Sunlight on your skin causes your body to produces vitamin D. More vitamin D in your body has been shown to prevent or reduce a number of illnesses and health problems. Exposure to direct sunlight in the mornings and evenings when the sunlight is not so intense is best. Too much sunlight can be bad too, causing skin cancer, which brings me to another method of health care that cost nothing.

Shade: Whether as a big floppy hat, or under a cool porch on a hot summer day shade can save your skin from wrinkles and skin cancer, and keep you cool to avoid sunstroke. And of course shade, unlike air conditioning, costs nothing. (But you could go an air conditioned library, store, or the mall and enjoy their air conditioning at no cost to you).

Fasting: Fasting has been shown to provide a number of health benefits It lets your digestive system rest, helps remove toxins in you system. Some sources recommend fasting one day out seven. You must drink plenty of water while fasting, (according to Tim Brantley in his book ***The Cure*** for example).

Water: Water is the true elixir of the Gods, able to cure disease almost by itself in some cases: Writes Brantley: "Carlos stomach burning and his ulcers were instantly corrected with water. What a simple solution. ... The more water that Carlos and I drank, the better we felt. We realized that water was instrumental in washing toxins away." Other drinks: pop, alcohol, even milk in some cases may be bad for you. And of course water is available free in most places. Studies have shown municipal tap water to be as clean as bottled water. McDonalds offers a spigot for free filtered water among its pop selections.

Relaxing: Avoiding stress is proven to be good for health. Living your life stress free is much more possible if you can avoid financial worries and burdens - perhaps by living Zero Cost.

Meditation: Costing nothing but proven effective in many ways that improve your health including lowering blood pressure, controlling your appetite, managing stress, dealing with emotional problems, calming your mind, finding inner peace, and achieving sense of well being and happiness. A good introduction to meditation and all of its benefits may be found in the book by Dr. Dean Ornish ***Reversing Heart Disease*** pages 226 to 243.

Cheap health care methods: not free but still very cheap:

Home remedies for illnesses have realized increasing effectiveness, sophistication and scientific validity over the years. Books and magazines are numerous:

Examples: ***Prevention*** magazine and dozens of books such as ***Natural Home Remedies*** published by Rodale Press.

Organic Housekeeping by Ellen Sandbeck has many healthy and cheap methods that can affect your health: Examples from her book:

Replace home pesticides - many of them not adequately tested, especially on children - with natural non-toxic remedies. For example: Use baking soda and powdered sugar for cockroach infestations, not toxic chemicals.

Use ordinary soap for hand washing and bathing. Antibacterial soaps are not any more effective than ordinary soap in controlling bacteria, and may cause bacteria to develop tolerance to antibacterial agents.

To live ZCL you must pay extremely careful attention to your health including diet, dental care, and safe behavior. Nevertheless, health can be the biggest single obstacle to ZCL. All the cheap or free health benefits provided by your body and nature may not be enough to keep you healthy. There are too many uncontrollable variables. Even practicing the best lifestyle and methods of preventive medicine you can get sick or injured. Health care costs and/or health insurance costs can take your entire income and savings making ZCL impossible. Thousands of people in this country are reduced to homeless destitution by these costs every year. You must take advantage of whatever government health care programs you are eligible for. Living ZC your income may be low enough to qualify.

Hard words on health: If you take care of yourself and do all of the things recommended by the best medical advice, and you stay healthy; you ought to pay less for health insurance and be rewarded, be compensated. If you abuse your health you ought to pay more. Health insurance is not set up that way however, in general, but it ought to be.

Health Savings Account: If you stay healthy living a ZC lifestyle and buy conventional health insurance, you are paying for all the people who don't take care of themselves. To assure health care for yourself, you could start and fund a 'health savings account'. Use interest and dividend income from the account to fund your ordinary health expenses. $40,000 would earn you perhaps $2,000 a year after inflation if prudently invested. If a big health expense hits you can tap into the account to cover it.

Catastrophic health insurance: It would be a good idea to buy catastrophic health insurance to cover unexpected health care costs that could wipe you out financially. Your carefully built comfortable ZCL homestead might be taken away from you, leaving you destitute and back in the homeless circumstance of chapter 3. You can hope charity and government programs cover catastrophic expenses, but they might not. Sadly, Medicaid will only cover you if you have virtually no assets: $3,000 or less, guaranteeing destitution if you are hit by massive medical bills and are not wealthy. It is a shortsighted program that may leave you cured but destitute. Hence the need for catastrophic health insurance.

Medicaid: Is it good public policy to strip a person of all of his assets, assets that let him live independent and self-sufficient because he gets sick? Living with $3,000 in assets, in any comfort, even living almost Zero cost is impossible. He would have to hide assets or give them to relatives, to keep them from the debt collector. Or go on welfare. Reducing a person to welfare from a state of self-sufficiency seems absurd policy to me. These laws need to be revised to let folks keep basic assets sufficient to live a comfortable ZC lifestyle despite catastrophic health care costs.

In getting health care shop around. Unfortunately there is not much competition in health care. (To be fair health care does not lend itself easily to market competition. Do you really want the cheapest heart surgeon you can find?) At each office ask what medical and dental exams and treatments will cost. Take advantage of free and income based health clinics. Get generic versions of drugs.

If you work at staying healthy and safe you should be able to spend much less than conventional health insurance would cost you per year.

You must take thorough and meticulous care of yourself including not taking any unnecessary risks in sports for example. Not that you should live in perpetual caution and fear while enveloped in safety equipment. That in itself, the stress and anxiety of it; could worsen your health. But, you should take prudent measures and engage in safe pursuits.

Dangerous sports vs. healthy sports: There is a sad tendency for certain kinds of people and organizations to take very healthy and inexpensive sports and activities and push them until they become expensive, unhealthy and dangerous. Certain personality types, perhaps deficient in self-esteem seem to go for these deadly sports.

Mountain climbing is a good example. Hiking and climbing in the mountains can be very healthy. The longest-lived peoples in the world live in mountains. But it may be pushed too far. Apart from the danger of falling, mountain climbing without oxygen in the so called "Death Zone" above 17,000 feet, the body undergoes steady deterioration and dangerous illnesses may develop as the body breaks down; illnesses such as cerebral edema (leakage of fluid into the brain) and pulmonary edema (leakage of fluids into the lungs).

Care of your teeth:

Like health care, costs for the dentist can derail your attempt to live zero cost. You must take meticulous care of your teeth. Folks living on the cheap sometimes just let their teeth go. But it is a false economy. Bad teeth and gum disease have been proven to make you vulnerable to other diseases, weaken your immune system, even shorten your life. Save the cost of fillings, caps, bridges etcetera and you can save a bundle.

Brushing and flossing once or ideally, twice a day is the first step to keeping healthy teeth. Concentrate on the back teeth on the side away from the cheek. It's where most problems develop. Use a fluoride mouthwash after brushing.

Even with brushing, plaque and tarter build up on your teeth. Plaque and tartar removal is vital to healthy teeth and gums. Tartar removal is apparently not a do it yourself project. You must have your teeth cleaned every 6 months for about $50. You can buy a tool similar to one type of tool dental hygienists scrape with; and looking in a mirror try to scrape the hardened tarter off your teeth yourself. I have tried it but not long enough to determine if it works. Dental hygienists spend years learning their trade, and don't clean their own teeth, so do-it-yourself teeth cleaning may not be practical.

Cleaning:

Cleaning and sanitation are vital parts of health of course. How can they be made zero cost? The outdoors is self-cleaning through natural processes, natural cleaners such as rain, snow, wind, sun, decomposition and biodegradation. These are excluded from houses and so folks must dust, wash, flush, and remove garbage. But we can use the free cleaning provided by nature too. One example: Rain-washing clothes, towels, bedding, carpets is entirely practical.

Hanging dirty clothes out on the clothesline before a rain and then letting them be dried by the sun and wind works well. I've done it many times and it leaves items clean and smelling fresh. It is an excellent example of practical extreme thrift. (Dry permanent press clothes in the shade or they may yellow).

Diets:

Food is discussed here under health because to live comfortably and zero cost, eat for health, not for pleasure. Timothy Brantley in his book ***The Cure*** writes:

"…It didn't matter whether you call it sickness, unhealthiness, disease, or anything else. It was all about eating and drinking the wrong things over an entire lifetime."

You can eat a healthy diet for one dollar a day; possibly even for 150 dollars a year: How? In general - eat mostly vegetarian. Buy basic staple foods in bulk. Buy concentrated milk, dry milk, 50-pound bags of whole wheat flour, oats, beans, and brown rice. Sprout grains at home to increase their vitamin content. Make your own pop and save a bundle: Just add sugar and yeast to water. Never buy pop again. Supplement your diet with homegrown organic garden and orchard produce such as broccoli, garlic, spinach, cabbage, blueberries, apples, ginger, oregano, basil.

Sprouting is an easy and inexpensive way to greatly increase the vitamin content of grains. Most whole grains can be sprouted. To sprout, you need a glass jar with a cover water can run through but not the seeds such as a piece of cheesecloth. Soak the grains overnight, then pour out the water and two or three times a day wash the grains as they grow by pouring water into the jar and swishing it around then pouring it out. This removes any possible mold growth and keeps the grains moist.

Here are a few examples of diets: without going into the medical details from Dean Ornish, N. V. Perricone, Randall Fitzgerald, and J. S. Sachs:

A healthy diet according to Dean Ornish: His diet is the only one proven to be able to reverse heart disease as explained in his book ***Reversing Heath Disease***. You must eat a near zero fat diet including almost no nuts, cooking oil, eggs (except egg whites), cheese, meat, or fish.

What can you eat? Most fruits and vegetables, egg whites, non-fat dairy products: milk, dried milk, yogurt, and cottage cheese. His books list the foods he advocates and presents recipes.

A healthy diet according to Nicholas Perricone from his book ***The Perricone Promise:*** Wild caught salmon. Hot peppers for sinus relief. Nuts and seeds: flaxseed, brazil nuts raw in the shell. Make yogurt and kefir. Eat plain yogurt and plain kefir with no thickeners or stabilizers or sugar sweeteners. Eat beans and lentils. Lentils cook quicker than beans: only 20 minutes for red lentils. Grow sprouts: for instructions see the web site ***www.sproutman.com***. Broccoli sprouts are especially recommended.

For health, Perricone states, avoid foods high on the glycemic index, that have high sugar content and so called 'fast carbohydrate foods' that break down quickly into sugars in your system: These include white bread, white rice, potatoes, pastas, sugars and corn syrup. Instead eat food that have a low glycemic index and are 'slow carb foods' such as whole grain breads and pasta, and brown rice.

Healthy foods according to Randall Fitzgerald from his book ***The Hundred Year Lie*** subtitled 'How food and medicine are destroying your health'**:**

Fiber rich foods: oat bran, beans, lentils, apples, citrus fruit, barley, peas, carrots.

Bladder cancer prevention foods: Broccoli especially broccoli sprouts, cabbage, cauliflower, brussel sprouts, kale.

Magnesium rich foods**:** beans, seafood, apricots, bananas, spinach, broccoli sweet potatoes, seaweed, seeds.

If you cross referenced these and other diets and ate only foods listed as healthy for each diet not much food would be left to eat, it would seem. Then throw in the food allergies some folks have to grains containing gluten (gluten is in most grains), milk, and certain vegetables, and it gets even worse. Still, there are some foods most diets agree are healthy. Some examples: egg whites, plain non-fat yogurt, most berries, lentils, sprouted seed and grains, some vegetables - especially broccoli, and herbs and spices such as garlic, oregano, turmeric, curry powder, and basil.

In her book ***Good Germs, Bad Germs*** Jessica Snyder Sachs explains that many, even most germs are beneficial; that there are 100 billion "good" bacteria protecting our skin and 15 trillion in our intestines that we need to process food. Antibiotics can ruin these good bacteria and render us vulnerable to drug resistant super-bugs. She paraphrases Scott McEwen - veterinarian at the University of Guelph in Canada writing "We might make greater progress by shifting wholesale back to more traditional styles of farming. Studies consistently show that animals raised on small "family" farms need less antibiotics and carry fewer drug resistant bacteria."

Sach further writes "…research shows that simply increasing dietary fats - especially fish oils and olive oils – eases the symptoms of many chronic inflammatory disorders and helps prevent the inflammatory damage seen in arteriosclerosis."

Food stamps, called EBT and in the form of a credit card like card are generous if you don't buy junk, if you don't fall for the agribusiness garbage they sell as food. The danger of free food whether from EBT, human services agencies, or charities such as gleaners is that they can undermine your will and ability to efficiently provide your own food. For example: Why make bread when you can buy it? Yet bread machines are cheap and plentiful, take much of the work out of making bread, may be obtained used for a few dollars - and homemade bread may cost pennies a loaf.

You can grow your own produce at home using organic methods that don't use chemicals and pesticides (although there are natural toxins to watch out for, such as in corn). Organic foods cost more if you have to buy them. I believe they are healthier.

Gardening is discussed more in chapter 5 on 'Homesteading'. Here is a little more detail: You may want to try the 'Mittleider Method' as explained and advocated by Jim Kennard on his web site ***www.mitleidermethodgardening@yahoogroups.com***. This method of gardening uses trace minerals and chemicals to improve natural soil. Using micronutrients can greatly increase productivity of most soils. The Method also relies on water holding planting beds, simple water saving watering systems and greenhouses. Even sandy desert soils have produced bountiful crops using these techniques. The Mittleider Method is not strictly organic but does not use pesticides and herbicides. It has sometimes been called the "poor man's hydroponic" method of gardening. Productivity is about half that of a pure hydroponic system but setup and operating costs are much less. Possibly 8 pounds of produce might be realized per square foot of garden area at a cost of $5 per square foot to set up for the first year and much less thereafter.

6.4 LOCATION and LAND:

Here I will talk about location, land, and some ways they may affect house design and construction.

Location:

To achieve comfortable ZCL you must have a good location. Your place must be safe and secure where no one will bother you. High crime areas, irritating or fussy neighbors, and draconian building codes and officials can make comfortable ZCL difficult. Crime rate you can investigate online. Do a search in google, for "crime statistics". Neighbors you won't know until you move but look at the character of the neighborhood. Is the area all trophy homes meant for show, or do homes look more utilitarian? Is every yard immaculate, or is there some 'disorder' here and there. Do residents use their yards for practical activities such as gardening?

Housing costs are absurdly high in some areas. Don't move there. If you must move there, perhaps because of a good job, consider buying land and building. Perhaps you can homestead at first as described in chapter 5. Of course, if you have a good job I think you'll be less likely to be aiming to live ZC. But consider, in our volatile job market things can change.

Location considerations for homesteading described in chapter 5 are entirely applicable to comfortable ZC living. As stated there (but worth repeating) an ideal location might be near a small town but outside public sewer and water area. Thus you avoid the annoying regular fees for these services. You will have your own private well and septic system with a tank and drain field.

Warm Climate: In the south ZCL may be easier. Heating bills may be minimal. It may be cheaper to build a house. There is little or no frost, so a shallow and inexpensive foundation is possible. Cost for clothes may be lower – no heavy winter coats and boots needed. There is a longer growing season so you can grow your own, or buy locally grown fresh produce almost year round.

Heat in the summer: Air conditioning costs may be reduced or eliminated (ZCL style) by proper house design using shading with trees, air flow, ventilation, fans, cooling towers, etc. More on this later. In hot dry climates adobe houses have long kept folks comfortable at virtually no cost.

What to avoid – when is an old house beyond saving: Bad soil under the footings: sinking and sliding on an eroding beach or hillside (all to frequent in west coast mountain areas), or in a flood path. Sometimes footing water drainage pipes are in clay soil and blocked with age so water collects adjacent to foundation walls and freezes – and buckles the foundation walls. Damaged basement walls may be repairable or convertible to a "Michigan basement" or crawl space.

On floodplains - where land may be cheap build an elevated house - as would have been a good idea in New Orleans. But make sure you have secure footings. Don't put footings where soil can turn to mush and move. In these places; a floating house - a houseboat may be possible. 'Shanty boat' style houseboats that normally sit on block-and-timber piers but float when floods come are described by Harlan Hubbard in his book ***Shantyboat.*** Living on a floodplain in a suitable house may make it possible for you to use land that is useless for most purposes and therefore cheap or even free.

Land: If you build:

Land Area: Your site must be large enough to support the activities necessary for ZCL: greenhouse, garden, garage workshop if you have a car, storage places for foraged stuff, food-processing facilities, etc. You may wonder, what is a reasonable land area needed to practice comfortable ZCL. After consideration of all of the above needs, we are in a position to estimate this:

Land area for food production:

See the discussion on page 180, 181, and 182 for land area needed to provide food. As noted there, growing high energy content crops such as beans, corn and possibly some wheat; - hydroponic solar greenhouses totaling 1,000 square feet could provide all of the high energy food one person needs for one year.

Or, more easily than growing high energy foods - you can grow food to sell or trade such as lettuce or tomatoes. Greenhouse and garden areas of 2,500 square feet producing an average of 4 lbs. of food per square foot per year could produce a total of 10,000 pounds of food, worth $1 a pound or more or $10,000 – more than enough money to buy food for a family of 4. I estimate about $4,400 per year would buy all of the food needed for a family of 4 if bought with efficiency – no pop or junk food for example –leaving $5,400 to cover other expenses such as property taxes, insurance, toilet paper, etc.

How much space is required for a driveway, parking for two cars, a garage with repair tools and facilities. (But you're going to have one car or even none, living ZC right?). Possibly you could have parking and repair space in a raised basement, to really save space. About 1,000 or 2,000 square feet of land area is needed.

House area about 28 x 40 feet = 1120 square feet.

Yard space for play area, patio, deck, pathway, etc. = 1,000 square feet.

Total minimum area: 2,500 + 2,000 + 1120 + 1000 = under 7,000 square feet.

A 70 x 100 foot area = 7,000 square feet = only 1/6 of an acre minimum if efficiently used. A larger area, perhaps ½ acre or about 22,000 square feet would feel more spacious. On a half-acre, a larger than minimum area may be devoted to each use. Several acres would be a spacious luxury from a ZCL perspective, and you may have to pay more property taxes.

"A rood of land (quarter acre) is sufficient to grow all potatoes and other vegetables and some fruit for the year's use, say for a family of five. Half an acre would be an ample allowance. Such a piece of land may easily be cultivated by anyone in the odd hours of regular work and the savings is naturally large from not having to go to the shop for everything of this nature that is needed." Edward Carpenter ***England's Ideal***. 1909.

6.5 SOLAR FARM: On a half-acre:

Every year, about 10 billion BTU of energy fall on a half acre of land at 40 degrees north latitude in the Midwest, and more in the west where it is sunnier – excepting the Washington and Oregon Coasts. If it sounds like a lot, it is - equal to 71,000 gallons of gasoline.

Here, is a suggested layout for a half-acre farm. Note that everything is placed to maximize efficiency, practicality and usefulness. Nothing is meant for show, or to impress the neighbors. There are no vast useless lawns, ornamental trees, decorative architecture or landscaping. If the layout ends up charming or beautiful it is because the practical often is more pleasing to the eye than the useless.

Summary of areas for each use:	**Square feet:**
House including porches decks and patio	2,000
Garage and workshop with storage	1,000
Parking area and driveway	1,000
Greenhouses	2,000
Gardens	2,000
Fruit and nut bushes and trees	1,000
Compost and mulch piles	500
Storage areas and sheds	500
Paths and walkways	1,000
Lawn and play areas	3,000
Pond	1,000
Woodlot, natural areas, wild places	6,000
Total:	22,000

Illustration # 11 below shows the possible layout of a half-acre farm.

This layout for a **Solar Farm** is one possible example of the full realization of a **personal economy** (or P.E.) as introduced in chapter 1.

I like to think – when actually built – that it could be the equivalent in the economic world of the **personal computer** (or P.C.) in the computer world.

In fact I believe the P.C. could go a long way towards making the realization of a P.E. possible - helping in all aspects of P.E. creation including finding methods that work through web searches; designing systems using design programs such as CATIA; buying components through E-bay (and countless other online sites); and operating systems such as greenhouse hydroponic climate control, watering, and nutrient flow after the P.E. is built. Your P.E. could be almost an extension of your P.C. – your computer stepping out into the real physical world to actually help you do practical tasks - instead of being used for an endless parade of useless time wasting activities.

For decades people have imagined that computers would make possible the creation of robots that would perform many of the tedious tasks of the world (and later maybe more sophisticated tasks). Someday, that may be, but here I suggest a more modest intermediate step in which your P.C. helps create your P.E.

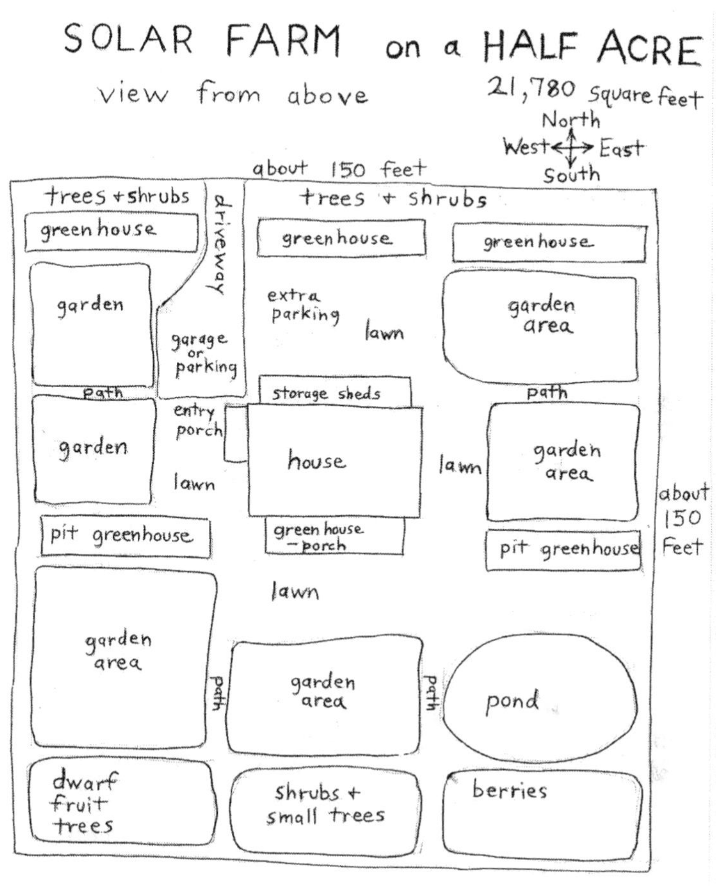

ILLUSTRATION # 11: SOLAR FARM

Explanation of the layout:

A backyard facing south is ideal but not absolutely necessary. Whatever side of the house faces the street; the south side of your house is needed for solar panels for electricity generation, solar greenhouse, solar water heater, possibly a solar cooker, solar water distiller etcetera.

Additional structures adjacent to the house include deck, porch, patio, and storage sheds.

Around the house and accessory structures is a ring of lawn and play areas. This ring of lawn can serve as a firebreak and allows access around the yard for vehicles if needed. Pathways define the edges of the lawns and provide access to the diverse uses of the adjacent areas. Outside the ring are gardens, greenhouses, compost and mulch piles, storage areas, sheds (wood shed, garden shed, storage sheds) garages– workshop, and pond.

Near the property limits are hedges of fruit and nut bushes and trees, woodlots and wild areas. Some of these areas may have multiple uses: compost piles and bins may be placed beneath the trees of the woodlot, parking and the driveway and parts of the house and garage may be beneath solar space heating panels and photovoltaic cells. Paths, walkways, lawn and shade loving vegetables may be partly beneath trees.

A note on cost: Lots of adequate size and orientation (backyard facing south would be ideal) can still be found at reasonable cost near small towns. In Michigan, for example, modestly sized lots near small towns may be found for a few thousand dollars.

Farming Solar Energy - Methods:

To develop your homestead to a situation where you can live in comfort at almost Zero Cost, you need create a solar farm. Ordinary modern conventional farms and the old time farms were devoted to farming crops. Your farm will be devoted to farming the sun. Conventional farms harvest the sun – in the form of crops at an efficiency of about 1/4 of 1 % or 0.25%. This modern solar farm could harvest the sun at an efficiency of about 4% or 16 times more efficiently than conventional farms.

Along with enhanced ordinary crop growing the solar farm will have a host of systems to harvest the sun.

As stated above, 10 billion Btu of energy falls on a half acre of land a year at 40 degree North latitude, (central Midwest) equivalent to 71,000 gallons of gasoline at 140,000 Btu per gallon.

Btu: What is a Btu? It stands for a British thermal unit abbreviated Btu and is a commonly used measurement of energy in the utility industry. A kilowatt-hour of electricity equals 3413 Btu of energy. For reference: the average family uses about 10,800 kilowatt-hours of electricity a year equivalents to 37 million Btu and home heat for their home averages 150 million Btu of energy a year in the central Midwest.

Other measurements of energy exist: langleys, calories, kilocalories, kilowatt hours, joules. In this book I will convert everything to Btus to make comparisons between systems understandable.

So anyone with a half acre of land can claim to be well off - with gasoline costing anywhere from $2.00 to $4.00 a gallon his land gathers $140,000 or more of solar energy every year. However, it is possible to use only a small percentage of the 10 billion Btu falling on your half acre - small, but enough to let you live zero cost.

And, if you are not careful, solar energy can be a trap. The costs for some systems can be so high relative to the return - you would be better off putting your money in the bank even though bank savings are partly eaten by inflation.

Techniques:

The new frontier is not space, or under the ocean but your own backyard. And, the new pioneer is you, expanding in to your yard to harvest solar energy for food, fuel, heat, light, electricity and materials. And if you become healthier doing the work necessary to harvest the sun; all the better for you.

What percentage of 10 billion Btu can you expect to harvest?

Corn: If you planted your entire half-acre to corn you could expect to harvest about 25 million Btu as food or fuel (50-plus bushels x 450,000 Btu per bushel). That is equivalent to 0.25% or one fourth of one percent - obviously a very low percentage. 50 bushels of corn processed into ethanol fuel could yield about 150 gallons with 67,000 Btu per gallon or 10 million Btu total as ethanol fuel - about one tenth of one percent conversion efficiency from 'raw' sunlight – a lower percentage than raw corn. But there are other methods of harvesting solar energy using current technology that are far more efficient. In the solar farm I propose here, about 4% overall efficiency or 400 million Btu are used, including 15 million Btu of energy in the form of food. These 400 million Btu are enough to meet the food, house heating, electricity, and vehicle fuel needs of a family of 4.

Components:

Tree canopy as woodlot and orchard.

Yard – lawn, play area, paths, walkways.

Grain field – could be wheat, oats, barley, millet, or other grain crop.
Garden and bean field.
Solar heated greenhouses – 6 greenhouses averaging 350 square feet each.
Solar cells: (photovoltaic cells) for electricity production.
Solar space heating system for house – encompassing south roof and walls.
Algae pond for bio-fuel – or possibly distillery for alcohol fuel.
Solar water heater – adjacent to south side of house.
House, garage and driveway – part of solar cell array installed above.

Solar Farm: Detailed table of Components:

Solar half-acre farm with estimated energy use per year:

Land use & note number	Land area sq. ft.	Total Solar Btu	Used solar Btu	Efficiency
Tree canopy & orchard -1	7,000	3,220000,000	2,600,000	0.15%
Yard-grass& walkways-2	4,000	1,380,000,000		
Grain field -3	3,000	1,380,000,000	1,380,000	0.1%
Garden -4 bean field -5	1,500 500	690,000,000 230,000,000	1,840,000 765,000	0.2% 0.33%
Greenhouse-6 Food-7	2,000	920,000,000	184,000,000 11,000,000	20% 1.2%
Photovoltaic System -8	2,000	920,000,000	92,000,000	10%
Solar space heat -9	1,000	460,000,000	92,000,000	20%
Algae pond -10	1,000	460,000,000	18,400,000	4%
Solar water Heater-11	100	46,000,000	18,400,000	40%
House and garage -12	1,000	460,000,000	0	
Total -13	23,100	10,000,000,000	422,385,000	4.2%
Food total -14	7,000	3,220,000,000	14,985,000	0.5%

Note: This table presents a rough approximation only. Accurate measurements and full realization of solar farms is a matter for future pioneers like you. The total area equals more than a half-acre (21,780 square feet) because solar cell arrays can be installed above buildings, driveways, garages, porches, decks, and walkways.

Notes:

1. Yield: 1/6 cord of wood a year as firewood. Tree canopy leaves after falling are useful as mulch and compost for garden and/or greenhouse: the solar energy made useful from this process has not been determined in any study I could find – research is needed. Orchard fruit energy content not determined: more research is needed.
2. Yard yield: grass clippings, (like leaves) useful as compost/mulch. Solar energy made useful not determined.
3. Grain field yield: 225 pounds of grain a year. Grain field straw after winnowing is useful for straw/mud brick making or as compost.
4. Garden yield: 4,000 pounds of produce per year. Plants convert solar energy to plant material, or biomass at about 1% efficiency, but only one third to one tenth of that becomes edible food in open field gardening.
5. Bean field yield included in garden total. Beans are more efficient than most plants at converting solar energy to food: 0.33% or 1/3 of 1%. Compare this bean field of 500 square feet to Thoreau's bean field of 2 ½ acres as described in Walden.
6. Solar greenhouses collect and store solar heat and protect plants from the extremes of climate thus making it possible for plants to produce more than open field gardens. Yield at 5 to 10 pounds per square foot – 10,000 to 20,000 pounds of food per year – to eat, trade, or sell.
7. Solar greenhouses may increase food production 5 times over open field production. Greenhouses may use semi-hydroponic methods such as the Mittlieder method. Some systems have realized 10 times increases over open field production.
8. Solar cells – photovoltaic: provide electricity for house and for electric vehicle energy for short-range trips –and provide a surplus that can be sold back to the electric company. Array is placed in part over house and garage roof, and driveway. Yield: 27,000 KWh of electricity per year.

Solar cells are currently too expensive to be practical for ZCL but are included because they may become economically practical within a few years.

9. Solar space heat is only useful in the winter, spring, and fall which reduces the useful solar gain. (Some solar energy systems store summer solar heat for winter use but the method was not used here because these systems require massive heat storage capabilities).

Solar space heat consists of: 'passive systems' for house direct gain and 'active systems' with thermal mass storage to store excess heat gain on sunny winter days for use on cloudy days.

The system would be located on the south side roof, walls, and attached lean to structures (such as a porch) of the house

10. Algae pond yields 184 gallons of biofuel for long range vehicle trips. Algae ponds are not yet practical technology but are included here to show what may be possible.

Another type of pond - for fish production may be practical but is not considered here. See work of the '**New Alchemy Institute**' in their books and online. As an alternative to an algae pond an alcohol distillery might produce vehicle fuel - as described more below.

11. Located on the south side of the house on roof slope or as lean-to adjacent to house. A solar water heater can make extremely efficient use of the sun because it provides useful energy all year round whenever the sun shines – thus the 40% efficiency.

12. This area consisting of the north facing slopes of buildings does not provide any solar gain.

13. A half-acre is 21,780 square feet. The total shown can be more because solar cell arrays can be placed in part over buildings, driveways, porches, decks, and walkways.

14. Food total consists of garden, bean field, grain field, and greenhouse production added together providing about 4,400 pounds of food for 4 people plus 10,000 to 20,000 pounds of food (approximately) to sell or trade.

A source of vehicle fuel, in place of the algae pond listed above could be a distillery producing alcohol fuel. Note: if corn is the feedstock for the distillery and 200 gallons of vehicle fuel are needed per year – about 2/3 acres of land would be required - so the solar farm would have to be larger, or the corn bought off site. Some distillery feedstock could be obtained from the ½ acre solar farm. Refer to the following book for details:

David Blume in his book ***Alcohol Can be a Gas*** proposes a 'Micro Distillery Model Farm' in Chapter 12. He proposes integrating a host of material/energy flows in a 'permaculture system' centered on alcohol production in a distillery. He writes "alcohol production should be part of an overall diversified farm design." His farm produces - to sell: alcohol, mushrooms, worm castings (as fertilizer), live fish, fish emulsions, and greenhouse organic vegetables. The farm integrates sunlight, water, carbon dioxide, nitrogen from the air, woodlot, wood, wood ash, cornfield, distillery/fermenter, methane bio-digester, and spirulina algae.

Blume writes that 3 standard 30 x 100 greenhouses with 7,200 square feet of useable space can grow 3 pounds of produce per square foot per plant cycle, grow 3 cycles per year or 9 pounds total per square foot per year = 65,000 pounds total selling for $2 to $4 per pound (the value of organically grown crops) possibly realizing $120,000 to $240,000 per year.

Blume states that the Archer Daniels Midland research Greenhouse in Decatur Illinois grows 10 crops of lettuce per year.

Most of the book discusses converting and running your car on homemade or co-operatively made alcohol. Get and read this huge, complex and fascinating book for a cornucopia of methods and ideas applicable to ZCL.

Blume references other books applicable to a ZCL Solar Farm:

Solviva 'How to Grow $$500,000 on One Acre and Peace on Earth' by Anna Edey (Trailblazer Press 1998). In New England she made $180,000 in 8 months producing salad alone.

MetroFarm: The Guide to Growing for Big Profit on a Small Parcel of Land by Michael Olson (TS Books 1994). The book describes how the author grows an organic salad mix on a city lot in Berkley California making hundreds of thousands of dollars per year.

6.6 SHELTER:

ZCL house design and building is worth another book. Here I will summarize and go into some details on house design that can minimize construction and living costs.

Most folks buy houses or have houses built that are totally unsuitable for achieving ZCL. They have thin 2x 6 or even 2x 4 walls; many, even most window on the north, east, and west sides of the house, and no un-shaded south facing roof or walls that can be modified to make use of solar energy. Sadly, most recently built houses are built for show and are commonly called 'trophy houses', meant to show off your opulence to your neighbors. They have expensive 'just for show' cosmetic and styling features such as elaborate entryways and front halls, soaring two story ceilings, and sprawling layouts.

If you must have a 'trophy house', locate and design it so improvements making the house suitable for ZCL can be made should your circumstances change. I discuss this idea a little more on page 250 & 251.

If you plan to buy a house rather than build, look carefully for a house that can be modified to be suitable for ZCL. For example: look for a large backyard facing south that gets plenty of sun in winter. More on this below.

General layout of house and yard:

In a cool or cold climate, best would be to have the back yard on the south side of the house, with the south wall of the house receiving good sunlight in winter, so you have places for solar panels, attached solar greenhouse, and a solar water heater.

The old extended family living on one site was a great idea appropriate to ZCL, perhaps not all officially related. Society today pulls people apart. It atomizes and divides families, parents, children, siblings, partners, and friends because jobs, schools and recreations are spread all over the landscape. An extended family household might help people get back together again.

Idea: design your house to make it easy to add a separate apartment in the building at a later date. "Mother in law" apartments were common in old houses; whether for relatives or to rent for income. Second floor or basement apartments were very common in old inner city neighborhoods. Try to provide for a separate entrance, kitchen and bath in your design. Zoning ordinances may prohibit a separate apartment in suburbs and trophy home subdivisions. Possibly, hide it and don't tell the authorities. If you rent out the apartment, look for good tenants, assess them carefully.

An important design problem is: a large house is wanted for all of the spaces useful for ZCL, but a small house is wanted for energy efficiency, low cost, and low taxes. To deal with this problem, a good solution is to build extensive unheated spaces for low cost storage and other spaces that are occasionally heated for workrooms – heated only when used. Consider even a barn-like house. Build: a useful attic space (by not using trusses), a raised walk out basement, attached unheated storage sheds, floor-to-ceiling shelves and an oversize 2-story garage. The Old Dutch and German houses were and are huge - combining many functions. Old New England farms combined most of their buildings into one huge rambling collection of attached buildings so folks need not go outside in winter to do chores. Danger of fire, perhaps militated against this idea being used elsewhere.

House design:

General size, shape, and layout:

The core of the house should be compact and simply shaped. Easy to design equals easy to build. Design a simple rectangular exterior shape with shed roof or gable (two sheds back to back). Keep roof pitch shallow: 6/12 or less to be easy to walk on, put roofing on, and repair

However, keep in mind a smaller house may end up costing more to live in, just as a smaller boat might (as Annie Hill explains in her book) because it may not have room for the facilities and spaces needed to maintain a comfortable ZCL lifestyle.

To keep the house simple in shape and compact, but with adequate square footage: Have a raised basement and a useable attic and therefore don't use trusses. Thus you have a 3-story house. This saves on the most expensive components, roof and foundation, which are minimized relative to floor area. A raised basement makes the basement space useful as living space because large windows can be placed into the basement walls. You can design the house to appear like a 1 story house as Jefferson did when he designed the Monticello, with the upper floor incorporated into roof lines and the raised basement partly hidden by earth berms and vegetation.

A good house layout for ZCL would be 28 x 40 foot rectangle on three floors, with the lower and upper floors initially unfinished and therefore not counted as part of the living space for property tax purposes. Possibly, style the house to suggest an old colonial house or even a barn. Aim for practicality, comfort, simplicity, ease of maintenance and construction, not appearance.

Illustration # 12 below shows a practical house design suitable for ZCL.

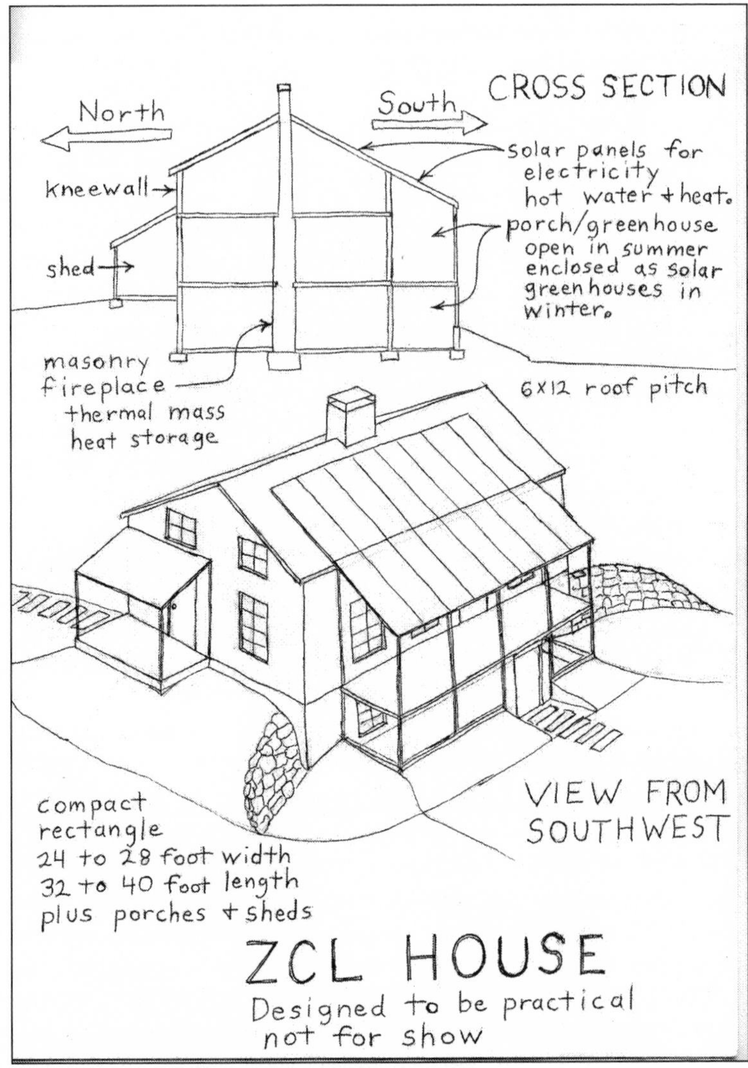

ILLUSTRATION # 12: ZCL HOUSE

Use Solar Energy: Make use of solar energy whenever possible. Dozens of good books exist on this topic so I won't repeat what they say here:

Examples of solar books: They all include some discussion of natural cooling.

***Natural Solar Architecture:* A Passive Primer** by David Wright, 1978

The Passive Solar Energy Book by Edward Mazria, Rodale Press 1979

The Passive Solar House by James Kachadonian, Chelsea Green Publishing 2006.

A solar home with attached or integral (built in) greenhouses has advantages: Near zero heating bills, places to grow fresh pesticide free food, warm outdoor-like spaces to visit in winter.

Solar heat is not effective on cloudy days so thermal mass is needed to store excess solar energy on sunny days for use on cloudy days. A backup heating source is needed if the thermal mass cools down too much, perhaps after an extended period of cloudy days. For ZCL a good method of back up heat would be an efficient wood-burning stove burning foraged scrap wood and downed timber. Good choices for a stove: Ianto Evan's rocket stove or one of the many types of masonry stoves developed in Eastern Europe. More in this below under 'Utilities'.

Design the house around the thermal mass of a fireplace/furnace in cold climates. Design the house around natural cooling systems such as a cooling tower in warm climates.

Floor plan:

Design to make possible multiple uses of rooms and make possible changes in room use.

Main floor: 1 bedroom, bath, kitchen-dining room (country kitchen), living room.

Upper floor: two bedrooms, study or extra bedroom, bath, storage

Basement: raised, with large windows: library, workshop, storage, half-bath (no bath tub, sink and W.C. only), utility room with furnace, water heater, washer, washtub, circuit breaker box.

Large basement windows add air and ventilation, and provide direct access to the outside. Place most of these windows along the south side of the house to gain solar energy for heat. Make insulated shutters to close over these windows at night or on cloudy days.

Keep the interior simple and plain minimizing wall area.

Linen closet with shelves may cost $500 if a carpenter does it. Get a cabinet from a garage sale and put it in the space, or shelve it yourself from scrap or foraged lumber.

Make the walls of rooms all useable for storage by obtaining or building moveable furniture – so you can move it to get to the storage.

Build Dutch closet beds: beds in enclosed nooks with curtains across the access opening. I call them 'Scrooge beds' as in "***A Christmas Carol***". They keep a sleeper warm without layers of blankets by trapping body heat within the nook - in a house that cools down at night.

Have lots of nooks alcoves, and hideaway corners: Examples: sleeping nook, pantry, dining alcove. Use curtains, not doors over some of these spaces. Another example: the English 'Inglenook' a semi enclosed space in a kitchen/living room adjacent to a large fireplace, that keeps folks warm without having to sit close to the fire.

Converse of this concept: design large multipurpose spaces. Example: the Japanese traditional style of house, which has moveable panels, shoji screens or curtains to divide or combine rooms as needed.

Build steps with a landing at the halfway tread for safety in case of a fall. Note: going up and down steps is good exercise

Build a kitchen, pantry and food processing area with adequate space for a yogurt maker, kefir maker, seed sprouter, food dryer, mushroom grower, seedling trays and lights. The country kitchens of old farmhouses provided space for these activities.

House construction details:

A house doesn't move, and is therefore simpler than a car, probably 10 times simpler having 1/10 as many parts, (not counting individual nails). Building a house is within the skills of most folks, I believe.

Foundation:

Consider a post or pier foundation rather than a basement. It is much cheaper.

Or, have a raised basement - making basement space more useful.

Frame:

Houses of frame lumber can be built by hand with the proper methods and tools by one person with an occasional helper. The book ***Working Alone*** by John Carroll explains how.

The lowest cost, fastest to build house method is to use plywood sheets and 2 x 4 or 2 x 6 framing on 2 foot centers.

Keep spans for joists and rafters short: 12 or 14 foot long joists and 16 foot rafters are smaller, cheaper, lighter, and easier to handle than longer lumber.

Build your house frame based on a modular frame of 2-foot centers (space between studs, joists, and rafters).

Build 2x6 walls or double 2 x 4 walls; which will be 10 or 12 inches thick with a 4 inch gap between the double walls – to allow thick wall insulation.

Roof:

Build a basic gable roof

Use ridge pole and rafters rather than trusses to allow useable attic space for storage or as space that can be finished and lived in later.

Design a 6/12 pitch or less for ease in walking on during construction and ease of repair.

Siding:

T111 siding, or plywood with battens siding are the cheapest, fastest to build and simplest siding because sheathing and siding are combined in one material.

Insulation:

At least 6 inch thick walls, even 12 inch walls to allow more insulation are not that much more expensive. You can build a double 2 x 4 walls with a space between, all filled with insulation. The outside envelope needs to be well sealed against air infiltration through cracks. Vapor barriers are needed on the inside face of insulation, adjacent to the drywall of the heated space.

Metal Brackets:

Wind and earthquake safe design can be cheap and easy by using metal brackets. Use them for strength, especially at the rafter-to-wall joint.

Materials:

Use basic natural materials salvaged, foraged and recycled wherever possible. A lot of stuff is out there, often free or low cost: doors, windows, cabinets, etc.

Get materials from houses being torn down. The TV show 'Extreme Makeover' always disturbs me. In the process of house wrecking they destroy quantities of good materials. But taking apart a house by hand to save the materials can be extremely labor intensive. Efficient methods to take apart an old house but save the materials are needed.

Look for a **Habitat for Humanity** store in your area as a possible source of materials. Prices are low. Buying there benefits the charity, and yourself.

Accessory facilities:

The barns of the old farms dwarfed the houses. Today, a house designed for ZCL may need extensive facilities that almost envelope the house: solar cell arrays, greenhouses, solar water heater, tool sheds, repair garage, food processing facilities, ponds or cistern, storage spaces, sewing room, computer room, home office.

Build an attached greenhouse built so it can also serve as a summer porch by designing framed glass panels that can be removed or opened in warm weather.

And another solution to needed accessory facilities is the ubiquitous shed. Old farms, you may have noticed, have lots of sheds.

Workshop: It is essential to have one on your site.

Projects to do in your workshop: building greenhouse components, repair and recycling of items, car building and repair. To have a workshop, you want to locate in a neighborhood where there won't be complaints or zoning problems, or put your workshop in a secluded place where it won't be noticed. Tools might be mostly hand tools. Put your workshop adjacent or attached to your garage so the garage may serve as a large work space when the car is pulled out.

Garage: If you have a car, have auto repair facilities and a heating system in your garage, or means of cooling it in hot climates. Idea: If your garage door faces south, have a solar garage door: with translucent (but not see-through) panels that let the sun in. Build an overhang above the door to keep the high summer sun out.

Storage: You need lots of it to live ZCL.

In the attic: dry but cold - clothes, toys, tools, supplies, small appliances, boxes, camping travel sports furniture, books

In the basement: damp, warmer - lumber, firewood, bags, garden pots, bottles, cans, jugs, metal scraps, plastic containers

In sheds: fuels, batteries, bikes, garden and yard care tools, potting soil.

In the garage: car repair tools

Create various storage spaces indoor and out - covered and not for various foraged and stockpiled stuff

Outside under cover: Lumber, firewood

Outside in the open but concealed or neatly kept: blocks, bricks, stone, gravel.

Greenhouse: See chapter 5 for a discussion of greenhouses. Here from a chapter 6 'comfortable living' perspective are some more details:

Idea: create a computer operated solar greenhouse. A 'solar hydroponic greenhouse' of 14 ft. x 20 ft. can gross $8,000 /year, earning almost $30 per square foot - and cost only $2,000 to setup. The booklet ***Home Hydroponic System*** by John Duckworth explains how.

Possible greenhouse heating system: a rocket stove burning scrap lumber and logs. (A wood shed or covered storage is needed to keep the wood dry). Build heavily insulated mud plastered straw bales on three sides of the greenhouse. Use plastic or plexiglas with insulated shutters on the south side.

Build an insulated floor using cheap insulation such as layers of waste plastic. Build a shallow frost proof foundation for the greenhouse to save $. Modern building codes such as the Michigan Residential Code based on the International Residential Code describe this type of foundation. Use inexpensive treated 8 ft. landscape timbers as posts that the greenhouse roof frame and rafters to rest on.

Ideas to minimize homestead insurance, mortgage costs and taxes:

House insurance:

Build an "everything proof" house. Or, "everything proof" your current house. Don't have any house insurance.

Injury lawsuits: If you take reasonable care of your property: that is - keep it safe; you should be safe from lawsuits over personal injury that occurs on your property (which is the big selling pitch of the insurance industry). To be everything proof you must consider location, design, and construction methods to guard against a host of dangers: fire, flood, wind, earthquake, people falling, toxic materials, etcetera And there is always something no one ever thought of before. You may think you need insurance for such things, but insurance companies are likely to have a clause in your contract so they don't have to pay out on unanticipated losses.

And during the construction process you must assure safety: no boards with nails sticking up anywhere, no use of toxic materials, no unguarded holes children or pets could to fall into - and much, much more.

Methods to achieve a house you may consider not insuring: Ianto Evans style cob house of mud and straw but larger and more elaborate. And/or build a straw bale house: straw bales sealed in clay coating are unburnable: far safer than a wood frame and drywall house. Floors may be of compacted puddled clay - softer that concrete, dirt cheap. Roof of metal: steel with a steel frame. Roof tied to the walls with metal brackets for strength against wind, tornados, hurricanes. Rocket stove heating system built of stone and clay - nothing to burn or catch fire and chimney exhaust temperature so low it won't burn your hand (the heat of the fire is almost all absorbed by the thermal mass of the chimney walls. You must build where there are no floods, and assure good drainage around the foundation. And, build where earthquakes are weak or nonexistent. You may be able to live in more risky areas if you reinforce the walls with rebar or bamboo 'pins'.

Use GFI (ground fault interrupter) protected electrical circuits throughout the house. Use no natural gas or propane in the house – thus avoiding gas leaks, asphyxiation, and fire dangers.

Keep the interior of the house uncluttered and simple and be careful to have no protruding hard or pointy furniture or fixtures. Have furniture with rounded corners, made of soft and giving materials. No glass tables or glass cabinet door faces. Build the walls and floors of soft and giving materials to prevent injury from a fall. Bare concrete walls and floors are not recommended for this reason. Keep down the use of curtains, fabric furniture, rugs etcetera that may easily catch fire. Store flammable items and materials, books, extra clothes and bedding, newspapers for recycling, etc. outside of the living space. Store gasoline and similar substances in a separate shed well away from the house. Keep your yard free of hazards: sharp objects hard surfaces, holes that could trip people, boards with nails.

Possibly buy or make soft items - upholstered furniture, pillows, bedding, clothing, curtains, and rugs, of treated fireproof or fire resistant materials.

Do these things and you may be able to forget about house insurance. (But if you try this idea, and get sued or lose your house don't come to me. See disclaimer at the beginning of the book).

Inside air quality can be low due to cooking, cleaning agents, out-gassing of building materials such as plywood and paints. Therefore to assure clean air for health: provide adequate ventilation to your home - possibly using an air-to-air heat exchanger that brings in clean outside air while recapturing the heat in outgoing warm air.

It is possible to get carried away with this as you can see. But a little thought and caution can cut your dangers way down with little expense or effort.

Mortgage:

To live comfortably ZC or LC you want to own your own house free and clear, that is - with no mortgage. A mortgage and the interest you must pay on it can eat your money and a huge chunk of your time in the form of the work you must do to earn that money.

Methods to eliminate the mortgage: Sell your current house and buy a smaller cheaper one that you can buy mortgage free with the equity already built up in your current home. Or, get a home equity loan on your current home and use the money to buy materials and support you while you build another house. Then sell your current house - using the equity you have in it to pay off the mortgage and the home equity loan. That is what I did.

Note - economic events overtook this book as I was writing it. Today, millions of people have mortgages on their homes that are larger than the market prices they can get for their homes, another words, negative equity. Discussion of this topic from a ZCL perspective will have to wait for a future edition of this book. Now, consider perhaps walking away from the millstone around your neck and if possible buy one of the myriads of smaller cheaper houses that are currently widely available on the market at a discount – where you can start building some real equity.

Property taxes: on your house: To paraphrase the ancient saying - death and taxes are the only certainties in life. Because it's not in government's interest to take poor, low income often retired people's houses for taxes thus turning independent people into dependents, some tax relief has been written into law. Nevertheless under Michigan property tax law - for example - about the lowest tax you can expect to pay after refund of part is about $800 a year. To live without having to work for money to cover this expense you would have to have $16,000 invested at a 5% return after inflation (about 7% to 8% before inflation).

More on property taxes:

Buy or best, build a modest house and you may keep your property taxes down, plus your income may be low enough that states with a progressive tax system may refund some of the $ you pay in property tax. In Michigan the refund is a maximum of $1200.

To keep your property tax appraisal down, keep down the ostentation, things done for show. If you are going to sell and move then make cosmetic improvements but otherwise keep down your taxes by keeping the building inexpensive. That doesn't mean uncomfortable or shabby.

Government cost: As a long-term way to keep down your property taxes, you can work to hold down the cost of government. Participate in government. Encourage economies. Government could practice many ZCL methods such as zero energy use buildings, using efficient vehicles, etc.

6.7 CONVERTING YOUR HOUSE AND LOT TO ZCL:

Millions of people bought homes unwisely, hoping to make money by the appreciation in value of their homes - rather than doing anything useful. A lot of folks have lost or will loose their homes. If it looks like you are going to be able to keep your home consider converting it to a ZCL style homestead.

You may have a huge hurdle, a big mortgage and no way to get that monkey off your back and probably an oversize house on which you pay high property taxes. Possibly you could sell and move to a smaller house.

In the suburbs you may have an advantage; a big lot with unused space (used for grass and landscaping). You have room to create gardens and greenhouses. You may have to fight or ignore city hall and neighbors to put in full height greenhouses, but may be able to put in hatch or pit style greenhouses that have a low profile, without objection.

Then, give up restaurants and learn to prepare your own home-grown food.

In large 2 and 3 car garages you can set up auto repair equipment. Of course you'll have to learn how to fix your own and certainly get a car that is easy to fix and cheap to run. (Sadly these may be in short supply soon).

And stop buying imported junk and start buying stuff that can be used to make and process other stuff.

Folks living in the city should see the work of the Farralones Institute where on an absurdly small lot they accomplish wonders. And as mentioned earlier, John Duckworth's 24 x 14 hydroponic greenhouse costing $2,000 to set up can produce $8,000 of produce. Most folks could fit a few of these on even the smallest lot, perhaps as a house or garage addition to avoid stupid laws limiting the size of free standing structures. Or set up a system in an unused room of your trophy house.

Discover the south side of your house - whether there's any sunlight there and retrofit solar energy using structures: greenhouse, panels to heat living space, water heaters, and photovoltaic solar panels that create electricity. And throw in a solar cooker to use in place of that gas grill.

Cover windows with insulated shutters at night to save more heat.

In your over-large house, shut off rooms, heat only part, and use those unheated rooms to store stuff that can be recycled or used for future projects: scrap lumber, tools, fertilizer, etc.

Build or convert your fireplace to a masonry heat-storing fireplace as described in the book: ***Finnish Fireplace: Heart of the Home*** by A Barden and H. Hyytiainen.

These are just a few examples. Dozens of techniques described in this book might be applied to converting a conventional house or trophy house to ZCL.

In the future maybe, banks will loan mortgages - not for houses meant to impress the neighbors and display affluence, or houses stuffed with useless luxuries; but for complete operational solar farms that produce food, energy, fuel, and materials on the site – solar farms that generate more than enough cash flow to cover the cost of the mortgage and provide the owner with a comfortable if not affluent living – in health, safety, security, and solvency regardless of the performance of the larger economy.

When millions of productive, real-wealth-creating solar farms replace the wasteful, wealth destroying trophy house subdivisions, then perhaps the mortgage, financial, and economic meltdown of the current era will permanently become just an unpleasant memory.

In the future maybe, the value of a home will be determined not by the square footage, number of rooms, architectural ostentation, and neighborhood real estate prices, but on the quality, completeness, efficiency and productivity of the solar energy systems on the property.

6.8 UTILITIES:

In this subchapter I will cover cooling, heat, thermal mass, electricity and photovoltaic systems, light, refrigeration, solar cooker, washing and drying clothes, sewer, water, garbage, waste materials, phone and Internet

Cooling:

Build a house that can make use of natural cooling methods, or modify your house to be naturally cooled to eliminate or at least reduce air conditioning costs. Comfortable, naturally cooled houses - without air conditioning - have been built in South Florida. One example may be found in the architectural magazine ***Dwell***, June 2001 page 64 article entitled '***Miami Murder Mystery***?' by John Lantigua. Natural cooling methods include: shading of windows with awnings and/or trees, large casement style windows to catch breezes; house up in the air to catch breezes and let air flow underneath, and large well ventilated attics. Another method: vertical ventilation of living spaces with fans and/or cooling towers or courtyards that exhaust air and heat upwards, above the house, pull air from the sides, and create a cooling air flow inside.

Heat:

Wood can be the cheapest and method for heating your home – a lot of wood can be foraged for free in the form of pallets, downed and dead trees, demolished houses, etc. Heating with wood, however, can be a tedious, time-consuming chore that can become 'hard thrift' as I described in chapter 2.

Therefore, to reduce the chore and time requirements of heating your house with wood: design a system so you have to start a fire and burn wood only every other day – through the use of plenty of thermal mass - and design the house around it. Have thermal mass in the form of a massive masonry wood-burning furnace in the center of the house - as is done in traditional homes in Scandinavia, Eastern Europe and Russia. These systems are expensive, but worthwhile – by freeing you from the tyranny of perpetually maintaining a wood fire in the winter. The book ***Finnish Fireplace; Heart of the Home*** by A Barden and H. Hyytiainen, (Finnish Building Center 1993) is one source.

As an alternative, at lower cost, even very low cost, design your house around a 'rocket stove' that uses earth as the thermal mass. Ianto Evans in his pamphlet ***Rocket Stoves to Heat Cob***

Buildings describes how, for very small houses. For larger houses you will have to scale up his system. Realize this however. Evans book does not describe a system sized for a conventionally sized house. You are entering uncharted territory.

Thermal mass:

Here are the thermal mass requirements for a system requiring a fire only every other day:

Thermal mass storage capacity needed for 2 days - 500,000 Btu per day are needed to keep the house comfortable (20,000 Btu per hour) or 1,000,000 Btu for two days. Estimate for a well insulated house on an average winter day 30 f day, 20 f night with basement walls and floor insulated on the outside and underneath.

Calculations: (skip this if you are overwhelmed, but is only simple multiplication). Temperature difference between house and thermal mass: 20 degrees, heat storage per cubic foot 22 Btu per cubic foot times 20 degrees or 440 Btu per cubic foot x 2,500 cubic feet of area in thermal mass as concrete, stone, brick, about the area of a masonry fireplace in the center of house plus the basement walls and floors.

Formula: c x t x a = heat storage capacity

c = Btu heat capacity of concrete/stones per degree per cubic foot of material = 22

t = temperature difference of thermal mass heated or charged, and discharged.

85f to 65f = 20 degrees f.

a= area of thermal mass = 1,000 cubic ft basement walls, 500 c.f. floor, 1,000 c.f. masonry fireplace or other internal basement walls of concrete, brick or stone or 2,500 cubic feet total.

solution=: 22 x 20 = 440 x 2500 = 1,100,000 Btu.- enough for two days.

Electricity: and alternatives to electricity.

Our ancestors lived with-out it. Living without it is almost inconceivable today. The Amish still do it.

Photovoltaic Systems: producing electricity from the sun.

These systems are expensive but cheaper than a few years ago and coming down in price. A 4 kilowatt photovoltaic system could generate about 5,000 kilowatt-hours (kWh) in the Midwest U.S., about half of annual need for an average house. If electricity is bought from a utility company at 12 cents per kWh, 5,000 kWh is worth $600. A 4 kilowatt system currently would cost about $36,000 before tax credits and $32,000 after. Worldwatch reports prices may decline by 50% by 2010. A system costing $16,000 and saving $600 a year has a simple return on investment (not counting the cost to borrow money or the interest the money could earn if invested) of $16,000/$600 = 3.8%. Over a 40 year life of the system producing 5,000 kWh per year x 40 years = 200,000 kWh total. The cost per kWh equals 200,000/16,000 = 12.5 cents, almost equivalent to the utility company price. These numbers are derived from the article '***Solar Energy:* Why it's better than ever'** by Scott Gibson in ***Mother Earth News*** August/Sept. 2008. Dozens of books and web sites exist on these systems, including homemade versions. Discussion of Photovoltaic systems could easily take over this entire book. I'll leave more research up to you.

Light:

Light bulbs: In the average home, the electric light bill is 10% of the total electric bill. .Fluorescent bulbs use 20% of the energy required for incandescent bulbs and last years longer. Problem: mercury (in a small amount but any amount is unhealthy) is necessary in fluorescent bulbs. If broken they can contaminate your house. Better, perhaps to use numerous small task oriented conventional bulbs, or go to the new LED 'light emitting diode' bulbs that use no mercury.

No electric lights: One option, get up with the sun and go to bed at sundown. Have a **'reading window'**; a Chinese idea, a window on the north side of the house (like old drafting and art studios) where the light intensity is best for reading. Reading beside it is absolutely zero cost. Don't make the window large. Install an insulated shutter to be closed over the window at night in winter.

Refrigeration:

Efficient refrigerator: A chest style refrigerator is more efficient because the door is on top, so the cold air inside doesn't drop out on the floor every time it is opened. Chest type refrigerators are made by Sundanzer available at Real Goods. Summit Appliances sells chest type refrigerators from their web site. Sun Frost makes side door refrigerators that are 5 times more efficient than conventional types by using thicker insulation, smaller compressor, and improved defrost methods - also available from their web site. These appliances are expensive, but over their service lives save a lot of electricity and money justifying their cost. An inexpensive chest type freezer may be modified to serve as a refrigerator by using a thermostat timer – normally used to make a freezer serve as a beer cooler.

You can reduce the operating cost of your refrigerator or freezer when it's cold outside. Bring that cold into your refrigerator. Low tech method: set out water in containers that won't break when it water freezes such as plastic milk jugs. Bring those in and put them in your freezer and refrigerator if it is not too full. But don't over-fill your freezer or refrigerator, as air must circulate inside to work efficiently. In summer put jugs of cold water from a well in the refrigerator.

Living without a refrigerator/freezer is discussed in more detail in chapter 5 on homesteading. Here are a few more ideas:

Old time methods:

Ice box: was an insulated wood cabinet like a small refrigerator. Inside were four shelves: two upper two lower. A block of ice was placed on the upper right or left shelf. The ice melted to a tray in the bottom. Ice was replaced every three or 4 days.

Ice room: Heavily insulated room set in the ground (originally sawdust between wooden frames) opened in winter - closed up in summer. Water in tubs in the bottom freezes in winter when vents are opened - stays as ice until next winter thanks to the insulation.

Modern adaptations of these might be possible saving much of the electricity used by a conventional refrigerator. Devices to keep the temperature more constant such as temperature activated switches opening or closing vents to the outside depending on outside temperature could be used.

Create a cool (literally) pantry using temperature control devices - temperature activated vents to the outside that bring outside air into the pantry in cool weather.

Solar Cooker:

Possibly place a solar cooker in a solar greenhouse adjacent to your kitchen. On a sunny day most dishes could be cooked in a solar cooker at virtually zero cost. A solar cooker could be made of scrap materials, even a cardboard box insulated and using aluminum foil to reflect heat into the box. Solar cookers of many different designs may be bought at the website of the store Real Goods. See ***www.realgoods.com***. Real Goods sells a host of other alterative energy devices: solar water heaters, refrigerators, photovoltaic systems, etc.

Hot Water:

Warming tank: Water out of a well or city pipes is cold. Pipe it to a tank where it can warm up to room temperature before going to the water heater tank thus reducing energy use. Instead of heating 45-degree water to 120 degrees, the water heater need heat only 70-degree water.

Solar water heater: A further step, besides a warming tank is called the batch type solar water heater. It is the cheapest and simplest type of solar water heater. Simply, before entering your hot water heater, well or city water is piped into a black painted tank set in an insulated box adjacent to the south side of your house. The box face facing south is covered with glass. At night and in cloudy weather an insulated shutter is closed over the glass. Real Goods sells batch water heaters. Or, a web search will turn up a number of plans for homemade versions.

Demand type of water heater: Here, you have no tank full of water loosing heat and energy. Only when water flows is it heated. Initial cost is twice that of a tank type of water heater. You save 20% a year so it pays for itself in 5 years perhaps.

Micro savings: In winter don't drain bath water and dishwashing water until it cools down so heat and moisture are given up to the house.

Clothes washing:

Washing machine: Used washing machines, sometimes needing repair may be bought cheaply. Buy models that are relatively easy to repair by the owner such as Whirlpool, Kenmore, and Roper (which are brands of whirlpool).

Clothes dryer: A clothes line or drying rack (or a tree branch) is as old as clothes and still effective, and causes less wear on clothes than a dryer. The tumbling action of a dryer wears clothes out. In winter, clothes dry quickly on a line or rack in an out of the way space in the heated part of your house, because winter air even in a house may be quite dry. If you have one, dry clothes in an attached solar greenhouse.

Sewer, Water, Garbage, Waste materials.

Don't locate where you must pay for city sewer and water. Have a well and septic tank system to save utility bills: Build a septic tank system that can be converted to a biogas facility at a later date. This may only require an extra capped pipe into the septic tank.

Biogas containing methane, (natural gas) is produced by bacteria as it decomposes or 'digests' plant and animal (human) waste in a tank: in this case your septic tank The gas rises to the top of the digester tank and may be collected in another tank above the digester tank for use as fuel. In China some farms use this fuel for cooking. The left over digested material is an excellent fertilizer.

As an alternative for a septic system, consider the rarely used, but once universal and environmentally friendly (if built correctly) composting toilet. See the book ***Goodbye to the Flush* Toilet** by Carol Hupping Stoner and ***The Humanure Handbook*** by Joseph Jenkins. A composting toilet system can be extremely cheap to build and work well, fitting in with ZCL goals. Sadly, local ordinances may prohibit them in most places, so you may have to put in a conventional system and install a composting system 'on the side', perhaps even surreptitiously. Or, you could try getting the government to change the laws.

Human waste really ought to be given back to the land (after composting to kill pathogens) - a common practice in Asia.

Food wastes from the kitchen should be added to a composting system or biogas facility to produce fertilizer for garden use.

Many other kinds of wastes can serve as garden mulch: shredded newspaper, grass clippings, leaves as describe in chapter 5 on homesteading.

Phone and the Internet:

Having no phone can save $500 a year, quite a chunk of change from a ZCL perspective. Attempting comfortable living you may insist on a phone (my wife does).

Ways to save: If you must have a phone, and have internet service to your home, get VIOP (voice over internet phone) service for around $300 a year. (But, it requires DSL or cable connection, which will cost you more and wipe out your savings).

Set up or join a shared phone system if you live in co-op housing, a co-housing community, or some apartments - to save on phone bills.

See chapter 5 if you haven't read it for internet access without the $120 or more cost for an internet service provider by using a library computer and 'burning' CD/DVDs as needed at the library to take home - or get a 'flash memory stick' that plugs into your USB port.

6.9 MISCELLANEOUS

Contents: I will consider these diverse categories here: clothes, kitchen, bath and cleaning, household, yard and garden, media and 'Last Penny Items'.

This chapter repeats chapter 5 except I will expand on chapter 5 a little. Here I aim for greater comfort, less emphasis on survival.

Okay, assuming you've got all of the other costs of living under control, now consider miscellaneous expenses. These are possibly the most difficult to eliminate living ZC because there are so many diverse items. Each expense is small but they rapidly add up and like taxes seem never to go away.

Extraordinary lengths may be required to eliminate every miscellaneous expense. There are a myriad of "little" expenses and a myriad of methods to deal with them. All together, these tasks can become formidable.

Some processes and methods may not be worth the time and trouble. You may find it easier to build up savings or investments to provide $ from interest or dividends to cover these costs.

Clothes:

Learn to sew and buy cloth rather than finished clothes. Look for sources of used clothes: garage sales, flea markets, salvation army, recycling centers.

You can often find barely worn good quality used clothes that are better than cheap new clothes and a fraction of the cost. You'll have to get used to wearing clothes other people may have worn. It may feel funny at first. Wash them twice and hang them outdoors to dry.

Socks: 30 pairs of socks are used per person per year or 120 pairs for a family of four, a lot of socks to buy; too many to hand knit. Idea: Needed are materials and patterns to make socks out of cloth that is folded and sewed - possibly a pattern for 'tube socks'. Maybe a special cloth 'sock cloth' (not sack cloth) needs to be invented. How can socks be made to last? One method: go barefoot, feet don't wear out. Go barefoot indoors at least to save sock wear.

No Socks: Wear sandals or shoes without socks. Sandal and no socks are common and practical in warm climates. In cold climates make moccasins to wear under boots. Moccasins last much longer than socks. Moccasins last longest if never worn in direct contact with the ground. For year round use outdoors protect moccasins with shoes made of discarded tires – the moccasin serve as liners as described by Thomas Elpel in his book ***Participating in Nature***. These are, Elpel asserts, the most comfortable, long lasting, versatile hiking footwear you can have. Elpel also describes making socks out of felt in the book.

Kitchen, bath and cleaning:

Soap: Does soap help? Washing your hands with soap and water reduces the risk of diarrhea by 45% and other severe intestinal infections by 50%.

Adding antibiotics to soap. This is a case of improving on perfection: only the result is the product is worse. They can charge more for the product but ordinary soap is just as effective against germs. "Over the years researchers have consistently found that antibacterial soaps are really no better than good old soap and water. At least five studies have confirmed this." From ***Never shower in a Thunderstorm*** by Anahad O'Connor 2007 by Times Books. She continues, "One of them published in the Journal of Community health in 2003, followed adults in 238 households for nearly a year, all of them in New York City, where levels of dirt and germs are legendary. Month after month the researchers found no difference in the number of microbes that turned up on the hands of people who use either antibacterial soap or regular soap. Nor do sanitizing gels work any better than soap. Further, these soap additives might contribute to the emergence of resistant bacteria and the residue, washed down the sink might pollute the environment. The U.S. Food and Drug Administration is considering putting restrictions on their use and marketing.

Dandruff control: Fennel tea can be used as a dandruff shampoo - described in more detail on page 199.

Toothpaste: Make a paste of baking soda and salt followed by 3% hydrogen peroxide rinse – the rinse diluted with 50% water to 1 ½%.

Mouthwash: Use 1 teaspoon of salt in 4 ounces of water. This is as effective as purchased mouthwashes at killing germs and cleaning the mouth. Salt water is also useful as gargle, and nose drops.

Natural cleaning agents may be made from inexpensive basic materials:

Disinfectant cleaner for table tops, kitchen and bath counters, windows, etc - vinegar followed by 3% hydrogen peroxide. Use squirt bottles and a wash cloth to distribute.

Vinegar: you can make your own vinegar: ***The Vinegar Book*** by Emily Thacker (Tresco Publishers, 12th edition 1996) details how.

Wood ash lye: also called potash lye is a natural detergent, a true zero cost method for washing utensils, clothes, even your body if diluted. To make it, place ashes in a porous container. Then drip water through the ashes into another container below.

Household:

Batteries: Get toys and devices that do not require batteries: Get rechargeable batteries and a charger.

L.E.D. flashlight: sometimes called a Faraday light that works through the motion of the light in your hand or a crank. Cost $20. You must have $ to buy items like this, but money used to buy money saving equipment is, from a ZCL perspective a good investment.

Yard and Garden:

Garden seeds are an investment that returns many fold - always a justifiable ZCL expense. Seed packets may be bought for 10 cents (1/10 of the ordinary price) in January at many hardware and garden supply stores as they clear their inventory for new spring packets.

Media:

The internet is replete with free programs and information useful for ZCL.

Free music, games, movies, and programs of all sorts can be downloaded from the internet. Books and web sites exist that describe how. Or, make friends with computer geeks to learn how.

One path to free programs you can download is through a program called 'e-mule' obtainable from the web site of the same name.

You can set up a free web site at Yahoo.

You can download a free internet search engine called ***'monzilla firefox'*** from the web site of that name.

'***Linux***' can be downloaded free and used instead of Microsoft for your computer operating system saving you the cost of buying Microsoft products.

Magazines: Libraries subscribe to dozens, even hundreds of magazines you can read for free, and back issues may be checked out like books.

Last Penny Items:

Saving the last penny: As I said above, the time and effort needed to avoid spending money on these items, to squeeze out every expense; might not be worth the trouble. Instead of living comfortably, you may become trapped in an endless treadmill of tedious tasks, (the reason why few folks practice self-sufficient farming, I believe). It may be easier to save and invest money and use the interest, dividends or capital gains earned to pay for some of these items.

If you want to squeeze more expenditures out of your budget, here are zero cost alternatives for some of those 'last penny items'.

Hand and body soap and lotion: Use plants as sources such as soapwort - described in chapter 3.

Paper towels: use wash cloths instead, or make your own paper towels from free materials - by crumpling and thus softening newspaper or phone book pages, or any scrap paper. Used but still clean paper towels may be set on a small drying rack. Get extra napkins at fast food places. They always give you more than you need but most folks just throw the extras out. Save yours.

Cloth napkins and washcloths: make them from scraps of old clothes.

Toilet paper: Billions of people don't use, can't afford toilet paper. What do they do? And what did folks do before toilet paper. One method: The 'botna', used in India, looks like a teapot - but without a handle or lid. A small plastic or metal watering can would work. Thoroughly crumpled paper of any kind – to soften it - also works. Thin phone book paper, catalog paper, and newspaper work best. Someone needs to invent a device that quickly and automatically crumples discarded paper – ***voila!*** Free toilet paper for billions of people. Also advisable, a method to remove the ink without ruining the paper.

Water saving: Efficient water use is especially important in a dry climate: see the web site: ***frugal about .com*** for methods.

6.10 MOBILITY:

Contents: **page:**

Introduction:

This subchapter is a big part of this chapter because mobility can be a difficult problem if you are trying to live ZCL in comfort. A car is expensive, but living with no car may restrict your mobility. I will explore ways to minimize car expenses in the first part of this subchapter and alternatives to the car in the last part.

If you don't plan to have a car, or you have zero mechanical interest or aptitude you may want to skip the section on cars.

Automobiles make zero cost living difficult. Certainly don't buy a new or expensive used car. Payments and depreciation are huge traps that will eat your money.

With a car, if you think must have one, achieving zero cost living is possible only if you save and or invest many dollars and devote the income to the vehicle. Car economics are very bad from a ZCL perspective. Remember the discussion in chapter 5. A new car will cost you \$5,000 or \$10,000 per year or more for all costs - requiring perhaps \$100,000 to \$200,000 dollars invested and earning a 5% return per year after inflation. A used car may cost you \$2,000 per year - requiring \$40,000 invested at 5% per year after inflation - if you have a number of abilities including the ability to drive with efficiency, drive very safely, and do in a thorough manner your own maintenance and repair. It may cost you more, much more if you do not have these abilities. And, you must be able to obtain low insurance rates – usually possible only if you are older and have a good (or perfect) driving record.

Transportation is an intractable problem in most modern American Cities. They are overrun with cars. Fewer cars on the road would be a very good thing. If you must have one, to live low cost if not zero cost, you need a safe, easy to repair, high miles per gallon car. Can you buy such a car? No. Later in this chapter I'll discuss the possibility of building your own car.

Now, I will discuss the possibility of buying an old used car and modifying it at low cost to achieve these goals.

6.10.1 Bangernomics: Old used cars:

What is bangernomics? 'Banger' is a British term for an old car. Bangernomics means buying and operating an old car on the cheap. There is a web site ***www. bangernomics.com*** that goes into the idea in detail.

To practice bangernomics you buy vehicles that are easy to repair or have that reputation. Possible vehicles from the web site and from personal experience - cars that are easy to fix and designed to be simple:

Ford Model 'A'.

Ford Falcon (conceived and intended by Robert McNamara to be a 'simple car').

Early Ford Maverick (a re-skinned Falcon).

Ford Econoline Van 1963 170 cubic inch inline 6 engine.

Opel Kadett 1965.

Opel Rekord 1959.

Valiant mid 1960's 1964 170 CID 163 3 speed column shift.

Dodge Dart with 61c manual transmission.

Old Toyota Corolla.

Cheverolet Chevette diesel may be cheap to buy and operate, but is not very safe. Diesel engines may be difficult to repair - in part because of the very high toques used on bolts.

Chevrolet Chevette diesel discussion. You may be able to buy one for $500 to $1500 used. Convert it to run on biodiesel. You may obtain 55 miles-per-gallon if converted. Cost to convert: a few hundred dollars. Buy locally produced biodiesel or make your own. A web search will reveal numerous websites and books available that show how. To deal with the safety issue: reinforce the pillars and doors, replace the glass with polycarbonate plastic, and add a roll cage. Your annual costs to operate this vehicle may still be $2,000 per years unless you can repair it yourself and produce your own bio-diesel. Then, you may be able to reduce your cost to $1,500 per year or less.

If a car is not mechanically perfect but is easy to repair and service it is good choice for ZCL: Example from personal experience: Dodge (Mitsubishi) Colt vs. Oldsmobile Omega to replace the Alternator. For the Colt cost was $110 for the alternator and bolts were hard to remove. For the Omega: the alternator was only $30 and it was easy to remove and replace.

Insurance saving method: If you are not using your car on a daily basis, perhaps only monthly or on an occasional road trip – perhaps because it is a second car - put the insurance in suspension. Activate your insurance only when the car is going to be used.

Vehicles to avoid:

Front wheel drive complicates everything. CV joints, engine and transmission crammed into small inaccessible spaces that allow no room to work.

Vans can be a problem: all the engine and transmission components are crammed into the small front-end space - so they may be hard to access, especially with front wheel drive.

6.10.2 Car Maintenance and Repair:

Living low cost, you can expect to have a fully depreciated rusty ‘banger’. Driving around in an old car is like gambling. Anything could go wrong at any moment. Expect it and prepare for it. Expect to be stranded someday so carry the necessities. Carry appropriate stuff. Tools, warm clothes in cold weather, water in the desert, etc.

As described in chapter 5 under utilities, you can get a free cell phone that only dials 911 to carry for emergencies. Simply google “free cell phone” or “free emergency cell phone” to bring up a list of sources.

Car repair is a tough subject. As you may suspect, cars are generally not made to be easily repaired by the owner operator. (Another reason not to own one). Even a list of all the systems and component and what could go wrong with each makes a thick book. A car has10 times more parts than a house, 5,000 parts or more to go wrong. Having your car fixed by professionals can be expensive. To live ZC you’ll have to fix it yourself, a big problem.

Maintaining your teeth and your car are a constant battle. Health and homes are more forgiving. Car repair costs (and dental bills), can ruin your budget and any chance at ZCL.

Needed is a vehicle designed from the ground up to be serviceable, that can be assembled in a garage from off the shelf components, mix and match. I'll discuss this more below under 'Homemade Car'.

Car problems and repairs can be a frustrating mystery and yet the fix needed may be cheap and simple. Example: Ford Escort Wagon from personal experience: A rust hole in the rear left corner let dirt get into the fuel shutoff switch; (that shuts off fuel flow in a crash). The car would not start. No one could figure it out including engineers and car repair technicians. It was fixed when I sprayed 'WD 40' liberally through the rust hole into the chamber (and over the dirty fuel shutoff switch thus cleaning it), and then covered the hole with duct tape. A film of oil over most parts in an old car can be a good thing.

Keep all bolts lubed everywhere. If rusty, soak and lube. Look. Get under the car and look for rust and get oil on it. Don't let brake caliper bolts get frozen with rust. But keep oil away from belts and CV boots – and brake pads and discs. Door bottoms rust out - as do door frames beneath the doors, and floor pans. Keep the weep holes in doors and door frames clear and spray oil into them occasionally..

Look for cars with low torque requirements on bolts or, if you try to make repairs at home; you may need an air compressor gun to get bolts off.

Keep the underbody and possibly the lower body panels coated with rustoleum or other rust preventing paint

A few basics on old cars: Things people don't do but should.

Check the oil weekly. Keep it full. Watch the oil gauge or 'idiot' light. If the light comes on stop immediately. You may be burning or leaking oil until it has become too low for the engine to operate without damage. If you drive with an idiot light on you are an idiot.

If the temperature idiot light turns red, or temperature gage goes into the red stop immediately and turn the car off. You may have a coolant leak or blockage. Let the engine cool down, add more water (distilled is best but add any you can get) and then possibly you can drive a few more miles to a place where you can get the engine cooling system fixed.

Gauges are better than idiot lights. You can see temperatures and pressures rise. Bad – to have an idiot light suddenly go on, with no warning.

Repair garage:

If you want to live ZC, and you are going to own a car you should repair it yourself. Therefore you must create a repair facility with tools to do most auto repair jobs. In a cold climate you need a garage that can be heated when repairs or maintenance is necessary in winter.

Build a repair shed or garage 10'x 20' minimum. If of minimum size, have plywood walls designed to be removable in summer/ hot weather for ventilation and ease of access.

Tools:

2 floor jacks to make tire rotation possible.
air compressor and sockets.
electrical testing equipment.
grease pit.
engine hoist chain with reinforced shed rafter/ frame structure.
welding equipment.
Look for used tools.

Rebuilding the engine and transmission is best left to pros but I've seen them removed in an ordinary garage, taken to repair shops or exchanged and then reinstalled. You need to be able to haul the engine and transmission out of the car and around in the garage. An engine chain hoist can be attached to garage rafters - extra supports may be necessary for the garage frame – saving the need to buy an expensive engine hoist sold at auto parts stores. The auto parts store hoist is on wheels, however, so it can easily be moved around in a garage. It may be possible to build your own – make a web search.

Car repair in the home garage:

This book cannot be a repair manual but here are some tips. Get books on how to repair your car: published by Haynes and Chilton available at auto parts stores and many libraries. Also, find web sites on it. Study the books and see if you think you could do the things they describe.

You may be able to rent or even borrow tools and diagnostic devices from car shops like Auto Zone for some jobs.

My experiences with car repair: I am not mechanically inept, but have been unable to do simple jobs on certain vehicles or else have spent hours on jobs that I expected to take minutes. Here are a few repair jobs you should be able to do and problems you may encounter: There are always unanticipated problems not mentioned in any books such as rusty or heavily torqued nuts and bolts you can't get off.

Changing oil: Oil pan bolt won't come off. When finally loose, you are likely to get oil all over your hand as you finish unscrewing it.

Brakes: rusty bolts, stuck calipers bolts on brakes.

Exhaust-muffler assembly: all rusty and bolts immovable.

Instrument panels: disassembly may be intractable puzzles, difficult to service with inaccessible heater fans, instrument, wires, and air ducts. You may need a repair book for your car to do this.

Belts: alternator, fan, power steering, air conditioning: It is difficult to get the belt tension right in hard to access front wheel drive transverse mounted engines.

Serpentine belt: replacement is doable by the amateur, but it may be hard to get to and move the 'tensioner pulley'.

Repair jobs that are hard to do or you can't do without expensive special equipment makes a long, long list: The automatic transmission for example, is not repairable by the amateur – it is extremely complex. Don't have one. Get a manual transmission and learn to drive a stick shift. A manual transmission is repairable by an amateur, and has many fewer components to go wrong. And, when the clutch wears out it is possible for an amateur/owner to replace it, though it does require 'dropping' (lowering) the transmission. Someday a genius will design a clutch that can be replace without dropping the transmission.

Rebuilding a Banger:

Unfortunately in the Northern United States salt used on roads eventually ruins most cars. Even plastic body Saturns have a metal underframe that will rust. Better to get a southern car to rebuild.

Body rust discussion: is a car repairable, worth repairing?

Consider the structural integrity of the car. Do a do-it-yourself string test (see the web site http://0costlivng.com) to determine if the body frame is still square.

Is the frame/body sound?

Frame rails are separate from the body on most trucks. They are integral to the body of a 'uni-body' car or van. These must be intact or be reinforced on a uni-body car or the structure of the car may be compromised.

Assure that the door frames have integrity. They often rust out at the bottom.

Reinforce the frame and any rusty areas with square steel tubes, brackets, and plywood.

Quarter panels and doors are repairable or replaceable on uni-body cars.

Rusted through floors: use plywood panels cut to fit and bolted down. These panels must be airtight to keep unhealthy, even potentially deadly fumes out of the interior. If the exhaust pipe runs underneath, protect any plywood from heat with a metal cover attached underneath the plywood, or fire could result.

Check engine attachment and suspension attachment points.

Replace broken windshields with plastic or polycarbonate windows: Sheets of plastic can be gently curved in conic sections to fit windshield spaces. Or, get a replacement windshield at a junk yard.

The book ***Drive it Forever*** by Bob Sikorsky has a list of causes of engine wear and ways to reduce it:

Causes of engine wear:

Prolonged time between oil changes.
Frequent short trips especially in cold weather.
One cold weather start equals 500 miles of warm engine travel.
Neglected EGR systems, PVC valves, and O2 sensors
Corrosion due to acid.
Abrasive wear due to dirt and dust.

Ways to reduce engine and vehicle wear while driving and parking:

Smooth, even, minimum braking while driving.

No revving, no fast sudden acceleration: causes stress and oil loss on bearing surfaces.
Minimize idle time: after 30 seconds shut it down.
Reduce A.C. use when in slow and stop-and-go traffic.
Don't coast at high speed: bad for differential gear teeth load.
Drive 35 to 45 whenever possible for maximum mileage potential.
Never pump the accelerator to start.
Avoid short trips on very cold days.
Idle engine 1 or 2 minutes after a prolonged highway run to dissipate heat and alleviate hot spots.
Park and walk.
Avoid dirt roads.

Engine:

The Sikorsky book contains a long list of ideas to improve engine efficiency and reduce maintenance costs. I will summarize a few here, but there are many more:
Use a radiator cover in below 0 weather such as a sheet of vinyl or cardboard.
Get a low back-pressure muffler or even a dual exhaust with a scavenger tip.
On the header get individual exhaust pipes for each cylinder.
Change and flush the coolant and add coolant lubricant oil.
Add a transmission oil cooler.
Add a high performance intake manifold.
Add a capacitive discharge or electronic ignition.
Add a thermostatically controlled electric fan.
Add magnetic drain plugs for the oil pan, transmission, and rear axle with a magnesium element for the oil.
Add a vacuum gage.
Convert the engine to run on LPG and LN to reduce engine wear.
Set the dwell first, then the timing.
Do an exhaust gas analyzer test at a repair garage. Check for a 15 to1 air/fuel mix.
Use only distilled water in the radiator and battery.
Add water miscible oil to radiator water to lube the water pump.
Use a 50/50 mixture of antifreeze and water in the radiator.
Get a locking gas cap.
Check for intake manifold leaks, check at the gasket.
Look for loose vacuum hoses: listen for a loud hissing.
Rear axle lubricant; check and change.

Test transmission fluid: red/ light brown = okay, dark = change. Front wheel bearings: clean and repack with fresh grease, never just add grease.

This list, suggesting that you must be rather devoted to your car to really "drive it forever" is another strong incentive to abandon use of the automobile altogether. You can see not owning a car and not having to repair it eliminates costs and from a ZCL perspective saves a lot of time and money.

Trip minimizing methods: To save gas and wear on your car.

Combine trips.
Go to closest the location you can find for any given task. To find locations use the phone book and/or internet before you go.
Plan ahead, take no spontaneous or convenience trips.
Shop online. Shop by phone.
Have things delivered or mailed, look for free delivery.

Improving gas Mileage:
Get a high miles-per-gallon car: These may not be easy to repair and are not very safe in accidents with larger vehicles, as I will discuss below. The Geo Metro is a good example.
Get a Chevrolet Chevette diesel. Convert it to bio-diesel and you could use waste cooking oil from restaurants for fuel.

The cheapest and most effective way to improve your gas mileage is to change your driving habits. A few methods:
Don't speed.
Go easy on the brakes.
When you see a light turn red ahead take your foot off the accelerator and coast to a stop.
Use a rolling stop at stop signs if you are comfortable with it. (It is illegal and could get you a ticket.)
Time traffic signals.
Inflate tires to the maximum pressure.
Never idle, shut the vehicle off after 7 seconds.
Keep the vehicle empty, added weight lowers miles-per-gallon.
Remove car top carriers and other fixtures outside the vehicle body.
When parking, try to park so you don't have to back up to leave, park facing out.

Car insurance discussion: discounts to ask your insurance company for.

$1,000 deductible - or higher if offered.
multi car - if you have more than one car.
no accidents in 3 years
no tickets in 2 years
driver age over 50 or 55 – older folks are safer drivers.
completed a driver training course – take one.
completed a defensive driving course – take one.
anti theft devices – add them.
low annual mileage – drive less.
air bags.
anti lock brakes.
daytime running lights.
joint auto and homeowners insurance – get both at the same time.
long time customer.

6.10.3 Alternative Fuel:

David Blume in his book ***Alcohol Can Be a Gas*** explains in a thorough and detailed 600-page book how to make alcohol and how to convert your vehicle to alcohol (or alcohol gasoline mix). He describes different still methods and sizes from micro stills to community based large operations. In his history chapter, he explains that the Ford Model T and Model A were designed to run on alcohol or gasoline. Ford believed farmers could produce alcohol fuel for their own vehicles - and a surplus to sell thus increasing their income and independence. Backed by a very experienced author and full of practical ideas and methods, Blumes' book is well worth reading for anyone attempting ZCL.

6.10.4 Homemade Car:

You can't buy houses and cars of the kinds needed for ZCL but have to build them or modify existing ones. The idea of building your own car from off the shelf or foraged, scavenged and junkyard parts can be an intriguing but very difficult challenge.

There is one book that explains how to do this. And, the book has spawned dozens of web sites. The book is ***Build Your Own Sports Car for as Little as L250*** (U.S. about $500.00) by Ron Champion. In the book he explains how to build a small British style

2-seat sports car loosely based on the Lotus 7 by the famous British designer Colin Chapman. 'Locost' is the name of the car built in the book. The car has a frame of one-inch square tubes welded together and covered with removable aluminum, sheet steel, and fiberglass panels. All components are easily accessible. The locost is built cheaply by buying a junk car for parts; spending perhaps $150 for engine, wire harness, wheels, steering system, brakes, suspension, etc. These may have to be rebuilt before use. More savings are realized by keeping the car simple, for example: Aluminum body panels can be left unpainted. A dipstick cans serve as the fuel gauge. Junkyard and automobile flea market parts are used whenever possible, including windshield, steering wheel, lights, seats, instruments, etc.

Here are some options to consider in building a locost-like car:

Possibly use a fabric cover over the frame, or plywood panels.

Build a four-seat version.

Build a bolt-together, not welded locost. Or a bolted and braised locost built on a jig to assure accurate frame position. Braising may strengthen a bolted-together joint.

Build an 'extra-safe' version of a locost as described below.

Building a car is technically difficult, though the Champion book makes it look do-able. Build it yourself and probably you can fix any part of it yourself.

Another ZCL style car is the Dawson-Issigonis 'Lightweight Special' built in the 1930's. It was a race car built with hand tools on a shoestring budget. Of course we are not interested in building a race car, but this car suggests what is possible.

Weighing only 587 pounds, 38% of that engine weight, it was built using so called 'monocoque' construction (body and frame all of one piece) using two beams of plywood faced with aluminum sheet; with torsional (stiffness preventing twist) strength achieved by integrating everything possible: engine, large tubular cross members, front suspension bearers, seat pan, and final drive gearbox. Springs were made using rubber bands, with swinging half axles and wishbone type radius arms.

Another option for a ZCL car: Rebuild a junker car: A method that is halfway between a homemade Locost and merely repairing an old banger.

Idea: Start with a banger; then simplify it as you rebuild it.

Simplification of a car: some possible techniques:

Use generic parts.

Stabilize rusty areas, then use square tube frame reinforcement for strength (in areas that may be lost to rust) and crash safety. Possibly use bolt-together rather than weld reinforcements to reduce the level of skill needed.

Make body panels easy to remove: so all components and systems are easy to access.

Use tabs on windows to open them rather than cranks or electric motors.

Use plastic/polycarbonate windows, they can add structural integrity to the frame (a glass windshield/windows add almost no integrity/strength to a car frame).

Use 1930s' style windshield of two flat panes forming a 'V' - or use gently curved plastic windows formed as 'conic sections' rather than hard-to- form compound curves.

Have no doors. Step over the side of the car to enter, as in the 'Locost'.

Use an air-cooled engine – no radiator, hoses, water pump, antifreeze required.

Do not use power steering or brakes - manual may be adequate in a small car.

Have all components light, compact, and easy to remove for servicing and replacement

Simplest suspension: torsion bars as in the old Volkswagon Beetle.

Car Design:

Car design, from a ZCL perspective, is worthy of another book but here I'll summarize some ideas:

Cars and the transportation system built for them are not well designed. Through the 100 years of existence very little has changed that improves the situation; much has changed that worsens it. Serviceability, safety, durability, reliability all have deteriorated. Cars have masses of unneeded gadgets and systems: 4 wheel drive, styling that undermines aerodynamics, excessive horsepower and speed. Many, even most, components of cars are either over or under engineered. Compared to the efficiency, low cost, and simplicity of bicycles; cars are hopelessly inferior. (In fact I believe all other transportation systems are inferior).

Car design goal: a truly safe, efficient small car. Complete and detailed designs for such a car must wait for other books and/or web sites. Here, I will make some suggestions.

Safety

The flag law of old England was right. It was a law requiring a man on foot to walk in front of their (then huge) steam carriages to warn of their coming. Now it is considered a foolish anti-technology law. But millions have died, and tens of million have been seriously injured by automobiles. Thousands of cars have been designed to be stylish, fast and comfortable. No cars have been designed to be really safe. In the future folks will consider contemporary attitudes towards car design and safety the way we look at the plagues and 'cures' for diseases of the middle ages.

The safety of any car, especially a car you build yourself must be the central consideration of the design from the beginning. All cars today are designed with safety considerations weighed as just one factor among many. In fact, safety I believe; should be the starting point of any car design, and be the most heavily weighted design consideration. The other systems and components of a car ought to conform to the requirements of safety. This is especially true in a small, light, efficient, high miles-per-gallon car. If you are in a small car and are hit by an SUV, you are 8 times more likely to die that the SUV occupants. An SUV safe small car is needed. None exist now.

In fact, SUVS are not really safe even for their owners. The danger of rollover is real and due to simple physics: higher and narrower equals less stability. The incidents of rollover of ordinary low riding cars are very low and almost nonexistent for low, heavy wide cars.

Needed are small cars built strongly enough to survive intact the impact of an SUV from any direction. So, structural reinforcements and crush zones must be designed into the car to give you a chance in a collision with larger vehicle.

A Safe Car: How a safe car ought to be created.

The auto industry has pushed the idea that weight equals safety. But the reality is structure is the key to safety. Consider lead vs. a diamond. Lead is denser and heavier, but smashed together which would remain intact? The diamond would prevail because of its structure while the lead would be flattened and broken.

So, a safe small car must begin with a strong structure. Needed is an impenetrable structure, possibly a diamond-like web of triangulated tubes.

A safe small car might resemble an elongated onion: a series of layers. The core layer might be soft, but hold the occupants in place in an accident. Then a hard impervious impenetrable layer protecting the occupant from intrusion by the hard elements of other vehicles, then a crush zone wrapping all around the car, then a soft outer layer- a soft thick skin to protect others if the car hits them; whether pedestrian, cyclist, or other vehicle. These layers must encompass the "greenhouse" or upper half of the car. Most deadly to a small car is SUV "overrun' meaning the SUV runs right over a small car because of its height, crushing in the weak and vulnerable upper half of a small car. Small cars hit from the side by SUVs has resulted in the hoods of the SUVs impacting the heads of the occupants in small cars. Polycarbonate window glass might strongly reinforce the greenhouse.

Possibly masses of Styrofoam or similar material could serve several purposes, as a crushable material for crush zones, for the soft inner layer, next to the occupants, and for the soft outer skin.

More details: outside the impervious layer design break away components - such as the engine, held by sheer bolts (bolts that break or 'sheer' away in an extreme crash) to throw off weight and dissipate energy in a crash, as in racing cars.

More details: inside the impervious layer, 'child seats' for adults might be added; tight fitting seats that wrap around the sides of the occupants, working the same way as child seats protect children.

Five point seat belts as in some aircraft and in race cars hold the occupant more securely than ordinary three point belts.

And crash helmets as in racing cars, and on bicycle riders, should always be worn while driving.

Ideal would be: riders in tandem, not side by side, thus allowing generous zones to the sides for all of the layers suggested above. Accidents statistics reveal that the safest place to be in an accident is the middle rear seat because of the wide areas all around to take the impact forces of an accident.

Source: June 27, 2007 ***"A cars middle back seat may be least desirable but is the safest."*** University of Buffalo study by Detrich Jehle, M.D. U.B. associate professor of emergency medicine. Jehle notes: "...passengers sitting in the position have a much larger "crush zone" than rear-side seat passengers in rear–side impact crashes. The crush zone is an area of the car designed to collapse in an effort to absorb some of the impact from a collision."

Look at racing cars, and though you're not going to race, do what they do: safety cage, roll bars, 5 point seat belt, helmet, break away components (including the engine in a drag racer).

So, to create a ZCL car, you might create a Ron Champion like 'locost' car but design it to maximize safety. It might be a two-seater with driver and passenger sitting in the middle, in a tandem configuration. An outer frame all around might be designed to crush on impact and thus absorb and dissipate some of the forces of a crash. The outer frame could be built high enough to absorb impact from a larger vehicle to deal with the 'overrun' problem. A strong inner cage could enclose the occupants all around as a final barrier against overrun.

Illustration # 13 below shows a design concept for a safe small car suitable for ZCL.

Idea: for a safe fuel - that is not flammable or explosive: Shelled corn. Shelled corn might be an ideal fuel; useful as protection in a crash, hard to light, will not explode. Is a car fueled with shelled corn possible? We use corn to make ethanol today, but processing costs are huge. Possibly corn could heat the boiler of a revived steam powered car.

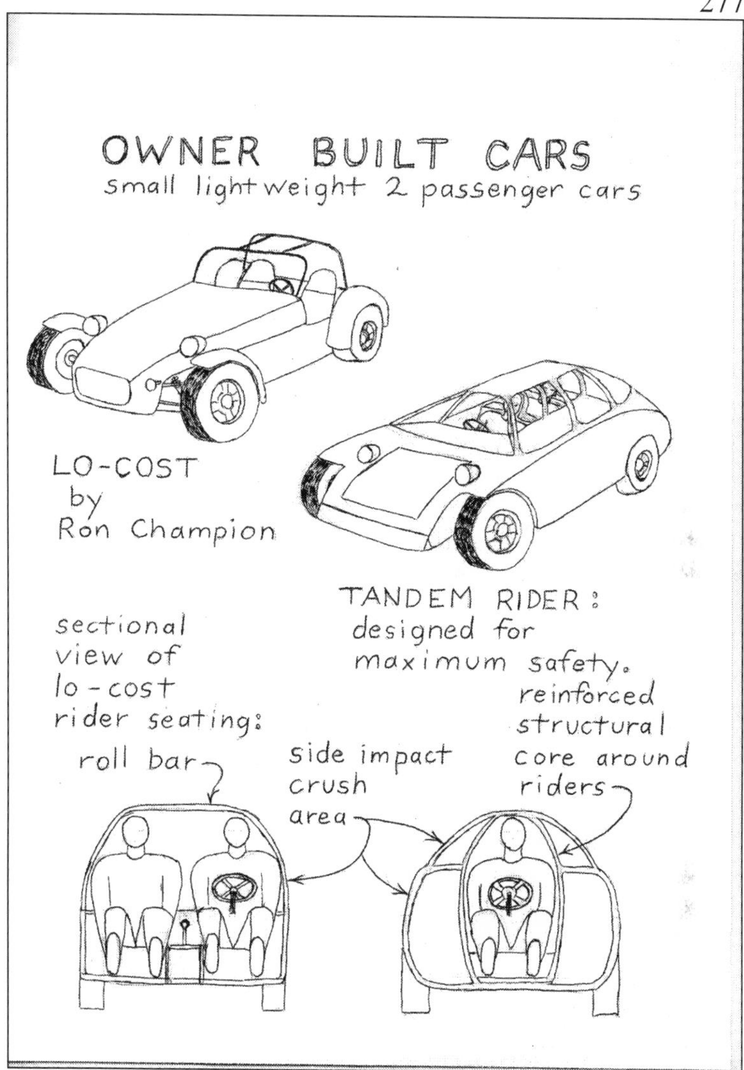

ILLUSTRATION # 13: OWNER BUILT CARS

Electric car

Here, I will consider the suitability of an electric car for ZCL. An electric car has limited range compared to a gas or diesel vehicle, going only 40 miles or less before requiring recharging. For a ZC lifestyle where you are not taking long trips, electric may work well. An electric can be simpler than a car with a gas or diesel engine, and perhaps less of a maintenance and repair nightmare. As you might expect, a whole new set of problems crop up. Examples:

getting maximum life out of the battery pack; and replacing the battery every few years.

Of course, you must have electric service to your homestead. You might consider a home electricity producing system such as solar cells, wind generator, water turbine, wood fired steam engine and generator, etc. These cost a lot, too much perhaps for a ZCL practitioner. And theses systems will have more maintenance demands.

Energy cost: electric vs. gasoline car: An electric car may use only 0.5 kilowatt-hours (kWh) per mile. At 10 cents per kWh that's only 5 cents per mile. A gasoline fueled car may cost 10 cents per mile with gasoline at $3.00 per gallon and car getting 30 miles per gallon - twice as much as electric.

Conversion to electric: a short summary. A search on the internet will turn up dozens of web sites about building or converting to an electric car. One example from ***ecomodder.com/blog/a-672-electric car***: Two novices converted a Geo Metro to electric for $672. Motor, parts and batteries came from a used fork lift (which they sold for scrap metal). They achieved 40 miles per hour and 9 to 15 mile range – suitable for local shopping trips. Another source: ***Electricity4Gas.com*** claims you can make a conversion for $300 using reconditioned batteries and motor. Their e-manual cost $50 and the promo sounds too good to be true, so be warned.

Summary of steps: To give you an idea of what is involved.

Get a banger car as donor: station wagon, hatchback or pickup with no rust, manual steering, manual brakes, manual transmission, strong suspension, rear wheel drive.

Remove: engine, carburetor, exhaust system, air conditioning, radiator, fuel tank, heater core and ducts, ignition instruments.

Keep: manual steering, manual brakes, suspension, wheels, rear wheel drive. speedometer and cables, manual transmission

Rebuilding:

Lighten car and strengthen frame

Build:

- wooden battery trays using plywood and metal brackets with a plastic liner
- electric engine motor mount
- controller mount
- generator mount
- provide an I.C. engine mount if a hybrid.

Buy a battery pack: New lead acid batteries at $60 each and 50 lbs. each x 14 batteries = $840 and 700 lbs.

The weight of these components installed in the car must be roughly evenly balanced between front and rear wheels.

A 'series hybrid electric car 'is a modification of a pure electric car to include a small gas engine that extends the range by charging up the battery pack. The car components such as battery packs, gas engine and generator, and electric motor can be distributed in the vehicle between the front, center, sides and rear of the car for good balance and accessibility for repair and maintenance. The battery pack can be kept smaller and lighter than the pack in a pure electric car, thus saving weight. A series hybrid electric can be designed to be a simple car, much simpler than factory built 'parallel/series' hybrids such as the Toyota Prius.

A number of series hybrids have been built by individuals. A great example is ***1993 Update: David Arthur's' Amazing Hybrid Electric Car*** interview by Matt Scanlon in The ***Mother Earth News*** June/July 1993.

China and Cars: Imagine our roads being used by four times the number of cars we have now. That would be China with cars. China has the same land areas as the U.S. but four times the population. Therefore cars will never be as widely owned in China as in the U.S. or their land would choke on them beneath paving for roads and parking. Car free cities must prevail - dedicated to walking, biking and mass transit. And, most of the rest of the world must do the same. Even countries with room for more cars today can expect to be choked by cars as their populations grow. So the automobile as we know it likely will not be the predominant mode of transportation in the future. So now I will consider alternatives to the car suitable for almost zero cost comfortable living

6.10.5 Motorcycle:

Safe Motorcycle:

In general, motorcycles are very efficient machines, lightweight, simple, compact.

They can be clean running with a 4 stroke or an electric motor. But they have two problems: they are not 'all weather' and they are not safe among the masses of steel that occupy the roads:

cars, SUVs and trucks. Possible, it seems are designs that deal with these problems. Here are a few suggestions:

The rider might ride low, be a "low rider" for balance and to allow a compact safety cage to be wrapped around him. Of course a weather protecting cover or cab may be wrapped around the safety cage. A low machine with a cab could allow improved aerodynamics compared to a conventional motorcycle and thus get better fuel mileage. Perhaps the advantage would be offset by greater weight of the cab and safety elements.

If you are in an enclosed cab, what about when you stop, won't you tip over? That can be solved and has been solved in other designs with small flanking wheels that automatically lower when the motorcycle stops.

Safety elements to add: helmet, headrest, tight fitting seat, seat belt, safety cage with roll bars, crush zones/crumple zones, interior padding, ultra light materials and structures, designed possibly as a kit that can use an existing motorcycle as a starting point. Of course all of this may wipe out any cost advantages a motorcycle has over a small car.

Illustration # 14 below of a '**cabinscooter**' (a term that is originally of German origin) show how a safe motorcycle might look.

Electric moped considered: Cheap to buy and operate. - it could be practical if you don't go out much in bad weather, or live where weather is usually good, and don't have to travel far to shopping, library, etc. Possibly, like a motorcycle, it could be adapted for all weather use.

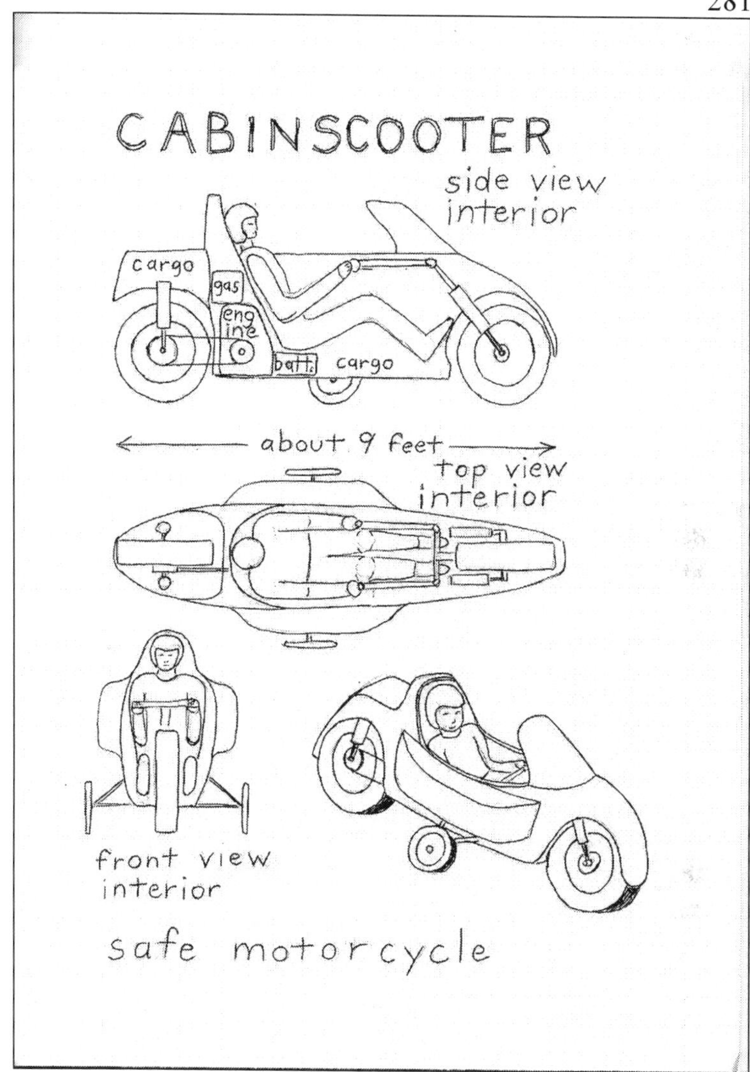

Illustration # 14: CABINSCOOTER

6.10.6 No Car:

Introduction

Having no car can be a huge step towards ZCL.

Living without a car is a whole challenge by itself. It is a foreign experience for most people, except for childhood and teenage years before obtaining a drivers license. Most folks have forgotten what it was like. Distances expand, bus schedules become important and time must be spent waiting for a bus and standing around perhaps in cold or rain.

On the other hand bills and worries contract: reliability, worrying about whether it'll start, repair costs, flat tires, traffic tickets and automobile accidents are no longer important. Keep your car for emergencies, perhaps. But don't drive it, leave it sitting outdoors or park it in a garage if you have one to keep it in better condition. Or sell it for dollars towards ZCL. Cancel your insurance. Insurance, especially for young people can be a heavy burden. It can cost thousands per year; all the more reason to cancel it. A huge amount of money can be saved and a huge step taken towards ZCL. Only use the car in an emergency like a run to the hospital. It is possible (of course) to drive without insurance but don't do it. If you do it, obey every traffic rule to the letter and don't have any accidents. You'll probably be the safest driver on the road if you do this. If you are caught, a judge may take a real emergency situation into consideration when deciding on your penalty. Penalties are heavy if caught.

How does it feel to not have a car? Distances expand. You feel like you live in a bigger world, another world in many ways. You find more intimate places and unexpected places. You are free from various costs, legal fees, gas, maintenance, repair, parking. Accidents associated with cars and driving are partly avoided; (though walking or biking around you still are vulnerable to the steel behemoths.) The ease of getting around is increased in some places: you don't have the problem finding a place to park.

Places where people can get away from cars and /or get around without them have sometimes become the most desirable and interesting places to live and visit while places overrun with cars have declined in appeal. People flock to pedestrian only streets in downtowns, cities emphasizing mass transit and bicycle use such as Ann Arbor, Michigan, and places devoted to horse drawn vehicles and bikes such as Mackinaw Island.

The Amish have a good idea. They rely on horses and buggies. They have the expenses of buying horses (or raising them) and equipment, of horse feed (or growing their own feed), of veterinarians and horse medicine, but these costs together are a small fraction of the costs of a car. If you choose to live in or near Amish country you could adopt some of their practices. It should be easier to use horses there because car drivers are more used to them, and suitable horses and equipment will be available.

Locations to look for to live without a car or to minimize car use: Locate where work, shopping, recreation and leisure are nearby; near enough to walk or bike. Choose very carefully. Consider locating in or near a small or medium size town: not rural, suburbs or big city. Locate, perhaps beyond sewer and water utility range to save those assessment, but close enough to get to library, post office, farmers market, co-ops, jobs, stores, etc. University towns may be more interesting. There may be more going on, many clubs and groups better cultural and recreational opportunities. You could try sneaking into large classes, they won't notice. Colleges and associated clubs and activities may be more insular and inaccessible to a student who is not enrolled, compared to universities. And, possibly look for economically depressed towns, for cheap land and housing costs.

The following is repetitious of ideas I've stated elsewhere but for emphasis, worth repeating:

Small towns may be a good option, with everything close together. The finest library of do-it-yourself literature I ever saw was in a small farmer-oriented town.

Why not rural? Living 'way out in the country' or in a wilderness area you may suffer from isolation, and boredom. In a remote area, getting around to all the places you need to go might be difficult and expensive. Things will be too far away to bike or walk, and so you must have a car and drive it long distances.

Why not cities? Large cities have become spread out, and so impractical to traverse by bike or walking. Mass transit may be either expensive or inconvenient and time consuming to use. Crime can be high so you may have difficulty finding any peace whether physical peace or peace of mind. Lots may be small and homes and neighborhoods crowded. There may be few or no places to hike.

Why not suburbs? They are usually too spread out, everything too far apart, boring, may have strict standards for lawn care, strict zoning ordinances, not bike or pedestrian friendly.

I am sure there are exceptions to these situations, so don't automatically rule any of them out, but choose carefully after a long and detailed look at a place.

No-car alternative: Keep a car in the garage in running order to use only for emergencies, or to be activated and insured only when needed like a vacation trip. Or, have no car insurance and take a risk on occasional trips; driving very carefully at or below all speed limits, obeying all traffic laws to the letter of the law and going in good weather during daylight only. But, sad to say you never know what will happen on the road. Roads are extraordinarily dangerous places with huge machines careening about driven by people distracted by cell phones and sometimes drunk. Even without insurance you'll have costs and fees for legal plates and a drivers license unless you dare to avoid these too. It could land you in jail. And, repair requires skill, practice, training and experience.

6.10.7 Bike:

On the other hand, bike or pedestrian travel in an automobile permeated world have their own dangers. Biking through a town in twilight or at night may be harrowing.

But bike mobility is tremendous. Even owning a car, I sometimes bike through neighborhoods and places I'd never go by car or can't go by car. Poke into odd corners of a community. A bike is the ultimate foraging device. No parking problems. Go around traffic jams. Living in Ann Arbor, Michigan in the 1980s I was able to bike three miles downtown in a 20 minute easy ride including stop signs and lights. No helmet in those days. A car would've taken 15 minutes plus time to find an often nonexistent or costly parking place.

Ken Kifer traveled a steady 10 miles per hour, 60 miles a day for months on end - tens of thousands of miles total on bike vacations as he describes in his web site ***www.Kenkifer.com.*** I'll summarize some of his suggestions here: He recommends a 'Touring Bike' with a long wheel base and load carrying ability; with attachment points on the frame for panniers, fenders, and a wide even range of gears. He says a good rain suit should always be carried.

Cost comparison: Bike - 1 or 2 cent per mile (for tires, tubes, repairs, etc.- according to Ken) verses Car - 45 cents to $1.25 per mile.

Speed comparison: Walking 3 mph, bike 10 mph, automobile 25 mph in the city. A bike with electric assist may achieve 15 miles per hour.

All Weather Bike:

There's a need for all weather bikes and adaptations to existing bikes to make them useful in bad weather, (seasonal training wheels or skis for icy roads in winter, maybe?) Living ZC, in really bad weather you don't have to go out. You can 'cocoon' (stay home).

An all weather bike might involve the design of a fabric enclosure over a lightweight frame that surrounds the rider, and perhaps a heating device. The upper half of a fabric cover might be made of clear flexible plastic, with the lower half of opaque plastic. The drive chain might have a cover. An electric motor and battery might provide power assist. Very useful - an automatic wheel stand that drops when the vehicle stops. Or, an all weather bike design might take the form of an enclosed recumbent three-wheeler – with two wheels in front for stability in turns.

Because bikes are compact and light, indoor bike parking may be a practical alternative. Get your place of employment to let you bring your bike indoors - into or near your office or work station. And, get local government and businesses to provide covered bike parking spaces.

The ***Art of Cycling*** by Robert Hurst thoroughly considers the use of the bike as a commuting, shopping and all around transportation device. It can work for many people. And to repeat for emphasis, every car off the road is a good thing. Biking can be near zero cost. Used bikes can sometimes be picked up for free on trash days, or bought for a few dollars at garage sales.

A bike is the most efficient transportation system ever. On pavement a bike is 5 times more efficient than walking, another words uses 1/5 as much energy as walking to cover the same distance, (and is easier on the feet). Bike friendly cities are listed in ***Bicycling*** magazine - March 2006 issue.

Traveling and vacationing by Bike: Carry all of your supplies. Each item is worth an extensive discussion beyond the scope of this book: I just want to introduce you to the idea. Ken Kifer traveled 3000-mile trips with two wool blankets and a tarp. His web site goes into his methods in extensive detail. Keep your supplies light and simple: tent tarp, bug proof canopy, sleeping bag bike chain and lock, tinder or stove, warm clothes, rain gear, cooking pots, dishes, silverware. Food: flour, nuts, beans, water to drink, wash tub. Camp in places where you can remain well hidden such as dense woods. Forage for some of your food on the way: wild plants such as apples, berries, mushrooms, in season.

Live in a pedestrian, bike, and mass transit friendly city, (and car unfriendly) and realize huge benefits: No car needed = big savings. The city is likely to be compact, and have diverse businesses and public facilities. People may be healthier because they are walking and riding. Children may be safer. Pollution may be low. University towns often have these characteristics.

As stated in chapter 5 the best location to live ZC may be a small town where most of the places you need to go are within walking or biking distance: library, post office, a few key stores for the basics you don't make or grow. A rural location may not be the best location for most people because a car with all of its associated costs may be necessary.

6.10.8 Walk:

Wrote Grace Halsell in her book ***Los Viegos***, "The viegos of Vilcabamaba have never been handicapped by the wheel as a mode of transport. They own no cars or bicycles. Nor do they have horses or burros to move them over the rugged landscape of the Sacred Valley. They simply walk. They walk to work and they walk home from work. That necessity enriches and strengthens them."

Note how unpleasant it is to walk or bike beside automobile choked roads. Noise, danger, and thousands of strangers eyeing you as they whip past you. The best places to walk or bike has always been where cars have are excluded.

Interviews from the ***Foxfire*** series of books:

"We had freedom back then. We was free. .... "It's fast time now y'know. Ever'thing's flyin'. These automobiles runnin' to and from ever' corner of the world. ......You can't walk along the highway'r'nothin'. You ain't got no freedom 'r'nothin'." Hillard Green age 79 in1966 ***The Foxfire Book*** page 376

"I never did try t'drive a car. My mule is th'way I got around. Used t'ride him t'Otto (North Carolina) t'get groceries..... Course you couldn't do that now. Theres's too many cars on th'road." Maude Shope age 76 in 1969 ***Foxfire 2*** page 18.

If you want to take up walking, what can you do about this? Find places to walk that don't require walking next to busy roads. For example, walk on dirt roads, along railroad tracks, on service roads behind shopping malls and industrial developments, through parks, cemeteries, vacant lots, undeveloped land, and through woods, thickets, valleys or hills on private land where the owners can't see you. You may be trespassing at times, but you are just passing through and doing no harm. You will rarely, maybe never be challenged. If you are, don't panic or run, explain what you are doing, and you probably will be allowed to continue without further challenge. You may be asked to go back the way you came. If so, comply cheerfully. After all, you are trespassing and could be arrested, fined or jailed. (Though it has never happened to me despite 40 years of trespassing).

Another option: Live in a region of mountains, state and national forests and parks, and generally less population density - where cars are less prevalent.

One more option: Live in a region of lakes, waterways and/or islands where you can boat to town or countryside.

6.10.9 Mass Transit:

Curitiba, Brazil built a fabulous bus system instead of freeways. Separate networks of roads were built for exclusive use by busses. Cars were from prohibited from these roads. It is easier to get around town by bus than by car, so people that have cars leave them at home. Type in 'Curitiba' in google and you will find web sites describing life in this wonderful city.

6.11 RECREATIONS and VACATIONS:

"No mon no fun" the saying goes. Is it true? Free or very cheap recreations are plentiful.

Have fun without spending any money? I can think of a way but we're not going there in this book.

This section is a challenge to write. Most folk - certainly most Americans think you have to have money to have fun, the more money the more fun. To convince most Americans otherwise is probably impossible. Nevertheless it is possible to do plenty of adventurous and exciting things without much money. Some of the most adventurous people on the planet live virtually zero cost already - devoting the few dollars they have to their passion. They do things the well off, dependent on their dollars and paid help could never do, wouldn't dream of doing. Rich effete William F. Buckley sailed across the Atlantic Ocean all right, but not without a big boat and an extensive inventory of appliances and electronic equipment (that was continually requiring expensive time wasting repair). Contrast his voyages with those of Annie Hill in her book ***Voyaging on a Small Income***. Consider mountain climbers like Ed Vesture living in poverty and climbing a new mountain every weekend or John Krakauer who, nearly penniless, attempted a new route up the

Devils Tower as described in his book ***Eiger Dreams***. Real adventures are not to be compared to the costly artificial recreations of theme parks and tourist trap resorts.

Visiting Disney Land/World always makes me feel let down. The artificial look and feel of it is endemic. Fake mountains, rivers, trees, adventures. Stuff for sale shoved in your face at every turn. And, not much fun. Little short rides. A day there leaves me with a sense of the overwhelming oppressive unreality of the place and awakens in me a longing for real adventure. Perhaps that is its one redeeming effect.

On a hike or bike journey you may find unexpected routes, encounter surprises, discover interesting places out in the real world. Make your recreations and hobbies useful and productive. Make your hiking or biking vacations foraging expeditions. Hiking along railroad tracks may lead to interesting and valuable finds. barrels, apples, berries, barrels, bits of scrap iron and steel scrap lumber firewood.

Instead of boring exercise equipment, try gardening in summer and a greenhouse in winter. In surveys, gardening is already listed as the number one recreation in America.

Interesting cheap or no cost recreations:

Ultra light hiking: means to hike and camp with the minimum equipment perhaps only 10 or 20 pounds including food. This is a fascinating topic I don't have space to explore in this book. Do a web search and you will find dozens of web sites with techniques to make your own equipment.

Biking: good used bikes may be had for a few dollars or sometimes free. Biking is an ideal foraging method: a large territory may be covered. With carrying pouches a bike can carry some foraged items. Bike may easily be hidden or chained up for exploring further on foot.

Kayaking: buy or build – (plans may be found on the web) a folding kayak that can be carried by bike or backpack while hiking, or on mass transit . Used boats, kayaks, canoes, sailboats may be found at low prices in want adds or on the web.

Sailing: very cheap once out on the water but docking and trailering may cost (for tow vehicle and the gas for it). Many inexpensive used boats can be found, sometimes parked in a yard for years. Look carefully and ask around. If you have an inexpensive way to keep a boat near the water, such as on a beach for free, then great cost free boating possibilities open up.

Pursuing your recreations through organizations can save you a lot of $; examples; the Scouts, hiking and biking clubs, American Hostels Organizations (formerly American Youth Hostels), senior citizen clubs, etc.

Look for free events and activities in your community: concerts, fairs, shows, farmers markets, sporting events, etc.

Other recreations: the Library, Internet, Hobbies, Sports, are discussed elsewhere in this book.

LONG or permanent VACATIONS

You may live your life as if on vacation and yet live very low cost, if not zero cost. If you have a house, sell or rent it out to a carefully chosen tenant and then travel for a while. Perhaps you can save and invest enough money to have a secure steady but modest income while you travel. You might live a gypsy lifestyle on land or on the water.

On Land:

Motor homes are very expensive and gasoline costs overwhelming. Old used motor homes are plentiful and cheap, often with low mileage because their owners used them much less than they expected. But, even sitting unused vehicles deteriorate, in some ways more than a vehicles being used - if not properly maintained. Also, gasoline costs are huge regardless of vehicle age. For example the old but often still good 'Trans Van' (with fiberglass body) can get only 8 miles a gallon.

Another option if you want to travel with your home might be a van towing a trailer. Vans can get 16 city, and 24 miles a gallon highway; less if towing a trailer, of course.

Old vans in decent shape are very plentiful. A van can carry plenty of stuff, and possibly tow a lightweight aluminum pop up camper trailer. Such a rig may be easier to maneuver in towns than a big motor home. Plus the trailer can be left at a campground and the van taken to town or that recreation site. To keep down gas costs go to one spectacular spot and then don't drive around. Hike, walk, bike, or take the park shuttle.

Design of a Gypsy Van: If you have some skill at carpentry and sheet metal vehicle body work you might customize an old van with pop out panels. A roof pop out could allow full headroom inside. Crossways, vans are too narrow for most adults to sleep in. (Of course they could sleep "kitty corner" or lengthwise). A side pop out could allow room for your feet. A rear pop out with steps to ground level might serve as a "living" room. I suggest pop outs (that can be closed up) rather than fixed expansions because these add weight and reduce gas mileage by increasing wind resistance.

Camping for free: Find two lane rural roads with wide wooded rights-of-way. Number designated state highways sometimes have these wide rights-of-way. Look for places to pull off where you can get well into the woods and be hidden from the road. Also, you can stop at night at freeway rest areas -but they are far less quiet or comfortable.

For land travel consider forgoing four-wheel vehicles altogether. Ken Kifer repeatedly traveled multi-thousand mile journeys by bicycle at minimal cost. His web site ***kenkifer.com*** describes in extensive detail how he did it and how you can do it too. For example, he thoroughly explains how to find free good camping places. (It is very easy to conceal a bike and small tent away from the road.)

Of course countless folk swear by motorcycles but I have no experience with them. Safety worries me. And new motorcycles are expensive.

It seems to me a modest (and quiet) motorbike taking slow rural back roads might make possible an interesting and cheap vacation. Even at 25 miles per hour a day's ride could take you hundreds of miles for a few gallons of gas.

On The Water:

Refer to chapter 4 on seasteading for more details on living on the water. Here I will discuss vacationing on the water.

Yachting in general has always been ridiculously expensive. But it can be cheap, perhaps the cheapest way to travel while vacationing.

A number of authors explain how to achieve this. Annie Hill in her book ***Voyaging on a Small Income*** explains how to sail the world on a modest sail boat without an engine. Lin and Larry Parday in numerous books and articles, also sail without an engine.

I don't have the guts to cross an ocean and if you don't either you still might voyage extensively at minimal cost among islands, and along coastlines and rivers. Dan Hookum in his book ***The Simplistic Sailboat*** describes taking his young family on month long leisurely vacations in a $600 homebuilt sailboat. They cruised the San Juan Islands of Puget Sound, often traveling only a few miles a day island- to-island. (Dans' experience was mentioned on page 212 but worth repeating).

Harlan Hubbard describes river drifting in his book ***Shantyboat***, drifting engineless down the Ohio Cumberland, and Mississippi Rivers. The waterways of the world provide highways to vast, often empty spaces. "A hundred thousand miles of practically deserted seacoast (exists).along the Alaskan and Canadian shoreline…" wrote Ken Neumeyer in his book ***Sailing the Farm.***

Fast motorboats and large houseboats, of course can suck huge amounts of fuel. But a small outboard on a hull designed for steady low speed travel can be efficient as the books and boat designs of **Phil Bolger** explain. Old used fiberglass sailboats have become plentiful and cheap. Since fiberglass never rots they can last many years. The Great Lakes in particular has a surplus of such boats whose owners, tired of sailing speed moved to powerboats. Such boats can be got for a fraction of their original cost. Look for 30 foot length or a little more. Boats that size frequently have full 6'2" headroom and adequate space for comfort. Larger boats get more expensive to buy and keep, and harder to maneuver. Look for sailboats with shallow draft, which vastly expands the area you may travel. A shallow draft sailboat with a centerboard that can be raised, and with a tip up outboard motor makes it possible for you to ground the boat - whether on tidal flats or river sandbanks. On rivers where trees may overhang your course, consider leaving the mast and sail at home and motoring. Or, take mast and sails with you and modify the mast to allow quick and easy lowering and securing on deck. On the sailing boats of Holland this is common so they may pass through canals and under the numerous bridges. For ways to do this see the article 'Tabernacles and Hinged Mast Steps' beginning on page 58 in the magazine ***Small Boat Journal*** - January 1989 issue.

Perhaps you will go south for the winter and north for the summers along America's inland waterways. Such journeys can be near zero cost as you drift south on river currents, and sail north along the coast. Take short ocean voyages to the Bahamas and follow endless chains of Islands across the Caribbean, or follow the

Texas coast to Mexico and beyond. Don't visit the expensive marinas. Throw your anchor down anywhere you find shallow protected water.

6.12 COSTS:

How much money do you need? What is the cost to achieve comfortable ZCL? I will consider three alternatives: a full cost path, a low cost path, and a minimum cost path to ZCL. Costs are estimated for an individual or a small family:

Alternative 1: Full cost path to ZCL: Buying a house and operating a car.

You already have some assets, equity in your house and some savings. Here is what you might expect to spend to set up a ZC lifestyle:

Own your house free and clear	$150,000
Homestead improvements (see note 1)	20,000
Food growing and processing facilities (note 2)	2,500
Car purchase and 'fix up' cost: (note 3)	2,500
Car operating expenses (see note 4)	40,000
Medical and dental costs (see note 5)	40,000
$ saved to cover remaining expenses (note 6)	60,000
Total	$315,000

Notes:

1. Homestead improvements mean systems to minimize or eliminate utility costs such as extra insulation, solar space heat, solar water heater, efficient appliances, etc.
2. For greenhouses, garden, food processing equipment.
3. Old used car 'fixed up'
4. Car expenses savings account pays $2,000 a year from interest or dividend income for operating expenses: gas, insurance, repair, maintenance, and license fees.
5. Health savings account pays $2,000 a year from interest or dividend income for ordinary medical expenses and serves as a reserve for emergencies. Catastrophic health insurance would be a good idea to protect you from the bankrupting medical treatments lurking in our health care system. This may cost you $200 a month

or $2,400 a year, however, adding another $50,000 to the savings listed above.

6. 'Remaining expenses' include property taxes, home maintenance, house insurance, phone and internet, recreation and vacation, and miscellaneous costs.

Alternative 2: Low cost path to ZCL:

$315,000 is a huge sum for someone working in the service economy. Can it be done for less? Yes if you work at it - build your house and live without a car. Build your own house using 'sweat equity' – meaning doing most of the work yourself. Or, better yet build your own house as part of a co-op or a co-housing community dedicated to ZCL.

Land	$25,000
Build your house (see note 1)	50,000
House improvements (see note 2)	10,000
Food growing and processing facilities (3)	2,500
Car free: walk, bike, bus pass (note 4)	2,500
Medical and dental cost (see note 5)	40,000
$ saved to cover remaining expenses (6)	60,000
Total	$190,000

Notes:

1. Buy land and build your own house doing most of the work yourself. Buy a house in a low cost area. Or, buy a handyman's special and how-to books.
2. Building a new house to use solar energy to achieve zero heating and electricity costs rather than converting an existing house to use solar, you might save half of $20,000 expected cost for a solar space heating system, solar water heater, solar electric panels, etc.
3. For greenhouses, garden, food.
4. This is a 'Travel savings account'. It covers the cost of maintaining a bike and the cost of a bus pass from the interest or dividend it pays - estimated at about $10 a month.
5. Health savings account to cover $2,000 per year in expenses.

To live ZCL you must work conscientiously to maintain your health and you must live with great care. Medical costs whether for insurance or treatments can wipe you out at ZCL levels of income and assets.

6. Locate where property taxes are modest, perhaps $1,000 a year after state property tax credits.

Alternative 3: Minimum Cost Path to ZCL:

Land: (see note 1)	$10,000
Build your house: (see note 2)	40,000
House improvements (see note 3)	5,000
Food growing and processing facilities (4)	2,500
Car free: walk, bike, bus pass	2,500
Medical and dental costs (note 5)	10,000
Property taxes (savings to cover)	10,000
$ saved to cover remaining expenses (6)	10,000
Total	$90,000

Notes:

1. Land could be much less.
2. Owner built house: a basic compact no frills house. Or, buy a fixer upper- handyman's special near a small town.
3. For zero heating and electrical costs - Owner built wood stove based heating system, solar greenhouses built using foraged materials and low cost methods, and owner built solar electric (photovoltaic) electricity generating system.
4. For greenhouses, garden, food.
5. $10,000 in your health savings account yields you only $500 a year from interest earnings (at 5% return after inflation) for health expenses. You had better stay healthy. Young you may get away with this amount. Old, possibly not. You may have to rely on free clinics, income based clinics, and government programs.
6. For remaining expenses - you must do more, much more than in alternatives 1 and 2 – rarely spending $ and practicing most or all of the techniques described in chapters 2 through 5.

Your recreations and vacations must be almost free: hiking, biking, camping, canoeing, camp cruising by boat.

Your cost of living is low - so when you earn $ from job, business or investments you may save (avoid spending) a large percentage of your income that you can put towards going 'up-the-ladder' of these alternatives: improving your house and land, building up a health savings account, etc. Gradually you can add systems, appliances, and tools that further reduce your living costs and/or save you time such as a roto-tiller, and even (the horror) a car.

Budget Per Year:

Comfortable Living budget: no car option. Add $2000 for operating a car.

Shelter	
property taxes	$1,000
maintenance	100
insurance	300
Utilities	
Electricity	0 (net)
Water and sewer (see note 1)	0
Phone	300
Internet	200
Transportation -no car	200
Food (see note 2)	0 (net)
Health care	2,000
Miscellaneous (see note 3)	1,200
Recreation & vacations	1,000
TOTAL: (see note 4)	$6,300

Notes:

1. Well and septic tank and/or compost system.
2. Garden and greenhouse surplus is traded for food not produced on site or foraged.
3. Miscellaneous includes: clothes, kitchen and bath, household, yard and garden, media,
4. $6,300 requires $126,000 invested at 5% net return after inflation. Assume inflation at 3% so an 8% return before inflation is needed with the extra plowed back into savings.

The Poor Millionaire:

Ken Fischer in his book ***The Ten Roads to Riches*** writes, "A million's not much anymore! A million invested well kicks off about $40,000 a year in cash flow ... - not enough to feel rich."

An individual with a million dollars seeking an investment with only moderate risk - might get 7% per year. With inflation at 3% he will realize only a 4% net return after inflation or $40,000 a year from his million dollars, not exactly a generous income. $40,000 per year might be barely enough for an average family living a conventional lifestyle. One million used in a ZC lifestyle would be more than adequate, however.

A millionaire is liable to have expensive toys, a big house with high heating bills, inefficient gas guzzling SUV and/or a fast sports car that is expensive to insure.

A skillful ZCLer might be able to live better than the millionaire in many ways stretching his dollars way, way farther. Any idiot can merely buy stuff and spend dollars to meet his needs, but real skill is needed for ZCL. You must plan ahead, not just buy for convenience.

Example: cars:

The millionaire may buy a new car every year. Depreciation costs (decline in the value of the car), insurance costs, gas, etc, will = about $10,000 per year.

A ZCL practitioner maintains an old car that gets high miles per gallon doing most repairs himself and buying only basic insurance = $2,000 per year.

Or, ZCL a practitioner walks, uses a bikes and occasional bus = $200 year or less.

Of course it is possible for millionaires to use their dollars to achieve ZCL. How many would? How many would even be capable of doing it, have the will to achieve it? They are not likely to have developed habits of frugality. They may have no generalized skills, be too proud to buy used, be too impatient to shop around or forage.

Some wealthy folks are frugal. People consider them to be eccentric cranks. Better for us all, I believe, if millionaires lived with frugality, instead of wasting the earths resources (and driving up cost for everybody) with big houses, extra houses (seven in the case of John McCain), gas guzzling cars, extra cars (Jay Leno has 30), and polluting, fuel wasting frequent jet trips all over the world.

6.13 RAISING $: To maintain a comfortable ZC lifestyle:

At last you reach a point where you can't or won't reduce costs any more. Perhaps you must have a car and won't or can't move to where a car is not needed so you are stuck with $2000 per year minimum cost. And, of course there are taxes.

Then you must save or invest to get interest or dividends, start a business or get a job. Of course, living almost zero cost, you can save even at service job wages.

What to invest in:

Money is eaten by inflation. As I've said elsewhere in this book, but needs to be emphasized, money loses value just sitting in your pocket or under the mattress. Putting money in the bank only may keep the value of your money even with inflation, earning maybe three percent interest or a little more while inflation eats it at an equal three percent average per year.

Trying to beat inflation: To get a higher return and beat inflation you might try investing in the stock market. Unfortunately stock that may pay higher returns – through dividends and/or increases in the value of the stock – have higher risks. You could lose all or part of your original invested dollars chasing after higher returns. You might also try investing in real estate, or starting a business. Again, the risk can be considerable.

Better and safer than money in your pocket, under the mattress, in the bank, or in bonds or stocks - is to invest in knowledge, in skills, tools and supplies that reduce your living costs and/or allow you to set up a business.

Businesses:

A business that is a natural extension or expansion of an activity practiced to achieve ZCL may be the best alternative. In my situation, study, research, and recording methods of ZCL were expanded into this book. But countless other methods present themselves.

Expand your greenhouse areas to grow organic produce that is saleable at a higher price than non-organically grown food: grow and sell a surplus and use the money earned to cover your food costs for the food types you don't grow.

Design and construct efficient ZCL houses and solar farms for others. Having built your own, you have experience at it.

Expand production of something you make for yourself: If you're no salesman and many of us are not and you can't sell it, you can still use the product yourself or use it in a trade, perhaps.

Electricity production from solar cells: sell the surplus (that usually will occur on hot summer days when air conditioners are running) back to the electric company. Called 'net metering' in some places, this is already possible, with laws and technology available. A device called an 'inverter' makes this possible. You will have to ask the power company in your area about it, and possibly lobby your government to make it permissible.

Computers have become cheap and easy to use and ease the business tasks of planning ahead and rationalizing accounting, production, marketing, sales, inventory, storage, shipping, and handling. The uses you make of your computer may be expandable into a business - such as accounting.

Look for and set up a business operation that, although it may pay at a low rate of pay per hour, is steady, constant, and automatic, and therefore over time, a considerable number of $ may accrue. Ideal would be a business that requires only a modest investment and doesn't require much monitoring. Electricity production from solar panels as described above may fit this concept - as the cost of these panels decreases. Install more panels than you need for your own electricity consumption, and let the electric company pay you for the surplus your panels produce. An oversized system will make your electric meter run backwards as your surplus builds up. I call this a 'sorcerers apprentice' business after the Hans Christian Anderson story and Disney cartoon, where the system and income flow roll on endlessly. You need do essentially nothing but cash checks and perhaps dust off your solar panels occasionally.

A list of more business possibilities: You will have to research these:

Auto repair in your home garage.

Computer system set up, operation and repair.

Biofuel production: alcohol, biodiesel, methane, and/or feedstock for biofuel.

Making or repairing clothes.

Bird seed, pet food.

Plants: seedlings, cuttings, potted plants, fertilizer such as worm castings.

Make/grow and sell: sprouts, yogurt, kefir, dried vegetables.

Download - from the internet to sell: books on CD/ DVD or printed out on your home printer, or music or movies on CD/ DVD; or house plans, craft instructions, car repair manuals, home and appliance repair manuals, etcetera.

And, the internet can expose even a modest home business to world-wide sales. You just need something to sell that you can sell for more than your costs. The book ***The Long Tail*** by Chris Anderson details the possibilities.

A business to install, operate, maintain, and repair solar devices and greenhouses.

Helping other people attain ZCL.

Home based publishing.

Recycling trash: more could be done with our mountains of trash, I believe.

The Dutch during the heyday of their trading enterprises stored grain in the attics of their houses, not for consumption but for trade, and to keep it close and safe. Hearing of a famine in some part of Europe they filled their ships with grain and sailed there as fast as possible – expecting higher prices. They saved lives, and made a profit at the same time. Perhaps, like the Old Dutch, you could save or store food or other things that varies in prices with the seasons and economic vicissitudes: selling when prices are high.

On-site storage facilities may need to be extensive for your business. You may need shelves, display cases, bins. Possibly you need a place to keep things you sell through the Internet. And, you need places to keep things accumulated while foraging

Zoning laws might restrict you so learn what these are in your area. If you can't work within the laws, you may need to conceal or disguise your business from government officials and possibly from neighbors. Discovered, you may have to move your business. And, you may need to work to change zoning laws to make them friendlier to home businesses.

Note: From your local building department: Find out the minimum shed size you can build without a building permit. Also, find out if a polyethylene plastic roofed structure is considered temporary and therefore, no building permit is required.

Your business may require a home office, computer, filing cabinets, workshop, repair shop, a place to perform services, etcetera.

Rental unit: As mentioned earlier, a rental unit in your home - with separate entrance, kitchen, and bath; could provide income and pay property taxes.

Stock Market:

Books on the stock market claim that over the long term a prudent investor might make 12% a year. 12% per year is the long-term average growth in the values of stock. Inflation takes an average of 3% per year so you are left with 9% net growth. In the cost and budget estimates above I assumed only a 5% return average after inflation. Unfortunately, all-to-often, stock investments don't pan out (literally). You can lose your carefully husbanded savings. Possibly you could realize 9% per year average in relative safety by investing in an index fund for the NASDAQ or the S & P 500 over a period of decades as suggested by Burton Malkiel in his book ***A Random Walk Down Wall Street***. At 9% you would need considerably less savings to assure a $6,300 annual income: only $70,000 rather than the $126,000 listed in the table above.

Stocks to buy: Stocks are notoriously unpredictable and the best experts get it wrong, usually (it seems) just after you've taken their advice. Malkiels' book explains that it is not just our own ineptitude. The market is quite random. The book recommends buying stock index funds only when stocks are beaten down and price-earning ratios are low - and then hold for years, even decades. Buy when price-earning rations are low, when the economy is in recession. You may have to wait years for these opportunities (while your money depreciates in value in a savings account due to inflation). If you buy individual stocks, buy stocks with a combined growth plus dividend value appreciation of 12% or more. A reasonable dividend of perhaps 3 to 7% helps secure the stock price. A high dividend may not be a good indicator of company value. The company may not be growing because it is in a mature industry that does not have much growth opportunity, and therefore must pay out a high dividend to attract investors/stockholders.

Because of the vagaries of the stock market; I must reiterate again, it may be best for you to invest in knowledge, tools, land and buildings that can reduce your living cost and support a home business.

Real estate: The recession of 2008 sadly revealed that it is no longer true that real estate always goes up. Ordinarily it is a good investment. Land and houses near small towns – towns outside of easy commuting distance to growing big cities and suburbs - never rose in value as much as suburban and big city properties. These may be good bargains. You may have a more difficult commute to a job if you have one in a big city or suburb, but living ZC you may not need to take a job there. You can sell locally or travel to suburbs or the big city only on weekends to sell products, perhaps at a farmers market. If close enough, city and suburban residents on week end drives may come to you.

VIGNETTES:

A day in the life a person already living zero cost in comfort.

Upon waking up, I have a big first decision, sleep in or not, an option I have because I live Zero cost. If I had been up late last night as I sometimes am on some project, I will sleep in, but not today.

For breakfast I have mayapple fruit forged in the woods yesterday. They are at their summer peak. I drink green tea grown in my greenhouse. I have slices of toast cut from homemade bread covered with homemade blackberry preserves. The blackberries were foraged from the woods too.

In the morning, I clean house using cheap, safe cleaners: vinegar, baking soda, hydrogen peroxide, wiping with rags of recycled materials.

I start dinner in a pressure cooker that cuts energy use and cooking time in half compared to conventional cooking - but I take one more step. I set the pressure cooker in my solar cooker on the deck on the south side of my house. Through the day, while I'm gone, as the sun intensifies my dinner will cook at zero energy use and cost.

Next I work in my greenhouse looking for garden pests, checking the operation of my automatic watering system, and picking greens to use for lunch. My greenhouse gives me abundant off season produce, some I exchange at the food coop for food I don't grow. I no longer need or use food stamps although my income makes me eligible.

Then, putting on my wide brim hat, I go out to the yard to work in the warm summer sun. I weed my patches of edible flowers - and pick a few leaves to eat. I split some firewood – not need until winter – but cutting and splitting wood it is useful exercise anytime.

Before lunch I bike to the neighborhood produce co-op. There I exchange some of my greenhouse greens for a mix of produce to make a salad. I make and eat the salad right at the co-op. After eating, I put in an hour of work at the co-op preparing produce for sale or trade, stocking shelves, and updating accounts kept on the co-op computer. It is a pleasant interlude of mental and physical work.

After lunch I bike to the library. It is trash day, as I ride I keep my eye out for stuff thrown out. I notice a house under construction with a dumpster outside full of scrap lumber. I don't need it but struggling friends do. I stop to write a note on my pocket PC.

At the library I use one of the library computers to answer e-mails (I have a reserved time). Then I do an Internet search for free stuff on ***freecycle.com*** and finally, I look for garage sales listed online. I have no phone but rely on e-mails, public phones, or use my friendly neighbor's phone when I must talk to someone. I save $500 a year.

Home again I get the mail. There is one bill in the mail from the electric company. I open it to find they owe me money and have sent me a check because the solar panels on my roof have fed more electricity into the power grid than I used last month. My house is designed to be cooled naturally, so I need no air conditioning. During the sunny days of summer when my solar panels are producing their maximum I don't need the power, but the electric company needs more since other folks are running air conditioners

I get the pressure cooker out of the solar cooker and dinner out of the pressure cooker. I cooked beans - traded with neighbors for squash and peppers. I make a green salad of turnip greens radish greens and foraged wild spinach (sometimes called lambs quarters or goosefoot). Dessert is sweet potato pie – no sugar added relying on the natural sweetness of the sweet potato for taste.

In the evening I go to a meeting of the local 'Thrift Club' dedicated to helping members save every penny. I am a charter member, and a celebrated local authority. Currently our group is looking for ways that the local government might save money by practicing ZCL methods.

In the late evening I watch TV – a PBS show on making methanol fuel from weeds, crop wastes and algae. (Maybe, someday I'll begin producing my own fuel and build a car). My reception comes from a homemade antenna (so I save the cost of cable) that can be rotated like the spars of an old sailing ship – from the ground to get the best reception. Using this contraption I can a dozen stations in different directions from my homestead.

Tomorrow evening I'll be at the community theater where I'm a writer, actor, cameraman, and sometimes spectator.

Bedtime, it is a warm night. I go out to the low 8 x 6 foot screened sleeping platform out in the garden next to the pond. The garden windmill turns in the night breeze, pumping water that trickles down the little waterfall next to the pond (and waters my garden). Waterfall and night bugs serenade me as I curl up in bed reading. For light I use a battery-powered lamp, the batteries recharged during the day from a solar panel on my porch. My energy cost is zero – again.

In the cool autumn nights to come when I sleep indoors again, I will throw scrap lumber in the rocket stove along with a few sticks from the yard and light it, creating a hot and fast burning fire, a blast of heat for an hour into the thermal mass of the stove flue. When the fire burns out; the heat will be stored - to be released slowly through the night.

ZCL through a year of life:

Spring: I pursue the bloom of garage sales and flea markets. I hunt for them on street, internet and newspaper (reading the paper at the library). I prepare the soil, plant gardens, get the greenhouses up to full production in the warming weather. I take long walks in the (bug free until June) woods enjoying the resurgence of life.

Summer: I visit farmers markets buying or exchanging produce. In the fine weather I build things outside: solar panels, garden sheds, greenhouses, root cellar, pond improvements. I forage for edible wild plants in woods and fields. I take long vacations to beaches, mountains and wilderness.

Fall: I harvest produce and dry, can, freeze and otherwise stockpile food. I cut down trees and carry, cut up, split, and stack logs under cover for use as firewood. (But I use wood cut last year for this winter's heat – wood should be allowed to dry six months or more under cover).

Winter: Thanks to my wood burning stove, solar heating system and heavy house insulation, my heating bill is zero. On sunny winter days the sun alone heats my house effortlessly. But in cold cloudy weather I must work: carrying in wood, starting and maintaining a fire, and removing ashes (for garden fertilizer). Someday I might use these ashes to make soap. I begin indoor building projects: parts for a future car, house remodeling, making clothes and furniture. I work in my greenhouse, harvesting out-of-season produce that commands a high price at the local market. I practice 'cocooning', staying home when blizzards strike. I do my planning and organizing for the year, get my financial accounts in order - determining how much I spent, how much I saved, and what and whether I can do better next year. Should I build another greenhouse? Do I have the space, time, and money?

***

CHAPTER 7: SOCIETY PRACTICING ZCL

Outline: **Page**

Introduction:

This book has concerned itself primarily with individual and family ZCL up to now. What would happen if dozens, thousands or millions of folks working together lived ZC? This chapter will consider that possibility, discussing how societies might practice ZCL - going from small to large organizations, and from short to long periods of time.

The practice of ZCL may evolve. At first individuals here or there may attempt a few, then more ZCL methods; then families; then finding each other, groups doing things in co-operation. Next, larger and more formal organizations: co-operatives, businesses, communities, cities, regions, and nations might gradually adopt ZCL practices.

From perfecting your **personal economy** described in chapter 6, you may now work to develop your 'L.E.' - your **local economy.** Just as servers connect personal computers allowing them to share information, programs, ideas, etc. - your local economy can be developed to connect your P.E. to the P.E.s of other folks - letting you share, co-operate and coordinate production of things and services not easily produced on your own.

Note: this is not the course of most economic development. More usual is specialization of local economies to produce good or services for export to the national or global economy and the atrophy of local production for local use.

7.1 GETTING TOGETHER

Informal or organized groups dedicated to ZCL could make a huge leap forward, could really open up possibilities the individual alone may not have, multiplying their capabilities through research, teaching, learning, making things, sharing, bartering, trading, foraging, etcetera.

Some examples: An organization can find and make use of previously ignored or unrecognized resources beyond the abilities of individuals or families to handle. Specific Examples: Taking apart buildings for materials ordinarily destroyed and hauled to the dump. Sharing equipment to collect, deliver and process large quantities of recyclable materials such as compost, mulch, scrap wood, scrap metal, appliances, etc. Buying things in bulk and dividing them up, reducing costs for members. Conducting classes in basic skills: sewing, leatherworking, woodworking, car repair, house building, computer use, web site building. Sharing rides, supplies and equipment to create almost free recreational activities such as hiking, camping, biking, canoeing, small boat cruising.

Confluence: A confluence seems to be a kind organization well suited to groups in the early stages of attempting ZCL. Quotes from Bert and Holly Davis in a magazine entitled 'Dwelling Portably'. January 1991 as discussed by A. J. Heim in her book ***Car Living Your Way***.

"For a while the past year, Holly and I were with the Oanfi Confluence ('Oanfi" means: 'Our arbitrary name for it'. Those in it did not have a name for it that we heard.)

"A confluence is an informal clustering of friends who dwell portably (or mobility) within easy travel of, (but seldom right next to) one another.

"Unlike gathers, caravans, or treks that are temporary, a confluence may continue indefinitely.

"Unlike most networks whose members live far apart and interact mainly by mail or phone, members of a confluence are close enough to meet often, share rides, help one another, etc.

"Unlike intentional communities which require management, a confluence can free flow, because differences can be handled by moving or avoiding. For the same reason, one confluence can accommodate a wider range of dwelling-ways, lifestyles, family types, interests, etc. than can one community.

"There can be … confluences with backpackable accommodations, live-aboard vehicles or boats, and temporary apartments or cabins. There are confluences in the backwoods, in farming areas, and in large cities. More than a million people (our guess), though most probably think of their connections as 'my friends and I' rather than as a type of (non) organization. Some confluences are composed of recent immigrants with common ethnic origins. Others center around strong shared interest such as surfing, bridge construction, computer hacking, a type of music, etc.

"All members of any one confluence probably have about the same amount of mobility. Though members may not move very often, some portability or at least temporariness seems essential if there's to be involvement without domination. (Most settled people prefer to live well away from their relatives and friends, even though that keeps them from doing much together; and to be cordial but uninvolved with any neighbors; lest they rub them the wrong way and create enemies - a horrid prospect where no one can move easily. When settled neighbors do get involved, they usually need formal rules or rulers to handle disagreements).

"Most confluences are fuzzy. They lack definite boundaries in space, time, or membership. In Oanfi, the one family we became involved with had some friendly neighbors (or neighborly friends) who, in turn, had other friends, some of whom the family knew and some they didn't. Furthermore, everyone moved around and came and went. (Oanfi folk lived in vehicles.) Most confluences are difficult to contact or to join … there's …no recruiting officer, visitors center, or admission procedure.

"Some of its members felt that Oanfi lacked togetherness. But to us, the amount of swapping/sharing of skills and equipment was impressive, especially because it sees to happen spontaneously, with no exalted guru or long winded councils telling everyone what to do."

Imagine if you will a confluence, or countless local confluences dedicated to ZCL. Able to teach, swap skills, share things and generally help each other, ZCL might become more easily realized, practical, and widely adopted. Confluences might be the natural basic units of organization for a widespread society dedicated to ZCL.

Problems in human social relations:

In the process of creating an ideal community problems between folks can be expected to arise: In particular personality conflicts; simply, certain people don't like each other. How can this be overcome? Like so much else in this book, it is the topic of another book or shelf of books. Here I will merely draw attention to the problem.

To survive and accomplish tasks, an organization requires that folks get along at a certain level no matter how much they dislike each other. To keep work going forward, sometimes folks must suppress their true feelings or at least avoid acting in uncivil ways. But suppression of your true feelings can makes things worse later, when the full force of your true feeling come out all at once. Mutual festering hatreds, I suspect has been the cause of countless organizational failures from family dissolutions to lost wars. Can folks be totally honest without ruining social relationships and organizations? Can honesty be achieved without hatred? I can imagined this exchange:

"I hate you".

"Well I hate you."

"Okay, we agree we hate each other. Now let's work together anyway".

Possibly, despite mutual hatreds and dislikes, admission of the fact and some maturity - ability to suppress certain feelings (such as the desire to murder the other person) could allow the organization to work. Though we grow to be adults, we are all like children to each other inside. In our reactions to each other it is not possible for us to totally suppress the child within.

Early organizations devoted to ZCL may develop into more formal organizations; perhaps forming a homesteading association and buying a large acreage together (land is cheaper to buy that way) and dividing it up or beginning a co-housing community.

7.2 CO-HOUSING:

What is it?

Co-housing is a formal organization of people working together to build and maintain their own community - usually using laws created for condominium associations. 40 families is a common community size. Co-housing communities usually exclude automobiles, relegating them to parking spaces and garages on the periphery, and rely a bikes, carts, and walking within. Communities may have all one type of house: townhouses for example, or separate single family houses, or a mix of housing types. They may share a laundry, workshop, computers, and recreational facilities in a central 'common building'. They may share tools, skills, vehicles and rides. They can create an enriched environment and lifestyle beyond anything even the wealthy could obtain with mere money: a group of sharing caring neighbors. And though some co-housing communities are expensive, they can be low cost.

Most co-housing communities are homes for families. A few have facilities and space to produce things and carry on businesses. A productive – rather than just habitation oriented co-housing community can offer a tremendous opportunity to practice ZCL. A production oriented co-housing community might cut the cost, and speed up the time needed for folks to set up a comfortable ZC lifestyle because land and development costs can be **shared**. For example, one well for water, rather than individual wells for each family could save $. I can imagine co-housing communities devoted to producing most of the things needed to live in comfort: food, health care, vehicle fuel such as bio-diesel, electricity, clothing, entertainment and so on.

ZCL Co-housing design:

I am going to discuss Co-housing design for ZCL in more detail here because it really is one of the best paths to achieve ZCL. I'll be repetitious of stuff already said about pursuing ZCL as an individual or a family, but perhaps it helps to emphasize the point. The difficulties are very great, not the least of which is assuring everybody is honest in the group and people get along.

This new community could be designed from the start to achieve ZCL: By the end of construction, residents may have few dollars left in savings; but have complete facilities to practice ZCL, even for small miscellaneous items – and so not need much money. In a commonly owned community building residents might have a large kitchen and dining space used for occasional shared meals (or to rent out), extensive food processing equipment (ovens, freezer, food processors, etc.), wood and metal working shops, facilities for making clothes, soap, furniture, and a hundred other things, car repair garage, elaborate computer room, media room with big screen TV, a system to store solar energy collected in the summer for use in the winter (called an annual heat storage system), storage space for stockpiles of things bought in bulk on sale at low cost for use in the future, and much more. These shared facilities allow individual houses to be modest and inexpensive.

Health care: Because a co-housing community can be compact with many shared facilities, on-site medical care facilities may be possible that can take care of residents – including people with long term debilitating illnesses.

A group health insurance that co-housing residents buy into together may be practical to save money. Residents may be solicitous of each other's health and well-being because they live in a community that **shares** health insurance costs. They may help each other when sick and in overcoming bad health habits like smoking or obesity - thus reducing the cost of health care and use of health care professionals.

Construction cost:

Co-ops and co-housing might make possible a lower investment to achieve a comfortable ZC lifestyle; less than the $170,000 or more suggested in chapter 6 on 'Comfortable Living'. Using sweat equity to build the community, sharing diverse facilities and skills, possibly $125,000 might be enough. Land costs for multifamily or a single-family house with lot might be $20,000 or even $10,000 for each lot, much higher in some places, lower in others. Putting aside the problem of a site (a whole book in itself), bulk buying of building materials for the community should save at least 10%. Building your home yourself, paying for it as you go along, called sweat equity can save at least half to two thirds of the cost of home construction.

Future residents sharing or teaching skills and working together during construction in carpentry, plumbing, electrical, heating systems to save labor costs could reduce or eliminate the use of expensive professionals. (They can drain away your hard earned money - charging you many times the dollars-per-hour you earn at your job). You may have to borrow money, get a line of credit and/or credit cards for plans, land, tools, materials, building permits.

This use of credit – for things that will eventually shrink your cost of living is a far, far better use of credit than the usual use of credit: purchases of imported junk, new cars, or a mortgage where your payment mostly goes to cover interest. If you are renting, consider getting out of rent as early as possible by moving to the site, camping out there and applying your rent money towards the building of your community. And, if you live on site, you can more easily use your spare time building. A step beyond camping - future residents might set up a dormitory structure on site first, perhaps a future barn, where they might live and save expenses while building their community.

What could the final cost be for each family of setting up a ZCL co-housing community? Possibly:

Land	10,000	
Material	30,000	see note 1
Parking and garages	2,000	see note 2
Common house	10,000	
Common barns	2,000	see note 3
Permits	1,000	
Utilities	20,000	see note 4
Savings	50,000	
Total:	$125,000	

Notes:

1. For a modest house of 1,000 square feet.
2. Some residents may not need a car but a garage would still be useful for various ZCL needs.
3. and various outbuildings
4. Including solar energy systems

The money in savings is needed to pay taxes and items not produced by the community - $50,000 netting $2,500 a year if invested at a 5% return (after inflation). Living ZC in a co-housing community residents might fairly easily, over time be able to increase the amount in savings as inflation rises.

$125,000 might seem like an unattainable sum to save for folks on a service economy wage, but by practicing the techniques in this book with resolve and diligence I believe it is quite possible.

7.3 CO-OPERATIVES: A new economy of co-ops.

What are co-operatives (or co-ops):

Co-operatives are organizations created to undertake buying selling, and/or the production of goods and/or services. Co-ops are formal legally incorporated organizations, owned collectively by the members who share in any benefits. They are usually non-profit, and may be democratically structured: electing boards of directors who then choose and administer managers, employees, and volunteers. Credit Unions are examples of a common, widely established form of co-op.

Co-ops may be competitive, just as businesses are competitive over membership, prices, services, and quality of products.

If people are to achieve any kind of economic stability I believe they need to be co-owners and participants in the local economic institutions they depend on. My experience banking with large private banks illustrates this. With irritating frequency the ownership of these banks changed. In consequence they were changing their name, changing policies, changing lending practices – usually for the worst for customers. I switched to a credit union.

Kinds of Co-ops:

Consumer co-ops: These are the usual kind of co-op today. A group of folks get together to buy in bulk and then divide it up. They may look at how products were made, not just prices, before they buy - taking into consideration the impact on the environment and the working conditions and pay of workers.

Producer co-ops: Rare today. They are a great challenge - making them work explores almost new territory in human social co-operation. The common opinion is that production of things requires bosses, and autocratic hierarchical economic organizations – to keep peoples 'nose to the grindstone'. A producer co-op based on voluntary cooperation among people creates a new level of difficulty and complexity for a co-operative organization. A new level of maturity and responsibility would be required of folks. I want to call attention to the problem in this book, a thorough examination of the problem would require another book or maybe a shelf of books.

Producer and consumer co-ops would combine the functions of both.

Multi task multifunction co-ops may be hard to manage and may take up much time and energy. The computer and web sites could help, making communication and co-ordination easier.

A key principle of co-op operation: Keep meetings few, short and to the point. Co-ops tend to devote vast amounts of time and resources to group meetings that may accomplish little and make participants feel that their time and talent was wasted.

In a co-op, the incentive of individual profit, that is; profit not shared with others is removed. But, the incentive of shared cost savings remains - and could be substantial.

Consumer/producer/co-housing co-ops combined: An organization for the future that may offer great advantages:

On one site, multiple activities could be going on. Face to face interaction could exist between the makers of products and the buyers/users – something that is extremely rare in this society. In some ways the ancient economy of the pre-industrial village might be recreated - with workshops producing items of cloth, wood, metal and perhaps plastic. Food processing might be undertaken in a co-housing kitchen as community gardens are harvested.

The co-op is an underused method of economic organization with, I believe, great potential to enhance ZC living.

Advantages of Co-ops for ZCL:

How can a co-op contribute to ZCL and cut or eliminate cost?

- The 'cost of profit' is eliminated. Benefits could be widely shared by local residents, not siphoned away by business owners and stockholders who may live a continent away.
- Local control of basic economic enterprises is assured, (a co-op is **NOT FOR SALE** – no distant owner can take it over and outsource production), economic stability is possible, secure local jobs can be created and kept.
- If incorporated as a non-profit organization taxes may be reduced or eliminated.
- They can research products and buy the best at a fair price, and not buy foreign products made by children in sweatshops or polluting industries.
- Sharing of facilities and resources is made more possible. For example, as co-owners of enterprises folks might make use of equipment during non-working hours such as tools, machines, computers, offices, etcetera.

- Some, many products are more efficiently produced at a large scale. Co-ops make it possible to achieve scale economies without handing production over to private businesses and corporation motivated by profit and not the best interest of a community.
- Work could be made interesting, even fun, with everybody doing their share of onerous tasks. Since everybody has to do them, everybody has an interest in making them more pleasant, or eliminating them through social or technological innovations.
- ZCL co-operatives may be well suited to people spit out by corporate capitalism, people who are not business types, not anxious to commercialize everything and everybody; people marching to a different drummer.

Co-ops and government:

Some readers may decide that these networks of co-operatives I am proposing is a kind of Communism. But, I do not propose co-ops as mere arms or departments of government - as in China and the old USSR - but free, independent coops: independent of government and big business - and in friendly competition among themselves over members, prices, product availability, quality and type, and efficiency of operation.

Government may be involved with Co-ops to regulate them where needed: for example reviewing health, safety, and accounting practices. A State might establish a Co-op Commission to oversee co-ops.

Governments that are friendly to co-ops and seek to encourage them may pursue new policies: They might create laws that encourage people to join, (without coercing them) with tax incentives for example. Non-profit status should help.

Co-ops verses Business:

This topic, worthy of more discussion than I present here will be addressed in the web site **http://0costliving.com**

Businesses are institutions that exist to make profits. The business economy uses the profit motive to gets things done. Though widely heralded as the greatest economic idea ever, serious problems exist in an economic system based on this motive. Greed as the motivator fails to use, even undermines the 'sense of community' that many, (not all) people feel. Instead 'all- for-one, one-for-all', an attitude of 'everyone for himself' can prevail. A co-op based economic system can make use of the sense of community - can make sharing, folks helping each other, and social responsibility more possible.

Big box retail businesses, full of imports can devastate local businesses. They don't buy locally. They can't be bothered by the trouble of dealing with small producers, or short production runs of sometimes-unique products. Locally owned, locally producing businesses may have difficulty selling to or competing against big retailers, and go out of business. Local economic stability may be undermined. Co-ops could help market the products of small producers.

Corporations are all about convenience buying. What if co-ops could become convenient, more convenient than corporations? Then, perhaps they could prevail.

Co-ops might, by use of the internet, by selective buying from other co-ops, by buying locally, by buying large amounts for members and dividing it up (thus getting wholesale prices), by rational, long term, planned purchases and production operate with more efficiency than corporations.

Co-ops can provide economic alternatives to the stranglehold businesses can have on community economic life. (Examples exist of collusion in prices and wages among businesses that is unplanned and legal, but still amounts to price and wage fixing). Co-ops competing against businesses can create more competition and more open markets.

Here might be the ultimate key to ZCL. Co-ops with all of their advantages - as they develop increasing sophistication and ability - might gradually undermine and take over economic functions from the corporate/business/capitalist world. A quiet, non-violent revolution might occur as co-ops restore economic stability to communities ravaged by the global corporate capitalist economy. The transition could be peaceful, unless the global corporate capitalist economy perceives co-ops to be a threat and chooses to lash out – requiring co-ops to institute measures for self-defense.

A New Economic System: A new economy of co-ops - 'co-operative capitalism' not 'corporate capitalism' - might advance ZCL.

What: Networks of coordinated interrelated co-ops producing a complete – or extensive inventory of goods needed by a community..

Why: I believe the efficiency and cost savings of centralized large-scale mass production of goods is greatly overrated. Another book is needed to establish this fact but consider these thoughts: When the cost of management, marketing, shipping, overhead, are added in, local small scale production may be cheaper and advantageous in other ways. For example the problem of matching a production run to demand is simpler, and producing too much or too little for the market is less likely. A network of co-ops might create a rational, coordinated, and fair system of production and consumption in place of the current market driven system which when closely examined is rife with waste, inefficiency, unfairness, disorder and chaos.

How: The current free market system creates economic opportunities. So many local and national businesses in the United States have been wiped out or outsourced that there are "holes" and opportunities for locally made product of all kinds. With the application of new technologies these may be produced more cheaply than imports. Examples: clothes, tools, appliances, wood products. (Americans once were brilliant woodworkers; producing snug houses, functional beautiful furniture, and the fastest clipper ships in the world. Wood was the 19th century plastic.).

7.4 SMALL TOWNS:

Advantages for ZCL: Small towns as ideal locations to practice ZCL were described earlier in chapter 5 on homesteading. Here the advantages are considered in more detail:

In a small town all basic facilities and services may be close together; post office, police, fire departments, government offices, library, recreational/entertainment facilities, basic shopping for food, tools, materials; health clinic, and access to high speed internet service, vehicle repair facilities (if you have one), farmers market, etcetera. A small town that is the county seat may be an especially good location, with more complete government facilities- county library and social service agencies for example.

Therefore, residents may be able to accomplish many tasks without a car, making ZCL easier to achieve.

Small towns may be easier to run with care and efficiency than big cities. Big city government requires big bureaucracies, resulting in remoteness from citizens; anonymity of service providers and thus it may operate with less care and efficiency.

In the future, I like to imagine, some small towns might become dedicated to ZCL. They might, possibly through co-ops do these things:

• Create a **'universal factory'** able to produce small runs of many different kinds of products, able to quickly switch production from one to another as global and local demand changes.

• Create a Community college branch at the local high school and library, perhaps making use of traveling teachers and underutilized local folks skilled at topics useful for ZCL.

• Practice less expensive government, and assess lower taxes by using volunteers for some government tasks: a practice that is more possible in small towns.

• Create a **'Community energy utility'**: such as an electric company possibly using local alternative energy sources such as solar and wind; and a bio-diesel alcohol, and/or methanol plant using agricultural waste.

• Create a **'Community recycling center'** including activities such as using farm and yard waste as compost for fertilizer.

Sleepy, stagnant small towns may be the growth centers of the future in a ZCL society. Around theses towns, might develop a nearby 'suburban' ring of small farms ½ to a few acres. These farms might be close enough to walk or bike to town and (like the Amish) thus have no need for cars. They might be organic farms recycling almost all waste.

Small towns used to have a compact core, centered around the railroad station, with everything within easy walking distance. (Now all too frequently strip malls exist in the townships just outside the city limits). Schools were located in the center of town within walking distance of most students. (no busses needed – keeping school board budgets and taxes low). In a ZCL oriented town these arrangements might be recreated.

Today, parking lot requirements in zoning laws require extensive areas of parking around the old business cores of small towns. In the future, reducing these parking space requirements might help to keep the core compact so walking and biking is easier. Someday, with thoughtful and careful design, perhaps it may again become practical to ride horses, and use horse drawn vehicles in small towns.

7.5 CITIES

What if entire cities took up ZCL? What if one city already has?

One large city is practicing, in part, zero cost living; Curitiba Brazil. (Curitiba was mentioned on page 287, but worth reiterating). In Curitiba the transportation system has been made so fast and efficient, using buses on roads reserved exclusively for busses - that automobiles are rarely used in the city thus savings the residents a great deal of money, lowering their living costs, and raising their quality of life and standard of living. The streets of fifty blocks of the downtown area are entirely given over to pedestrians. No traffic jams, no dangerous cars among pedestrians. The city has been described as having third world costs but first world living conditions. Visit some web sites describing Curitiba. You'll be impressed. Just google 'Curtiba'.

Bike City:

Large numbers of folks attempting ZCL might want to try creating bike cities or adapt existing cities to be bike cities.

What are the advantages?

You could go everywhere without continually watching out for cars. You could travel around town without crossing rivers of rampaging metal behemoths. Children, wildlife, etc. could cross roads with less danger of being run over.

In a bike city three miles across with diagonal routes (as well as the common grid of roads), all destinations could be within a 20-minute bike ride. 8 or 10 mph is easily possible on a bike, almost as fast as the average speed of cars in most cities. 150,000 people could live comfortably within a nine square-mile square area (3 x 3 miles).

The city might feel open, spacious and even half empty - the land free of all of the space demands of automobiles and thus useable for other purposes. (In most cities half of the land is used for vehicles: for roads, parking lots, gas stations, driveways, junk yards, etc). In bike city much less land is lost under the pavement of the transportation system. Because bikes take up less space on streets than cars streets could be narrower - 4 lane roads cut back to two lanes. Freeways might become treeways - long beautiful parks - laced with bicycle paths. Less land would be required for parking, in fact not much parking area would be needed- parked bikes don't take up much space. The endless parking lots of strip mall shopping areas might be converted to green spaces or possibly solar farms – the pavement ripped up.

Bike city would have sufficient area within city limits - using the high intensity techniques of solar farms described in chapter 6 - to provide for all of the food and energy needs of the residents; and a modest surplus for export.

Bike city could be a healthy place to live. Frequently riding bikes, people get exercise, become fit and slim. Air pollution and the associated health effects could be reduced. Medical costs and health insurance costs might decline precipitously. No one would be killed or injured in an automobile accident. Car insurance would be unnecessary.

Horses might be put to use again. The Amish might move near bike city, and flourish building and selling carriages, wagons, horses, and gear.

Bike city might be quieter, much quieter, safer, cleaner, and cheaper to live in than a car oriented town. Bikes are cheap to buy and repair and no fuel (except food for the biker) is required..

It may be possible to design bikeways that are covered, for all weather capability, or bikes might be designed to be useable in bad weather, (enclosed three wheel recumbent bikes may work well for this).

Combining bike city with a bus system like Curitiba Brazil might create an unbeatable transportation system: Buses can carry bikes on outside racks - increasing the practicality of both. Bus routes and stops can be fewer and farther apart because bus riders - with bikes can travel farther and faster when they get off.

Perhaps, at the edge of town, parking lots for cars would be provided for visitors and residents who insist on having them.

Existing cities might be converted to bike cities through these steps:

- At the perimeter, build a ring road and peripheral parking lots. Ban all cars except emergency vehicles within the ring.
- Provide delivery truck access routes to businesses and industries - possibly limited to certain times of the day - possibly sunken (with bike paths, parks, buildings over).
- Within the ring, at slow speed, allow construction and utility vehicles to use roads.
- Eliminate and convert car-parking areas in town to other uses.
- Paved roads that are used only by bikes and emergency vehicles – might be narrowed – four-lane roads becoming two.

- Develop all weather bikes and bike routes. Build covered bike paths in the commercial center of town.
- Permit 3 wheel-motorized bikes when required by disabled residents.

In bike city you may be able to live for very low cost, in a splendid environment. You might live a better, richer life than wealthy folks can in more conventional communities.

Bike city could be, not an antiseptic suburb or 'new town', but a complete working community with clean industries, home businesses, backyard businesses, maybe even farms with some kinds of farm animals in town.

Suburbs converted to ZCL communities:

The lots of suburban houses are large enough to convert into solar farms as described in chapter 6. These suburbs converted to 'farms' would look quite different. No sweeps of immaculate lawn punctuated by ornamental plantings. House and yard would be modified to be productive and useful, instead of for show - to impress the neighbors. Instead, yards would sport collections of the facilities needed for a ZCL farm: solar greenhouses, vegetable gardens, arrays of solar cells, sheds and barns for storage and processing of various materials and crops. Carefully designed and kept these new farms might still be pleasant in appearance to the neighbors. (Useful and utilitarian things often are more aesthetically appealing than merely ornamental objects. For example: Van Gogh painted pictures of his plain room, of sunflower fields, of peasants at work. And in England Constable painted scenes of simple country life).

7.6 EDUCATION AND TECHNOLOGY:

Technologies for ZCL:

Old technologies for ZCL:

Of what use is history? One use is that in history you may discover how practical technologies were discovered. The women of ancient Rome washed their clothes in the Tiber River. Roman temple sacrifices, ash and animal fat ran into the river. Where women washed clothes downriver from these sites they discovered that their clothes got cleaner easier. Some unknown thought to combine ash and animal fat: Viola soap! Considering this vignette from history made me ask: really, how hard can it be to make your own soap? Not very hard. Maybe we don't need the over processed, overpriced, over packaged commercial products.

Caesar put heels on the sandals of his soldiers. Heels allowed them to march faster and therefore Caesar was able to outmaneuver and defeat all of his opponents. In a ZCL society that does a lot of walking, it is worth knowing that a simple modification to footwear allows people to walk farther and faster. What other simple modifications to basic everyday items in life have yet to be discovered that can really improve life?

New technologies needed for ZCL:

Inventions needed to make ZCL easier:

To live ZCL we need to design/invent tools, machines, systems, technologies that make possible small scale production - at home or as part of a local economy and at a cost competitive with imports - of the innumerable diverse things needed for a comfortable life. Go through a department store and think about how you could make, or substitute a home/locally made item for every item they stock.

Think about whether, and how you could build your own car, making a factory unnecessary, perhaps. Think about how you could build your car cheaply and efficiently using components ordered on the internet, or using items from your local building supply store, or using recycled parts. Someday, in a ZCL economy, there might be hundreds of car companies (as there were at the beginning of the automobile age).

More inventions needed:

Technologies that put your home computer to work in the real world – that make it do more than just process data such as:

- Computer directed clothes and shoe making systems. (Goodbye clothing imports).
- Computer directed food-processing systems. Examples: breakfast cereal making machine, granola bar maker, candy bar maker.
- Computer directed fuel-making systems: methane, methanol, alcohol.

• Computer directed systems that perform all of the tedious cleaning tasks required in the home and community: trash collection and recycling, dishwashing, bathroom cleaning, cleaning floors, etcetera.

Too many inventions, too many technologies have the negative effect of making people more helpless, more dependent on, more subjugated to business, corporations, governments, professionals and various ‘experts’ for products and services such as health care, car repair, most supermarket food, heating, plumbing and electrical systems of homes, etc. The best inventions, from a ZCL perspective; free people from these dependencies: the bicycle, the solar house and greenhouse, the personal computer, the internet, Linux, Firefox, etc.

New colleges/universities:

I believe that in some ways colleges and universities are vastly overrated today. Too often, they are an excuse for students to avoid going to work. And, college/university education may not be worth it for many students, who end up with huge student debts and low paying jobs.

Much, even most of what they teach is not applicable to the useful, practical aptitudes needed to live ZC.

But learning, reading and study are still important. For ZCL we need colleges/ universities that emphasize practical and useful knowledge. At a ZCL college there might be courses in the ‘art’ of foraging, of finding uses for waste materials, of building solar greenhouses of scrap materials.

And needed are ZCL oriented colleges/universities that research and develop some of the inventions needed as listed earlier.

It might be interesting, even fun to attend a university for free by sneaking into classes - in the big classes, no one will notice. In economics, you can learn about the ‘marginal utility of production’. In calculus learn the ‘differential catechism’.

Your sheepskin supposedly will open doors for you but if you are intelligent, capable and a good learner, you may be better off learning real world skills. Instead of getting into the door of a business that relies on a piece of paper because they have no clue how to judge a person, better perhaps to stay out of their door altogether - and use whatever skills you have learned through college to live zero cost and start your own business.

7.7 SOCIETY: A zero cost living society:

What would an entire society look like practicing zero cost living? A vast impoverished wasteland where no work gets done, and garbage is everywhere, perhaps? Or, a real utopia where everyone does what they want to do, and no one is compelled to do anything to pay for food, shelter, etc. But doesn't every society need to compel someone to pick up the trash, wash the dishes, clean the public restrooms, labor in factories, and do all of the other miserable awful jobs necessary to keep society going?

I believe, if an entire society practices zero cost living, they will invent methods to make all of these tasks unnecessary, perhaps in the case of trash for example, by not producing things that wear out or get obsolete and are not recyclable or repairable.

Also: when you insist on taking care yourself including sometimes mundane daily tasks and not foist them on others then, because activity and exercise are built onto your daily life you may be healthier and live longer, (and help reduce health care costs). This may include (with the help of new technologies), cleaning up your own messes, growing your own food, repairing your own car, and building your own house.

For example, a ZCL society might create a "Health Car".

A "health car" could be imagined and designed specifically to provide good exercise for the owner in the process of operation, maintenance, and repair. For example, instead of power steering, use manual steering thus giving your arms exercise while operating the car. Similarly, instead of electrically operated roll down windows, use the old crank type thus requiring you to stretch your arms and move around. A car that is repairable, easy to repair at home can be another reason for exercise (as well as less frustration) built into your daily life. Possibly, some cars could have pull or crank starts again, requiring exercise to operate. (But with a safety device to save your arm in case of backfire – which the old model T didn't have. Another new invention might be added to the list above - a safe crank starting method for a car).

Health, recreations and games:

Sports today are expensive, dangerous, wasteful and unproductive, especially the racings sports and fighting sports. I believe sports can be healthy, useful, productive, and very low cost.

In a ZCL society, people might play sports that accomplish something as they are played. A few sports may accomplish this already: hunting, fishing, hiking, biking -but may easily be made wasteful if the practitioner starts buying elaborate equipment and going to extremes. Examples of new useful sports: a competition to find certain wild foods in season, a foraging contest on a bicycle, a contest to build useful things out of waste materials.

Board, card, role-playing or computer games might be invented that teach the basics of ZCL. Imagine a board game in which the players collect cards as they move around the board, each card representing a skill or system needed to set up a comfortable ZCL lifestyle. Or imagine a ***'Sims'*** game in which the characters try to live ZC; or ***'Sim City'*** game where the goal is to establish a ZCL society.

Thoreau Game:

ZCL itself might be a fascinating challenge, an interesting competition, a sport, perhaps a reality show or game, a game dealing with the real world. Now that would be a worthwhile game, wouldn't it?

ZCL practiced as a game, a great game; I think ought to be named the 'Thoreau Game', after Henry David Thoreau, the writer of Walden, the quintessential book about living cheap and independent. The game would be a contest to discover who is able to live most comfortably while spending the least amount of money: starting from nothing, or perhaps with basic clothes and a knife or a few tools. Opening gambit, secure food and water, beg or forage, squat somewhere. Each contestant chooses a starting location; at the end the winner is the one with the most comfortable circumstance.

In this survivor game in the real world your prize might be merely good health, perhaps a little extra money and development of a strong self will.

Economic freedom and security

ZCL might be used to build a social safety and income net. Workers need not take low paying jobs that exploit them, but work only when wages are raised to an appealing level. The 'reserve army of the unemployed' as described by Karl Marx and others, that is used to keep down wages and keep up profits, may become "a reserve army of independent freemen', a labor force only available when employers can assure them an attractive income, perhaps as co-owners rather than employees in more democratic economic institutions sharing in decision making and profits.

A new way of living for the elderly

Instead of paying social security to an aging population, better might be to help set them up to live ZC. The activity and exercise needed might be of positive benefit to most of the elderly. Similarly, folks with disabilities could be helped to take care of more of their needs through a household or community set up to practice ZCL. Savings might be realized in health care costs.

And, instead of schemes to privatize social security and get folk to gamble their money in the stock market with all of its attendant variables and unknowns, investments in systems and facilities that make ZCL possible might be more secure and assure a better return on invested money.

Progress?

So called 'progress' has had the bad consequence of making a lot of work out of tasks that, formerly, were free and fun to do. For example: the Native Americans hunted the buffalo herds of the Great Plains – a challenging, exciting, way to obtain food and a host of other useful materials such as hides for clothes and tents. Buffalo took care of themselves - were able to survive, even thrive out in the open - were perfectly adapted to the grasslands and climate, migrating with the seasons to fresh grasslands Now cattle occupy the land on fenced in ranges, requiring winter feed and shelter, overgrazing the land, requiring the tedium or rounding them up and shipping them off, and the horror and abysmal working conditions of the slaughterhouses. Proposals have been made in recent years to remove the fences, restore the buffalo herds and their ranges, and allow seasonal hunting.

7.8 ECONOMY:

A ZCL Society might be based on a New Economy of market co-operatives.

What am I talking about? Networks and associations of privately owned and operated non-profit economic co-operatives including producer and consumer coo-ops as described earlier. The new economy might create a diversified network of local producer co-ops capable of providing all of the basic things people need: food, fuel, electricity, etc.

Co-ops might provide buyers and markets for locally produced goods.

Co-ops might consider setting up a local food-processing factory to handle and market locally grown crops: setting up a biofuel storage, marketing and shipping co-op, or a refinery processing methanol

One great thing about co-ops is that they are NOT FOR SALE and therefore can't be bought up, split up, and outsourced by big business thus destroying local jobs and the local economic base. And, co-ops could own natural resources - keeping them out of the hands of businesses that too often overexploit and exhaust those resources, take the earnings and profits away to line the pockets of stockholders and /or wealthy owners, and provide no benefit to the local community. .

Co-ops might keep down prices by providing alternatives to businesses (especially big-box businesses filled with imported goods and gas stations selling mostly imported oil), by providing competitive sources of supply, and by cutting out middlemen. Co-ops could maintain local alternative sources of supply to imports in case of price increase or actual cut off of supply. (Folks living ZC might buy locally even at higher prices to prevent the local economy from being undermined –because once local sources of supply are wiped out, then prices may rise for imports due to a lack of competition).

Through formal associations, co-ops might coordinate the operation of the local economy. By co-coordinating supply and demand: matching the needs - the expected purchases of members of the consumer co-ops with the products of the producer co-ops.

The government role in market co-op economy might be, in part, to provide a 'fence of laws' to help and defend co-ops and free markets from unfair competition by big businesses such as price gouging. Anther role might be to monitor for honesty in the financial dealings of co-ops. But government must be careful. It should not regulate co-ops such that they become a medieval style guild economy, which restricts supply of goods and services to keep up prices.

Possible economic consequences of ZCL if widely adopted:

Imports dry up
Savings increase
Corporations and big business shrivel
Prices become stable for basic human needs: food, fuel, land, housing.
Wages rise as people work at will and not out of necessity.
Technology replaces labor - eliminating obnoxious repetitious unhealthy low paying jobs
Illegal aliens stop coming; their services no longer needed because people take care of themselves. Illegal aliens may have to learn to live ZCL too.

Biofuel Economy:

In a future ZCL economy we might get all of our vehicle fuel in the form of 'biofuel' processed from algae ponds. Biofuel production and algae ponds have problems, technology has not quite perfected them today, (and detailed discussion of this is beyond the scope of this book). I want to mention them because they may fit well into a ZCL economy and society. Farms may become energy farms, producing not just food, but also energy in the forms of biofuel, methanol, ethanol, solar energy, as discussed in chapter 6.

If / when perfected, an algae pond may produce 15,000 gallons an acre. (An acre of cornfield might produce 300 gallons of fuel or less).

500 gallons of fuel production would require only 1/30of an acre equaling 1,452 square feet of pond. 500 gallons equals 50 million Btu of energy, enough to heat an efficient house in a midwestern climate for a year, or enough fuel to run a car for one year traveling 12,500 miles and getting 25 miles per gallon.

1000 square feet of pond per person per year might be enough for all basic needs. For the entire United States: 300 million people x 1000 square feet of pond = 300 billion square feet divided by 43,560 (the area of one acre) = 6,896,552 acres divided by 640 (acres in one square mile) = 10,776 square miles. Therefore an area of about 100 x 100 miles square could provide enough biofuel for the whole country: Algae ponds need not all be located in one region, but might be scattered and range in size from backyard ponds to farms with thousands of acres of pond.

Farm produced biofuel might be processed and stored on the farm, or at locally owned and operated co-operatives. Perhaps some small towns will have a municipally owned and operated biofuel refinery.

7.9 REGIONS:

Locations to try ZCL as individuals, families, groups, or formal organizations:

The Amish choose the places they settle with care: looking for regions that suit their needs: cheap fertile farmland, few cars on the roads, helpful neighbors nearby –usually fellow Amish. Just as certain places suit the Amish, some regions may be more suitable for practicing ZCL.

Evaluating all the regions of the Earth or even North America would take another book or two. Here is one example, to show you what to look for: Northern Canada south of the permafrost. The entire region is intolerably cold in winter. Mosquitoes and black flies infest the summer. The spring and fall are the most pleasant seasons. So why go there?

It is a hard country but may be a good place to practice ZCL. Small towns widely scattered exist, with rough but adequate road systems. In the plains, declining towns may have abandoned houses that can be saved and made habitable. In the eastern forests and western mountains wood suitable for lumber or firewood may lay unused along the roads. Land is cheap: 10, 20 or more acres may cost a few thousand dollars. Summers may be warm and sunny, but short. Greenhouses would be needed to extend the growing season. Hunting for deer, moose, caribou for food and clothing, and foraging for wild plants could be practical in this vast mostly wild region. In the Eastern half, vast networks of lakes exist where you can canoe, camp and fish. The book ***Living in the Woods for Pennies a Day*** by Bradford Angier describes the region in more detail. The book is old, published in 1972 but still useful. The reader should take note of the way he carefully evaluates each province and region of Canada and Alaska for their suitability for his lifestyle.

7.10 CONTINENTS:

Seasonal migration: a new ways of living

Take a seasonal journey by boat from the far north to the far south and back.

Build a summer homestead in Northern Ontario in the Nipigon Bay region on the northern shore of Lake Superior; or maybe near Black Bay or Thunder Bay. In the fall as the cold weather closes in, sail south on Lake Superior and the Great Lakes to Chicago and through the Chicago ship canal to the Mississippi, to the Ohio, to the Tennessee - Tombigbee river/canal system, to the Gulf coast to a homestead you build in the Florida Panhandle: upriver on the Apalachicola, the Escambia, or maybe the Suwannee. Winter there. Or, homestead in Nova Scotia, Quebec, or New Brunswick and sail down the Atlantic coast to South Florida and the Keys for the winter. (These areas are crowded and expensive so you may have to live on your boat).

Another vision: To allow seasonal migrations from the north to the south without use of the automobile, build great north-south bikeways and trail-ways free of cars leading from Canada to the Southern United States. The Appalachian Trail already could be used for the purpose by hikers in the Eastern United States. (I doubt anyone uses it for the purpose today). A series of north-to-south trails could be created further west possibly connecting up sections of existing trails. Perhaps trails could be created from Detroit to Pensacola, from Minneapolis to Corpus Christi, or from Seattle to San Diego.

Cross Country Foraging Paths:

Hiking/biking paths might be created from the north to the south that let travelers forage with the seasons, going south in the fall and north in the spring. Along these paths could be planted (or allowed to grow wild) edible plants that you may forage to supplement your diet, or perhaps provide for all of it. As the forager moves with the seasons he finds food ripening as he travels. Examples: raspberries in the Midwest in July, blueberries in the Canada in August. These trails might skirt or pass through chains of park lands set aside for the purpose. Thus, you could follow the season north in spring, and south in the fall foraging the ripening foods as you go.

***

CHAPTER 8: SOCIETY VERSES ZCL

Contents: **Page**

INTRODUCTION:

In this chapter I will examine the relationship, positive and negative, between folks attempting to live ZC and Society.

Why this Chapter? Two reasons:

First, because it will permit me to show in more detail why ZCL may be a good idea. As you will see, history reveals that human behavior and economic systems have been (and still are) volatile. The establishment of ZCL may serve as a defense against that volatility.

Second, because I want to show how economic and social forces and the vagaries of history make practicing ZCL difficult, even impossible sometimes. Folks attempting ZCL ought to understand, be aware of social/economic forces that may undermine their lifestyle.

You may imagine you can just build your comfortable ZCL homestead and/or community and relax. Not possible. Social/economic forces may undermine your life, as they did to the old American Farm Culture (as I will describe below) and all other cultures of the past that attempted to live with independence. Do not underestimate the difficulties, for most people Zero Cost Living will be very difficult to achieve.

I have organized this chapter from the perspective of time. I will examine ZCL verses society through time in three steps, going from the past - to the present - and into the future.

8.1 THE PAST:

Why History? The one thing that stands out to me, and probably to some other folks who study history a lot is how incredibly wrong, stupid and foolish people and societies have been – even when they were (supposed) winners – like the Romans. The fact is, history is chock full of blundering leaders - kings, presidents, politicians, generals, business executives, etc. From hindsight we can see their blunders with depressing clarity. And we might realize that we must be committing fresh blunders now - that we are too stupid to see, and folks in the future will look back at us as fools. But perhaps by understanding a little of history we can avoid or mitigate some mistakes.

As history reveals, sometimes society undermines thrift (and folks practicing thrifty ways of life), and sometimes embraces it.

AMERICAN HISTORY and Zero Cost Living:

The history of the 'Old World' (as it is called) of Europe, Asia, and Africa has plenty to teach about the conflict between society and people living ZC – but in the interest of brevity I will leave that discussion to another book. I will focus my discussion on America.

8.1.1 Early America:

Native Americans (inaccurately described as 'Indians') lived without money, off the land, as recently as 150 years ago. They lived in freedom and independence; hunting fishing foraging wild plants and growing beans, corn and squash. No one owned land as an individual, and a Native American could camp without cost anywhere within his tribal domain. (Today, places where folks might live rent, mortgage, and tax-free are non-existent – except for seasteading, or hiding in remote wilderness areas). The Native Americans taught the first European immigrants how to survive here: how to hunt, forage for native plants, and use medicinal herbs. They gave the settlers new seeds: corn, squash, beans, pumpkins and taught them how to grow them. They paid a heavy price for their kindness. Most died from European diseases. The European invaders killed or drove away the survivors and took their land.

Even before the loss of their land, trade with the invaders had undermined the self-sufficient lives of Native Americans. Steel tools and weapons replaced stone, and steel was paid for with fur. But the fur trade was not sustainable. Over time, the sources of fur were depleted, the land was "trapped out". To pay for the things they had become dependent on Native Americans had nothing left but the land they lived on and required to maintain their way of life. Sometimes they sold it for a pittance of what it was worth. Sometimes, with desperate bravery against hopeless odds they tried to defend it. They lost their land and frequently their lives.

Their fate reveals a sad, endlessly repeated trend in history. The trend has been for larger and more technologically advanced societies to undermine smaller, more sustainable, self-sufficient, thrifty, independent, but less technologically advanced societies – sometimes by invasion, sometimes by more subtle means such as trade; trade that may cause excessive exploitation of natural resources and destruction of the economic underpinnings of more 'primitive' societies. (The question of whether or how this trend may be countered will be considered in parts 2 and 3 of this chapter entitled 'The Present' and 'Three Futures'.)

So far, we are not too far removed in time from the ZCL society of Native Americans, and our land shows it. Compared to many long settled and overpopulated regions of the world our land is still relatively fertile and forested and well watered; despite dust bowls, clear-cut logging of mountainsides, imported tree diseases, pesticides, mine and industrial wastes, and increasing pollution as the kinds and uses of chemicals increase every year. It may be that we can still get back to the idea of living on the land, off the land, with the land - at ease and peace rather than in destructive affluence.

8.1.3 The American Revolution:

The Revolution got Americans out from under the thumb of others. Such an event, such a circumstance is exceedingly rare in history. A door was opened. Most revolutions, sadly, quickly returned the masses of humanity to servitude, under new masters if successful. But after the American Revolution that did not happen. For an extended time folks lived in freedom, if not wealth, almost without masters of any kind, and with only a thin veneer of government and taxes. The early United States was perhaps the most free and frugal society ever to exist on earth: The new nation did not have much of an army or navy, volunteer militia were the basis of defense. Government was minimal so taxes were very low. No class of nobility existed to waste resources and subjugate people, (with the one exception of slavery in the South). No big businesses/corporations or masses of subservient workers existed. No wealthy class was able to dominate politics and social life except for a limited time and in limited ways: With the presidency of Andrew Jackson, for example attempts to expand the power and influence of wealthy folks, and to create a moneyed aristocracy were temporarily pruned back.

8.1.4 American Farm Culture.

Next came the rise of what I call the "American Farm Culture". The spring growth of this new culture was formed before the Revolution, but it only came to full fruition, and only could come to full fruition after the Revolution. It was the original, the **real** American Dream. The Farm Culture was a way of life, not a business. It encouraged independence and freedom, not wealth. Folks commonly lived on what today we would call "diversified organic farms".

Wrote Richard Hofstadter in his book ***The Age of Reform:***

"In the very hour of the its birth as a nation Crevecoeur had congratulated America for having, in effect, no feudal past and no industrial present, for having no royal, aristocratic, ecclesiastical, or monarchial power, and no manufacturing class, and had rapturously concluded: 'We are the most perfect society now existing in the world.' Here was the irony from which farmers suffered above all others: the United States was the only country in the world that began with perfection and aspired to progress."

By the 1840s, The American Farm Culture was at its height. A vast nation was out from under the thumb of European or any other nobility. There were not many rich men, and even the rich men were not very rich. There existed a rough inequality based on ability and merit. Today, this idea: that inequality exists because of ability and merit, is one of our greatest cultural myths. It is a myth today, but then it was real. It is no wonder people loved their society so much, no wonder they fought so hard for it in the Civil War, and tried to extend it to the American West.

Railroads and factories were in their infancy. No catalogs of manufactured junk disturbed farmers. Horses, wagons, sailing ships, canals and towboats; beautiful, quiet and much loved provided most transportation. (Steamboats were already widely used too - sometimes blowing up, and fit into the social/economic system of the era without disruptive effects). On canals many individual owners operated towboats. Massive corporations/industries dominating society and striving to put people - either as employees or consumers - under their thumb did not exist. No moneyed aristocracy existed. Most folks were not yet chained to a money economy. They were able to work or not work for others as they chose. They could quit at will and go back to their farms when wages or working conditions did not suit them. Therefore wages were high in America - compared to the rest of the world.

Governmental power was very weak; taxes were low. Not much of an army existed. There existed an unprecedented democratic style of government. Disease was a problem but lack of crowding and limited communication kept it in check. There were no energy problems, virtually no pollution, oil and coal was not used. There were the sails of ships and farm animals for power, and a few windmills and waterwheels, and wood fuel for steamboats. And there was land in the west free or cheap and plentiful promising a really comfortable if not wealthy life for a hardworking family. Like the Native Americans who taught them so much; the entire society practiced a way of life that was near Zero Cost. Economic, political, and social freedom not seen in the world before or since pervaded society. The afterglow of that era is still felt in America.

A farmer in Jefferson's time said: "My farm gave me and my family a good living on the produce of it and left me, one year with another, one hundred and fifty dollars, for I have never spent more than ten dollars a year, which was for salt, nails, and the like. Nothing to wear, eat, or drink was purchased as my farm provided it all. I put money to interest, bought cattle, fatted and sold them, and made great profit!" (From Hofstadter ***The Age of Reform***).

Interesting that Thoreau found even this idyllic society restrictive, profligate and wasteful. But complain though he did, he was still able to live a thrifty, independent and untrammeled life in it.

In ***The Farm*** Louis Broomfield wrote: "**. . .** The vegetable garden was of the greatest importance. Out of it came not only all of the vegetables for the summer, but for the winter as well, for Maria would have considered it a disgrace to have bought food of any sort.

It had been part of the Colonel's dream that his farm should be a world of its own, independent and complete, and his daughter carried on his tradition. The Farm supported a great household that was always varying in size, and in winter the vegetables came from the fruit-house or from the glass jars neatly ticketed and placed in rows on shelves in the big cellar. The sweet corn was dried in the sun instead of being preserved, pasty and insipid, in tins, and not only did it retain much of its own delicious flavor, but took on something of the sun itself. And the strawberry jam never knew a vulgar kettle. It too was made by cooking it on the roof of the woodshed in the glare of the hot July sunlight."

In his book ***Eighty Acres***, about his childhood on a family farm in the 1930s Ronald Jager wrote:

"For all its storied simplicity through the years, the family farm involves, and conceals, complex economic orders. The system we knew relied upon a fine-spun network of interdependent strands: look closely and you see everything seems to depend on everything else. ...."

"....all the farms shaped up in remarkably similar ways: a half dozen standard field crops, some wasteland in pasture, at least two cash crops, six to ten cows, a team of horses, a hundred chickens, some pigs, an orchard, a garden, a woodlot. On every farm every one of those elements was tied to each of the other.... We hauled the hay that fed the cows that fertilized the field that grew the grain that thickened the milk that fattened the pigs that supplied the bacon that fed the family that hauled the hay. ...."

As you can see these farms were sophisticated and complete examples of '**personal economies**' defined in chapter 1. (Today the Amish continue to practice this kind of farming).

Threats to the existence of that culture loomed. Slavery permeated the South, which allowed the growth of an aristocracy. Railroads, a fascinating technological wonder at the time, were noisy, expensive and conducive to the growth of big powerful companies. Factories were expanding. Industry was waking up.

Native Americans (called Indians because of Columbus's great blunder) had their land taken by force. They fought hard to keep their land and lives, rejecting what was forced upon them. Pontiac, Tecumseh, Crazy Horse, Sitting Bull were a few of many heroic fighters. American culture tried to convert them to the farming way of life, believing it to be much superior to the vicissitudes of tribal war over hunting and trapping ground and the uncertainties of Indian life.

"The Indians can't continue to roam thousands upon thousands of miles of this continent merely hunting and warring on each other. Civilization is here." said President Madison in 1812.

The causes and prevention of most disease were not understood at this time. Nevertheless folks stayed healthy most of the time - in part because the population was widely spread and transportation slow. In the Civil War, huge armies (relative to the past), and concentrations of soldiers caused twice as many deaths from disease as from battle.

The American farming culture was eagerly practiced wherever possible and fanatically defended whenever necessary. Lincoln was its most perfect representative and eloquent spokesman. The Civil War destroyed the threat of Southern aristocracy and slavery. But the farming culture was undermined even as it won the war by the businesses and technologies needed to win it. A few folks were becoming rich, able to dominate the lives of others, and creating a new moneyed aristocracy. They promised convenience, efficiency, more productivity, low priced consumer goods, and tools/equipment to ease the heavy work load of self-sufficient farming. Farm culture could keep a family economically secure but the work was hard, and the appeal of these new devices was irresistible.

Thoreau:

Thoreau found plenty to complain about even in his (by ZCL standards) idyllic culture. He saw trends he did not like in the new American society: destruction of nature, railroads, the growth of wealth and of wealthy folks. Still, farm culture persisted for many decades. Thoreau also believed a new and greater society might be attained out of the idyllic nugget of 1840s America.

Thoreau lived in genteel poverty by choice. In his book: ***Walden*** he describes how he lived with simplicity and little money while building a cabin, planting beans, observing nature, and writing the journal that became his famous book. He knew freedom. He could take off any time for a trip or a cause and frequently did. And, he could leave at a moments notice. Without concern for money or schedules he could go hiking into forests and up mountains, boating on the Connecticut River, even go to jail to protest poll taxes and the

Mexican War. His writing is a solace to poor people. The impact of his ideas looms larger with every passing year.

Changes in Farm Culture:

Diversified farms, almost self-sufficient in the East - with the settlement of the Western plains - became monocultural grain exporting businesses. Farmers grew crops to sell, often only one crop, then bought everything else. Western farms were not a continuation of the old farming culture at all. Farming became a business, not a way of life. American Farm culture was once practiced by most of the population. The industrialization of the economy rapidly reduced millions of independent farmers to the status of employees.

Laura Ingalls Wilder in her book ***Farmer Boy*** makes a clear and simple statement. When Almonzo's mother was told he might take a job as an apprentice wheelwright (carriage maker), she says, "A pretty pass the world's coming to, if any man thinks it's a step up in the world to leave a good farm and go to town! How does Mr. Paddock make his money, if it isn't catering to us? I guess if he didn't make wagons to suit farmers, he wouldn't last long!" Oh it's bad enough to see Royal (her other son) come down to being nothing but a storekeeper! Maybe he'll make money, but he'll never be the man you (Almonzo's father) are. Truckling to other people for his living, all his days. He'll never be able to call his soul his own."

In retrospect, practitioners of the American Farm culture were naive and vulnerable, and were ruined while hardly knowing what hit them or how to resist. ***The Farm*** by Louis Broomfield: and ***Waiting for the Morning Train*** by Bruce Catton describe their eventual fate. To this day we hardly recognize what we had and what was lost, dwelling only on how convenient everything is today: fast food, cars, TV, as if they were the most important things in life. It was a culture not adequately defended after the extreme effort of the Civil War, and not being able to foretell the future, (as no culture has been able to do), in no position to preserve itself. Today we blandly say it was just progress, it was inevitable, history moves on. But is this true?

Demise of the American Farm Culture:

The pioneer farmers had more interesting, even exciting lives than did the workers/employees of later industrialized society. They faced the multiple challenges of exploring, moving-to and settling their fresh new country. Their workload was varied, requiring an interesting mix of skills and kinds of labor. They built their own homes, barns, fences, cleared fields, and made their own tools, furniture, clothes, toys. They could and did leave their new homes at will to go hunting for weeks at a time. They foraged woods and fields for wild foods. As described by the books of Louis Broomfield and Laura Ingles Wilder their culture was vibrant with fairs, dances, sports such as horse racing, and celebrations of the seasons.

But difficulties existed. Farming could be hard. The old farmers needed to practice thrift with fanatical dedication if they hoped to prosper. Many a farmer became anxious to get out of it, and quickly did when consumer products and factory jobs came along.

And when the old farmers retired they died quickly from lack of exercise and fatty diets of the era.

What did the old farmers know? What could they teach us today? Plenty.

They could teach us how to farm organically, use horses, preserve food without refrigeration by canning drying, fermenting, and building root cellars (as Thoreau did at Walden). They could teach us how to make tools, and process materials. Things few folks can do today or want to do. (The Amish still know how, and if asked with respect, will teach you).

All worthy of study. But we need to improve on what they did, using methods described in this book to avoid the trap of hard thrift described in chapter 2.

8.1.5 Rise of the Factory:

Adam Smith and the early industrialists made a discovery more momentous than any new invention of the time. People could be made to spend many hours a day at one tedious task and do nothing else. Men, women and children could be made to work at that single task for years with little or no complaint. The idea was pushed as far as possible: how long, how fast, how young, how cheap could people work. All other skills and abilities that an individual might possess withered, except the skills needed for tedious monotonous, slave-like jobs. Sweatshops proliferated. Chicago meat packing plants perfected them, described by Upton

Sinclair in his novel ***The Jungle.*** The factory system precipitated the demise of the American Farm Culture.

Here, I want to clarify the reality of the capitalist economy with its supposed efficiency as described by Adam Smith in his book ***The Wealth of Nations*** written in 1776. Let us revisit Smith's needle factory. Men, women, and children were required to work long hours and do nothing else and therefore buy everything else they needed. Other talents, skills or abilities they may have had languished. So when laid off they were helpless and unemployed. This is the unconsidered consequence of specialized labor created by Smith's capitalist economy.

Smith wrote: "I have seen several boys under twenty years of age who had never exercised any other trade but that of making nails, and who, when the exerted themselves, could make, each of them, upwards of two thousand three hundred nails in a day." ***Wealth of Nations*** page 14.

The nail makers – and pin makers made lots of nails and pins, and nothing else, and so develop no other skills, and when a nail-making or pin-making machine came along their years of accumulated skill become worthless and useless. They knew no other trade and so would have to try to take up a new trade at the beginning. (I am not opposed to technological progress, but I am opposed to economic systems and methods of production that condemn folks to bleak, servile, machine-like jobs).

In 1840 Edwin Chadwick, a famous British social reformer and colleagues were investigating the slums of Glasgow, Scotland to find the causes of a deadly fever. He …"ducked through a low doorway. …. "

"The passageway opened onto a courtyard…. In its center rose a vast dunghill, the product of the destitute who crowded into the rooms around it. Relying on a strong stomach and an unrelenting will, Chadwick made his way along a narrow path that skirted the courtyard and passed through a second corridor on its far side. He walked through it and found to his horror, a second courtyard, identical to the first with a second immense pile of human feces. …the denizens of this grim world, clothed in rags and tatters, crowded together for warmth, looked out at the intruders through hungry eyes."

There were "…. vast piles of human excrement in every courtyard."

"…. The desperate conditions inside the buildings matched the horrifying state of their courtyards. In one room, they found a group of women, huddling naked beneath a blanket. Their clothes, …were in use by their roommates. Without enough clothes for all the occupants of the room, the women took turns using what they had to venture out in the cold. …" from ***The Blue Death*** **by** Dr. Robert Morris chapter 3 ***'All Smell is Disease'.***

Here was thrift forced on people by the economic system, thrift of the worst kind – thrift in the form of grinding poverty.

No wonder, by the late 19th Century the Philosopher Nietche had his character - Zarathustra mouth the words "Better to rule in hell than serve in heaven."

But Lincoln had an answer, "As I would not be a slave, so I would not be a master."

This is the reality of Adam Smith's economics. It was and is only an excuse to concentrate, impoverish and exploit labor. It saves money for the manufacturer/owner, but avoids the real cost of a product which is the cost to provide a living wage and compensate the worker for the skills he must forgo to endlessly do the single task set before him. The skills, abilities, and knowledge of an assembly line worker may never be used. His working life is spent on a single narrow task. Everything else, he must buy. If he is laid off in this unstable competitive economic system he has no employment options except maybe, (if all the jobs haven't been outsourced) other equally tedious single task jobs that are useless for any other purpose.

The factory system sought to eliminate all craft, all skill from work, so unskilled workers could be to used get the work done at the lowest wage possible, and well paid skilled workers and their skills jettisoned.

Upton Sinclair in ***The Jungle*** wrote the story of how immigrants were taken advantage of and broken by the economic system of 1900 Chicago. It is a novel, but it was the real fate of many. Fast talking salesmen and ruthless businessmen took advantage of them. They took jobs with horrendous working conditions in meat packing plants. Though reforms have been made, the economic system is still all too much like it was then. There are plenty of lessons to be learned from this book. It can wake you up, show you what to expect from business, from corporations, from unrestrained capitalism. Don't let the fate of these poor immigrants be yours.

Thus came the age of the job, the employee, the manager, and the professional. Farming became a business, "agribiz", not a way of life - with employees, migrant labor, farm managers, big machines, huge acreages, overweight farm owners (from lack of exercise), all ties to the land broken, life splintered but an apparent vast increase in the flow of money and economic growth.

In the late 19th century the Grange movement, William Jennings Bryan, the Farm-Labor Party and others made a feeble defense of the American Farm Culture. But they had little idea of how to oppose the juggernaut of the factory system, big business, and unregulated capitalism.

Karl Marx compared French farmers to a sack of potatoes each alone and independent and unwilling or unable to co-operate. And co-operation was (and is) the key to their survival and survival of their culture; and so he put no confidence in their ability to create social change. Folks must cooperate **voluntarily** if they are to win or keep their freedom. The Chinese communists under Mao Tse-tung based their revolution on peasant farmers, and won – or so it seemed. Recent history has seen the unraveling of everything he attempted. His revolution was based on coercion, fear, and top down control of people's lives. It was a dead end in history.

8.1.6 The Dust Bowl:

The book ***The Worst Hard Times*** by Timothy Egan chronicles what American farming-as-a-business had become in the dust bowl of the American Plains in the 1930's. In an orgy of stupidity and unrestrained greed, farming as a business ruined millions of acres of productive grassland. The farmer/settlers there suffered unbearable experiences - dying coughing their lungs out with silicoses from breathing the dust.

In 1930 a man named Bam White attempted to settle on acreage in the heart of the region that succumbed to the dust bowl.

Egan writes: "Saving money from skunk skins, field labor, and turnips, Bam finally put together enough of a nest egg to get his own place. It was a half-dugout, not as deep as the typical hole in the ground; it measured fourteen feet by thirty-six feet, just over five hundred square feet of high Plains habitat for Bam, Lizzie, and the three kids. The roof was tarpaper, which shrieked like a hag in the spring winds. The walls were fingernail thin, and Lizzie said she could not live in a place so cold. Bam and the boys tried to insulate it, tacking pasteboard to the walls. They put in six layers, and now the place was sealed against the more severe exhalations of the High plains. The dugout was divided into two sides: in one half was a cook stove and table, the eating and cleaning area; in the other half were beds for Bam and Lizzie, a cot that the two boys shared, and a bed for their sister. The house had no water. No toilet. No electric power. It was young Melt's job was to haul in buckets of water for cleaning and cooking and to collect cow chips for the stove. "This place ain't much, Bam White would say, twisting the edges of his handlebar mustache, but it's ours, and dammit we finally got something here in Texas".

Now that was hard thrift.

His efforts were all for nothing. His farm failed in the dust bowl and he died of silicoses. His fate reveals that hard work, skills, thrift, and dedication may not be enough to succeed, or even survive. The contrast between his experience and that of the earlier pioneers in the East couldn't be more stark.

Most farmers were able to live comfortably by the standards of the time, but had to work long and hard - dawn to dusk and more - 7 days a week during planting and harvest seasons, and had a host of chores throughout the year.

In the factories workers labored maybe 10 hours a day 6 days a week. Their evenings and Sundays were free. Later 8-hour days and 5-day weeks became common.

8.1.7 Rise of the Dependent Classes:

Applying Adam Smith's economics and the factory system new wealthy classes arose in America; wealthy beyond the dreams of kings. These newly wealthy folks aspired to the arrogance and power of the old aristocracies of Europe. The newly wealthy required; besides factory workers, a host of dependent employees: accountants, salesmen, engineers, servants, and many more. A new middle class was created to do these jobs. Many a factory worker and farmer's son aspired to the new middle class white-collar jobs: varied, interesting, clean, no sweat required. These new jobs - with a regular paycheck coming in - seemed secure compared to the uncertainties of farming or factory work.

One big problem: this entire new economy was dependent on the new wealthy folks and their companies, and subject to their whims and faults, and all were subject to the vicissitudes of the free market; to the health of the overall economy. The old farmers were independent. When the economy turned bad they could fall back on home and local production. The new dependent classes did not have that option.

8.1.8 The Great Depression:

Before the great depression workers in the new factories had already lost many of the old crafts, skills and thrifty methods used in farming - woodworking, leatherworking use of horses and oxen, care of animals, processing food, and living without electricity.. Thrifty methods of travel, such as the last sailing ships and the men who could sail them were gone from the seas. (The old square-riggers were difficult to sail and maintain requiring dozens of men to climb aloft in all weather, too often to their death. But schooners; common on the Great Lakes and the coastal waters of America - worked from the deck, were easy and efficient to sail. But energy was cheap in those days and the savings of using sails was perceived as too much trouble).

In the depression the dependent classes were forced by circumstances to be thrifty and had forgotten how, and so were helpless and suffered in consequence. Most people lived in cities, and were used to buying everything. The farms of their fathers had been sold off and were long gone, along with the skills and will power needed to live there and work the land.

In the past during tough economic times, folks could and did go back to home and locally based industries/technologies. But, national industries/technologies had wiped out locally based industries/technologies so people had nothing to fall back on as big industries cut back. For example, horses were a cheap and practical means of travel before the automobile. They were cheap to keep on farms, eating farm grown hay and grain. And they reproduced themselves on your farm - no need for factories. But skill at using horses and industries supporting their use – leatherworking, carriage making - were gone. And masses of cars meant horses could not be easily or safely used on public roads anymore. They were not put into widespread use again during the depression.

In Germany, the helpless and dependent population turned to Nazism, Hitler, and surrender of all of their liberties.

But in America some of the old thrift was remembered and brought back - revived from 19th century farming.

Thrifty methods had survived in the mountains of Appalachia as described in the ***Foxfire*** series of books. Lifestyles of depression folks are well worth studying. Practitioners are still alive and ought to be interviewed. John Steinbeck was, perhaps, the premiere chronicler of depression life and a gold mine of methods of survival in such circumstances.

Steinbeck wrote "The Depression was no financial shock to me. I didn't have any money to lose, but in common with millions I did dislike hunger and cold. I had two assets. My father owned a tiny three-room cottage in Pacific Grove in California, and he let me live in it without rent. That was the first safety. Pacific Grove is near the sea. That was the second."

"People in inland cities or in the closed and shuttered industrial cemeteries had greater problems than I. Given the sea a man must be very stupid to starve. That great reservoir of food is always available. I took a large part of my protein food from the ocean. Firewood to keep warm floated on the beach daily, needing only handsaw and ax. A small garden of black soil came with the cottage. In northern California you can raise vegetables of some kind all year long. I never peeled a potato without planting the skins. Kale, lettuce, chard, turnips, carrots and onions rotated in the little garden. In the tide pools of the bay mussels were available and crabs and abalones and that shiny kelp called sea lettuce. With a line and a pole, blue cod, rock cod, sea trout, sculpins could be caught." From October 1973 ***Esquire: "A Primer on the Thirties***".

The economic stimulus of World War II pulled America out of depression. But still under war emergency – folks practiced thrift: There was gas rationing, and no new cars were being made so trains, buses and trolleys and even bicycles were extensively used.

8.1.9 Postwar Culture:

After WW2 thrifty living was remembered with horror, eagerly abandoned and gladly forgotten as new waves of consumer products flooded the country. For example, new cars, less practical and more expensive than the cars of the 1930's: with fins, ornate grilles, lots of chrome, and big engines became the style.

Next came the rise of what I call the 'Global Corporate Capitalist Economy' (the GCCE). American political, social and economic power dominated two thirds of the world called the 'free world' Communism dominated the other third. American businesses - and then businesses of many countries -expanded under the umbrella of American military power to become true global enterprises: global corporations. Challenges to the GCCE were met by war in Korea, Vietnam, and dozens other countries.

The GCCE was adept at maximizing profits, regardless of the consequences - whether to the environment, the folks working for them or the consumers of their products. Diseases such as cancer proliferated. New sweatshops were opened in third world countries. Unsafe products: asbestos, cigarettes, junk food and many others were produced and widely used. Auto accidents and their victims increased.

In the late 1960's and early 1970's, in response to the excesses of the GCCE such as environmental pollution and the Vietnam War came an era of rejection of commercialism and consumerism among young people. A back-to-the-land movement began, spawning hosts of new homesteaders, organic farmers, co-ops, and communes. These folks had no background in such things. Their parents and grandparents had taught them nothing about it, the skills needed had been long forgotten and most attempts fell flat on lack of skills, practice, tools, and the hard relentless work required to follow that life. These folks made naïve and feeble attempt to recreate some aspects of the old American Farm Culture. Sadly, that movement dissipated leaving hardly a trace.

Nevertheless, aspects of that antique farm culture might be brought to life again, incorporated into techniques for Zero Cost Living.

In the 1970's economic inefficiency, wasteful consumption, and declining production of American oil precipitated the 'energy crisis' causing lines to buy gasoline, spikes in energy prices, lowered thermostats and 55 miles per hour freeway speed limits; (that some folks still speak of with horror). Thrift was back in fashion. Solar energy, windmills, wood burning heaters, organic farming, and rural homesteading became popular.

In the mid 1970's some of us believed we were on the verge of a Solar Age. We would create an efficient sustainable civilization respecting nature - an age of Aquarius. But none of it came to be.

American society threw away 30 years that should have been used to develop energy independence, an important step towards ZCL. We are back in the same old rut, only deeper. Why? Were the thrifty initiatives of the 1970's just wrong? Then why are we back in the same situation?

In retrospect it is obvious that most people just didn't "get it." We believers in a solar civilization were naïve and trusting in humanity and in human reason. But people are after all, only human, and not always reasonable. The adherents of the GCCE were not so naïve; they knew only too well what people were like. We imagined efficiency had something to do with economics.

The fact is you can tell folks something a hundred times, teach them, show them and they still won't "get it." (But one good thing, eventually they "get it" and that may be happening now). In the late 1970's and early 1980's the American people and government were at their wits end, helpless to deal with economic stagnation and runaway inflation, stagflation it was called – and the energy crisis because they didn't know how to take care of themselves anymore. They hadn't known how to take care of themselves for a hundred years. The attempts some of us made to develop alternative energy, new communities, and just plain thrifty ways of life were insufficient. Most folks were uneducated and unprepared for so much change. But the GCCE could take care of people. And they did.

The position and power of the GCCE was restored, even increased. They struck deals with oil producing nations to get stable, and then cheaper oil prices – selling them weapons and part ownership in GCCE companies. The GCCE was able to cut back safety, social, and environmental regulations; reduce the power of governments; and weaken the power of unions. President Reagan broke the PATCO strike and all the other Unions saw their power undermined in consequence. (Reagan having been a democrat and a union man knew how weak they really were and how to break them).

The GCCE managed in the 1980's and 90's to stabilize the price of energy, to control inflation, to destroy the "evil empire" of the Soviet Union, to bring Communist China into the fold, to restore and even increase corporate profitability. They put thrift back in the box. What was thrift compared to all of the new goodies. The GCC came up with masses of useless junk folks were willing labor long and hard to get: trophy houses, sports utility vehicles, junk food, cable TV, video games, computers that became obsolete every two years, drugs. (Drug dealers are just global corporate capitalists who happen to sell their stuff outside the law. They are the worst version of the same breed). The GCCE was once again wringing $ out of working folks, strip mining money out of their hands.

But the day of reckoning was only put off.

In the 1980s and 1990s greed was back in fashion. Profligate waste was back in vogue. Inefficiency, extravagance and debt were hallmarks of life. Thrift was, like the era after World War Two looked on with horror - or else merely seen as irrelevant.

8.1.10 Recent history:

Profit was made king again. Greed was a virtue again. Unions became no more than a shadow of what they were. And thrift was irrelevant again along with everything that went with it. A lot of folks who had attempted thrift in the 1970s and 1980s decided it was just too hard. Energy conservation, recycling, eating healthy, organic gardening, solar home, biking to work – took too much time and effort. Easier to just forget all about it. Do your job, buy everything else and never bother to think of thrift, ever.

Then it all began to unravel. The economic order of the 1980's and 90's was unstable, and the day of reckoning was merely put off.

And in these wasted decades one good thing arose, personal computers linked to the Internet. Though 99 percent, indeed 99.9 percent of it was and is more useless junk, 0.1% is not, and is enough, more than enough to change things. Thanks to the Internet the old lost thrifty ideas and methods, and newly discovered/invented methods can be found and shared more easily than ever.

LESSONS OF HISTORY:

Here are my observations on how the course of human history may affect ZCL:

As history reveals, sometimes society wars on thrift and sometimes and sometimes embraces it.

Trend: Larger technologically advanced societies may undermine small more backward societies. The Romans overwhelmed the Gauls and Celts of Northern Europe. The Europeans overwhelmed the Native Africans, Asians, and Americans. Societies attempting to live ZC may find their lifestyles and lives under assault by larger advanced societies. ZCL societies, to survive, must consider if and how this social trend may be countered.

Trend: A society may evolve from a republic of free farmers to Empire - in the process destroying frugal ways of life.

This is a pattern of history that has been repeated over and over. The Dutch experience is described on page 349. Roman history provides another highly relevant example. The Republic with an army of citizen soldiers/free farmers on small farms became an empire with a professional army and a slave economy of huge estates. Free farmers were reduced to plebian dependents on the dole in Rome and other cities of the Empire, given bread and circuses: free grain from Egypt, gladiatorial game in the coliseum. It was a pattern of life repeated all over the Empire. The Roman people lost their ability to fight and defend themselves. They lost the ability to take care of themselves. Caesars' army of professional soldiers crushed the citizen armies of the Republic. The United States today seems to be in the late Republican phase of the Roman historical experience. Can the trends of a civilization be changed? Or is the common historical pattern of all past cultures inevitable. In the Civil War, the United States defeated the imposition of a system of outright slavery, and did not follow the Roman Empire down that path. Nevertheless, as in the Roman Empire, the culture of free farmers has disappeared. Is it possible to defeat the looming American Imperial culture?

In the United States, the goal of the early pioneers was self-sufficiency and independence, not wealth. If independence resulted in wealth; all the better but getting rich was not the goal. Getting rich was the goal of the conquistadors, an altogether different goal that dominated societies in Latin America. American pioneers were anxious to get out from under the thumbs of upper classes. They built the free farmer economy. They didn't have much money. They used barter and exchanges of labor. They worked together on projects to improve their lives mostly through government: on roads, canals, harbors, lighthouses. Their culture blossomed after the revolution. The free farmer economy was fanatically fought for and successfully defended in the Civil War. Lincoln was the archetypical embodiment of the culture of the free farmers. After the war the original American dream was replaced by the "get rich" dream of the conquistadors. The society of free farmers was gradually subverted and destroyed by the rise of monopoly capitalists/ industrialists with their factories, railroads, and mines; technologies that required masses of servile labor. And free farmers once again came under the thumb of upper classes, reduced to servitude as factory workers. The window was open for only a short time. Louis Broomfield, in his book, ***The Farm*** describes its rise and demise. The native, then pioneer, then farmer economy was swamped and made dependent and servile "employees"; Indians to reservations, farmers to factories and now factory workers to the aptly named 'service' jobs in the service economy that American is becoming. Aptly named because, though supposedly in service to customers, the employee is really in service to his corporation. People are reduced to economic dependence. The skills needed to survive independently are lost. A ruling class, an aristocracy in all but name lords it over America.

Societies attempting to live ZC will have to consider and deal with this trend of history.

Trend: as societies evolve and change – thrifty practices may be undermined– causing costs to go up. Wealthy, powerful folks and institutions developing new technologies strive to take over and exploit resources assuring them means to increase their wealth and power. Resources needed to live with thrift may be taken away from folks - and wasted on luxuries. So, things once free now cost money. Things that are free now may cost money in the future. Things once inexpensive are now expensive, and things that are inexpensive now may be expensive in the future.

Early America was not so poor, and we are not as rich now as conventional economic accounting would calculate.

Americans were not rich, but the cost of living was low. They could hunt, fish, forage and grow their own food. Free land was available for the taking. The active lifestyles and simple diets required of almost everyone kept us healthy and free of many modern diseases. Air, water and soil were free of pollution and pesticides. Transportation was slow but transportation costs were low: folks could walk, ride a horse or carriage, or sail. Grass was cheap, wind was free. Cities were compact so folks could get to most urban destinations in a few minutes by walking

How many things once free now cost $?

Once, you could drink water straight out of streams and lakes. Now it must be filtered to be safe. Once, land could be gotten for free, and many folks merely squatted on land, using it, but paying nothing for it. Now land costs a lot. (I believe we unwisely let it all be settled too fast). Once forests were vast and wood for lumber and firewood abundant. A pioneer could build and heat his house from the timber on his property for the cost of an axe and saw. It was cut over within a few decades. Once you could easily walk everywhere, now a car is usually required - roads have become unpleasant and unsafe to walk or bike along. Society sometimes (callously and thoughtlessly) wars on thrift - reducing or eliminating the possibility of it.

Countertrend: Thrifty societies thrive, wasteful societies decline.

Blessed with resources, frugal and efficient nations thrive - become prosperous. One example mentioned above: The Dutch. By hard fighting, like the Americans later against the British, the Dutch won their independence from the Spanish Empire. Free of Imperial chains, as frugality and efficiency became a stereotypical definition of Dutch character - followed an era of economic growth. Then came a golden age of prosperity, technological advances, and artistic achievements. They had fine harbors, timber for ships, and, as timber was cut, fertile farmland. By hard labor they won more farmland from the bottom of the sea. They exploited rich fishing grounds in the North Sea. The Dutch grew crops, fished, manufactured and shipped things other nations needed, created worldwide trade networks - and prospered.

Then the Dutch become profligate wasters, become inefficient. They overexploited, then exhausted local resources as population, wealth, and consumption grew. All of the local timber was cut, nearby fishing grounds were over fished. Now, timber food, and other resources had to be imported for a rapidly growing population and economy. Their worldwide trade networks were transformed into a vast empire that had to be defended. Ships were built for the navy, not fishing and trade. They had to fight expensive wars to keep their empire. At first the Dutch were victorious. But the financial burdens of military and naval power were too great. Thrift was no longer possible. A huge navy was needed, but could not be maintained. Wars were lost and Dutch power and independence became only history. Kevin Phillips in his book ***Bad Money*** describes the history of Empires including the Dutch, Spanish and British Empires in more detail.

Countertrend: Empires may decline into poverty – forcing formerly well off people to live with thrift.

Empires that have declined from wealth to poverty abound in history. A few examples: Roman, Spanish, Dutch, Russian, British, and Soviet Union. The Spanish had all of the gold of the New World and yet sank into national and individual destitution over the course of a century. The British Empire encompassed fabulous wealth and territory. It was said, "The sun never set " upon it. Yet it is dissolved and Great Britain, not so great anymore, became (for a while) one of the poorer nations of Europe. Consider the Soviet Union, an Empire in all but name. Although the people were never wealthy, the government somehow managed to support a huge military establishment for decades. The Soviet Union was replete with natural resources; oil, minerals, and a vast land area and yet went bankrupt. Possibly, if the Soviet government and society had understood and striven to practice ZCL they would have continued in economic solvency.

A THEORY OF HISTORY: Societies may evolve from freedom to servility and back again. As American and world history reveals, sometimes society wars on thrift and sometimes and sometimes embraces it.

Based on my study of history from a ZCL perspective, a theory of human social evolution suggests itself to me.

Generations long living under servitude and oppression eagerly seek and strive for freedom, regardless of personal and financial sacrifices. But later generations, having lived free, again consider submission and servitude, thinking more economic security and perhaps more wealth preferable to mere freedom. But once again, as servitude becomes oppressive; the old longing for freedom returns. Thus the European peasants eagerly swarmed to America to get out from under oppression. They sought independence and freedom. They did not expect to be wealthy - living in pioneer homesteads in the wilderness. Then the children and grandchildren of American pioneer farmers – tired of the work required to be self-sufficient on the old time farms - left the farms to work in factories and corporations, gaining greater security, but again living their working lives and in some ways their non-working lives in a new form of servitude. Their children, who see the limitations of the new supposed security, again long for greater freedom.

So the ages of human history alternate between periods when people seek greater freedom, and periods when they seek greater security. Folks are enticed into working for wages, and abandoning economic independence. Then, they become oppressed by the new economic regime and seek to escape from it.

Organizations of folks attempting to live ZC should consider where the larger society they live in is - in this oscillation in history and plan accordingly. For example, ZCL communities may thrive during eras when folks seek greater freedom, and languish, perhaps even feel under siege when people seek greater wealth and security in large and often coercive social organizations.

Summary of Lessons of History - that may affect attempts at ZCL:

Large advanced societies undermine small backward 9but thrifty) societies.

A society may evolve from a republic of free farmers to empire- destroying thrifty ways of life in the process.

The wealthy/powerful may take control of resources needed to live ZC – making them cost $ and undermine frugal lifestyles.

Thrifty societies thrive; wasteful societies decline.

Empires may decline into poverty – forcing folks to live with thrift who previously knew wealth.

Societies may evolve from freedom to servility and back again – creating circumstances that make practicing ZCL easier or more difficult.

How are these tides of history to be countered? I will consider this question in part 3 of this chapter ‘Three Futures’.

8.2 THE PRESENT: Where we are now.

Here, I will consider current social circumstances and social trends as they affect ZCL - making ZCL less likely, less possible and more difficult to achieve – or creating potentials and opportunities making ZCL more achievable.

8.2.1 SOCIAL CLASSES and ZCL:

Wealth and Poverty:

Wealth and poverty in a strange, but explainable way are similar in their effects on human behavior: Both can cause people to live without practicing or even attempting efficient thrift.

Poverty:

Folks living day to day have slight chance to practice efficient thrift. Their situation may make it hard for them to think and plan ahead, to save $, to find time and resources and to learn needed skills. They may be especially vulnerable to temptations - drugs alcohol, gambling, impractical pursuits, entertainments, and activities. Sometimes their behavior is the cause and sometimes the result of poverty. Physical and sometimes mental illness, personality flaws, an inability to save money, or hold a job, or take care of themselves are all part of this extremely complicated problem.

Folks living in poverty may practice thrift by necessity (as described in chapter 2) – too often hard thrift, inefficient thrift. Poverty - as many live it - is a wasteful, not thrifty, way of living. They may have no choice but to live in badly insulated houses or mobile homes, and operate old poorly maintained gas-wasting vehicles. They may be inactive, indolent, overweight, with bad diets, health problems and high health care costs (often borne by society). I have seen some working poor - through their entire lives - wasting the dollars they earned through long hours of hard work on stuff they can't really afford or don't really need: expensive entertainment systems, junk food, new cars; and more recently - overpriced homes.

And, sometimes they waste and destroy resources trying to secure the basics necessities –food, fuel, shelter; for example overfishing, overgrazing land, and destroying forests for firewood.

Wealth:

But the rich can be worse, much worse than the poor, from a ZCL perspective, because they have no incentive to practice thrift, to live without waste. So they buy huge houses, Hummers and SUV's, expensive clothes, trinkets and junk for the purpose of showing off their wealth and inspiring envy, make frequent jet trips all over the world, etc. Their attitude may be: if you've got it, why not spend it any way you like no matter what the effects. (When the wealthy waste resources such as fuel it drives up the cost of that resource for everyone. With plenty of money, they are less affected by their waste).

The modern world has seen the rise of wealthy folks; wealthy beyond the wildest dreams of kings or emperors of the past. Sadly, the wealthy can never have enough until a resource is exhausted or polluted whether it be land, energy, air or water because they must always try to be wealthier than their competitors, the other wealthy people they know - be top of the heap. So in the process the fish are stripped from the sea and the trees and minerals from the land and the bare soil is washed away. Rarely, do they practice a measured and sustainable economics, but too frequently - consumption to excess and exhaustion of resources.

The Middle Classes:

Middle class folks may be able to practice efficient thrift - with enough $ to plan ahead and avoid the inefficiencies of a day-to-day existence but not so many $ that they can ignore thrift.

Two middle classes have existed in America. The old independent middle class and the dependent middle class of more recent origin both described earlier in the 'History' section of this chapter.

The old independent middle classes: the farmers, traders, and small businessmen practiced frugality as a way of life. They lived almost ZCL lifestyles. The dependent middle classes: white or blue collar employees of corporations did not continue these practices; instead relying increasingly on credit and debt - for example: mortgages, home equity loans, car leases, credit cards, student loans, etcetera. The dependent middle classes live under hierarchies of bosses, in paternalistic and/or coercive social relationships as employees. They all-to-often are treated like children by the businesses they work for - and act like children in their patterns of consumption.

8.2.2 **CURRENT SOCIAL TRENDS:** and their effects on ZCL:

Trend: today, the dependent middle classes are in decline.

Wealthy folks, through the GCCE they own have become more wealthy and powerful in America than ever before. Billionaires have become the criteria of true wealth. Millionaires are merely middle class. Wealthy folks, whether they admit it or not increasingly aspire to be an American aristocracy.

In late 20th century America middle class blue and white collar workers had become well off thru hard work, unions, the power of their democratic government to impose conditions on the GCCE, and the ability of the GCCE to use some of their profits to pay Americans well (after all America was defender of the world order needed by the GCCE). Americans, though dependent; remembered the old liberties they once enjoyed, were uneasy in their servility and, with prosperity had become less servile, less inured to the jobs and demands of the CGGE.

The corporations, having gone global found cheaper, much cheaper and more servile workers offshore: workers anxious to take hard jobs for long hours at low pay. Sweatshops and child labor of Adam Smith's era; long abolished by law and social progress in economically advanced countries, are again raising their ugly heads in the outsourced factories of the poor countries.

Today, a host of forces undermine the dependent middle classes: Their jobs, wages, living expenses, and assets are being hammered as never before.

Jobs:

Jobs are outsourced to China, India, and everywhere else. A flood of cheap products imported from these countries – in almost every industry - undermine and destroy domestic manufacturing and still more jobs. Illegal immigrants take still more jobs from Americans – and force wages lower by flooding the labor market with unskilled worker willing to work for low wages. Manufacturing jobs, once 45% of jobs in America are down to 10%.

Local economies have become strip malls of chain stores such as Wal-Mart, packed with cheap imports that undermine local businesses and local production. (Though not the intended meaning: 'chain stores' are aptly named - you are chained and dependent on their products and jobs - without options when locally based businesses that might provide some competition are undermined and go out of business.)

Wages:

Most of the new jobs have been in the low paying service industry. Low paying service jobs are replacing manufacturing and high tech jobs. The median (not average) income of Americans has dropped by 15% in the last 5 years. (Average income is not lower because the incomes of the wealthy are up, while the incomes of employees - are down - averaging out to small gains in overall average income in America).

Living expenses:

While incomes remain stagnant or fall, prices for medical care, dental care, education, and in fact almost every professional service have increased.

Prices for oil and other commodities have surged in recent years, and though they have retreated again, they could leap up again when conditions change.

Overuse of credit cards has left folks in debt and paying high interest rates on their debts.

The dependent classes have difficulty practicing thrift. A consumer mentality exists. Constant barrages of messages by media, by neighbors, (by relatives including their own children) by society encourage folks to BUY. "The customer is always right." goes the old often quoted saying originally by Marshall Field. (But I would say "the customer is an idiot." The customer buys foolishly, stupidly, wastefully. The customer buys when he doesn't have to buy, always has, always will, maybe. The consumer is the frog in the pan of water that is slowly heated so he won't jump out until cooked. I urge you to jump out now).

Assets:

Falling home prices have reduced the value of their principal asset.

The values of gas wasting vehicles most folks own have declined.

Investments and retirement account values are in decline.

Middle class Americans have a negative savings rate, saving less than nothing – and increasing debt each year.

Savings:

Government, banks, and business claim they want folks to be thrifty and to save money. But in reality they do not. They want all of us to spend - to keep businesses profitable and taxes flowing.

No economic incentives to save exist. Savings interest rates are extremely low (near 0 in 2009). And, inflation eats the dollars you have saved, sometimes faster than interest earnings accumulate;

so savings are continually eroded by inflation thus further discouraging folks from saving $.

Years of low interest rates have had their effects. People have nothing in savings. Better than savings, I believe, is to put your dollars to work in ways described in this book.

GCCE vs. America: ("It's the end of the world as we know it." song by R.E.M.).

Today, under the pitiless assault of the GCCE, we are seeing the final brutal dismantling of the American Economy that existed since the rise of big business.

Dependence on corporations and businesses for jobs results in instability and insecurity for you and me and for the supply of the things we need to live.

America has become a weird, distorted society compared to the past, with good jobs evaporating like water, chimerical social stability, negative savings rates, and eroding standards of living. Everything is done for the sake of business and business interests, for profit, and to assure the lowest possible wages for employees.

Vast numbers of the middle class: millions of people are falling out of the middle class and into poverty.

Corporations profess freedom but practice subjugation. They want folks to be dependent on them for jobs and products. It is how they make money. It is not in their interest to see people live without buying their products (or working for them). For profit, their interest is to undermine anyone attempting to achieve personal economic independence (or practice ZCL). When they do not achieve a sufficient level of subjugation (as measured by profits) in the form of sufficient sales, sufficiently low wages and sufficiently high prices they will shut down or move their business to a place where they can realize higher profits. Today, corporations eagerly move production south or overseas – to employ the subservient, powerless, and impoverished populations of China, India, etc. Then they sell the products back to (an increasingly in debt) America.

The CGGE is in the process of outsourcing from America the production every good and service that they possibly can. The GCCE is abandoning a nation where people have, with centuries of sacrifice and successful struggle; won rights and freedoms - to go where people are without freedoms, without rights, poor and desperate and ready to work for any wages under any conditions, doing whatever is asked of them no matter how polluting, dangerous or destructive.

Unions:

Once there were strong unions in America, and they had the power to improve the wages and working conditions of their members (and even of non- members in their industries). They were able to mitigate the coercive and paternalistic excesses of the corporations and give members a voice in their working lives. Now, however, in the face of billions of desperate third world folks looking for any job and corporate ability to move work anywhere; union days may be numbered because they have insufficient power to prevent the outsourcing of jobs.

Once, unions were intended to have wider purposes than they have today - with trade schools, colleges, clinics, hospitals, recreational facilities, social safety networks from pre-natal care through retirement. These ambitions languished as unions fade from the social scene. Government has stepped in to provide these needs but very incompletely –leaving huge gaps. By practicing ZCL at a society wide level these gaps might be filled. For example: a ZCL style comfortable homestead could be the basis for an inexpensive and healthy retirement instead of relying on union/company pensions and social security – and living in idle indolence in retirement.

But there is opportunity in all of this: Middle class, and working folks threatened with poverty may look for help and an escape route from their worsening circumstances. They may be more open to new ideas, more willing to learn to work and to organize, perhaps towards achieving ZCL.

And, seeing the difficulties of others, seeing the 'writing on the wall', folks who still have assets and/or good jobs might consider creating 'parachutes' and building 'fortifications' against economic decline in the form of ZCL homesteads and communities.

Transition to a ZCL Economy: how might it occur:

In 2008 and 2009, occurred a collapse of consumer spending, and an economic crash rivaling the Great Depression. The dependent middle class experienced an acceleration in the decline of their income, wealth, and consumption.

By beginning some of the practices of ZCL perhaps a recovery can be implemented that creates a different economy based on an independent middle class. Money could be invested in systems and technologies that lower the cost of living and enhance long term economic security. (Investments in alternative energy achieve this to a limited extent). Investment could be expanded in community based economic enterprises such as in co-ops that produce, buy and sell products locally rather that on big businesses that make and sell mostly imported - or exported products. Investment in these businesses results in money flowing right back out of the economy again to buy imports.

8.2.3 POTENTIALS: AND OPPORTUNITIES:

Reasons for hope:

You can get a computer operating system called '**Linux**' for free. You need not buy Microsoft Windows. And, you can get Internet access software called ***'Monzilla Firefox'*** for free. These free software programs fit perfectly the concept of ZCL. They are another steps towards ZCL. The folks that labored over these great achievements worked for **NOTHING**. They did it for free. That fact alone is astounding in the modern world and a cause for hope. In the future such initiatives could, perhaps be expanded to encompass all of the technologies needed to live ZC.

Through the web millions downloaded free music through Napster and though that avenue is closed, other avenue have opened up. I have been able to obtain 'CAD' (Computer Aided Design) programs costing tens of thousand of dollars from friends who downloaded it from the Web. (I use the systems for practice at CAD design).

In addition to the computer, certain key inventions and technologies make ZCL possible, practical, even desirable. Some of them include: the bicycle, the solar house and greenhouse, heat storing stoves such as the rocket stove and masonry stove, and ancient methods to keep perishable foods without refrigeration.

Amish - I envy their economic freedom: no electric bills, no car costs, durable tools and equipment and huge barns dominating their houses, like the barns of the pioneers. They know where to put their money.

Credit Unions vs. Banks:

Banks may be internationally owned. They are bought and sold, merged and divested, thrive and go bankrupt as the economy and markets fluctuate. They change their names, change their policies and personnel, and invest according to the dictates of distant, even foreign corporate headquarters. They provide no economic stability.

Credit Unions are institutions well suited to people practicing ZCL. Unlike banks, they have real economic stability. They are locally owned and controlled, and invest in the local economy. They are islands of security and stability in a changing economy.

The Independent Middle Class

Imagine the rise of a new independent middle class - independent of the wealthy, the corporations, and the government: not rich not poor, not employee or employer. In some ways they might emulate the old independent middle class – the old American Farm Culture. The independent middle class might be able to manage their economy by using the personal computer and Internet to plan and coordinate production and sales rather than try to operate in the chaos, waste, and exploitation of the so-called "free market".

These new middle class folks, unlike U.S. 19th century farmers need to be aware of social forces that will try to undermine their way of life. The independent middle class would need to be conscious of economic history and have the will and ability to fight for their way of life.

This book suggests a path to create an independent middle class, not an easy path but one that may provide some shortcuts, may shove aside some economic obstacles.

The missing economy:

In most American industries local small scale producers are gone. And, recently, at the national level production of a vast array of products has almost disappeared including computers, electronics, furniture, clothing, toys.

In agriculture, middlemen have severed the ties between farmers and consumers. Local food processing industries for local use; are gone. Locally grown food is not preserved for winter. Instead, produce is shipped from California, Florida and South America.

But, one product shows what may be possible. Local breweries have come back into fashion. National brands or imported brews cannot compete in price or quality with local breweries.

The potential of local production: Local production may cost more; but supply disruptions and price monopolies are avoided and the vicissitudes of the global economy are mitigated. A society attempting ZCL might emphasize the development of local economies producing to fill local economic needs - rather than production for export to the global economy.

The New Independent Economy:

Mass Production vs. local / home production:

Mass produced products may initially be cheaper and more convenient than homemade products. But over time; as homemade and locally made products gets wiped out and forgotten; prices of mass produced goods rise due to lack of competition because there are few or no alternatives.

For example - from history: The car verses the horse.

At $240 for a new model and gas at 20 cents a gallon, and unmatched speed and convenience a Model T far outclassed a horse and buggy. Today however a horse and buggy costs a fraction of the cost of a new car. The old technology was wiped out and made impractical. Then the price of the new technology increased. Masses of cars - in car-choked cities became less pleasant places to live and travel in. Walking or biking became difficult, and it became impossible to take a horse on the road, (except in rural Amish country).

Meanwhile new technologies have made homemade products more convenient, simpler and cheaper. Examples: bread machine, yogurt maker, food dryer, (soap making machine anyone)? Mass production cannot match the price of homemade because they must include marketing, labor, and transportation in the cost of their products. In the future, I believe new inventions and technologies may make the price of home and locally produced goods more than competitive with mass-produced goods.

Examples today - from personal experience:
Yogurt: Homemade $.30 a quart. Store bought $2.00 a quart.
Bread : Homemade whole wheat $1.00 a loaf. Store bought $2.00 a loaf average.

Another example: A once extensive wood working industry in America - making a host of products- has been supplanted by imported particleboard and plastic items: furniture, tools, toys, and household items. Real wood was at one time even a component of automobiles. (Wood doesn't rust). Woodworking is healthy; good exercise, pleasant challenging, but (except in house framing) almost non-existent. Electric tools make woodworking easy. Wood is recyclable, renewable, biodegradable, non-toxic, easily modified and repaired. The industry is ripe for revival.

Another example: design clothing that is easy and simple to make and modify from basic patterns to fit several sizes. Early American clothes did that. They used suspenders, buttons rather than zippers, extra long pant cuffs, slip over shirts.

Needed are ideas, inventions, technologies, and methods that make home and local production more practical.

Technological innovation is important, but also important from a ZCL perspective is technological clarification and simplification. The car, for example from a ZCL perspective would be much improved if it were kept cheap, simple, (but safe) and repairable. Perhaps, as suggested in chapter 6, it could even be built by the owner. (Or, maybe small-scale community based car assembly factories might be created).

So, for most of the basic necessities of living:

The missing economy could be recreated. Local production for local use and consumption could be restored through community owned, co-operatively owned businesses and factories - resulting in import substitution - replacing imported products with locally made products– thus reducing imports. Needed is public policy to create and encourage local production at low cost. The emphasis – the overwhelming emphasis in fact - in public policy is on the exporting economy. But this results in more dependence on imported products as a region specializes in one or a few products and imports everything else.

Older technologies and local productive capacity should not be allowed to be lost due to imports or economic downturns - but kept handy as a basis for economic security - kept available for use if needed when prices rise too high or sources of imports are disrupted. Thus, the pressure is kept off any one system and competition is enhanced.

Examples:

Heating systems: Build natural gas heated homes backed up with wood and solar heating systems. The wood/solar alternative may be used when natural gas becomes expensive, thus keeping a brake on the price. A natural gas heating system is in general far more convenient to use than a wood/solar system – so if gas is cheap – why not have it available and use it. But, have an alternative in place when gas becomes expensive.

Transportation: Build transportation systems that provide alternatives: car, bike, mass transit. Old trolley systems were destroyed in many cities but where kept are invaluable today as in San Francisco. And mass transit systems - where newly built - are marvels as in Curitiba Brazil.

In his book ***Fields Farms and Workshops Tomorrow*** (1912) Petr Kropotkin wrote "Have the factory and workshop at the gates of your fields and gardens and work in them." Kropotkin, a Russian anarchist did not believe in the centralization of production in huge factories, but in dispersal, across the countryside of small factories. He believed this dispersal would help folks working in factories be more healthy, independent, self- sufficient, because they could also be farmers, or could easily get fresh food from nearby farms. And, they would be free of all of the temptations and problems of living crowded together in big cities. He may have been right. It is a topic for another book or a future edition of this book; but the idea leads me to imagine widespread networks of small co-operatively owned 'Universal Factories' (my name for them), that are adaptable, flexible and multipurpose and thus capable of producing many types of products in short production runs, produced as needed for local use and consumption. I imagine the production of clothing, furniture, tools, electronic equipment, automobiles and a hundred other items in each of these factories. The powerful and inexpensive computers we have today – with robotics thrown in, might make Universal Factories possible that can produce goods at prices competitive with mass produced imports.

8.3 THREE FUTURES:

8.3.1 Where we are not going any time soon:

Will we have a future of universal wealth and abundance?

Future superabundance? In the future will everybody be rich? No, the opposite is assured as a finite Earth groans under tens of billions of people. In the short run I believe we will have superscarcity. Oil is one example. We won't run out of oil. That is a fallacy. It will just become scarce and more and more expensive relative to the incomes of average folk.

Land is another example. The land area of the Earth is 57 million square miles. Population now is over 6 billion equal to 100 persons per square mile or about 6 acres per person. Of each person's six acres, 1 acre is ice, another acre is tundra, a half acre is mountains 2 acres are desert, and only 1 acre is habitable and able to produce food. World population is expected to grow by billions more in the next 50 years. To allow room for all these people, we must each reduce our economic footprint on the world. (Population growth is slowing, but there will be billions more people before it levels off).

Early humans and Native Americans could live zero cost because they enjoyed empty land and abundant resources. Now the crowded land may not be able to provide abundant resources for everybody, but only for the privileged and insulated few.

But if folks can use less land and energy per person to meet all their needs then the pressure of scarcity might be relieved. If we are really efficient - living ZC we won't be as much affected by scarcity. But crowding can make it harder to live ZC - land and resources are all claimed. For example: you may be able to make use of use vacant parcels of land - maybe by trespassing to forage for firewood or wild edible plants. But you cannot protect or preserve the resources on them. New subdivisions or roads wipe out your resources. You could forage on public land, but the problem with using public land (for example to gather firewood) is protecting it from overuse if more than a few folks take advantage of it.

U.S. population today is at 300 million. Do we want one billion or more - like China today? It could happen if illegal immigration is not controlled. (Before the recent flood of immigrants American population growth was near Zero.) Native Americans tried but were unable to stop immigrants. Someday we must take up their cause and find the will to control illegal immigration if we want to keep America from becoming as crowded as China.

Perhaps when humanity has developed the ability to use the resources of space: with lunar or asteroid mines, solar satellites, and zero gravity manufacturing superabundance will be possible, but that's in the far future. In the short term the cost of going into space will far exceed any conceivable return and only exacerbate the depletion of resources here on earth.

8.3.2 Where we seem to be going:

In the future, I believe, most people will live in poverty.

In the future, I fear; the wealth of the world will be more and more absorbed by the wealthy few. World economic growth will occur, but only a few will reap the benefit. For the vast majority of people personal wealth will decline.

Cheap labor, in seemingly inexhaustible numbers undermines the application of advanced technology to the production of goods. Why invent, develop and install expensive robotic technology when millions, billions of folks on increasingly overpopulated earth can be made to work long hours for subsidence pay. Wages, worldwide, will fall.

For employees, folks working for wages, per capita (per person) income in the United States, and the world will more and more resemble India or China over time. Life there goes on at an average per-capita income of a few hundred dollars a year. The U.S. economy of today is not a realistic model for the world. The working folks of the world will not see their incomes rise to the per capita income levels of the United States. Rather, median incomes of working people in United States will fall to levels common in India/China.

(In China, factory workers work six days a week and – according to many reports would work a seventh if offered. They are paid so little they must work long, long hours to survive. I don't believe we should buy the products they make. Make them get real lives instead of ruining and wasting their lives in tedious labor, and subverting our lives and ultimately our freedoms. For soon enough if their madness becomes the world standard of labor, we will all be required to work seven days a week).

The future American economy.

In the future if we continue current trends, I believe big industry, big factories and mass production will no longer exist in America. There will be no unions, and not many corporate offices either, because they will have moved offshore to avoid American regulations, avoid taxes, and get the lowest labor cost. A worldwide corporate aristocracy will rule the United States from afar. Big business will leave only small pieces of their operations in the U.S. - sales offices, services that can't be outsourced, and retail outlets. Also remaining in the U.S. will be local businesses selling to local markets – selling products that can't be outsourced, small-scale factories producing for local consumption, and perhaps local and highly specialized technology and craft type businesses selling on the internet to the worldwide market.

When the incomes/wages in America have been driven down, possibly near levels in India, or China, and working folks have become sufficiently servile and docile, then maybe, big industry will return.

8.3.3 Where we could go:

A ZCL society may offer greater security than can be offered by the volatile global economy. And, it may be possible by co-operation – practiced with diligence and efficiency - and by learning, sharing, good planning and design, and technological advances to make ZCL societies attractive to folks, more attractive than conventional lifestyles even in times when globalization and economic growth seem to be working for most people.

Genteel Poverty:

The incomes of folks living ZC may be low, and by the standards of the usual definition of the middle classes, ZCL folks may seem to be living in abject poverty. But living in the seeming poverty of ZCL could be a genteel poverty that needn't be unpleasant.

And, as the incomes of the American middle classes fall towards the world average, if folks learn to live cleverly - we need not live in abject poverty. In fact, if we do it right we may live better than we did with the wealth we used to have – and live not in grinding poverty, but; sloughing off of the old wasteful ways: opening up new opportunities for new ways of life. If we live ZC, with thrift we need not sacrifice much of our standard of living and we may maintain comfortable lives as our incomes decline. Indeed, rightly done, the quality of life could be enhanced. A family that can't live well on $50,000 a year today, may find it possible to live well on $5,000 a year in the future under a new economic system.

Way below the "poverty line" as defined today, but still way above the world average.

Though in the future you may live in seeming poverty you need not give up as much as you might think. The computer exemplifies this. New computers are becoming cheap, used computers are very cheap, you can use community computers at libraries and public buildings for free, and free wireless internet service may soon be widely available.

The original American Dream restored:

The American dream as it is understood today may be stated as "Go to America and get rich" or "In America if you are smart, talented and ambitious you can get rich." But this is a twisted, commercialized caricature of the original American Dream. It is the dream of the old Conquistadors revived - to go to America to find gold and then live a life of aristocratic ease on a hacienda (where servants take care of you and do all of the work). The original American dream was freedom, was getting out from under the thumb of anyone who sought to rule our lives; whether nobles, kings, clerics, politicians, businessmen, or corporations. The pioneer settlers did not go into the wilderness expecting to get rich, but to live free, independent, self-sufficient. The pioneers built their own houses, raised their own food, made their own clothes, medicines, soap, furniture, almost everything. Zero Cost Living, emulating the pioneers - is a pursuit of the original American Dream.

The Independent Middle Class:

The Independent Middle Class, practicing ZCL may free folks from the need for jobs, income and products from the wealthy, big business, and the GCCE. And, the Independent Middle Class could be insulated from the economic instability and insecurity created by the global markets and unstable economic system that is the GCCE.

The Independent Economy:

The Independent Middle Class would need to be supported by a new 'Independent Economy'. The Independent Economy might consist of networks of formal economic organizations including co-operatives, small private businesses, co-housing communities, farmers markets, community schools, health clinics, locally owned public utilities, public mass transit, etc. Together these economic organizations might constitute complete local economies able to provide, at the local level, for all of the basic human needs: food, shelter, fuel, electricity, etc. These organizations might be voluntary, democratic, private, and non-profit. Associations of these organizations might regulate and co-ordinate these local economies with the help of the computer and the internet. As in business oriented free market systems, competition over members, products, prices, service quality, etcetera might be ongoing between these organizations. It might be a regulated competition, perhaps in part government regulated, and in part self-regulated by private non-profit associations.

The free market global corporate economy may continue, but its negative effects might be mitigated at the local level, by the Independent Economy.

The Independent Economy may work towards the creation of a ZCL society - saving time, money, energy, and resources - using expanded versions of the techniques and systems described in this book for individuals and families.

CONCLUSION to the chapter:

The new ZCL society might emerge from the old corporate capitalist economy like a butterfly emerging from a cocoon. The great struggle of the new millennium will be to free ourselves from that cocoon, to get back our freedom. At an individual and personal level, and all together, we might free ourselves from the yoke of the corporations, the government where it is their handmaiden, the chaos and insecurity of the global market, the developing worldwide aristocracy of wealth, and the Global Corporate Capitalist Economy.

***

CONCLUSION to the book:

As you can see if you've read the whole book and not just skipped to the end, ZCL practiced conscientiously or in part by millions of folks could go a long way towards solving many of the host of social and economic problems looming over us - as suggested in the introduction to the book.

Trade deficits and imports:

ZCL folks don't buy much imported stuff. Home and locally based production replaces many or most imports.

Job losses because of downsizing and outsourcing:

These consequences of our unstable global economy may be cushioned by a more home and locally based economy. Locally owned, community controlled co-ops and businesses that produce food, energy, etcetera could assure job stability in our local communities.

Illegal immigration:

We do more for ourselves, jobs currently done by illegal aliens and so employ fewer of them. Instead of taking low wage jobs in America they may find it more advantageous to practice ZCL too.

Environment:

We practice local intensive organic gardening: use less chemicals and pesticides. We require less land for agriculture and more land can be left natural - more Amazon African, and Asian and American forests left intact. We rely less on agribiz for food and oil companies for energy. We reduce carbon emissions and reverse global warming. We reduce environmental pollution and degradation.

Social Security:

Living ZC, not so much money is needed for economic security. Retirement income may be reduced but folks may still live in comfort - maybe not take as many trips overseas or to restaurants but make more trips to local attractions and have meals with friends.

Welfare:

Folks learn to acquire assets they can use to take care of themselves - even though their incomes may be very low. Thus, less welfare is needed to keep a family comfortable.

Health care and insurance costs:

Health may improve because folks live more active lives doing useful things and eating for health rather than entertainment. Local and home-grown organic produce may be healthier and if more folks grow it - keep down costs for organic food - currently sold for double the cost of conventionally grown food. And, old folks living with younger families: recreating the extended family of the past - may be socially and economically beneficial all around.

Savings and investment:

Everyone agrees most Americans don't save enough. However; inflation eats away the value of your saved money, banks pay a small or nonexistent interest rate on savings over inflation, stocks are risky and volatile, and the government taxes some of your interest and savings income. Where's the incentive to save? Better to save and invest in the form of home and local productive assets that can reduce your living costs: organic gardens, greenhouses, tools, etcetera. But now I'm merely repeating the theme of this book.

Though the sale of electronic games may suffer, new growth industries may arise that equip and educate folks to take care of themselves.

Living ZC we could build up a new society and economy not dependent on big business, on global corporate capitalism on imports of energy or anything, or on the wealthy and on subservience to wealth and money. We produce basic needs for and by our community, neighbors, friends, and ourselves thereby establishing a stable and secure local economy, providing adequate income, a decent standard of living and high quality of life.

In my study of history I see a pattern where nations, cultures, even entire civilizations too easily abandon their earlier economic systems and move on to new ones which become expensive and difficult to maintain whereupon they collapse leaving them worse off than before.

The Dutch for example moved from fisheries and local trade to a far-flung empire with long distance trade and huge profits when successful. But their empire was vulnerable to interlopers and required military power, especially an expensive navy. So, after a few years of importance in the world, their empire collapsed and Dutch power and independence were destroyed. Their old economic bases gone, they devolved to a minor European power.

So too every empire, every great power, so too, the United States. We can, we should, recreate, maintain and improve our old economic bases so we may more easily keep our liberties when things don't go our way.

Americans practicing ZCL may be virtuous enough to rule an empire, but living ZC they will have no use for one. It would only ruin them. So, I believe, our task must be, not to build an empire, but to get rid of our empire, and keep any other empire from ruling the earth in our place.

I believe without equivocation that if we are to keep our liberties, be a free people we must free ourselves of dependence on corporations that, though they pretend to be the advocates, practitioners, and even the embodiments of freedom actually seek to set up a new absolutist aristocracy in America and the World and cause by their practices and methods and polices the diminishment of free folk everywhere to their servants and chattels. Always there are certain kinds and classes of people willing, even eager to give up liberties for greater security, for greater apparent wealth and power and therefore ready to serve this new aristocracy.

If you let the corporations, business, and government control your life, you may spend your life doing something useless, worthless, trivial, and meaningless. Don't do it! Life is a fabulous gift! Don't let the greedy, cold, and stupid make you to waste it.

Thoreau wrote, in ***On the Duty of Civil Disobedience:*** "Is a democracy, such as we know it, the last improvement possible in government? Is it not possible to take a step further towards recognizing and organizing the rights of man? There will never be a free and enlightened State until the State comes to recognize the individual as a higher and independent power, from which all its own power and authority are derived, and treats him accordingly. I please myself with imagining a State at last which can afford to be just to all men, and to treat the individual with respect as a neighbor; which even would not think it inconsistent with its own repose, if a few were to live aloof from it, not meddling with it, nor embraced by it, who fulfilled all the duties of neighbors and fellow-men. A state which bore this kind of fruit, and suffered it to drop off as fast as it ripened, would prepare the way for a still more perfect and glorious State, which I also have imagined, but not yet anywhere seen."

What sort of State did Thoreau imagine? The words of his books suggest it. I would be so bold as to venture it would resemble somewhat the culture and society I have suggested in this book.

Men and women who can really take care of themselves in a world full of people who only want to be taken care of whether wealthy, middle class, or welfare cases are in a position to help others to take care of themselves too. They could build a new world free of the baggage of a civilization in decay.

I am continually discovering new ramifications of the idea of ZCL. I believe and expect ZCL will become a way of life for millions, even billions of folk in the future. Like the ancients, and the Hunzas before 1965 money will become unused, or little used by all of these people.

If I am not heard by the current generations; may I be heard, like Thoreau, by the future.

My friend, do not worry about money, about becoming homeless and destitute, about food, shelter, or health. And, do not fret if you seem to have missed in life your share of wealth, fame and power. You have read this book and you know you can always live Zero Cost.

***

Candide by Voltaire:
Chapter 30 - Conclusion

It was altogether natural to imagine that, after undergoing so many disasters, Candide, married to his mistress and living with the philosopher Pangloss, the philosopher Martin, the prudent Cacambo, and the old woman, having besides brought home so many diamonds from the country of the ancient Incas, would lead the most agreeable life in the world. But he had been so robbed by the Jews, that he had nothing left but his little farm; his wife, every day growing more and more ugly, became headstrong and insupportable; the old woman was infirm, and more ill-natured yet than Cunegund. Cacambo, who worked in the garden, and carried the produce of it to sell in Constantinople, was above his labor, and cursed his fate. Pangloss despaired of making a figure in any of the German universities. And as to Martin, he was firmly persuaded that a person is equally ill-situated everywhere. He took things with patience. . . . . .

Pangloss, Candide, and Martin, as they were returning to the little farm, met with a good-looking old man, who was taking the air at his door, under an alcove formed of the boughs of orange trees. Pangloss, who was as inquisitive as he was disputative, asked him what was the name of the mufti who was lately strangled.

"I cannot tell," answered the good old man; "I never knew the name of any mufti, or vizier breathing. I am entirely ignorant of the event you speak of; I presume that in general such as are concerned in public affairs sometimes come to a miserable end; and that they deserve it: but I never inquire what is doing at Constantinople; I am contented with sending thither the produce of my garden, which I cultivate with my own hands."

After saying these words, he invited the strangers to come into his house. His two daughters and two sons presented them with divers sorts of sherbet of their own making; besides caymac, heightened with the peels of candied citrons, oranges, lemons, pineapples, pistachio nuts, and Mocha coffee unadulterated with the bad coffee of Batavia or the American islands. After which the two daughters of this good Mussulman perfumed the beards of Candide, Pangloss, and Martin.

"You must certainly have a vast estate," said Candide to the Turk.

"I have no more than twenty acres of ground," he replied, "the whole of which I cultivate myself with the help of my children; and our labor keeps off from us three great evils - idleness, vice, and want."

Candide, as he was returning home, made profound reflections on the Turk's discourse.

"This good old man," said he to Pangloss and Martin, "appears to me to have chosen for himself a lot much preferable to that of the six Kings with whom we had the honor to sup."

"Human grandeur," said Pangloss, "is very dangerous, if we believe the testimonies of almost all philosophers; for we find Eglon, King of Moab, was assassinated by Aod; Absalom was hanged by the hair of his head, and run through with three darts; King Nadab, son of Jeroboam, was slain by Baaza; King Ela by Zimri; Okosias by Jehu; Athaliah by Jehoiada; the Kings Jehooiakim, Jeconiah, and Zedekiah, were led into captivity. I need not tell you what was the fate of Croesus, Astyages, Darius, Dionysius of Syracuse, Pyrrhus, Perseus, Hannibal, Jugurtha, Ariovistus, Caesar, Pompey, Nero, Otho, Vitellius, Domitian, Richard II of England, Edward II, Henry VI, Richard Ill, Mary Stuart, Charles I, the three Henrys of France, and the Emperor Henry IV."

"Neither need you tell me," said Candide, "that we must take care of our garden."

"You are in the right," said Pangloss; "for when man was put into the garden of Eden, it was with an intent to dress it; and this proves that man was not born to be idle."

"Work then without disputing," said Martin; "it is the only way to render life supportable."

The little society, one and all, entered into this laudable design and set themselves to exert their different talents. The little piece of ground yielded them a plentiful crop. Cunegund indeed was very ugly, but she became an excellent hand at pastrywork. Pacquette embroidered; the old woman had the care of the linen. There was none, down to Brother Giroflee, but did some service; he was a very good carpenter, and became an honest man. Pangloss used now and then to say to Candide:

"There is a concatenation of all events in the best of possible worlds; for, in short, had you not been kicked out of a fine castle for the love of Miss Cunegund; had you not been put into the Inquisition; had you not traveled over America on foot; had you not run the Baron through the body; and had you not lost all your sheep, which you brought from the good country of El Dorado, you would not have been here to eat preserved citrons and pistachio nuts."

"Excellently observed," answered Candide; "but let us cultivate our garden."

-THE END-

SOURCES:

It would be possible to make a hundred page book of sources useful for ZCL. Here are a few. Some of these books I own and some are obtainable from a library sometimes using their exchange service with other libraries. Some are out of print. Look for out-of - print books on the internet, at garage sales and at flea markets where, following good ZCL practice, many of my books were obtained for a dollar or two.

Most magazines, web sites and books used as references in this book are already described right in the text so to avoid repetition and save space I have not included most of them here.

MAGAZINES These have good web sites with free articles.
Back Home
The Mother Earth News
Organic Gardening from Rodale Press
Hemmings Motor News Articles on old cars. Parts for sale.
Messing About in Boats
Small Boat Journal - long out of print. Look for copies in bookstores and websites selling old magazines.

WEB SITES These are all preceded by the usual "www".

Living Cheap News	by Larry Roth
The Cheap Page	Free information and sources for cheap house building methods.
Frugalliving.About .com:	Exhaustive tips many sent in by readers on cheap living.
Frugalcorner.com:	links to dozens of web sites.
Gutenburg Project.	Free books online.
Firefox	Free software for internet browser.
Monzilla	free software for web site building.
Linux	Free operating system software.
Craigslist	free advertising for stuff for sale.
Freecycle	Free stuff from neighbors.
Lehmans.com	Tools, supplies, products materials made and used by the Amish.
kenkifer.com:	Philosophy,bike travel and camping.
propertyroom.com	police auctions online – cheap stuff.

simpleliving.net	extensive writings on **'Voluntary Simplicity'**
thesimpledollar.com	great site, a cornucopia f tips including a great formula for cheap laundry detergent.
iwon.com	free web stuff.
webstakes.com	free web stuff.
freebiesisland.com	freebies.
OnlineBookTrader.com	book exchange often for the cost of postage only.
Titletrade.com	book exchange.
Paperbackswap.com	book exchange.
Ocw.mit.edu	all the course material for all the courses at M. I. T.
Sciencedaily.com	all of the latest science news.
Idle theory.com	google this for web sites on the value of idleness.
Thehomelessguy.com	musings and personal experiences of a homeless guy - Kevin Barbieux.
Whywork.org	self explanatory.
Benandjerries.com	example of a great website
Natural Building Colloquium	Straw bale other often low cost houses.
theengine2diet.com	persuasive advocacy of a vegetarian diet by a triathlon champion and firefighter.

Organic and health food sources online:

Sproutman.com	sprouts
Diamondorganics.com	organic foods
Heliosnutrition.com	kefir
Pomwonderful.com	pomegranate juice
Sambazon.com	acai
Mothernature.com	barley grass, wheat grass
Greenfoods.comwestbrae.com	beans
Organicfruitsandnuts.com	nuts and seeds
New-chapter.com	tumeric spice
Interhealthusa.com	berry extract

BOOKS:

I have not included publisher information on many of these books because you may easily track most of them down on Amazon, E-bay, or ABE books online. The title, and/or author should be enough information for you to find them.

PHILOSOPY

Walden by Thoreau

Down and Out in Paris and London by George Orwell Destitution and how to survive it

Doing Nothing by Tom Lutz 2006

Into the Wild by John Krakauer: 1996 about Chris McCandless's attempt to live free.

The Long Tail by Chris Anderson Online home based business possibilities.

The Farm by Louis Broomfield The rise and fall of the American Farm Culture.

No Shortcut to the Top by Ed Viesturs 2006 Mountain Climbing

Fields, Factories and Workshops Tomorrow by Peter Alekseevich Kropotkin 1912

GENERAL GUIDES

Living Well on Practically Nothing by Edward H. Romney

Living Well on a Shoestring by Yankee Magazine 2000

Alone in the Wilderness by Dick Prennke

Participating In Nature by Thomas Elpel

Botany in a Day by Thomas Elpel

Stalking the Wild Asparagus by Euell Gibbons

Permaculture any and all books on this subject.

Homesteading Adventures by Sue Robishaw

Sleep Close to the Fire by Jim Allen

How I Lived Seven Years without Electricity and Running Water by Esther Holmes.

HEALTH

Healthy at 100 by John Robbins 2006

The Hundred Year Lie by Randall Fitzgerald 2006 How Food and Medicine are Destroying Your Health.

Los Viejos by Grace Halsell

Clean and Green by Annie Berthold-Bond 1990 Cheap and natural cleaning ingedients

Feasting on Raw Foods edited by Charles Gerras
Home Remedies by Sid Kircheimer and ***Prevention Magazine***
Nutritional Healing by James and Phyllis Balk
The Engine 2 Diet by Rip Esselstyn: vegetarian triathlon champion.

SHELTER
$50 and Up Underground House Book by Mike Oehler
The Cobbers Companion by Michael G. Smith
The Hand Sculpted House A Practical and Philosphical Guide to Building a Cob Cottage by Ianto Evans, Michael G. Smith and Linda Smiley
Rocket Stoves to Heat cob Buildings by Ianto Evans
Straw bale books by Athena and Bill Stern
Little House on a Small Planet by Shay Salomon
How I Lived 10 Consecutive Years in Cars by Craig Roberts
Living Homes by Thomas Elpel

TRANSPORTATION
Build Yourself a Sports Car for as Little as L250 ($465 U.S.) by Ron Champion Haynes Publishing 2nd edition 2000.
The At of Cycling by Robert Hurst
kenkifer.com describing the bike journeys of Ken Kifer.
Drive It Forever by Bob Sikorsky 1997
Car Living Your Way by A.J. Hain
Google 'no car city' or 'car free city' and 'Curitiba' for web sites devoted to this topic.

GARDENS AND GREENHOUSES
All books and website on the ***'Mittleider Method'*** of gardening
Your Homemade Greenhouse by Jack Kramer
Building a Solar Heated Pit Greenhouse by Garden Way Publishing
Any Organic Gardening books by Rodale Press
Watering Systems for Lawn and Garden A Do-It-Yourself Guide by R. Dodge Woodson 1996
Drip Irrigation for every landscape and all climates by Robert Kourik 1992
Home Hydroponic System by John Duckworth - Papa Duck's Water Farm P. O. Box 1080 Weaverville, N.C.28787.

Made in the USA
Columbia, SC
20 February 2020

88189919R00228